LACROSSE IN AUSTRALIA

Lambton L. Mount and the Foundation Years

DOUG W. FOX – OAM

Copyright © 2021 Doug W. Fox - OAM

All rights are reserved. The material contained within this book is protected by copyright law, no part may be copied, reproduced, presented, stored, communicated or transmitted in any form by any means without prior written permission.

Every attempt has been made by the author to provide acknowledgement of the sources used for the material in this book.

The author welcomes corrections and new information: send to dougwfox@bigpond.com.au

Cover design and typeset by BookPOD. Printed and bound in Australia by BookPOD.

Front cover images:
Photograph of Lambton Mount circa 1863. Reproduced courtesy of The Western Australian Historical Society Lacrosse Action Scene depicting the 'Reds versus Blues' in Albert Park, Melbourne. Hand-coloured wood engraving from the author's personal collection. Originally published in black and white as "The Canadian Game of La Crosse in Australia" to mark the commencement of lacrosse in Australia. Illustrated Australasian News 4 September, 1876. P. 136

Back cover:
Photograph of Victoria versus South Australia match on 16 July 1904 at the Agricultural Ground, Sydney, New South Wales

ISBN: 978-0-6452671-0-5 (pbk.)

A catalogue record for this book is available from the National Library of Australia

Lacrosse in Australia

Contents

Foreword vii
Acknowledgements ix
Preface x

SECTION ONE: LAMBTON MOUNT

Chapter 1   Arrival, Gold and Pedestrianism 3
Chapter 2   Pastoralism, Glass Bottles and Civics 17

SECTION TWO: THE BEGINNGS OF LACROSSE IN AUSTRALIA

Chapter 3   The Beginnings of Lacrosse in Australia 33
Chapter 4   Reds versus Blues and the VLA 47

SECTION THREE: ACROSS COLONIAL BORDERS

Chapter 5   New South Wales 69
Chapter 6   South Australia 85
Chapter 7   Queensland 115
Chapter 8   Tasmania 129
Chapter 9   Western Australia 141
Chapter 10   New Frontiers, Decay and Revival in Victoria 161

SECTION FOUR: LACROSSE IN POST-FEDERATION AUSTRALIA

Chapter 11   The Early Years of Federation 185
Chapter 12   The Canadian Lacrosse Tour of Australia, 1907 207
Chapter 13   Club Development, Championships and Women's Lacrosse 249
Chapter 14   The Wartime Years 273

Postscript 289
Appendix 1 – Playing Rules for Lacrosse 291
Appendix 2 – La Crosse as a Rival to Cricket 307
Bibliography 313
Index 317

Foreword

As a young boy, when I first picked up a lacrosse stick and commenced an almost daily habit of tossing the ball against a wall, I had no inkling of how profoundly this unique sport would enrich and shape my life.

There was always a lacrosse stick around home as my father was a skilled and active player. During the winter months I looked forward to Saturdays when I could go and cheer for the Camberwell Lacrosse Club and watch my father play. He protectively resisted my pleas to join the club and play in a junior team until I was in my tenth year. "You're too young for Under 14s so it will be dangerous", he explained, but inwardly he was thrilled with the prospect and proud that I already loved the game. Every lacrosse father understands that.

He taught me how to apply linseed oil to the hickory frame of my cherished stick and rub neatsfoot oil into the hide and gut stringing to keep it supple. There were no plastics or nylons in lacrosse in the 1950s. The sticks were handmade by native American Indians and each one had its own balance and individual feel. Choosing a new stick was an occasion mixed with joy and anxiety. It had to feel well-balanced and 'right' but usually there was a very limited supply from which to make a choice. Players instinctively knew that a well-chosen and well-cared for stick would add confidence to their game and become a long-term friend. From the 1970s onwards the mass production of plastic sticks changed all that and players now enjoy innovative equipment which is robust, uniformly balanced and user-friendly.

Somehow, I convinced my very close friend, Hal Cutting, plus a clutch of others, to join me in that junior team during the 1950s. Winter Saturday mornings were spent piling into the cavernous innards of my father's Ford V8, and travelling to Glen Iris to be joyously muddied and battered. Playing sport in a team with mates brings rewards that cannot be experienced elsewhere.

In 1986, when travelling as an official with the Australian team for the World Championships, I was reminded of the special nature of the hand-made lacrosse stick when our party was invited as guests to the Onondaga Indian reservation in upstate New York. Oren Lyons, the legendary chief and advocate for the native American cause, gave a fascinating address after our group had enjoyed a meal in the reservation longhouse. With a traditional lacrosse stick in his hands, he spoke with emotion of its ongoing significance within the culture of his people and as a symbol of the game they had been pleased to share with the world. At that time, I recall my imagination being drawn back to the spectacle of 1876 in Melbourne when the first lacrosse was played in Australia. The dots had been connected. Oren spoke also of the important part modern lacrosse plays in providing opportunity for personal development, educational pathways and better futures for young native Americans.

Reflecting on that, I wonder what other sport could possibly have impacted on my own life as much as lacrosse. Glimpses flash by of dining at West Point Military Academy, living and playing at Yale and Cornell Universities, making a speech in the House of Commons in London and leading the Australian team on to the field for the World Championship in front of my own family and friends at the 1974 World Championships held in Melbourne. Every Australian lacrosse player who has had the good fortune to play at interstate or international level will have their own collection of memories that define the special qualities that the sport has brought to their life. Along the way lacrosse has been for me the spark for seeking to achieve, the source of self-assurance to take career steps and the fountain from which enduring friendships have sprung.

The other over-riding joy in my own lacrosse journey, has been the involvement of my family. This began with the birth of my brother Graeme in 1955, eleven years my younger. My birth mother had died when I was four years of age after she contracted poliomyelitis during the post-war epidemic which swept Australia. Before re-marrying ten years later, my father was left with the task of raising my sister, Beverley, and myself. He somehow managed, but welcoming a new mum and baby brother into our existence was life-changing. I am happy to apologize to Graeme for the untold number of hours which I inflicted on him, robbing his childhood while practising lacrosse, cricket and other sports in our backyard at Surrey Hills in Melbourne. He has never complained about that, or the many years he subsequently spent as one of Australia's greatest ever midfield/attack lacrosse players or the fifteen years he spent as a lead batsman in Victorian District Cricket.

The family participation continued with my own son, Russell, who also took to the game and flourished. I was able to proudly sit in the grandstands at Hofstra University, New York in 1992 and watch him play as part of the Australian Team for the World Under 19 Championship. In later years I was fortunate to experience the joy of coaching my three Melbourne-based grandsons in the one Under 11 age junior team at Camberwell. It doesn't get much better than that. Through all of the absent hours at lacrosse, my wife patiently waited, watched, helped and supported. Thank you, Sue.

This book is intended to document the events, people and places which shaped the beginnings and spread of lacrosse in Australia in the period from the first beginnings in 1876 up until the time when the sport was brought to an almost total halt by the First World War. These were the formative years for lacrosse in this nation. It progressed haltingly throughout these years and, but for a few wrong turns, could well have emerged to be a premier sport in Australia.

Instead, lacrosse has remained as one of the lower-profile, less populous sports for Australians, largely ignored by media and governments but retaining its own powerful lifeforce. Elsewhere in the world, lacrosse has experienced amazing growth in recent years and now seventy nations are affiliated with World Lacrosse, the international governing body. The sport is making significant steps towards inclusion as an Olympic sport in 2028. When this is achieved, lacrosse in Australia will gain the public profile and public funding it richly deserves.

Doug W. Fox

Acknowledgements

My thanks are recorded to the following for their valued contributions to this book:

- Research staff at national and state libraries and other archival sources for their willing assistance in locating, copying and arranging permissions for the reproduction of many of the photographs, illustrations and documents which are included in this book.
- Luke Oswald, Ian Toy, Graeme Fox and Damien Orr for reviewing selected chapters or sections of the manuscript.
- Shaun McKenna of Shaun McKenna, Digital Content Production for his professional expertise in photographing the premiership medals displayed in this book.
- Sylvie Blair of BookPod Publishing who steered the design, layout and publishing process.
- Lacrosse Australia Foundation for managing the marketing and distribution functions.
- Graeme Fox and Ferg Stewart for their general advice and assistance with proof-reading.

Preface

Pioneers are all around us, some flamboyant and vocal, others hiding in wait for their moment.

What prompts some people to spend their life as a seeker and creator is one of mankind's mysteries. If there was a simple formula, many would want to embrace it. Pioneering, however, is an inflicted rather than chosen existence, a driven life, interrupted by the highs and lows of accomplishment, but never satisfied.

For the true pioneer there can be no halting or turning back and there is no escape. The drive is intrinsic, unrelenting and never ending.

Lambton Mount was a true pioneer.

Lacrosse has a long and rich history in Australia. The undisputed pioneer and father of the sport was Lambton Le Breton Mount, an immigrant from Canada.

It was Mount's efforts that led directly to the first organized playing of lacrosse in Albert Park, Melbourne on the 16th of June in 1876.

Some accounts have claimed that Mount was a newly-arrived immigrant when he started lacrosse with a supply of lacrosse sticks brought with him on his journey from Canada. This is far from the reality. Mount had been resident in the colony of Victoria for some twenty-three years before he made a purposeful decision to start lacrosse as a new sport.

Mount was born at St Clair, near Montreal and came to Australia with his family as a fifteen-year-old in 1853. Like thousands of others from all around the world, the Mount family left their homeland for the colony of Victoria, lured to the Ballarat gold-diggings and the adventure of a new life in a young country.

Mount's role in the commencement of lacrosse has never been fully or accurately reported. For almost one hundred years the accepted folklore within lacrosse circles in Australia was that the game had gained its start through a chance encounter in 1874 when Mount wandered one day into Albert Park in Melbourne armed with a lacrosse stick and ball. The story went that the sight of Mount tossing the lacrosse ball captured the attention of a couple of local lads who eagerly took up the invitation to try their hand and subsequently roped in their friends. Erroneously, it was this understanding that led Australia to lobby the international lacrosse community to allow it to host a Men's World Championship in Melbourne in 1974 to coincide with what was thought to be the centenary of lacrosse in Australia.

Neither the year nor the story of the chance start were correct. In fact, the introduction of lacrosse came in 1876 as the outcome from a planned and carefully orchestrated campaign which was conceived, spearheaded and managed by Lambton Mount with help from other people. Why Mount started this campaign, and how he planned and succeeded with it, is the subject of later sections in this book.

Less patient readers may choose to jump straightaway to Chapter 3 and beyond, where the beginnings of Australian lacrosse are documented, but they will likely return to the early chapters on Lambton Mount for an understanding of the man and what drove him. The life story of Mount during the twenty-three years between his arrival in Victoria and the start of lacrosse in Albert Park in 1876, reveals much of the character of an ambitious and energetic man. His remarkable pioneering exploits across a range of fields read like a storybook. Similarly, Mount's twenty-three years after 1876, before he departed Australia to ultimately take up residence in England, are marked with extraordinary drive and achievement.

Mount lived through, and participated in, many of the significant milestones of early Australian history and he made his own mark in spectacular ways as a truly great Australian pioneer and contributor to life in the colonies. He was a vocal advocate for Australian Federation long before it was achieved in 1901, but he had by then departed the country so he never became a naturalized citizen.

Regrettably, Mount's story has remained largely unknown and his contributions to Australia have remained unsung. There has not been a written account of his life and achievements, the only summary of any substance being a short biographical piece in the Australian Biographical Encyclopedia.

It is hoped that this book, despite its primary focus on lacrosse history, will go some way towards putting the record straight about Lambton Mount.

SECTION ONE

LAMBTON MOUNT

Lambton Mount

This photograph of Lambton Mount (circa 1880) is housed in the Gold Museum in Ballarat, Victoria and at Dingley Dell, the cottage home of his friend, Adam Lindsay Gordon at Port Macdonnell, South Australia.

The photograph, reproduced courtesy of the Gold Museum, was donated to the Museum by Douglas Sladen, a friend of Lambton Mount and fervent admirer of the literary achievements of Adam Lindsay Gordon.

Sladen, a noted poet and author, was the first Professor in History at Sydney University in 1882 and was later responsible for having a bust of Adam Lindsay Gordon placed in Westminster Abbey in London to memorialize 'Australia's National Poet'.

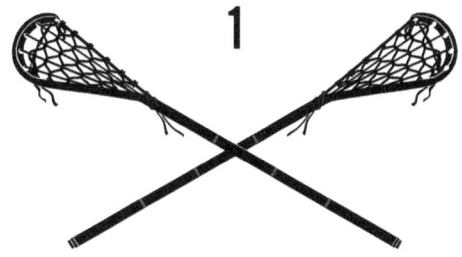

Arrival, Gold and Pedestrianism

Lambton Le Breton Mount was born in Montreal, Canada on June 10, 1837 and was aged fifteen years when he arrived in Port Phillip Bay with his family on April 20, 1853. He had five siblings, three older brothers, one younger brother and a younger sister.[1] His father, Dr. Henry Edward Magente Mount, was a qualified physician-surgeon who trained in London and subsequently practiced medicine as a general practitioner in Montreal. His mother, Emily Catherine Le Fevre, was the daughter of a French naval commander who, dissatisfied with Napoleon Bonaparte's rise to power, had abandoned France for Britain.

Little is known of the Mount's family life or circumstances in Montreal in the years before they decided on emigrating to Australia in 1853. Unfortunately, there are no known first-hand accounts in the form of family letters, diaries, photographs or other documentation. It has been necessary to piece together the biographical details of Mount's extraordinary life from what is available in newspaper reports, municipal records and government gazettes.

The Mount family home in Canada was at St Clair, a sprawling community strung out along the St Lawrence River some ten miles east of central Montreal. The children were educated in local parish schools and Lambton also attended high school in Montreal. Before departing for Australia, he may have started in some form of employment. It is likely that Francis, Harry and William, Lambton's elder brothers, had all finished their education, but there is no record of whether, or how, they were employed. His young brother, Julius was aged 10 years and his sister, Emma, was aged 5 years so both would still have been attending school.

Dr Mount was a respected physician in Montreal and maintained a well-established practice. When he later returned to Montreal in 1864 during a retirement trip with his wife, he was welcomed and honoured with a reception.

The decision-making which prompted the Mount family to pick up roots and transplant their lives to far-off Australia is not documented. Clearly, the family's imagination had been sparked by the news of the amazing gold discoveries at Ballarat and Bendigo which spread around the world in the early 1850s. The lure of a new life with untold riches in Australia caused a worldwide stampede for almost a decade and attracted many Canadians. In part the attraction was to escape from the cooped-up life of the factory worker....

> *"No factory bell to ring out and ring in, no gate to be closed to a second, and, to intimate that once shut 'No hope enters here".*[2]

The Mounts left from their homeland in January 1853 and sailed for Australia from the port of New Brunswick, USA aboard the "Fanny", a 120 ft barque.

Dr. Henry Mount, 1864
Photograph Courtesy of McCord Museum, Montreal

Their journey of emigration as a family involved a major commitment of time and finances and was not something that they were likely to retrace.

Dr. Mount sailed as the ship's Surgeon on the Fanny, a position which gave him free passage and some reduced fares for his family. His role during the voyage was busy and demanding, caring for 130 passengers and crew in crowded conditions with long periods at sea. Sickness was common on sailing ships and injuries to the crew were frequent, especially if the voyage encountered rough seas.

After an eighty-day journey around the Cape of Good Hope, the Fanny arrived at Port Phillip Bay in Victoria on April 20, 1853.[3] Here, Dr Mount was required for a time at the County Court in Geelong to give evidence in a stealing case brought against a ship passenger on the Fanny. Apart from the court appearance, the family spent their time in Melbourne making preparations for their trek to Ballarat.

Fortunately, historians have provided detailed accounts of what Melbourne was like in 1853 and what the journey to the goldfields entailed. In this account, the wonderfully crafted depictions provided by Weston Bate,[4] Geoffrey Blainey[5] and Geoffrey Searle,[6] and the paintings of S.T Gill,[7] have been used to re-create a sense of what the newcomers experienced.

The Mount's arrival into the youthful and haphazard city of Melbourne was likely to have been overwhelming. The port was poorly formed and overflowing, and the banks of the Yarra River were crowded by raucous newcomers, crammed in tents and makeshift huts without sanitation. The first task for the Mounts was to find temporary accommodation and then stock up on the supplies they

1 – ARRIVAL, GOLD AND PEDESTRIANISM

needed to get them to the goldfields and establish shelter and a new home. Some horses, a dray, a pony trap, tents, stretcher beds and bedding, kitchen and cooking utensils, water bags, cleaning items, paraffin lamps and picks, pans and shovels for mining were the essentials for those who could afford them. Bargaining with untrustworthy merchants and protecting the purchases from thieves were part of the hazards and excitement of the unruly circumstances in this rapidly growing city.

The journey of one hundred miles to Ballarat took three or four days over un-made tracks with overnight stops to eat, sleep and refresh the horses.

Ragged townships, dominated by rough-built hotels, had sprung up along the way to provide food, alcohol and lodgings for the travelers. Depending upon the time of year, the newcomers might experience extremes of wet and cold or unbearable heat with flies and mosquitoes to add to the discomfort. Ballarat itself was a straggling township of tents and small timber shanties spread out among the streams and gullies along which the hopeful miners had pegged their claims.

With a family of seven, which included two females, the Mounts would certainly have needed careful planning to provide any degree of comfort for their early days in this harsh new environment. From the records which do exist around this time, it seems that the Mounts initially set up a tented home on the hill in Lydiard Street East some half a mile north of the Ballarat city center. Dr Mount is recorded as having registered his professional qualifications in Ballarat and gained the right to practice medicine on the goldfields in May of 1853. Later, in 1857, Dr Mount built and lived with his family in a timber cottage in Doveton Street West, from where he based his medical practice. The cottage was replaced

S.T. Gill – On the Road to the Diggings
Courtesy of State Library Victoria

S.T. Gill – Cradling for Gold
Courtesy State Library Victoria

with a brick house by 1862. With five young and strong sons, the family was well-positioned to undertake the physically demanding work as gold-seekers.

It is unclear how long each of the Mount boys remained as miners or to what extent they succeeded in their search for gold and riches. The indications are that they were moderately successful but, in time, they all moved on to other occupations. Much of the richer discoveries of the earlier alluvial mining had been worked out by the time the Mount family arrived at Ballarat and the hunt for gold was increasingly turning to the tougher regime of digging shafts for underground mining.

Lambton passed up the diggings in October 1854 for a period of employment with a land surveying and mapping company.[8] This work took him across large parts of western Victoria and opened his eyes to the wealth and comfortable lifestyles enjoyed by pastoralist families. Later, in 1854, Lambton joined the Union Bank in Ballarat as a teller. Later, he switched to the Oriental Bank where he was promoted to accountant and subsequently served brief terms with the bank in the northeastern Victorian gold towns of Bendigo and Beechworth.[9] The bank added to his understanding of business and his clients further opened his eyes to the activities of successful businessmen and entrepreneurs.

As befitting his somewhat puritan and god-fearing upbringing, Lambton was a reliable and conscientious employee and avoided many of the excesses of life on the goldfields. When not at work, his time was spent horse-riding and accompanying his father on visits to attend patients in outlying areas or training himself for athletics which was soon to become his main recreation and an unexpected road to fame. The popular sports and pastimes of the day were cricket, horse racing, coursing, and football. These were largely foreign to Lambton. The pubs, sly grog establishments and gambling, which were the center of after-hours life for many young men, held no appeal for Lambton.

Lambton could not, however, have escaped the excitement of the politically-charged times on the goldfields or the important happenings around him which shaped much of Australia's history.

There was constant distrust of police on the goldfields and an unhappy interaction between them and the miners. In addition to maintaining law and order, the police were charged with collecting fees

1 – ARRIVAL, GOLD AND PEDESTRIANISM

and enforcing payment for the mining licenses which the miners felt were unjust. This led to altercations and arrests and, ultimately to the revolt by miners during July 1854 at the Eureka Stockade. Thirty miners were killed and many others were injured during the revolt and Dr Mount was called upon to treat some of the injured. [10]

Excitement of a different kind came to Lambton's world during 1860 when the Burke and Wills expedition party left Melbourne to explore the unchartered lands to the north and find a route to the top of Australia.[11] William Wills had come to the gold-diggings at Ballarat in the same year as Lambton. His father was also a physician and both were known to Lambton. The adventure of exploration was just the kind of challenge Mount found captivating. No doubt, he keenly followed the reports of the expedition and its eventual tragic outcome in the death of both Burke and Wills.

S.T. Gill – The License Inspection
Courtesy State Library Victoria

Throughout his early years on the goldfields, Lambton's family remained in or around Ballarat. His father Dr. Henry Mount, served on the Hospital Board and was appointed as the Coroner for Ballarat in 1854.[12] He relinquished this role after a year and built a local medical practice which he worked until retiring. He, and his wife, were well-respected citizens, actively involved in community cultural life and ongoing supporters of the Ballarat Hospital where Dr Mount served on the Board for most of his time in Ballarat. In 1864, at the age of sixty-two years, Henry Mount retired and travelled overseas with his wife, before relocating to live in Melbourne. Lambton's eldest brother, Harry, took up land for farming on the out-skirts of Ballarat and was active in the cricket, racing, football, and rowing clubs. Later, he was sentenced to five years in jail in 1870 after being convicted for his role in the unlawful capture and importation of natives from Fiji as labour for the Queensland sugar trade. Lambton's second brother, Francis (Frank), turned for a while to farming after leaving the hunt for gold, and, later joined Lambton in a pastoral venture in Western Australia, followed by a short-lived livery stable business in Ballarat and then a partnership with Lambton in a glass-making business in Melbourne. A third brother, Julius, joined the mounted police and ultimately left the district to go farming in eastern Victoria. By 1874, Lambton was well-established in business in Melbourne and none of the Mount family were still residing in Ballarat.

The Canadian Stag

A new life came for Lambton Mount when his talents in pedestrianism began to emerge in 1858.

Pedestrianism, or athletics as it is now known, was a keenly followed sporting pursuit in colonial Australia. It came from a long tradition in Britain where amateur and professional runners were lauded for their exploits and generously reported in the newspapers of the day. On the goldfields, wagering on match races arranged between the leading runners, was a regular pastime. Contests took place after working hours, or on weekends, and were popular spectator events with significant trophies and money prizes put up by promoters and hoteliers.

For a person to become a champion athlete, a favourable combination of attributes was needed: some natural talent and a mix of suitable physiology, determination, self-confidence and hard work at training. Lambton Mount possessed all of these attributes in abundance.

Mount was keenly interested in athletics and, being in a sedentary occupation with the bank, liked to keep himself fit and strong in his free time. He had been attracted to the 'Muscular Christianity'[13] movement that was followed by many young men at the time. Muscular Christianity held to the motto and discipline of 'in corpore sens' which believed in the health benefits of care for the body through good nutrition, an abstemious lifestyle and regular fitness and strength training. This cultural movement developed in England in the mid-nineteenth century and was embraced by public schools as character building for young men. The spiritual value of sports, especially team sports, was a centrepiece of the movement and was practiced at Rugby School and depicted in Thomas Hughes' 1857 book 'Tom Brown's Schooldays'. Mount was never one to engage in the raucous beer-swilling and gambling binges that were common among young men on the gold-diggings.

Mount had an ideal build for a speedy, endurance athlete. He stood 5'8 ½ inches tall with powerful legs and chest on a lithe frame.[14] No doubt, he was toughened by the time he had spent working the gold-diggings and riding the horse trails around Ballarat.

He would have been aware that he had good running speed and endurance but it is not known what prompted him to first engage in competition running.

The first record of Mount competing was on Boxing Day in 1858 when he won a hurdle race and a one- mile race at the Highland Sports, held at the Copenhagen Grounds in Ballarat.[15] A few days later, on January 1, 1859 he won a 300 yards race at the Buinyong Caledonian Highland Games.[16] The Caledonian Society fostered cultural and social interaction between Scottish immigrants. Its annual Highland Games were colorful community occasions with a grand parade led by men in traditional Scottish garb and followed by a festival of food, competitions, and fun. Large crowds turned out to enjoy the merriment and watch the running races which were interspersed with dancing, novelty events and highland contests of caber tossing, tilting, and shot putting.

Mount's race victory at Buninyong was a low-key start but, from that day onwards, his pedestrianism career blossomed and he rose to fame as the star athlete of the Ballarat goldfields. In early February,

1 – ARRIVAL, GOLD AND PEDESTRIANISM

Lambton Mount "The Canadian Stag"
Photograph Courtesy of The Royal Historical Society of Western Australia

Athletic Sports at the Melbourne Cricket Ground

he responded to a challenge for a race against Henry Bull over 600 yards.[17] Mount won easily and immediately put himself up against Jerry Emery on February 8 at the Copenhagen Grounds. Emery, an American-born professional runner, was regarded among the best in Australia. Mount was narrowly beaten in a desperate finish but his display drew the attention of shrewd judges and he was quickly embraced and dubbed the "Canadian Stag".[18] No further competitive running is recorded for Mount in 1859, but that was set to change drastically in 1860.

The formation of the Ballarat Athletics Club occurred at a meeting held at the Unicorn Hotel in Ballarat on February 2, 1860.[19] The club objects were stated as "encouragement of every athlete and the stimulation (by competition) of Ballarat athletes to excel in those British sports which tend to promote physical energy, agility, and endurance". These objects closely reflected the ideals of the 'Muscular Christianity' movement. A committee was established with James Lang elected as Chairman and Lambton Mount as secretary. The Copenhagen Grounds, a large open area attached to the rear of the Tannery Hotel in Sturt Street, were named as the training and competition venue for the new club. The publican of the hotel, William Boyd, was appointed to the committee. He was already an active competitor and volunteer in athletics with the Caledonian Society.

Mount's next experience of competition came on February 6th at the Melbourne Cricket Ground (MCG) where he ran, without winning, against the leading amateur and professional runners in Victoria.[20] He competed in the 300 yards hurdles, 440 yards steeplechase, and 440 yards flat race.

1 – ARRIVAL, GOLD AND PEDESTRIANISM

Two months later, the inaugural meeting of the Ballarat Athletics Club was staged at the Copenhagen Grounds. The premier event was the newly-established Challenge Cup over half a mile. Mount competed on the day, easily winning the 440 yards handicap and 600 yards steeplechase events against accomplished competitors.[21] In the Challenge Cup he ran second to 'Little Davey' Arnott. Mount's display prompted growing attention and he was immediately encouraged to take on more of the better-known professional athletes in the colony.

True to his muscular Christianity beliefs, Mount chose to run strictly as an amateur and he stuck with that position throughout his entire career. He was permitted to take travel and other expenses out of his winnings, but he donated the rest to local charities, frequently the Ballarat Hospital where his father was a director. Commonly, the money prize for winning would be supplemented by a trophy in the form of a cup or an elaborately engraved belt.

Mount quickly became part of the accepted system for arranging match-ups. Contests were either individual challenge races where the challenger offered to run against someone for a named prize, and within a named time frame, or where a runner put out an open challenge to run a set race at a set time against all-comers. Often, the challenges were issued by hoteliers or businessmen acting as promoters or acting as a manager for an athlete they supported. The rules of the Ballarat Club's Challenge Cup stipulated that the event would be conducted over the course of a year with challenges open to other athletes by giving one month's notice. Mount won the trophy on challenge during March of 1860 and held it against six separate challenges until the following June, to be the ultimate winner.

In other events during the intervening months, Mount swept all of the local amateur runners aside and excited Ballarat by beating most of the great professionals of the times: Alec Allan, Joe Whitely, Little Davey Arnott, James Joshua, Jerry Emery and others. He competed in different locations over various distances in flat races, hurdle races, steeplechases, and walking events. It was apparent that a new Pedestrianism star had emerged and Ballarat quickly embraced Mount as its local hero.

Lambton Mount c.1864
Photograph Courtesy of The Royal Historical Society of Western Australia

From 1856 onwards, Mount was employed in a regular-hours, day job with the Oriental Bank in Ballarat, initially as a junior teller/clerk and later as a bank accountant. Before his employment in banking, he had spent some months working with a land survey company run by Thomas Burr. Burr had been the Deputy Surveyor General in South Australia for some years and was the District Surveyor for the Victorian Government in Ballarat.[22] Burr was an inspiring man for Mount, having participated in exploration expeditions with Governor George Grey in South Australia, and been an attendee at the mass meetings of the Ballarat miners during the lead-up to the Eureka Stockade. Mount travelled extensively in western Victoria in this job, learning the skills of land surveying and contributing to a government- commissioned survey. During this time, Mount was impressed with the expanse of pastoral lands being opened up to squatters and the wealth which followed for those who were successful in securing leases.

His horizons were further opened through his time in the bank where he developed financial knowledge, investment skills, and a sense of ambition about what could be achieved in this 'land of opportunity'. He came into contact with a broad cross-section of society and, as his fame as a star athlete grew, his network of friends and associates, who mixed and worked in high places, expanded.

In Melbourne, another amateur runner had emerged who was also beating the professionals. He was Henry Colton Harrison, better known as H.C Harrison. Harrison had earlier spent time on the goldfields and was employed in the Customs Department at Geelong. Like Mount, he was a strict amateur and would not accept money from foot-running. The term 'professional' signified that an athlete was prepared to accept money stakes and wagers, not that they made their living from athletics.

Henry C.A. Harrison. Sketch by Ruby Harrison, T. Wills Cooke Collection Courtesy of National Library of Australia.

As Mount's athletic successes continued, journalists and promoters became keen to attract him to run in Melbourne and to pair him against H. C. Harrison. Harrison was a member of the Richmond Football and Cricket Clubs and was acknowledged as the father of Australian Rules football for his work with Tom Wills in formalizing the first set of playing rules for the code.

Not one to turn away from a challenge, Mount took the initiative and advised the newspapers that he was prepared to run against Harrison to determine the champion amateur in Victoria. He proposed an innovative, multiple-event format with the winner to be decided by the best of three races.[23] The nominated events were a 100 yards flat race, a 440 yards flat race and an 880 yards steeplechase over 3'6' hurdles. The offering was taken up by Harrison with one change, the reduction of the steeplechase distance to 600 yards.

1 – ARRIVAL, GOLD AND PEDESTRIANISM

Championship Pedestrian Race at the Melbourne Cricket Ground
Courtesy of State Library Victoria

The Melbourne Cricket Club Sports Committee set about promoting the match-up as the 'Championship of Victoria' and fixed the opening event for Saturday, June 15, 1861 at the MCG.[24] The contest caught the imagination of the public in Melbourne, Ballarat and also Geelong. Amid great fanfare, four thousand spectators turned out to witness the contest. The MCG was dressed up with marquees and food stalls in anticipation of a large spectator crowd.

Harrison was favoured in the betting and proved his worth by winning all three closely contested races in times of 10.5 seconds for the 100 yards and 54 seconds for the quarter mile. Mount was gallant. His efforts, and sportsmanlike acceptance of defeat, further boosted his growing band of supporters. Mount's performances against Harrison made such an impact that a group of Melbourne admirers banded together during September to present Mount with an inscribed gold watch as a token of recognition and appreciation. Mount was touched by the gesture and lifted his focus on reversing the outcome for the 1861 Championship.

Mount continued to compete with success in a variety of events and locations throughout 1861, but it took some time for a date to be agreed for the Championship against Harrison. Arranging time away from work became awkward when his role with the Oriental Bank was relocated to Bendigo. Eventually, agreement was reached for the contest to be held on Friday the 2nd of December at the Copenhagen grounds.[25] This was the biggest athletic attraction ever conducted in Ballarat and it did not disappoint. The band from the Ballarat Rifle Rangers added music to the occasion as five thousand spectators crammed into "the Cope" to witness the occasion and support their local hero. Mount and Harrison had agreed to donate the entire proceeds of the day, after expenses, to the Ballarat Hospital.[26]

In the opening 100 yards sprint race, Mount got away well at the start and led by two yards until the final fifteen when Harrison pushed to close the gap but failed by a foot. The run time was 10.5 seconds. Mount's supporters were elated and cheered wildly. Harrison squared the contest by outpacing Mount in the second event over 440 yards, leaving the steeplechase race as the grand finale. The format was 880 yards over sixteen hurdles, a distance which suited Mount. Harrison led the race until being overhauled at the final hurdle with Mount powering away to win as the crowd burst on to the arena to crown their new Champion of Victoria. Following the event, a sum of £100 was donated to the hospital and both Mount and Harrison were made Life Governors. The Championship of Victoria now stood at one victory each and a decider was needed.

In 1862 Mount again had a shift in his employment, this time to Beechworth in north-eastern Victoria. He was keen to defend his Champion of Victoria title but injuries, ill-health and some disagreement over venue caused a delay in setting a date. Both runners preferred that the final contest would be conducted in their home town and negotiations dragged on until an agreement was reached in favour of Ballarat during December. Famously, on one occasion during his time at Beechworth, Mount missed out on securing a coach ticket to travel to Melbourne and, instead, chose to run the journey. He accomplished this in four days, averaging 50 miles per day, and completing the trip ahead of the coach.[27]

The 1862 Championship of Victoria proved to be as big a public attraction as those of the previous two years. In front of a noisy crowd of five thousand at the Copenhagen grounds on Friday, 5th of December.[28] Harrison took the honours, winning the 100 yards by a yard in 10.5 seconds and the 440 yards in 53.6 seconds. The final race, the steeplechase over 660 yards, was declared a dead heat and then awarded to Mount when Harrison chose not to participate in a re-run. The times run by these two men in their three Championship meetings were impressive and compare well with the athletes of today when allowance is made for the grass track, the inferior footwear, and their less regular training regimes.

Harrison, in his autobiography, credited Lambton Mount as being his most formidable opponent and lauded the respectful and friendly basis on which they had competed against each other.[29]

Mount had proved himself as an athlete at the highest level and, although he competed on a few occasions in 1864, his mind was turning to other challenges and his life was about to branch out in surprising new directions.

1 – ARRIVAL, GOLD AND PEDESTRIANISM

Notes

1. Index of Passenger Lists for British and Foreign Ports 1852-1889, Unassisted Shipping Index, Public Record Office, Victoria
2. The Illustrated Melbourne Post, 9/08/1862 p.5
3. The Argus (Melbourne) 26/04/1853 p.4
4. Bate Weston. The First Generation at Ballarat. 1978
5. Blainey Geoffrey. The Rush That Never Ended: A History of Australian Mining, Melbourne University Press, 2003
6. Searle Geoffrey. The Golden Age -A History of the Colony of Victoria. Melbourne University Press. 1963.
7. Gill Samuel T. Victorian Gold Diggers and Diggers as They Are. Lithograph sketches. National Library of Australia.
8. Australasian Biographical Archive – Victorian Series. Humphreys H. M. Men of the Time in Australia, 1882.
9. Australasian Biographical Archive – Victorian Series. Humphreys H. M. Men of the Time in Australia, 1882.
10. Geelong Advertiser and Intelligence 4/12/1854 p.4
11. The Argus (Melbourne) 21/08/1860 p.5
12. The Star (Ballarat) 5/08/1859 p.3
13. Bell's Life and Sporting Chronicle (Melbourne) 30/07/1859 p.3
14. Bell's Life and Sporting Chronicle (Melbourne) 27/04/1861 p.2
15. The Star (Ballarat) 30/12/1858 P.3
16. The Argus (Melbourne) 5/01/1859 p.6
17. Bell's Life and Sporting Chronicle (Melbourne) 19/02/1859 p.2
18. Bell's Life and Sporting Chronicle (Melbourne) 5/12/1869 p.2
19. The Star (Ballarat) 1/03/1860 p.2
20. Bell's Life and Sporting Chronicle (Melbourne) 11/02/1860 p.2
21. The Argus (Melbourne) 11/04/ 1860 p.6
22. Australasian Biographical Archive – Victorian Series. Humphreys H. M. Men of the Time in Australia, 1882.
23. Bell's Life and Sporting Chronicle (Melbourne) 1/06/1861 p.2
24. Bell's Life and Sporting Chronicle (Melbourne) 22/06/1861 p.4
25. Bell's Life and Sporting Chronicle (Melbourne) 14/12/1861 p.4
26. Bell's Life and Sporting Chronicle (Melbourne) 21/12/1861 p.3
27. The Sydney Morning Herald 22/07/1931 p.8
28. Bell's Life and Sporting Chronicle (Melbourne) 6/12/1862 p.2
29. Mancini A. and Hibbins G.M. Running With The Ball, Lynedoch Publications< Melbourne.1987 p.108

Pastoralism, Glass Bottles and Civics

On the morning of December 11, 1866, the residents of the small coastal township of Bunbury in the Swan River Colony, awoke to the sounds and sights of 4,800 sheep being swum to their beach from a clipper laying offshore under anchor in shallow water.[1] Two men dressed as drovers and one in city garb were overseeing the operation.

On landing, the sheep spread in all directions into the dunes, feeding on grass and other edible foliage. Some, too weak to make the swim, were being ferried from the ship in small dinghies. The scene brought great excitement and amusement to the local children who rushed about the sandhills in efforts to help contain the sheep.

Under the drover's hats were Lambton Mount and Adam Gordon. The other man was John Peake, Mount's foreman for the venture. They had come from Victoria with 4000 fine merinos and 800 Leicesters.[2] Their mission, undeclared to the Bunbury residents before the landing, was to drove the sheep forty miles

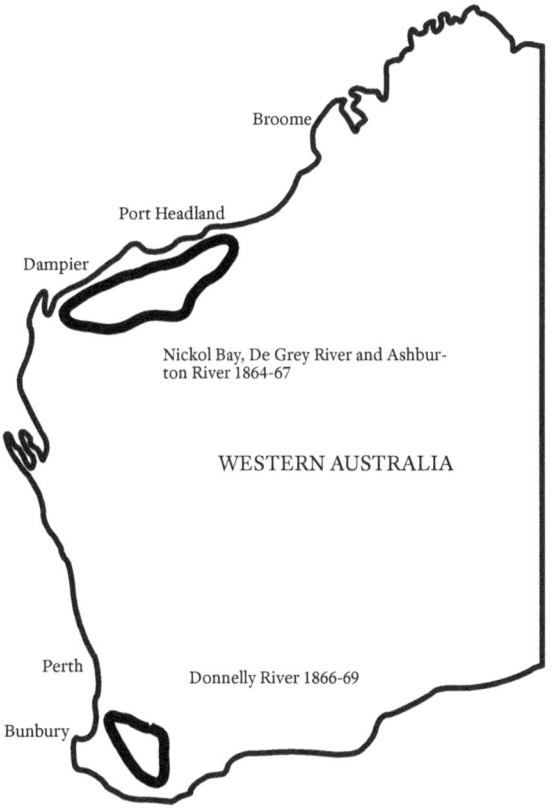

Map Showing Extent of Lambton Mount's Pastoral Activities in Western Australia, 1864-1869.

inland to seek a pastoral land selection on the Donnelly River country. Without fences, and with only a handful of horses and dogs, the task of managing the sheep was beyond awkward. Some of the animals, seemingly as stressed as their owners, escaped to unknown freedom and were lost in the sand dunes.

Mount's drover companion on the beach was Adam Lindsay Gordon, the famed Australian poet, horseman and statesman. Today, Gordon's bronze statue adorns a busy intersection in Melbourne, inscribed with a well-known stanza from his poetry:

> *"Life is mainly froth and bubble,*
> *Two things stand like stone,*
> *Kindness in another's trouble,*
> *Courage in your own".*

Other tribute memorials to him and his poetry are found in multiple places around Australia and in Westminster Abbey in London. Gordon was a friend of the Mount family in Ballarat and Lambton had spent many hours on cross-country horse-rides in his company. Now they were colleagues in a business venture.

So began Lambton Mount's second venture in establishing pastoral runs in Western Australia. His first venture, in partnership with his brother, Frank, in 1864, was located in the Kimberley country, two thousand seven hundred miles away in the northwest of Western Australia.

Both ventures occurred in places that were largely unexplored. Both ventures involved vast cross-country exploration with the hardships that went with months of rough living in the harsh Australian bush.

The Pastoral Dream

Mount's pastoralism ambitions can be traced back to his early years in Victoria where he studied surveying under Thomas Burr and assisted in the first trigonometrical survey of the western part of Victoria. Here, he was able to observe first-hand the lifestyle enjoyed by pastoralists and the massive wealth that was being quickly accumulated from wool.

In subsequent years, Mount spent ten years in banking, initially with the Union Bank, and then under the employ of the Oriental Bank, mainly in Ballarat. He studied with interest the role of the banks and the means used by financiers to fund business ventures. As his athletic career blossomed during the early 1860s, and his network of friends and acquaintances expanded, Mount was quietly saving his money and hatching a plan to join the pastoralists in an ambitious venture of his own. He was highly self-confident and displayed a sense of invincibility, no doubt garnered from the successes and adulation he had earned on the running track.

2 – PASTORALISM, GLASS BOTTLES AND CIVICS

During July of 1864, Mount was attracted to the public advertising and promotion in Melbourne of a company named the Camden Harbour Pastoral Association. The Association was being formed to "settle the very superior, well-watered pasture and agricultural country around Camden Harbour" in the remote, and unsettled, north-western country of Western Australia.[3] Mount may have attended one or more of the public meetings conducted in Melbourne by William Harvey, the promoter of the venture. The opportunity to be part of this venture was offered by public subscription with one hundred shares of £100 each and one hundred shares of £160 each to raise £26,000. Shareholder entitlements included free passage

Oriental Bank, Ballarat. C. 1863

by ship to the new lands, the opportunity to take up a lease of 20,000 acres of land at no cost for twelve years, one year's rations, a share of livestock upon arrival, no rent for four years and the right to purchase the land from the Government on favorable terms.[4] This was an enticing prospect for Mount and he turned his mind to a new life as an explorer and pastoralist. He appears not to have taken up any shares in the Camden Harbour Pastoral Association but its objectives and methodology closely fitted Mount's dreams of discovery and farming.

Lambton's brother Frank was also interested in Western Australia and the pair set up a partnership to pursue a venture of their own. Mount's research led him to a meeting in Melbourne with Captain Jarman whose ship, the Tien Tsin, traded out of Perth between Western Australia and England. Jarman had previously transported livestock to the area selected by the Camden Harbour Association but he advised Mount that a superior harbour existed at Nickol Bay, 400 miles to the south. Mount accepted this advice and spoke with an acquaintance, James Orkney, who was a wealthy Melbourne businessman, ship owner and Member of Parliament. Orkney's ship, the 435 tonnes 'Aurifera', was set up to transport livestock with a double layer of pens on the deck. Orkney was interested in the proposed venture and an alliance was soon established with the Mount brothers.[5] Further advice came through a government agent from Western Australia, confirming that there were large expanses of promising grazing land in the hinterland of Nickol Bay.

The Mounts and Orkney set about preparations during September and set sail in the Aurifera from the port of Williamstown in Melbourne on November 14, 1864.[6] On-board with Orkney were the Mount brothers, a few other men, plus supplies and livestock. Their voyage proceeded smoothly and the stock fared well. After a brief stop in Fremantle to pick up feed hay, the Aurifera reached Nickol Bay on the 20th of December. In a letter to the Governor of Western Australia, Orkney provided the following information:

> "The stock and stores are all landed, and we have been wonderfully fortunate – considering the long distance from Melbourne, having landed in fine condition 1509 sheep, 9 horses, 3 cows, and a quantity of pigs, goats and poultry. The vessel having arrived at neap tides we were necessitated to anchor a long way off, which caused considerable detention in the landing, and it was during that time that most of

the loss of stock took place, there being no free circulation of air, as when the vessel was sailing....... Mr. Mount and our party will be busy for the next two months travelling over the country and looking for available sites for present and future operations, and it is my intention to ship more stock from Adelaide or Melbourne on the Aurifera's return from Calcutta, and as the sheep will be of the same quality as the present shipment – fine wool merinos, I hope that this district will get a fair trial, and that in the increase of stock and production of wool, your colony will be benefited, as well as the pioneers of settlement in this untried part of Australia".[7]

After establishing a base with a holding area for the sheep, Mount and a colleague departed with horses and supplies to explore the hinterland in search of suitable land for a permanent settlement. Frank Mount and James Orkney remained at Nickol Bay to care for the livestock. Orkney subsequently sailed home to Melbourne when his ship returned after picking up cargo from India. Mount travelled many hundreds of miles during the next seventy days in a remarkable piece of exploration. The extent of his journey is revealed in the attached map.

The actual route taken is not known but he travelled from what today is Dampier, northwards past Port Hedland to the De Grey River and then turned south past Marble Bar and through the Hammersley Ranges to the Ashburton River, before returning past Onslow to the mouth of the Fortescue River. Finding a passage through the Hammersley Ranges was an accomplishment which the Australian explorer, Francis Gregory, had not been able to achieve during his expedition of 1861. Lambton and his colleague experienced amazing hardship on the journey; battling searing heat, scarcity of water, difficult terrain and threatening natives. Mount made three separate land selections involving 300,000 acres on the De Grey River, 100,000 acres on the Ashburton River and a further 100,000 acres at the mouth of the Fortescue River.

Mount later spoke glowingly of the land and the environment for farming, while noting that,...

> *"the land was excellent for pastoral purposes but has not as yet afforded any traces of mineral wealth..... An opinion has been expressed, however, that the territory is not a mineral one".*

As history would later show, Mount had failed to spot or suspect anything on his exploration journey that would have led him to discover the unimaginable reserves of iron ore and other mineralization in the Pilbara that today sustain the operations of Rio Tinto, BHP and Fortescue, Australia's giant mining companies. Had he done so, he certainly would not have been in Melbourne in 1876 to initiate lacrosse.

What Mount could not have known during the months when he was travelling to and exploring the Nickol Bay hinterland, was that the Cambden Harbour Association venture was turning out to be a disaster. Robert Sholl, an agent sent to Camden Harbour by the Governor of Western Australia to establish an administration base and undertake surveying for land allocations, reported back to the Governor in Perth that fifty-three members of the Association had left the place soon after arriving:

> *"Everything seems to have gone wrong with them. Before they could land out of the vessel that was chartered to convey them to certain wealth and good fortune, it struck a reef that was not marked on the chart, and went to pieces. They survived the shipwreck only to encounter worse misfortunes. The rich*

2 – PASTORALISM, GLASS BOTTLES AND CIVICS

and salubrious plains they had expected to cut up into sheep runs were nothing but a rocky desert, which would not yield them enough water for their personal consumption. The stock consequently began to die in clusters. The sheep, the pure merinos breed, wasted by hundreds. The horses would not eat the coarse and withered shrubs, or they ate them and were poisoned. There was no rain, and when rain did fall, those who escaped being scorched to death by the tropical heats, were chilled to death by tropical showers. A climate in which the nights are almost as bad as the days, and the tepid sea breeze has no effect on the thermometer, is pretty sure to bring disease with it, and accordingly the effects of it soon began to tell upon constitutions used to the genial seasons of southern Australia...... Of course, the result of all this is that the settlement will probably be abandoned".

By March of 1865, little more than a quarter of the Camden Harbour stock was still alive and half of the settlers had left or were waiting for a chance to return home or move south to the Nickol Bay area. By August, there was nothing left of the settlement.

An interesting aspect of the early settlement of the northwest venture was the desire by the Government to support the English transportation program and introduce the use of convict labour. This was an unpalatable prospect for many of the people who had come to settle, especially for those from Victoria where the issue had been the source of public debate and condemnation. For the government, low-cost convict labour was the least expensive means to the establishment of buildings and infrastructure needed to support a new settlement.

Adam Lindsay Gordon
Courtesy of State Library of South Australia

For Lambton and Frank Mount, there were multiple challenges in the Kimberley but they stuck to the task and established their stock on the three separate parcels of land selected during Lambton's initial exploratory journey. The venture proved to be more of a struggle than a success as they battled through two years of disastrous drought. Lambton left Frank in charge and returned to Melbourne in April of 1866, purportedly, to make arrangements for the importation of additional sheep. Instead, he hatched a new plan with his friend Adam Lindsay Gordon, to develop a second Western Australian pastoral venture two thousand seven hundred miles away, inland from Bunbury. Gordon was living in South Australia at this time and was a contributor, rather than the main driver or source of finance for this venture.

Why Gordon had chosen to commit his money and leave the eastern colonies is not clear. Always a restless and impetuous personality, Gordon's friends and acquaintances recognized that he was not at ease with his life at this time. Later, in a letter to a friend, Gordon confided as follows:

"I am awfully sick of the life I have been leading and the society that I have not been able to escape from. I can assure you that my chief reason for making that rash venture in Western Australia was a desire to escape from all my sporting associates and begin a new life in the bush. Still, I have done no worse than I should have done if I had kept away from here and killed myself with running after lost sheep and nursing doomed ones". [8]

For Mount, the move to Western Australia had been a relished, new adventure. For Gordon, it was more an escape for a fresh start.

After landing their stock and provisions at Bunbury in December 1866, Mount and Gordon commenced the task of exploring for suitable pastoral land. By chance, Gordon came across Guy Thomson, an old friend from his school days in England. Thomson was well-established on a farm at Bridgetown, 150 miles inland, and invited Gordon and Mount to stay with him there and rest their stock during their journey.[9] They took up the offer and Gordon spent almost a month there, hunting, riding horses and writing poetry, while Mount journeyed south on reconnaissance.

The group took up a parcel of 3000 acres for Gordon's sheep at Balingup Brook near Bridgetown and Mount erected 30 miles of dog fence to protect them at nights. In four days, 400 of the sheep went blind and had to be moved after feeding on lobelia grass, known locally as 'blind grass".[10] In 1867 the sheep were moved south to the Donnelly River where Mount had purchased a freehold block for a cottage and taken a lease on 50,000 acres. Soon afterwards, Gordon rode overland to Albany and returned to his wife, Maggie, in South Australia, settling for a time at Port Macdonnell, a small coastal village near Mount Gambier. Their home, Dingley Dell Cottage, is today a classified heritage building operated as a Gordon museum.

Mount worked hard, battling the elements to build and stabilize his pastoral operation. Concern for Gordon lingered on his mind. Gordon had clearly lost interest in sheep farming by this time and viewed the Western Australian venture as a complete financial disaster. In March of 1867, Mount put an ambitious proposal to the Government of Western Australia and encouraged Gordon to place a similar proposal before the South Australian government. They each sought a grant of £750 to mount an expedition to retrace John Eyre's historic journey of exploration across the vast Nullarbor desert to establish survey points for the building of a telegraph linking Adelaide with Perth.[11] It was a much-needed project that promised significant benefit for communications between the Australian colonies but it did not attract the requested government support.

Gordon's finances had been propped up by an inheritance which he had used to fund the failed pastoral venture. In May 1867, his daughter Annie was born at Robe and in June he published two volumes of poetry. Now he needed some regular income and he turned again to Ballarat and horses. In November of 1867, he took out a lease on the livery stables at the rear of Craig's Hotel and Frank Mount left Western Australia and joined him to help manage the venture.[12] This change brought some temporary joy to Gordon who was able to train and ride steeplechase horses, the source of his lifelong love of freedom and daring. He had been universally recognized as the best amateur steeplechase rider in Australia. Gordon's disposition, reflected in his poetry, had always swung between the highs of adrenalin-driven achievement and lows of melancholy that bordered on depression. He took to the racetrack again, ignoring injuries and the passage of time that had reduced his surety but not his daring. Unfortunately, tragedy struck for Gordon when his daughter of one year died in May of 1868 and, later, he was badly injured after a horse threw him into a gate, leaving him partly incapacitated. Neither he nor Frank Mount were good businessmen and the livery business was struggling.

In September, his wife left Ballarat and, soon after, Gordon settled his lease on the stables and left Ballarat to move to Brighton, in Melbourne.[13] Gordon continued his racing career in 1869, riding in Melbourne and in various parts of Victoria. In May, he won three steeplechase races in one day at Flemington and later in the year rode Babbler to victory in the steeplechase event at the Melbourne Cup carnival.[14] News came through at this time that two further volumes of his poetry, which he had used his last money to publish, were not selling well. Gordon took a shotgun onto the beach at Brighton and ended his life on June 24, 1870.

Mount had some success with his Donnelly River pastoral holding, winning First Prize for the Best Imported Fine Wool Ram at the Wellington, Nelson, and Murray Agricultural Society Show during November 1867.[15] However, like Gordon, he also become dispirited during 1868 and his mind was turning to opportunities other than sheep farming. A severe wet and cold winter, coupled with dingo attacks and further problems with blind grass, resulted in further heavy stock losses for Mount. By winter's end in 1868, only 1300 sheep were still alive at Donnelly River and the Kimberley selections in the north-west country had also failed.

During 1869, Mount sailed for India to fulfil a contract he had made for the sale of horses to the Indian army and with a plan to export Jarrah timber for the Indian government.[16] Misfortune struck on the sea voyage to India when a cyclone engulfed the vessel and twenty of his eighty-four horses were killed and others were injured. His principal objective of arranging for timber sales for railway sleepers in India failed to eventuate as Government funds were low and purchasing had been suspended for two years. On his return to Western Australia in November, Mount put his property and all stock at Donnelly River up for auction.[17]

PURE MERINO SHEEP.

Imported from Victoria.

TO be sold by *Public Auction* at the Bunbury Show on the 24th Nov. :— if not previously disposed of by private Sale—about 600 Merino Ewes 6 and 8 tooth ; and 47 Rams 6 and 8 tooth. Also about 500 lambs dropped in June last, 100 of which have been retained as Ram lambs. Any communication addressed to the undersigned at Bunbury will receive prompt attention.

LAMBTON L. MOUNT.

For Sale or to Let.

A RUN of 30,000 acres on the Donelly River, Nelson District, including 15 miles frontage of both sides, of the River, which is a strong running stream all the year round. The Homestead comprises 60 acres in fee simple, and a paddock of 1,100 acres, securely fenced with a very substantial and Sheep-proof, new mahogany four-rail fence. A Kitchen garden of 2 acres in good cultivation, half an acre of vineyard, two commodious huts, substantial stockyards, and every convenience for carrying on either a large cattle or horse station, the country being most luxuriantly grassed and well watered. There are also 40,000 bricks ; 35,000 feet sawn timber, assorted sizes ; 45,000 shingles ; 4,000 slabs ; 3,000 palings ; 1,000 pieces of fencing ; 6,000 laths ; and various other timber suitable for a fine dwelling. The Homestead is situated on the River 24 miles from Bridgetown, from which there is a good road, and about 65 miles from the Vasse by the Warren Road. Any communication addressed to the undersigned at Bunbury, will receive prompt attention.

LAMBTON L. MOUNT.

Mount's time in Western Australia had come to a close. He had not made the mark on Western Australia that he planned. Today, the only record of his stay is a small stream named Mount's Brook which flows into the Donnelly River.[18] After he sold the land and left the area, Mount's property became known locally as Mount's Ruin until the new owners formally re-named it as Mount Leeuwin.

In 1869, Lambton arrived back in Ballarat leaving an unsuccessful and largely un-documented legacy of pioneering and exploration in Western Australia. Curiously, during May of 1865, while Mount was battling un-cooperative sheep in outback Western Australia, his former running adversary, H.C Harrison, was captaining a football team against Tom Will's team on the Richmond paddock in Melbourne. This was a year before Harrison and Wills combined to draft the set of playing rules that were adopted as the standard for Australian football.

Glass Bottle Manufacturing

The Ballarat Star newspaper carried a brief report in December, 1869, stating that Lambton Mount had been seen in Ballarat and was contemplating setting up a business. Following his return from Western Australia, he was about to transform his life in a radically new direction as a pioneer in glass-making, a relatively new industry for Australia. This was a brave move as there is no evidence that Lambton had any knowledge or experience in glass-making. His brother Frank, who was 19 years of age when he left Montreal in 1853, may have worked for a time in glass-making.

Until this time, the Australian colonies relied upon the importation of glass and glass products from England and Europe. There was good demand for glass but the intricacies of manufacturing and the lack of experienced glass tradesmen had always made it a risky proposition for Australia. A few people had dabbled in local glass production but had struggled. The earliest was the Victoria Flint Glass Works,[19] started at Sandridge (Port Melbourne) in July, 1868, by Messrs. Thomas and Young who were tradesmen with expertise in glass-making. Their business lacked capital and remained small, producing only a limited variety of glass products.

Soda Bottle Produced at Emerald Hill Glass Bottle Works

In 1869, some Ballarat investors joined the float of a company to manufacture glass bottles under the name of the Melbourne and Ballarat Glass Bottle Company.[20] The company opened with great fanfare on 6th April 1869, when an 'omnibus,' pulled by four grey horses, transported the company directors from Collins Street to inspect the factory. The factory occupied six acres of land adjoining the Yarra River at the end of Victoria Street, Hotham in the area which is today the Melbourne Docklands. The river provided ease of transport and the nearby beach at Sandridge (Port Melbourne) provided good quality sand for glass manufacture. It is unclear whether any of the Mount family were participants in this new company but they were certainly aware of it and interested in the opportunity of manufacturing glass.

2 – PASTORALISM, GLASS BOTTLES AND CIVICS

Melbourne Glass Bottle Company's Works

In September 1870, the Flint Glass Works was taken over by Mount & Co. a company formed between Lambton and Frank Mount and their father, Dr Henry Mount.[21] The new company retained the employees of the previous business and employed Lambton Mount as Manager until August of 1871. Frank Mount subsequently operated the plant until selling out in 1872. Before this time, Lambton branched out on his own with a £2000 public float and established the Emerald Hill Glass Bottle works on a site close to the Flint Glass factory.

At the outset, his main production line was soda bottles in the form illustrated. The glass had a distinctive green tinge caused by a high concentration of iron in the sand drawn from the Sandridge beach. Lambton was, as usual, energetic and innovative and his business began to thrive. He lacked the capital needed to bring the latest glass-making equipment and techniques from Europe, but he could see the need and potential.

Two entrepreneurial investors came to Mount's aid in 1872. They were Frederick Grimwade and Alfred Felton. Both were wealthy and well-connected within business circles in Melbourne. Between them, they had established and built a joint business as importers and distributors of pharmaceuticals. They had also started a rival bottle-making plant at South Melbourne but they had no hands-on experience and had failed to find a good manager. In July of 1872, they approached Mount with a proposal to merge his plant with theirs and to take over as Manager of the expanded enterprise, located on Graham Street, Sandridge.[22] They made it clear that they supported Mount's vision of researching and importing the latest technology. Mount accepted the offer and, in October 1872, sailed to England on a mission to buy the latest glass-making equipment and bring a team of highly skilled tradesmen to Melbourne. He travelled extensively in England and also in Europe before returning to Australia in April 1873 in company with a team of new employees who were experienced Scottish and English glassmakers.

Under Mount's guidance, the Melbourne Glass Bottle Works expanded and diversified its product range. Managing the bottle-makers who Mount had recruited in Europe soon proved to have its challenges. Mount had contracted each of the glassblowers to work on a piece-work basis, with daily minimums to be achieved. Some of them took a liking to Australian beer and annoyed Mount by finishing work early to head for the pub. He retaliated by docking their pay and then successfully fighting court cases until he brought the work team under reasonable control.[23] William Boyd, the former publican and proprietor of the Copenhagen Grounds during Mount's athletics days at Ballarat, was employed to manage the factory as it expanded in size and added further workers.

As the business expanded, Mount's status within Melbourne society also increased. Riding horses and sleeping under the stars had made way for the business suit, networking and marketing. In 1871 his link with the Melbourne Cricket Club had been re-kindled when he was appointed as a member of the MCC Sports Committee, tasked with introducing and conducting healthy recreations for young men in the colony. He joined his friend, and former adversary, H.C Harrison on this Committee and participated for many years as an organizer and judge at athletic events and Sports Days.

Mount's innovating talents were displayed to the fullest in his role with the Melbourne Glass Bottle Works. Felton and Grimwade were careful to protect new techniques that gave their business a competitive advantage and Mount submitted twenty or more patent applications during his years with the company,[24] including:

- 1873 – Improvements in the construction of furnaces for the manufacture of glass.
- 1878 – Improvements in the stoppering of aerated water bottles.
- 1879 – A certain invention for improvements in the stoppering of aerated water bottles.
- 1884 – Improvements in steam boilers.
- 1884 – An improved glass melting furnace.
- 1885 – An improved method for utilizing the waste heat from furnaces.
- 1889 – Improvements in glass furnaces
- 1893 – An improved stopper for bottles, jars and other receptacles principally adapted for those containing vegetable substances in preserving liquids.
- 1895 – An improved multi-tubular feed water heater for locomotives and other boilers.
- 1895 – Improvements in or relating to tunneling with the aid of compressed air.

2 – PASTORALISM, GLASS BOTTLES AND CIVICS

Mount continued to manage the Melbourne Glass Bottle Works at Sandridge for twelve years until, in 1885, Grimwade and Felton decided on a major expansion. They asked Mount to continue as Manager at the Graham Street plant while overseeing the design and building of a major new plant across the Yarra River at Spotswood. The new plant was opened in 1890 but not fully completed until 1894. Mount subsequently managed the Melbourne Glass Bottle Works at Spotswood for the next eight years before resigning in 1898. He had travelled again to Europe in 1878 and in 1882 to research the latest glass-making trends and equipment and recruit further expert artisans.

In Melbourne, Mount became a prominent and respected member of the Melbourne business community and was active in the Victorian Chamber of Manufacturers, serving a lengthy term as Vice-President and for a period as Chairman.[25] In September of 1878 he was appointed as a Commissioner responsible for arranging the 1880 Melbourne International Exhibition and again in January, 1887 he was selected under the authority of the Governor of Victoria, Sir Henry Loch, and the Chief Secretary, Alfred Deakin, to the role of Commissioner for the Melbourne Centennial Exhibition.[26] These appointments were crowned with a Gold Medal and one year later he was appointed as an executive member of the Royal Commission to make arrangements for representing Victoria at the Paris International Exhibition of 1889.[27]

When Mount first came to live in Melbourne in 1870, he stayed with his parents in their home, in Orrong Road, Caulfield. After his marriage to Mary Glynn in June, 1874 in Melbourne, the Mounts moved to the gracious Belgrave Terrace house in Emerald Hill in the fashionable locale of St Vincent's Place, in the close proximity of Albert Park. Emerald Hill (later South Melbourne) was located on higher ground than the surrounding swampy ground which extended southwards to Sandridge (Port Melbourne) and the wharves on Port Phillip Bay. This locale was removed from the industrial works and factories being established along the Yarra River and had become the residential area of choice for a cluster of more well-to-do business and professional families.

An indicator of Mount's social and civic elevation came when he and his wife were invited by the Governor of the colony as guests to the Governor's Levee, a glittering social occasion. Mount had established himself as a man of influence in the affairs of Victoria. He was never backward in having his say on civic and political affairs, often writing letters to newspapers on issues of the day. He was vocal in support of Australian Federation and excise tariffs to support the growth and protection of local industry. In his role with the Melbourne Glass Bottle

Belgrave Terrace, Emerald Hill

*Lambton Mount c.1878
Photograph Courtesy of The Gold
Museum, Ballarat, Victoria*

Works, he employed skilled men to manage sections of the expanding and highly successful operation.[28] These included Thomas Garnsworthy and Stan McNeilage, family names that would later become prominent in the Williamstown Lacrosse Club.

A most significant occasion so far as the sport of lacrosse is concerned, came in September of 1875 when Mount was invited as a guest to view the playing of the Victorian Football League match between Carlton and Melbourne. It was at this game that Mount reflected on the lacrosse he had witnessed during his boyhood and concluded that lacrosse was a superior game.

The awkward financial times which came in the first half of the 1890s impacted the bottle-making business. Mount battled with labour disputes and his management style was being increasingly questioned by Felton and Grimwade. By the late 1890s, Mount was showing signs of looking for new challenges.

Harrop, in his book "Good Things Came from Glass", summed up Mount's contribution to the Australian Glass Industry thus...

> *"The design and construction of the new plant represents Lambton Mount's greatest contribution to the birth of an Australian glass industry. The scale of operation which he planned and implemented set MGBW in a league beyond all other Australian glassworks".*[29]

During 1898 Mount resigned and moved to Sydney to oversee renovations at the Waterloo Glass operation, and then to New Zealand to oversee the building of a glass bottle works in Wellington. After the turn of the century, he worked for a while in South America before moving to England where he supervised glass works buildings in Leeds and Manchester. He made London his home and spent the remainder of his life there, continuing to submit patent applications for new techniques in the glass industry. He made a return trip to Australia in 1903 before returning to England where he died in London in 1931 at the age of 95 years.[30]

His legacy was extensive in Victoria and, of course, included his decision and subsequent determined action to introduce the sport of lacrosse into Australia. As the following chapters of this book reveal, he managed the lacrosse aspects of his amazing life with the same hands-on skill that he had applied to all of his endeavours. Before arriving in London, Mount, true to his preparedness to not stand back when the occasion demanded, was active in rescuing and saving the lives of fellow passengers when the ship on which they were travelling to England, was sunk at Perim Island in the Mediterranean Sea.

2 – PASTORALISM, GLASS BOTTLES AND CIVICS

The South Melbourne Bowling Green at St Vincent's Place, Emerald Hill

In London, his daughter, Violet, emerged as a leading opera singer and performer. From time to time, Mount was able to reminisce on his extraordinarily full life when friends from Australia made contact on visits to London. Unhappily, there is no evidence of his family having retained the letters, diaries, trophies and other memorabilia that would have documented the detail which it seems will forever remain buried.

Notes

1. The Inquirer and Commercial News (Perth) 28/12/1866
2. West Australian 15/07/1936 p.8
3. The Daily News (Perth) 24/06/1922 p.11
4. The Inquirer and Commercial News (Perth) 14/09/1864 p, 3
5. Sydney Morning Herald 27/04/1866 p.3
6. Perth Gazette and West Australian Times 18/11/1864 p.2
7. The Inquirer and Commercial News (Perth) 26/04/1865 p.3
8. The West Australian 7/04/1936 p.12
9. West Australian 11/04/1936 p.20
10. West Australian 11/04/1936 p.20
11. West Australian 7/04/1936 p.12
12. Kramer L. Australian Dictionary of Biography vol.4, 1972 pp. 267-269
13. Kramer L. Australian Dictionary of Biography vol.4, 1972 pp. 267-269
14. Kramer L. Australian Dictionary of Biography vol.4, 1972 pp. 267-269
15. The Inquirer and Commercial News (Perth) 25/12/1867 p.1
16. Australasian Biographical Archive – Victorian Series. Humphreys H. M. Men of the Time in Australia, 1882.
17. The Herald (Fremantle) 6/11/1869 p.3
18. The Herald (Fremantle) 6/11/1869 p.3
19. Ballarat Star 31/12/1870 p.2
20. Ballarat Star 6/04/1869 p.2
21. Ballarat Star 31/12/1870 pp. 2-3
22. The Argus (Melbourne) 9/12/1873 p.4
23. Harrop. Mal 2008 Good Things Come from Glass
24. Australian Government National Archives 1873-1895
25. Australasian Biographical Archive – Victorian Series. Humphreys H. M. Men of the Time in Australia, 1882.
26. Australasian Biographical Archive – Victorian Series. Humphreys H. M. Men of the Time in Australia, 1882.
27. Australasian Biographical Archive – Victorian Series. Humphreys H. M. Men of the Time in Australia, 1882.
28. Harrop. Mal 2008 Good Things Come from Glass
29. Harrop. Mal 2008 Good Things Come from Glass
30. Sydney Morning Herald 22/07/1931 p.8

SECTION TWO

THE BEGINNGS OF LACROSSE IN AUSTRALIA

The Beginnings of Lacrosse in Australia

Lambton Mount took a bold step during 1876 when he publicly revealed his intention to pioneer lacrosse in Australia. Horrie Webber, in the introduction to his 'History of Lacrosse in Victoria", noted that [1] ...

> *"Such athletic pastimes as immigrants from countries other than Great Britain brought with them survived with difficulty against the traditional Anglo-Saxon pastimes such as horse-racing, cricket, football and rowing. Of those that retained their particular characteristics and retain to this day a loyal though perhaps esoteric following, is Lacrosse."*

The population at this time had no knowledge of the sport and there was no photography or film to provide visual images to assist in the understanding or promotion of the game. Public communication about activities and events relied upon newspapers, supported occasionally with hand-drawn sketches or, at best, costly lithograph illustrations. Even the assembly of people in groups was challenging. Before the widespread advent of rail and tramways, travel was reliant upon walking, horse-riding and horse-drawn vehicles. It was not surprising that, when lacrosse commenced in Melbourne in 1876, it developed in a tight geographic cluster.

These circumstances did not deter Lambton Mount. As a young man, Mount had constantly demonstrated that he was never one to sit on his hands if he had either the idea or the desire, to start a new venture. His impetuous nature led him at times into risky pursuits from which he often had to retreat. These included his pastoralist ambitions in north-western Australia and later at Bunbury; his plans with Adam Lindsay Gordon to explore and survey a telegraph route across the Nullarbor desert; his short-lived tilt at exporting timber and horses to India and the failed livery stables business in Ballarat.

Mount was always prepared to give new ventures a go, but equally happy to admit when things were not progressing as hoped and abandon them if need be, sometimes at a very significant personal and financial cost. In his most successful ventures, Mount demonstrated that he was well-prepared, strategic and persistent.

Mount's Letter to the Editor

Towards the end of 1875, with his business affairs well-established and thriving, Mount's pioneering drive was surfacing afresh.

In April of 1876, Mount wrote a letter to the Editor of the Australasian Newspaper,[2] declaring that he was intending to start lacrosse as a new sport in Victoria. Surprisingly, Australian Rules football was a key ingredient in his decision and timing. Australian football was itself a young sport, played by increasing numbers of young men and followed by throngs of spectators. The newspapers of the day gave good coverage to football but also to the limited number of other outdoor sports that had been transplanted from the homelands of immigrants and had managed to establish a foothold in the colonies.

Mount's letter to the newspaper was published on April 8, 1876. The letter, which is reproduced in full below, revealed his admiration for lacrosse and included a number of important insights, including his view that lacrosse was a superior game to football.

> "THE GAME OF LA CROSSE.
>
> THE EDITOR OF THE AUSTRALASIAN.
>
> Sir,
>
> *Very many years ago, when a small boy in Canada, I used to watch, with rapturous excitement, the Red Indians, tribe against tribe, play the game of La Crosse, and always yearned impatiently for the time when I should be big enough to play also, for then it was a select game, and small boys did not aspire to more than imitate it in a bastard manner by shinny, or shinty, or hockey, or whatever you like; but migrating to this colony while yet a lad, the feverish scenes of the golden days completely banished it from my mind, until about six months ago, while witnessing the final match of the season between the Melbourne and Carlton football clubs, it occurred to me what a much superior game La Crosse was, and I then resolved to take steps to initiate it in Victoria. By the following mail I sent a message to Canada for 40 La Crosse sticks, and the rules of the game.*
>
> *Now follows a strange coincidence. By the incoming mail from England arriving here about the middle of December last came the **Illustrated London News** dated October 16, 1875, containing a large picture of 'The Game of La Crosse as played in Canada, and on page 375, a description of the Game, and some interesting remarks thereon, which, with your permission, I will now copy.*

3 – THE BEGINNINGS OF LACROSSE IN AUSTRALIA

'This excellent outdoor pastime is the national game of Lower Canada, where it was learnt by the French from the Indians, before the English conquest. Mr. W. Cruickshank, of Toronto, up to which city it has passed from Montreal, contributes a sketch which requires but little explanation. Two goals, each 6ft. wide by 6ft. high, are placed several hundred yards apart, between which are the players of the respective sides, opposed to each other in pairs. The ball is started by the captains exactly in the middle of the field, and play begins. The position of the players is now entirely at discretion, or subject to the directions of their captain. The ball may not be touched with hands or feet but is shovelled off the ground or caught "on the fly" by a crosse, which is a very primitive racquet-bat of Indian manufacture. The crosse-stick is about 4ft 6in long, and has a large curve on itself at one end. From the tip of this curve to about the middle of the straight part there is a cat-gut "leading string," and the interspace is netted with gut, so that you have a kind of racquet, only the net-work is wider and longer, and the handle is longer. The goals may be from 150 yards to a mile or more apart, according to the number playing. The object of the game is to urge the ball between the posts by means of the crosse. You must not touch the ball with your hands, but must always stop it, pick it up, carry it, and throw it with your crosse. An average throw is 150 yards, but one of 200 yards has been done. The ball is of India rubber sponge (for solid India rubber would be too heavy) weighs about 4oz, and must be between 8in. and 9in. in circumference. With skillful players on both sides the game may be protracted for hours the ball going almost through the goal many times. When caught by the keeper it goes to the other end of the field 'with a whiz like a stone from a sling, for a moment putting a new aspect on affairs. "When a runner is pressed he will toss the ball up, then wheel round and catch it at the back of his pursuers, or play it into the hands of his supports, as shown, in the sketch. That the game is of Indian origin accounts for its being all running and dodging. Some of those people were engaged in a match lately played at Toronto, which resulted in favour of the Indians.

It is said that next spring 13 Iroquois Indians and 13 Canadian gentlemen propose to make a tour through England, Ireland, and Scotland, in order to show how the game should be played. We are assured that a match between these two teams will be worth going to see. Many noblemen, members of Parliament, and other gentlemen have promised their support. The late General Sir James Lindsay expressed a great desire to see the game introduced into our public schools. The Montreal La Crosse Club has the honour of having the Prince of Wales and Prince Arthur as honorary members. Both Princes were delighted with the games that were played before them at Montreal. The game has been tried during the last summer by the members of the Thames Hare and Hounds Club on Wimbledon Common."

"Well, Sir, it is not very probable that the 13 Iroquois Indians and the 13 Canadian gentlemen above mentioned will visit Australia to show us how the game is played; neither is it necessary, for, from the foregoing explanation, and from my own recollection and knowledge of the game, I feel assured it can soon be played as faithfully and as well here as in Canada. My object in now writing to you is to give publicity to the game, and prominence to the fact that I intend calling a meeting of my friends and acquaintances, and others anxious to initiate the game, at the Port Phillip Club Hotel on Wednesday, April 12, for the purpose of establishing the Melbourne La Crosse Club. I have a genuine Indian La Crosse stick in my possession, which I will produce at the meeting. It is a simple, light, and inexpensive affair, and similar ones can, I think, be made here for about 7s.6d each. In the meantime, I am daily expecting to hear of the arrival of the 40 ordered from Canada. The sponge India rubber ball and the ordinary goal posts and flags comprise the rest of the simple paraphernalia necessary to play this game. A tolerably level ground, 11 swift and *dexterous men, staunch and true, on each side, "and the shouting throng, to incite you along," will display you a game electrifying in its phases; and highly interesting to the spectators.*

LAMBTON L. MOUNT."

For sports observers of the time, Mount's letter and the idea of starting lacrosse may have appeared to come out of the blue. Not so. Apart from the flashback to his boyhood and his observation about the game being superior to football, there was a raft of influences and pre-conditions that prompted Mount and made the timing right for lacrosse.

Background Influences

During the height of Mount's athletic career in 1863, the first account of lacrosse in Australia appeared as an article in four separate newspapers during March and April, including The Age and *The Leader* in Melbourne and *Bells Sporting Life*. The article, titled "A Rival to Cricket" was a copy of an extremely detailed review of the sport which had been published in *Chambers Journal* in England (reproduced in Appendix 2).[3] The author argued that lacrosse was a better game than the main English outdoor sport of cricket and ought to be introduced into England. At the time, Mount was well-known as the Canadian Stag, the athletic hero of the Ballarat goldfields. He was probably surprised and pleased to see the newspaper articles on the sport he relished from his homeland, but the urge to start lacrosse was far from his mind at this time as he was absorbed in athletics. His ambitions were also focused on his hidden desire to become an explorer and pastoralist. The time was not right for lacrosse, but perhaps the Chambers article planted a seed.

It was not until November, 1867 that any further item of substance on lacrosse appeared in colonial newspapers. This time, the Geelong Advertiser published a glowing account from London of the appeal of the sport when two teams of Iroquois natives from Canada toured and played exhibition games.[4]

"LA CROSSE.

Captain Johnson brought over eighteen Iroquois Indians in the Peruvian, last week, for the purpose of introducing the national game of Canada into England. The Iroquois tribe inhabit Lower Canada, near Montreal, and several of Captain Johnson's company were the same that performed the game before the Prince of Wales when in Canada in 1860. On Tuesday last a private performance took place at Beaufort House, Walham-green, under the patronage of Lord Eanelagh, at which members of the press and a few friends only were present. The Indians looked very smart, dressed in their blue and red drawers, the chiefs of each side being distinguished by feathers in their caps and other ornaments. As regards the game itself, it greatly resembles our hockey, with the exception that the ball may be caught in the network of the "crosse." This instrument consists of a hickory stick about six feet long, and bent at the end very much like a bishop's crozier. Over the crooked part a network made of deer skin is loosely stretched, but not in a bag shape, nor yet as tightly as the gut of a racquet bat. On this network the ball may be caught and carried till knocked out by the; "crosse" of some opponent. In fact, this feature of the game.is very like catching the ball in the rugby game of football and running in with it till a "scrimmage" ensues. The goal posts consist of two poles six feet high, with small-flags on the top, and placed six feet apart. The distance of one goal from the other is optional; a game is won when one side drives the ball through their opponents' goal posts. No player is allowed to wear spiked shoes, and the Indians all preferred moccasins, which certainly seemed to hold on the turf as well as our spiked cricket shoes. The ball is made of hollow Indian-rubber and must not be more than nine nor less than eight, inches in circumference. It must not be caught, thrown, or picked up with the hand, except to take it up out of a hole in the grass, to keep it out of goal, or to protect the face. If the ball is accidentally put through a goal by one of the players defending it, it is the game for the side attacking that goal, If the ball be put through a goal by one not actually a player, it does" not count for "or against-either side. The players are not allowed to "hold each other." nor grasp an opponent's "crosse," neither may they deliberately trip or strike each other. A match is decided by winning three games out of five, unless otherwise specially agreed upon. The players are designated as follows 1st. Goalkeeper, who defends the goal, 2nd.'Point,' who is first man out from goal; 3rd. 'Cover point', who is in front of point; 4th. 'Centre' who faces in the centre of the field; 5th. 'Home', who is nearest the opponents' goal. The remaining players are termed fielders. The game is one which we think is likely to become very popular in England, as it constitutes a kind of "summer hockey." It is a pastime which requires great speed and endurance, especially when "running in" with the ball after catching it on the crosse. One thing is allowed, contrary to our English rules of hockey and football, viz., pass on to a competitor on one's own side who is near the enemy's goal. In football this is generally called "being before the ball." and the player to whom the ball is passed is not allowed to touch it until an opponent has played".

This 1867 tour prompted the establishment of lacrosse clubs in England and Ireland and, shortly after, the England Lacrosse Association was formed.

It was also in this year that George Beers, a Montreal dentist, took steps to westernize the native Indian game by establishing and publishing a set of playing rules and actively pushing for the sport to be adopted as the national game of Canada when the Dominion was proclaimed on July 1, 1867.[5] After Federation in Canada, the sport advanced from six clubs to more than eighty clubs in less than six months and Beers became acknowledged as the "Father of Modern Lacrosse". Lacrosse also established a foothold across the border in the United States, buoyed by the accounts of Royal patronage and the return home of men at the close of the American Civil War.

In October of 1870, the Canadian Illustrated News heightened Mount's sense of what was happening in lacrosse when it published a lithograph depicting a match between the Montreal Lacrosse Club and a team from the Caughnawaga Indians who he had watched as a boy near his home.

Dr. George Beers
Image courtesy of Canadian Lacrosse Hall of Fame

The family home of Mount's boyhood was at St Clair, Montreal, a village on the banks of the St Lawrence River

Lacrosse Match between the Montreal Lacrosse Club and Caughnawaga Indians, 1870

some ten miles east of the city centre. Here Mount came into contact with the large population of St Regis Indians who occupied reservation land along this stretch of the St Lawrence. It is not clear how much he had handled a lacrosse stick during this time, but he had watched closely and, as young boys are want to do, had imitated the game with friends using makeshift equipment.

Following Mount's move from Ballarat to Melbourne to set up the Hotham Glass Works at Sandridge in 1869, his reputation as a businessman and his visibility as a prominent figure in the colony advanced steadily. Mount's social and civic connections were also on the rise. In 1872 he had been appointed to the Sports Committee of the Melbourne Cricket Club (MCC)[6] to work initially with John Hammersley and R. W Wardill as the organizing group to promote athletic sports events on the Melbourne Cricket Ground, which had been ailing. The charter of the Sports Committee included the establishment and conduct of healthy sports for young men in the colony. The Committee was re-formed in 1872 with H.C Harrison, V. Cameron and Bill Slade joining Mount. This group revitalized the Athletic Sports meetings with stronger publicity, professional athletes, musical bands and promotions to attract lady spectators. Mount remained on this Committee until the late 1870's when it was disbanded.

In May of 1872, Mount attended a Special Meeting of members of the MCC which had been called to consider a proposal to support the visit to Australia of "an English eleven of gentlemen cricketers" which was to include the legendary W.G. Grace. Mount was simply an onlooker on this occasion but his exposure to, and interest in, sports promotion was growing.[7]

3 – THE BEGINNINGS OF LACROSSE IN AUSTRALIA

Further written accounts of lacrosse appeared in Australian newspapers from time to time but none of the positive posturings about the merits of the sport caused anyone to seek to import it into Australia at this time.

By late 1872, Mount's successes in manufacturing glass bottles and inventing new techniques for the industry had come to the attention of two of Melbourne's leading businessmen, Alfred Felton and Frederick Grimwade. They approached him to manage and develop their Melbourne Glass Bottle Works at Sandridge and he accepted. Subsequently, in October of 1872, they sent him on a business trip to Europe to research the latest glass-making equipment and hire skilled artisans.[8]

During his time in England Lambton Mount witnessed first-hand the interest and growth of lacrosse. There were 182 lacrosse clubs in the British Isles by 1882 and a North v South contest was part of the fixture.[9] However, the time was not right for Mount as he was heavily committed to his business venture to build a new glass works for Felton and Grimwade.

Two years later, news came late in 1875 that George Beers was organizing a lacrosse tour of England and Europe by teams from Canada. Beers assembled two teams for the tour, the first a group of 18 Caughnawaga Indians, and the second, a team of white players from the Montreal Lacrosse Club. They departed from Canada on April 29, 1876.[10]

To mark the event and help educate the public, the London Illustrated News published a lithograph in December, 1875, entitled "The Game of La Crosse as Played in Canada".[11] As accounts of the venues and matches played by the touring Canadian teams came through, the world took notice of lacrosse and Lambton Mount's aspirations for the sport in Australia were affirmed. Lambton Mount did not miss the opportunity to draw attention to this prominent international tour. The Canadians played sixty games during the passage of three months in cities which included Belfast, Dublin, Glasgow, Edinburgh, Newcastle, Manchester, Sheffield, Birmingham, Bristol and London. The highlight of the tour was the hosting of an exhibition game by Queen Victoria at Windsor Castle on June 26, 1876, just ten days after Mount's first gathering of interested recruits in Albert Park in Melbourne. Reports indicated that the Queen had enjoyed the colourful occasion and presented medals and autographed photographs of herself to the participants while Big John Baptiste, the Mohawk Chief and Captain of the Caughnawaga team, made a humorous patriotic speech.[12]

Preparations for a Start

Mount's letter to the Australasian Newspaper in 1876 was a clear statement of intent to start lacrosse. While the letter provided an overview of the nature of lacrosse and advertised the public information meeting to be held at the Port Phillip Club Hotel, what it did not reveal was the depth of prior planning which had been undertaken by Mount and others.

Some of what Mount did in the lead-up to his letter and the initial public meeting remains as conjecture for it is unrecorded and lost in the passage of time.

What is known from the letter is that Mount had taken steps to place an order for the import of a shipment of forty lacrosse sticks from Canada, together with balls and a copy of the playing rules. What is not revealed is that he had sourced a local firm to make some lacrosse sticks by copying a genuine hand-made Indian stick that he had in his possession. He had either acquired the stick from one of his overseas business trips or imported it earlier from Canada. In early 1876, Mount approached Henry Upton Alcock, a colleague known to him originally on the Ballarat goldfields and later as a fellow member of the Melbourne Cricket Club. Alcock had established a successful business in Melbourne making billiards tables, the firm of Alcock & Co. Billiards was a popular pastime among the more well-to-do families of the colony and Alcock had the equipment and skills to bend and shape timber as well as Royal patronage. This was an obvious choice when Mount went seeking someone to manufacture lacrosse sticks.[13]

Alcock used Australian mountain ash for the lacrosse sticks and delivered an initial batch of twenty or so sticks early in June of 1876. Prior to this, Mount had started the task of recruiting a nucleus of local young men and getting them enthused about the adventure of learning the skills of this curious new game.

The first of these initial recruits to handle a stick was George Beech, a local young man, seventeen years of age, who resided in Emerald Hill, close to where Mount had his residence. The timing of Beech's first episode of catching and throwing a lacrosse ball is not known but it seems likely that it occurred early in April in Albert Park using the genuine Indian stick copied for production by Alcock & Co. Beech became one of the keenest players in the early years and helped to expand the game in Victoria and later to introduce it into New South Wales after his employment took him to Sydney in 1883. Beech was widely recognized as the 'Australian father' of lacrosse.

3 – THE BEGINNINGS OF LACROSSE IN AUSTRALIA

Alcock's Billiard Table Manufacturing Establishment in Melbourne, 1870's

A small nucleus of other interested young men soon emerged and in a short time Mount had a group of five individuals eager to play and be part of the new sport. Among them was Amos Norcott, the eighteen-year-old nephew of Henry Harrison, Mount's great adversary from his athletic days and a colleague on the MCC Sports Committee. Also in the initial group were George Mitchell, aged eighteen, nineteen-year-old Jim Barclay and Canadian brothers, James and William Statter, who all lived and worked locally. James Statter had played lacrosse in Canada among some of the best players of the Dominion and Mount quickly seized on him to share his skills. Mount himself, despite now having reached the age of thirty-nine, was keen to play and he joined the group in some early skills sessions in Albert Park, with James Statter leading the coaching.

Some thirty years after this time, George Mitchell wrote the following letter to the Argus Newspaper[14] to correct what he regarded was an inaccuracy in a story which the paper had run on Lambton Mount and the beginnings of lacrosse in Australia:

> *To the Editor*
>
> *In your interesting account of the welcome to the Canadian lacrosse team recently, there is an omission which I beg permission to rectify. Mr. J. Statter of Emerald Hill (now South Melbourne) who was a Canadian, started the game, and showed us how the noble game is played. This was about 30 years ago. Quoting from memory the first members of the club were Messrs. J. Statter, L.L. Mount, C.H. Norcott, C.R Parsons, J. Barclay and myself.*
>
> *Yours etc. George Mitchell, Geelong*

Mitchell, it seems, made his observation based on his recollections of being coached in lacrosse basics by James Statter. He was seemingly oblivious to the extensive background work that Mount had done in planning and initiating the beginnings of lacrosse.

Co-Ordinating Committee

Once Mount had decided to initiate lacrosse, he set about gathering a group of influential colleagues around him to pool ideas and develop a strategy for publicizing the venture and attracting young men who might be interested in becoming players. A coordinating committee was formed at a meeting held on April 12, 1876 at the Port Phillip Club Hotel.[15] This hotel, located in Flinders Street, Melbourne, across from the main railway station, was a popular gathering and meeting venue in central Melbourne for sporting and other community organizations.

Port Phillip Club Hotel, Flinders Street, Melbourne, 1870's.

George McCormack, a well-regarded Canadian-born barrister and former lacrosse player, was appointed to Chair the coordinating committee. He and Mount were joined by an impressive group of experienced sports enthusiasts with wide-ranging business backgrounds. They were all friends of Mount and most lived close to his home in Emerald Hill and close to Albert Park.

In its beginning years lacrosse was very much an Emerald Hill affair. The men who orchestrated the game came from Emerald Hill and a large proportion of the initial playing group also resided in Emerald Hill (South Melbourne as it later came to be more commonly known) or its precinct. Emerald Hill grew as a suburb on an expanse of higher ground, conveniently close to Melbourne but removed from surrounding swampy land and the residences of workingmen in the precincts of Port Melbourne and Sandridge. It developed a reputation as a fashionable Melbourne suburb inhabited by many of the city's well-to-do and influential citizens.

The initial coordinating Committee included:

- **George D. McCormack,** Canadian by birth Barrister living at Coventry Street West, Emerald Hill
- **John (Jack) Conway**, aged 54 years, a former Australian Team test cricketer and Carlton Football Club captain who lived nearby to Mount in Emerald Hill and was a good friend. Conway was a driving force in the South Melbourne Cricket Club and worked as a journalist, covering cricket, football and racing for The Age, Australasian, Leader and

Sydney Morning Herald newspapers. In 1875 he had successfully promoted and managed a tour of Australia by the English Cricket Team. Two years later Conway promoted and arranged an Australian Cricket Team tour of England. His media networks, public relations skills and administrative flair, made him an ideal ally for the challenge that Lambton Mount had set for himself.

- **William Boyd**, an experienced hotelier and businessman who Mount had known from his early athletic days in Ballarat. Mount had so much respect for Boyd's people-handling skills and judgement that he had for many years employed him as Foreman to oversee the tradesmen at his Melbourne Glass Bottle Company factory. Boyd lived at Park Street, Emerald Hill, close to Mount.

- **Thomas J.D. Kelly** - aged 31, Intercolonial and International cricketer with the Melbourne Cricket Club who later became the Under-Secretary to the Treasury & Controller of Accounts in New South Wales. He lived a short distance away in St Kilda.

- **Owen C. Williams** – aged 29, cricketer and Hon Secretary of East Melbourne Cricket Club and a Victorian Cricket Selector. One of the promoters of the Victoria v All England match played on the East Melbourne Oval in 1874. An accountant who later became a Senior Manager in the Bank of Australia.

At the initial meeting of this Provisional Committee, Mount took on an interim role as Secretary and Treasurer and the others agreed to help with arrangements to establish the Melbourne Lacrosse Club and to actively seek young men to join as playing members.[16]

Three weeks later a further meeting was arranged on the 26th of April at the Port Phillip Club Hotel and the Provisional Committee was expanded into a broader Management Committee.[17] The promotions strategy was proving to be effective as by this time more than fifty members had enrolled as intending players. The new Committee of Management comprised the original group plus the following:

- **William Riggall** - aged 33, an accomplished cricketer with South Melbourne Cricket Club and prominent Melbourne solicitor, later to become Principal of Blake and Riggall, Melbourne Law Firm.

- **John. A Donovan** – celebrated footballer, player and Captain of Carlton Football Club until 1874, later Vice-Pres of Victorian Football Association and Hon Secretary and President of St Kilda Bowls Club.

- **Henry (Harry) Frederick Boyle** – Aged 29, legendary Australian cricketer and also a good baseballer and Carlton footballer. Prominent player and committee member with the East Melbourne Cricket Club. Victorian cricket representative from 1872-88 and a member of the first Australian team to tour England in 1877. Harry astounded English cricket by taking 6 wickets for 3 runs and 3 for 14 in a match against the MCC at Lords and went on to tour England with the Australian team a total of six times, the last as Team Manager in 1890. His employment was as Principal of Boyle and Scott, a sporting goods business in Melbourne.

- **William (Bill) Wakeham Gaggin** – aged 28, famed East Melbourne cricketer during the late 1860s and 1870s, representing Victoria, NSW and Tasmania. One of the "Old Jolimonters". Later he became an official of the Treasury and an Honorary Life Member of the Victorian Cricket Association.

- **Frank E. Allan** – aged 27, cricket legend with the South Melbourne Cricket Club and hailed as the 'bowler of the century". Later a member of MCC Bowling Club and Chief Inspector of Vermin, Victorian Public Works.

- **William (Bill) James Runting** – aged 37, stalwart Secretary of the South Melbourne Cricket Club, recognized in 1875 by the Leader Newspaper as "the premier cricket administrator in Australia". Well-known in Melbourne business and social circles as a principal in the Accountant and Land Agent Firm, Runting & Wright. Later in life, he held senior positions with the Federal Institute of Accountants, Swan River Brewery Company, Barrier Mining Company, Masonic Lodge, Melbourne Philharmonic Orchestra and served on the Kew Borough Council including a term as Mayor. President of Victorian Cricket Association in 1882 and founding President of Glen Iris Lacrosse Club in 1928.

It is noticeable that Mount started lacrosse with a strong connection to cricket. This was deliberate and strategic. He figured that lacrosse would provide an attractive winter sport for cricket players as an alternative to the rough, and often unruly game of football. Apart from the direct link to large pools of young men in cricket clubs, Mount was also attracted to the prospect of access to the high- quality ovals and fenced facilities managed by the leading cricket clubs of the day. Outside of the Melbourne Cricket Club, South Melbourne Cricket Club and East Melbourne Cricket Club were the premier clubs in the colony. The South Melbourne Cricket Club playing membership numbered 375 in 1876 and contained numerous players and officials who were happy to assist lacrosse.

Only two meetings of these founding Committees are recorded in newspaper accounts but the sequence and nature of the events that followed indicate that some careful promotional planning had been put in place.

The initial public meeting that Mount had referred to in his opening letter to The Australasian newspaper took place on Friday 9th of June at the Port Phillip Club Hotel. The attendance was heartening and lacrosse sticks were distributed to the attendees to practise with before the initial get-together to start the sport.

The Leader Newspaper reported as follows[18]:

"LA CROSSE.

The Melbourne La Crosse Club held a meeting last evening, at the Port Phillip Club Hotel. A number of the La Crosse sticks were distributed, and the balance will be left in charge of the caretaker of the South Melbourne Cricket Club ground, Albert Park, where those members who have not yet selected their sticks can procure them. It was determined that practice should he held every afternoon within Albert Park, but

3 – THE BEGINNINGS OF LACROSSE IN AUSTRALIA

that Tuesday and Friday afternoons would be specially set apart for practice, and that the first scratch match between the members would be held next Saturday, at half-past two p.m."

Lacrosse in Australia was underway.

High on Mount's agenda at this time was the task of getting the lacrosse equipment right. By May of 1876 Mount had been eager to get underway but the date for the intended start was delayed while he waited for the first batch of the locally-made, Alcock lacrosse sticks. Twenty sticks were delivered in early June and Mount placed an announcement in the newspapers advertising that lacrosse was to commence in Albert Park on Saturday 17th June, at 3pm. The Australasian newspaper subsequently reported as follows:[19]

"The first practice game of the newly formed La Crosse club took place on last Saturday afternoon, in Albert-park. The unfavourable nature of the weather militated against the attendance of the members, of whom between 16 and 20 put in an appearance. There was, however, a fair attendance of the public present, who were anxious to see and learn the mysteries of the new game.

Owing to the rules of the game not being as well understood there was an amount of awkwardness exhibited by some of the players which will not be noticeable when further practice is indulged in. One or two of the players attempted to strike the ball with the crosse, which resulted in that implement of warfare coming to "smash". They should remember that the ball must be slung out of the net-work attached to the stick, and not propelled by means of a blow. The new sticks answered well in the hands of those who used them properly, but, ere long, a good stock of better crooks, together with balls and Co& will arrive direct from Canada, the home of the game. During the week a few of the awkward squad have been out practicing with crosse and ball with the view of getting into good form before the next practice game.

Melbourne La Crosse Club will play a scratch match this afternoon at 3 o'clock. Members are requested to be present not later than that hour so as to choose sides.

The La Crosses ordered from Canada are daily expected by the American barque Obed Baxter. Those made here are a very good substitute, though of course hardly up to what the imported ones are expected to be".

Disappointingly for Mount, the locally made lacrosse sticks failed to perform as well as hoped. Australian mountain ash proved to be more brittle than the hickory timber used in the sticks made by the Indian tribes in Canada, so breakages were high. Afternoon practice sessions and Saturday matches continued at Albert Park as best they could and, as the Leader newspaper hinted after the second Saturday gathering on the 24th of June, the shipment of sticks from Canada was eagerly awaited.[20]

"There was a fair muster, with some fresh blood added to their numbers, on Saturday afternoon, when good practice was indulged in. Messrs. Statters, Sheppard, Cameron, Lyons and a few others are continuing to display marked improvement at the game. The new la crosses daily expected by the Eben Baxter, from Boston U.S., will be distributed to the members, and when more skill at the game is acquired, and a suitable costume adopted, the game will doubtless become very popular. The club meets every Saturday, at three p.m., at the Albert Park, in that portion nearest to the Albert Park Railway Station."

Already there were some players starting to show out. Daily weekday practices were held in the late afternoon at Albert Park and gave the most enthusiastic players the opportunity to quickly progress their catching and throwing skills. Some of these young men would later become instrumental in taking lacrosse to other parts of Australia.

The Melbourne Lacrosse Club adopted a uniform of "blue cap, white jacket, blue knickerbockers and white stockings" which players quickly took to as a distinctive lacrosse look. They split into two groups and added red caps to distinguish the opposing teams for weekly scrimmage matches between "The Reds" and "The Blues". These matches were played each Saturday afternoon in Albert Park until October 1876 before a summer recess was decided, bringing to a close the first season of competition lacrosse in Australia.

Notes

1. Webber, Horrie. The History of Lacrosse in Victoria. 1994. (Unpublished). Published posthumously in digital format as "A History of Lacrosse in Australia, 1876-1994" with editing and additions by John Nolan and Bill Gray.
2. The Australasian (Melbourne) 8/04/1876 p.13
3. The Leader (Melbourne) 7/03/1863 p.15
4. Geelong Advertiser 1/11/1907 p.3
5. Weyand A.M & Roberts M.R The Lacrosse Story. Baltimore 1965 pp.17-19
6. The Australasian (Melbourne) 21/09/1872 p.13
7. The Australasian (Melbourne) 18/05/1872 p.12
8. Harrop Mal Good Things Came From Glass. Melbourne University Press, 2008 p.16
9. Weyand A.M & Roberts M.R The Lacrosse Story. Baltimore 1965 p.105.
10. South Australian Chronicle & Weekly Mail (Adelaide) 21/12/1878 p.18
11. The Australasian (Melbourne) 8/04/1876 p.13
12. Ovens & Murray Advertiser (Beechworth, Victoria) 5/10/1876 p.4
13. The Argus (Melbourne) 11/09/1875 p.5
14. The Argus (Melbourne) 26/07/1907 p.4
15. The Age (Melbourne) 13/04/1876 p.3
16. The Age (Melbourne) 13/04/1876 p.3
17. The Leader (Melbourne) 24/04/1876 p.12
18. The Leader (Melbourne) 10/06/1876 p.19
19. The Australasian (Melbourne) 24/06/1876 p.13
20. The Leader (Melbourne) 24/06/1876 p.12

Reds versus Blues and the VLA

Lacrosse had made a start in 1876 but it was by no means secure.

The playing group was dedicated but small and the sport would not be able to attract the public attention or appeal needed to grow until the skill levels were lifted. Mount and his colleagues understood that a plan was needed to get lacrosse to the next stage of development. They may have hoped, but could not assume, that the sport would capture immediate public attention and grow of its own accord.

As it turned out, there was no stampede. Participant numbers reached a total of forty-eight in 1876 and scrimmage games were organized each week around the thirty or so players who attended on any given weekend. Regular accounts of the weekly lacrosse matches were published in the *Leader* and *Age* newspapers throughout 1876-1878 as the sport slowly established. These reports were generally brief and usually recorded only the surnames of the players so it is difficult to definitively identify, or research, the lives outside lacrosse of all of the young men who were the original lacrosse players in Australia.

Participants were assigned to either the "Reds" or "Blues" but there was some shifting between teams to balance their strength when improving players became dominant, or when the numbers were uneven due to absences or injuries. The forty-eight participants in the inaugural year, and their main team affiliations, were as follows:

Reds: W. R (Bill) Adams, Alic Anderson, Balderson, J.G.(Jim) Barclay, G.M (George) Barthold, George Beech, Robert (Bob) Clouston, Edgar, S. Eville, Fitzgerald, Jonathon M (Jack) Fraser, Fry, W.A (Bill) Lyons, Mathews, Jim. McHarg, Percy S Mercer, George. Mitchell, Morton, Nicoll, Louis Pirani, Sheppard, Sinclair, Jim T Stabback, William Statter.

Blues: P. Cameron, Chapman, J. Chessell, C. Cotteril, Percy, M Eville, William J. (Bill) Fookes, Forbes, Joel Fox, Fuller, Claude.T Harper, William.C.E (Bill) Heale, Harry. C Jones, Lloyd, R.F. Macallister, Mallinson, Lambton Mount, Mountwell, Amos Norcott, Charles. R Parsons, Robinson, Thomas Statter, E.C (Ted) Tribe, Turnley, Walker.

A mapping of the residences of this playing group reveals that the start of lacrosse was very much an Emerald Hill affair. A high proportion of the inaugural players lived in Emerald Hill (later known as South Melbourne), within short walking distance of Albert Park and close to Lambton Mount's home in St Vincent's Place. For those who didn't live nearby, travel to Albert Park from Melbourne and suburbs was available via train, using the St Kilda line which had operated since May of 1857. The playing field used for lacrosse was located a short distance from the Middle Park Station. By 1876, Melbourne had a railway network that serviced Williamstown, Essendon, Brighton and lines which extended to Geelong, Ballarat, Bendigo, Wodonga, Maryborough, Ararat, Portland and Echuca. Ease of movement around Melbourne was further developed when the establishment and expansion of inexpensive private and government horse and cable tramways commenced from 1884.

Reds versus Blues matches continued at Albert Park on Saturday afternoons during the winter playing season, April to September, throughout 1876. A similar schedule was repeated for 1877 and 1878.[1]

Rules, Uniforms and Equipment

The playing rules of the Montreal Lacrosse Club were adopted with minor amendments. These were close to the original rules laid down by Canadian, George Beers, the founder of the 'modern' form of the game.

The rules were formalized and printed in 1879 when the Victorian Lacrosse Association (VLA) was formed. A copy of these original playing rules is included in Appendix 1. In summary, the key elements of the game played by the Reds v Blues and subsequently by the Victorian Lacrosse Association competition, were as follows:

Team   - Twelve players assigned as Goalkeeper, Point, Cover Point, Centre and Home. Others were termed fielders, and later named Left and Right Defense and Attack.

4 – REDS VERSUS BLUES AND THE VLA

Field - No defined boundaries with goals set any distance apart as agreed by the opposing captains. Goalposts eight feet in height capped by flags and six feet wide. Play permitted behind the goals.

Equipment - Crosse to be any length to suit the player, have a maximum width of one foot and be strung so as not to prevent dislodgement of the ball.

Face-Off - Ball faced off between opposing centre players to start the game by tossing it in the air and after goals are scored. A ball thrown out of bounds to be faced off at the nearest point in bounds.

Scoring - Goal scored when the ball is thrown between the goal-posts from the front. The match is decided by the greatest number of goals during the time of play decided on by the captains.

Rough Play - No deliberate striking with the crosse, tripping or shouldering an opponent.

Once the initial attempt to have sticks made locally had proved to be unsuccessful, crosses and balls were imported from Canada. The three-month delay involved in the importing process often proved to be a barrier to club start-ups and growth in future years.

These basic playing rules adopted by the VLA were later used by other Australian colonies with some local amendments. The rules were, however, a frequent point of discussion and contention between the colonies and states until a national governing association was formed in Australia in 1932. Until that time, agreement on playing rules and rule changes was achieved by inter-colonial or inter-state conferences.

Although inexperienced as a player, Lambton Mount was a keen and effective participant throughout the three years of the Reds v Blues matches. He organized and generally captained the Blues team and was often mentioned among the best players. Bill Lyons was the regular captain and organizer for the Reds. Scoring was generally low with winning scores rarely above five goals.

Newspaper reports of games were regular but typically comprised not more than a few paragraphs like the account of the action published in the Leader during September, 1877:[2]

"The best game that has yet been played took place in Albert Park on Saturday afternoon. For many Saturdays past a decided improvement has each day been noticeable in the play, but for genuine skillful play last Saturday's efforts far distanced all previous ones. The ball was faced for by Adams and Jones. Adams wrestled it from Jones and passed it on to Eville, who was playing on the right wing. He directed it towards Mount, but Chapman ran in first and took it up the field to Jones, who was well checked by Walker. The ball was now for some time kept in the centre, and some capital play was shown by Jones, Adams, Walker, Eville and Barclay. Chapman now came to the rescue and passed it on to the red's goal. Lyons then got possession of it, and made a shot for goal, which, however, went wide. A few minutes afterwards he made another shot, this time with more success. In about ten minutes afterwards he repeated the dose, scoring the second goal for the blues. The reds now rallied, and Mitchell, Beech and Norcott made a gallant attempt to score a goal, but the blues' defence men were on the alert, and repulsed

their efforts. Some pretty play now took place between Cameron, Mitchell, Chapman and Norcott, which resulted in Norcott scoring a goal for the reds by a good long shot. The blues now rallied, and, fully bent upon winning, kept the ball playing about the red's goal for some time. At last Barclay succeeded in putting it through. Chapman a little while afterwards scored the fourth, and Parsons a little before time the fifth. Statter made a grand rush a little before time, and it is very probable had his crosse been in good order he would have scored a goal; as it was, it went only a few inches wide. No other goal having been got by either side; the blues were declared the victors by five goals to one. Parsons, Chapman, Cameron, Fraser, Jones, Barclay, Reade and Lyons were conspicuous by their exertions for the blues, and Mount, Mitchell, Norcott, Beech, Heale, Walker, Eville, Adams Cottrill and Statter did good service for the reds."

Without the visual help of photography, only written descriptions, sketches and lithographic engravings were available as means to explain and depict the game to interested public. The Illustrated Australian News acknowledged the presence of the new sport in Melbourne with the following lithograph illustration of the spectacle in its publication of September 4, 1876.[3]

The Canadian Game of La Crosse in Australia.

The playing uniforms adopted by teams during the colonial years of lacrosse in Australia were modelled on those used by clubs in Canada and subsequently developed in England. Standard outfitting included a jersey and long knickerbockers made of woollen-based flannels, woollen stockings, a short-peaked cap and shoes with cleats. Colors were restricted mainly to combinations of navy blue and

4 – REDS VERSUS BLUES AND THE VLA

white. Navy blue dyeing of cloth was first undertaken in Victoria around 1872 at the Victoria Woolen Manufacturing Mill,[4] on the banks of the Barwon River in Geelong by Robert Kaufmann, a German-born artisan who was the great grandfather of the author. Methods of dyeing cloth in other colors were developed later and rarely used for jerseys until the 1890's. Alternative and brighter colors were possible for the playing cap and stockings where cotton and silk were sometimes mixed with wool. The cap was used as the distinguishing item for opposing teams until it faded from use early in the 1900s. Throughout this account, the playing colors of teams and clubs have been recorded wherever known.

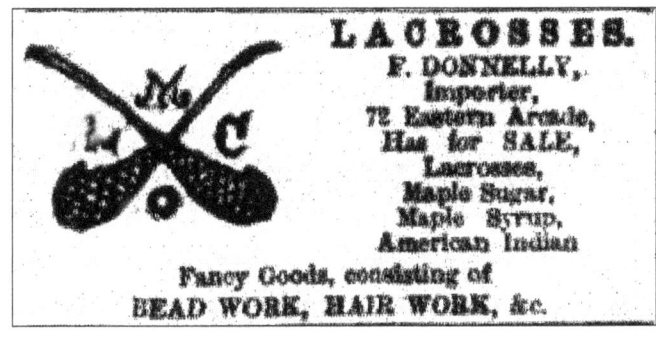

Despite a few unsuccessful attempts at local manufacture, the key item of playing equipment, the lacrosse stick, remained the North American hand-made item imported from Canada. The early growth of lacrosse was often compromised by a lack of sticks or a delay in waiting for shipments to arrive. Curiously in the late 1870s, the supply of lacrosse sticks in Melbourne came through F. Donnelly, in the city Eastern Arcade, an importer specializing in goods from Canada whose main lines were Maple Syrup, Maple Sugar and Indian beads and hair.[5]

By the end of 1878, lacrosse had established a presence in the colony of Victoria but, its relatively tight geography and restriction to Albert Park meant that it was not widely seen or understood within the broader population of 280,000 residents of Melbourne at the time.

It was clear that Lambton Mount and the pioneer players had an eye to future expansion. Whilst the program was largely based in Albert Park, a few attempts were made to showcase the sport at other venues. Games were recorded at Royal Park and St Kilda Cricket Ground, and, on September 28, 1878 the sport was taken to Geelong and played on the Corio Cricket Ground.[6]

Outside of Australia, the Australian Cricket Tour of England in 1878 raised the stakes for lacrosse when the team played a friendly match watched by 800 spectators in Montreal on their journey home. The Team Manager, Jack Conway, an Emerald Hill resident who was part of Mount's initial committee to plan for the introduction of lacrosse, sent a revealing report home...

> *"Cricket is not a popular game in Montreal, but lacrosse evidently is, for some of the contests, we are informed, especially those with the Indians, draw an attendance of 8,000 or 10,000 persons".* [7]

This observation about the popularity of lacrosse in Canada was not new information for Lambton Mount as he had experienced it himself. However, it seems to have been a signal for Mount that the game could be expanded and succeed in Melbourne beyond the limited format of the "Reds v Blues".

Some of the participants in the first few years of lacrosse in Australia took to the sport and played each week, rarely missing a single game. Others were less enthusiastic and played on an irregular basis or participated only for a short time before dropping out. For lacrosse, the important players were those

that re-appeared in the following years and became the backbone of future clubs, or moved to other colonies and helped initiate the sport elsewhere. They were true pioneers of lacrosse in Australia.

Apart from a few players, like Thomas and William Statter, who had previously played lacrosse in Canada, most of the participants were introduced to and learnt the game in Albert Park. Those that stood out as players were possessed of superior athletic talent or spent more time working to develop

Saturday Afternoon Holiday Amusements in Melbourne

their stick-handling skills. The leading players among the Reds and Blues were Bill Lyons, George Beech, Amos Norcott, Bill Adams, Lambton Mount, Jack Fraser, Jim Barclay and Jim McHarg.

When the Illustrated Australian News ran a pictorial feature in July, 1879, depicting the recreational pursuits of Melburnians, lacrosse was included among the key amusements along with cycling, shooting, quoits, sailing, bowls, football, theatre, horse-riding, coursing, hunting, and sight-seeing at the zoo, the National Gallery, and the theatre.

The Victorian Lacrosse Association

The Clarence Hotel, located on the south-eastern corner of Collins and Elizabeth Streets in Melbourne, was the venue of a historic meeting for lacrosse on Tuesday March 25, 1879.[8]

Clarence Hotel, Melbourne, 1879

About forty lacrosse players attended the meeting which had been called by Lambton Mount. After three years of weekly 'Reds versus Blues' matches with a core of thirty or so regular participants, the time had come for change. Mount chaired the meeting and a decision was soon reached that the players should split their numbers for 'the good of the game' and form four separate clubs and a coordinating Association, the Victorian Lacrosse Association (VLA). It was agreed that the clubs be called Melbourne, Carlton, Fitzroy and South Melbourne.

Clearly, there had been some prior discussion on these arrangements after the 1878 season. The new clubs had been pre-determined as two delegates to lead and represent them at the VLA were named at this meeting for each new club as follows:

Messrs. Jim Barclay and Jim McHarg (Carlton), Harry Jones and Bill Lyons (Fitzroy), Dave Fox and Amos Norcott (Melbourne) and P. Cameron and Bill Fookes (South Melbourne). Mount was elected as Chairman of the Association, Barclay as Treasurer and Lyons as Secretary, and it was agreed to adopt, with minor changes, the Laws of Lacrosse set down by the Montreal Lacrosse Club.

Immediately following the formation of the VLA, each of the clubs set up practice sessions and placed newspaper advertisements for club meetings, inviting intending and new players to attend. At these meetings, the clubs appointed office bearers and decided upon their playing colours. The opening of the playing season and the inaugural inter-club lacrosse competition in Australia was scheduled to start on Saturday April 27, 1879. To meet the deadline, the 'old players' in each club needed to recruit new young men and build their numbers to fifteen or more active players to ensure that they could meet their match obligations.

The club system, which has defined the sport in every Australian state since that time, was born with the following officials appointed:

Melbourne: Vice Presidents – L.L Mount and C.R Parsons, Secretary/Treasurer – G. Beech, Committee – W.A Lyons, Norcott, T. Statter, D.H Fox and Balderson, Captain – C.R Parsons, Vice-Captain – L.L Mount

Carlton: President – John Munro MLA, Captain – J.G Barclay, Secretary/Treasurer – C.T Harper, Committee – J. McHarg, Edgar, Fraser, Eville, and Batten

South Melbourne: President – Andrew Lyell MLA, Vice Presidents – W.J Mountain, Dr Wm. Barker, Secretary/Treasurer – E.C Tribe, Captain – W. Cameron, Committee- Fookes, Mallinson, Holloway, Turnley and Anderson.

Fitzroy: President – H.P Fergie, Captain and Secretary - Bill Lyons, Treasurer – Harry Jones, Committee – Messrs. Clouston, Dobbinson, Finlay, Heale and Peddington

Reporting under the Indian *nom de plume*, 'Caughnawaga', the Leader newspaper gave good coverage to the opening games and made a separate report on the progress and prospects for the game, with special attention given to the issue of rough play[9]...

> "The Association has adopted a code of playing rules directed to the end of making the game more gentlemanly and freer from roughness. On this head I feel it my bounden duty to make a few remarks. Roughness has never been, and so far as I can see will never be, essential to good play; in fact it is quite otherwise – the experience of all competent judges goes to prove that the players who make a special study of rough play never can hope to become proficient in the more delicate and dexterous points of the game. Let a swiper ask himself the question 'to what good purpose all this swiping and flailing?" and he will, without much twisting and turning of the matter over in his mind, arrive at the conclusion- to no good purpose. It is positively necessary that a player, when checking, should retain the most pertinacious control over his crosse, and this he will find it impossible to do if he indulges in the "swipe" or "sledge-hammer" mode of checking. The loss of a thorough control of his crosse places him at a considerable disadvantage, and his opponent, a wily player doubtless, fails not to avail himself of the opening, and probably scores a goal for his side, or materially assists towards scoring one. Young players will do well to cultivate a gentlemanly and scientific style of play, leaving roughness altogether in the background."

The recruits, known as 'apprentices' or 'prentice boys' were an unknown quantity when matches started. Some had practiced assiduously and others were very raw, having been drawn to the new excitement by their friends and work colleagues. The parent club, Melbourne, played in the inaugural game against South Melbourne at Albert Park and Carlton met Fitzroy at the Fitzroy Cricket Ground.[10]

4 – REDS VERSUS BLUES AND THE VLA

Fittingly, Lambton Mount scored the only goal in the match at Albert Park, leading his charges to a 1 goal to nil victory. Prominent players for Melbourne were Statter, Mount, Beech, Balderson and Griffin while for South Melbourne Mallinson, Fookes and Rodier distinguished themselves.

The teams for this match were:

Melbourne: *(wearing colours of navy blue guernsey, white and red)*	C.R Parsons (Captain), L. Mount (Vice-Captain), Beech, Bennett, Balderson, C. Cottrill, H. Cottrill, Fox, Gregory, Mathews, Morton, Norcott, and J. Statter. Emergencies: Griffin, Bure and Neate
South Melbourne: *(wearing white guernsey, navy knickerbockers, light blue stockings and cap)*	Fookes, Mallinson, Tribe, Rodier, Anderson, Kellett, Ford, Raine, Turnley, Holloway, Cameron, Eville and McKee. Emergencies: H. Knight, W. Buckhurst.

The other game resulted in a 2-all draw with both teams having a large number of players making their first appearance at lacrosse. The following players participated:

Carlton: *(wearing colours of navy blue and white)*	J. G Barclay (Captain), Whitehead (Vice-Captain), Armstrong, Batten, Edgar, P. Eville, Fraser, Green, Harper, Martin, Millett, McAinsh, J. McHarg, McKenzie, and Sinclair. Emergencies: Corteen, S. Eville, Cole
Fitzroy: *(wearing colours of grey and blue)*	Fookes, Mallinson, Tribe, Rodier, Anderson, Kellett, Ford, Raine, Turnley, Holloway, Cameron, Eville and McKee. Emergencies: H. Knight, W. Buckhurst.

The goal-scorers were Sinclair and Fraser for Carlton and Pryde and Lyons for Fitzroy.

The 1879 season progressed through fourteen rounds of fixtured matches with no formal finals matches. Carlton headed the table when the wind-up was reached in September. When compared with other sports, promotional activities to expand the game were not especially to the fore in 1879. Towards the latter half of the playing season, two public exhibition games were conducted using a 'Combination Match' format in which the best eight players from each club were selected and combined into two opposing teams, Melbourne/Fitzroy and South Melbourne/Carlton. The second of these matches was played on the Melbourne Cricket Ground and used as a season-closer during early October. Response was less than hoped for with only 300 spectators paying the sixpence admission fee.[11]

Australian football, by comparison, was active and innovative with its promotions. On Tuesday, August 2, 1879 the first-ever football match under electric light was played between the East Melbourne Artillery and the Collingwood Rifles at the MCG. Under the co-ordination of Lieutenant T. Draper of the Army Engineers Corps, five first-class steam engines produced the largest display of outdoor lighting ever witnessed in Australia. Two military bands and a 20-man tug of war added colour to the novelty on the night.[12]

Newspaper support for the VLA and the new club competition was reasonable but modest throughout 1879. The Age, The Argus, The Herald, The Leader, the Australasian and the Weekly Times all carried reports on lacrosse and sometimes published team selections for the coming matches. The better players for the year came mainly from the 'old hands' that had spent the previous years developing their craft in the Reds and Blues competition. The shift to a club-based format proved successful with a total of around 100 participating players but the challenge for the 1880s was to expand the number of clubs and players.

The Eighties

Suggested New Image for Lacrosse, Australasian Newspaper 1880

At the commencement of the 1880 season, an unsuccessful attempt was made to have the playing rules changed to widen the goal-posts.[13] As justification for the change, the Melbourne Club pointed to the low scoring in games and their record of two wins, three losses and nine draws from a total of fourteen matches during 1879.

Apart from Melbourne, each of the other clubs experienced strong increases to their playing lists but there was no attempt to enter multiple teams and no new clubs emerged. Some amusing, external advice on how to grow public support for the game came during July from the Australasian newspaper.

Writing as "An Outsider", the Australasian journalist reviewed the sports played in the colony and concluded that football stood way ahead of any other activity. Football was drawing crowds of 13,000 spectators and gates of £400 with large numbers of young women attending to enjoy the gladiatorial spectacle. Lacrosse, it was concluded, needed help[14]...

> "Up to the present time this game has been played, as a rule, to empty benches. The 13,000 to 14,000 spectators are conspicuous by their absence, and youth beauty are 'nowhere' on the ground. I have an idea – I may be wrong – that if the able youths who indulge in lacrosse would adopt some picturesque costume - say, the dress of the Iroquois Indians who are dabs at the game - good houses would be the rule, and the sixpences would come rolling in. This suggestion I present free of charge, and if the gentlemen concerned would kindly glance at the engraving given above, they would, I am sure, at once see the immense advantage of going in for a little of the show business"

4 – REDS VERSUS BLUES AND THE VLA

When the close of season came in 1880, Fitzroy headed the table with Melbourne in second place. The first mention of trophies for lacrosse came from the Melbourne club where Mr. Bennett donated three items to be awarded within the club to the best players for the season. James Statter, Dave Fox and George Beech were the recipients.

At the first Annual Meeting of the VLA, held at the Clarence Hotel, on Saturday, April 24, 1880, the following office-bearers were appointed:[15]

> President: John Wagner
>
> Vice Presidents: Lambton Mount and Bill Fookes
>
> Secretary: Bill Lyons
>
> Treasurer: Jim Barclay

The President, John Wagner was a Canadian born businessman who had come to the goldfields in the 1850s and subsequently built a highly successful coach building and transport business.

Pro-active promotions by the VLA brought some lacrosse growth in 1881 when two new clubs, South Yarra and Collingwood, were added to the VLA membership. Bill Lyons provided direct help to get South Yarra formed and Joel Fox and Morton (Melbourne), agreed to play with South Yarra and help develop the new young players. Similarly, George Beech left his home club, Melbourne, to coach and play at the newly formed Collingwood club, where he was appointed as Captain. Both new clubs performed creditably in their first year and each went on to later become VLA premiers, but neither lasted more than a total of ten years before disbanding or going into recess.

Two important names came to prominence in Victorian lacrosse in 1881; Joel Fox with the Melbourne Club and Phillip Shappere with the Carlton Club. In later years both became long-serving dynamos within the promotion and administration of the sport. Recognizing the stimulus which would come from a trophy to acknowledge the premier team at the conclusion of the club competition, Phil Shappere, an importer and manufacturing jeweller, donated a silver goblet as a VLA trophy. This trophy was won, and retained, by the Fitzroy Lacrosse Club.

In 1881, the VLA made its first attempt to influence some regional growth when it arranged for 28-30 of the best players in the colony to play an Exhibition Match on the 24th May at Kyneton, 45 miles north-west of Melbourne.[16] Diabolic weather ruined the spectacle and, after a thank-you dinner at the Junction Hotel, the players returned to Melbourne by the 9.12 pm train. No new club resulted from this venture, but Kyneton did form a team some years later.

In April 1882, it was noted that a group was practising lacrosse on a vacant allotment adjoining the Royal Saxon paddock in Ballarat.[17] Arrangements had been made for the VLA to send a group of 26 players to Ballarat for exhibition matches on Easter Friday and Easter Monday. A preliminary meeting to form a club in Ballarat was held at Antcliffe's Hotel on the 18th of April with 20 men attending. The meeting resolved to form the Ballarat Lacrosse Club, the first regional club to be established in Victoria.[18] Subsequently Amos Norcott attended a practice session in May to provide coaching for

the new Ballarat players. Unhappily, this new club failed to take the field apart from some practice sessions, apparently due to a lack of suitable lacrosse sticks. A further four years would pass before a club was re-formed and lacrosse at Ballarat became a reality.

In 1882, Phil Shappere presented another premier team trophy, this time a fine engraved silver urn which was to be retained by any club that won it twice. South Melbourne Lacrosse Club won the competition in successive years, 1882-83 and was presented with the award. The trophy carried an inscription acknowledging the then President of the VLA, Mr James Balfour MLA. Balfour was an appointed figurehead but did not have any active involvement in the administration of lacrosse. Curiously, the South Melbourne club added an extra inscription to the trophy and awarded it to its two best players who were considered to have been responsible for the premiership success – George and Weymyss Gordon. The trophy was theirs to retain and was not seen again for 134 years until it turned up on a public auction site and was eventually purchased by the Victorian Lacrosse Foundation and donated back to the Victorian Association in 2019.

The Shappere Urn

In recognition of the outstanding administrative career of its original donor, the trophy was re-named as "The Shappere Urn" and established as a perpetual trophy to be awarded to the individual, club or group that does most to grow lacrosse in Victoria each year. The inaugural winner of the award in 2019 was Nick Anthony from the Melbourne University Lacrosse Club for work he had done in building a national lacrosse competition among Australian universities and colleges. The award was not presented in 2020 when the parent Association, Lacrosse Victoria, was forced to cancel all competitions due to the worldwide coronavirus pandemic.

Some club growth occurred in 1882 with the addition of the St Kilda club in March and Richmond Lacrosse Club. Both played for just one season. Richmond disbanded in 1883 and joined with an expanded group to form the East Melbourne Lacrosse Club. Access for lacrosse to the well-located East Melbourne Oval (adjacent to the Melbourne Cricket Ground on the city side) appears to have been the rationale for the merger. The St Kilda players threw in their lot with the South Yarra and South Melbourne clubs. South Yarra ultimately became the most successful of the new clubs, re-naming for a short time as St Kilda, and then emerging as a force in later years until its disbandment a few years after the World War. East Melbourne competed in the 1883 competition, expanded to two teams in 1884 (Reds and Rovers) and played in 1885 before disbanding.

In November, 1882, Lambton Mount witnessed first-hand the exposure and public adulation that top level sport could bring in Australia when he travelled home with the Australian Cricket Team on a voyage of the Pacific mail steamer RMS City of New York from San Francisco to Sydney via New Zealand. The Australian Cricket team had completed a highly successful 38 match tour of England, winning all but 4 matches against first-class teams and beating the All-England eleven. The team included Mount's friend, star cricketer, Fred Boyle, who had helped Lambton when he set up his promotions committee for the introduction of lacrosse in 1876. Mount, and another Australian cricketer, George Bonnor famously almost missed the ship when it was forced to wait for them and was late sailing out of Auckland for Sydney on November 20, 1882. The team was lauded and given a lavish and triumphant welcome when it arrived back in Australia.

Further pictorial content depicting lacrosse was published in the Australasian Sketcher in 1882 in the form of a lithograph engraving. This depiction is reproduced in Chapter 6.

Significant Developments

Many significant developments came during 1883.

The first was the action taken by South Australian, Alf Wilkinson in arranging a public meeting in Adelaide to initiate lacrosse. Wilkinson had been inspired by the contact he had with lacrosse when he visited the Gordon family in Emerald Hill, Victoria in mid-1882. Wilkinson's Adelaide bid failed initially but was the first sign of a colony outside of Victoria showing an interest in the sport.

The second important event in 1883 was the formation of the Melbourne University Lacrosse Club at a meeting held at the University on Wednesday 25th of April.[19] The Melbourne University Club started slowly, then prospered as a premiership club during 1897, 98 and 99. The club has survived to the present day as Australia's oldest continuing club, along the journey producing many fine players and administrators. It is, arguably, the oldest lacrosse club in the world that has remained in continuous existence, its ongoing presence since 1883 broken only by brief periods of forced recess during the World War years of 1914-18 and 1939-45. Harvard University Lacrosse was established two years earlier than the Melbourne University club but it experienced a brief period during the 1890s when it went into recess and did not field a team.

From the outset, the club was afforded strong support by the academic staff of the University, but was structured to be run by the student population. The following were the founding fathers of the Melbourne University club:

Patron: Dr. Hearn

President: Professor McCoy

Vice Presidents: Professors, Strong, Halford, Siklington, Marron, Andrews and Smith

Captain: John Parnell

Hon. Secretary/Treasurer: R.W Smith

Committee: Messrs. Tyers, Rogers, Reade, Horne, Chase, Parnell and Smith.

The decision to form the University club in late April of 1883 left little opportunity for team preparation but an enthusiastic group of players enrolled and managed two practice sessions before their first VLA scheduled match. The playing colours were a blue jersey, white knickerbockers, blue stockings and a blue, white and black cap.

The University club played its first-ever match with a team of novice players on Saturday 5th May, 1883 against South Yarra at Albert Park and was soundly beaten by 6 goals to nil. The inaugural playing group included Messrs. Bromfield, Clendlahem, Horne, Joske, Parnell, Kenny, Pitcher, Reade, Ross, Smith, Wingrove, Vaughan, Faney, James and Wilson. [20]

John Parnell served as University Captain for seven years and was a member of the second Victorian team in 1889, before pursuing a military career in which he became Commandant of the Duntroon Military Academy, was promoted to Major-General and cited as CMG OBE., and then retiring to serve as Administrator of Lord Howe Island.[21] Other notables in the inaugural University team included Fred Wingrove who moved to Perth and became a founder of lacrosse in Western Australia. Later notables, who commenced their lacrosse in the pioneer years with University, included John Latham and the Murray brothers, Cecil, Hugh and Noel. Cecil Murray played with University in the late 1880s, before transferring in 1891 as a founding member of Caulfield where he became a champion attack player and triple premiership Captain. Subsequently, in 1897, he moved to help form the MCC club.

The earliest team photograph of the Melbourne University Lacrosse Club during the colonial era is from 1897 and is reproduced below. Of particular note is the length of the strung sections of the Flannery lacrosse sticks and the lack of any pocket in the stringing.

The third development of note during 1883 was the promotion and commencement in Victoria of regional lacrosse at Sandhurst (Bendigo). This followed an exhibition game organized by the Association in the gold-fields town on Monday, May 28, 1883 during the Queen's Birthday weekend.[22] Twenty-eight players from six of the VLA metropolitan clubs travelled by train to Bendigo and played at the Camp Reserve as part of this promotion. Despite wet weather, they were watched by some 900 spectators. Later, on Thursday evening, 31st of May, twenty-five young men attended a meeting at Bailes London Hotel and voted to form the Bendigo Lacrosse Club. The entrance fee was set at 2s 6p, and the playing colours selected as red cap, navy blue guernsey and knickerbockers and red stockings. At an adjourned meeting one week later, the following office-bearers were elected: President – Mr A.S Bailes, Vice-Presidents – Messrs. A. Joseph, W.G Jackson and W. Bruce, Secretary- A. Allsop, Treasurer – A.S Bailes and Committee – J. McLean, C. Hunt, T. Skues, W. Honeybone, W. McLean and A. Bishop. Alf Bailes was a local Council member and later Member of the Victorian Parliament representing Sandhurst.

The Bendigo Club played internal matches and was active in seeking to spread the sport among nearby towns in the Bendigo District. It had good support from the local media which highlighted the qualities and skilful, but non-violent, nature of lacrosse compared with other sports.

> *"In playing lacrosse the muscular action is not confined to any particular part of the body, as in other games, but brings into play the arms, legs, and body, develops self-reliance and awakens the energies of all players. It is totally different to cricket or football, and possesses many novelties which constitute in a great measure the beauties of the game.* [23]

4 – REDS VERSUS BLUES AND THE VLA

Melbourne University Lacrosse Team 1897

The Bendigo Advertiser subsequently published a full copy of the VLA playing rules on Saturday, 2nd of June.

In July, the Bendigo club played an exhibition match at Castlemaine and followed this with a match at Canterbury Park in Eaglehawk on August 2, 1883.[24] Lacrosse came more prominently to public notice in Bendigo during August when the Melbourne University club agreed to send a team to play against the locals. The Fife and Drum Band of the Industrial School marched through the streets to herald the match at the Upper Reserve on the 22nd of August, and later played at intervals throughout the game. The University won the game by 3 goals to nil and the players were entertained at a Dinner Dance at the Metropolitan Hotel before returning to Melbourne by train. A club operates today at Bendigo and participates in the winter inter-club competition organized by the governing Association, Lacrosse Victoria. Its existence has been precarious and transient, but the Bendigo Lacrosse name has survived despite long periods of recess, the interruptions of World Wars and the difficulties of operating in isolation, one hundred kilometres from Melbourne.

VLA Premiership Medallion 1884

The year 1884 brought further growth in Victoria. Nine teams competed in the 1884 VLA fixture which included two teams from Collingwood (Reds and Blues), two teams from East Melbourne (Reds and Rovers) plus Fitzroy, Melbourne, University, South Melbourne and Bohemians. South Melbourne claimed the premiership and their players each received silver medallions presented by Phil Shappere.

The Bohemians Lacrosse Club was formed in 1884 when the Carlton club resolved to discontinue and rename as Bohemians.[25] The name derived from a fashionable cultural and lifestyle movement that had been founded in 1875 and gained a strong following in Melbourne among a section of young men at the time. The Bohemian Club drew its members from the same families as the exclusive Melbourne Club and saw themselves as elegant and cultured sportsmen, playing cricket in summer and performing theatricals during winter. Through their dress and their artistic interests, they strived to create a persona that set them apart from the rigidness of Victorian Melbourne. Their membership included Tom Roberts and Frederick McCubbin of the Heidelberg School of painters, Marcus Clarke, Adam Lindsay Gordon and captains of industry which included Russell Grimwade. Jim Barclay moved the motion to rename the Carlton Club as the Bohemians and

Depiction of Lacrosse in the USA 1884

4 – REDS VERSUS BLUES AND THE VLA

"Hard Pressed" Lacrosse in Canada, Harpers Weekly, 1888

Phil Shappere, Jim Fraser, Bill Batten, Claude Harper, and Phil Mercer all were elected as part of the new committee. The club played with mixed success during 1884 and struggled in 1885 before merging with Fitzroy. Later, many of the Bohemians were involved in the establishment of the Hawthorn Lacrosse Club, founded in 1893. The Bohemian movement itself began to fizzle around this time and faded from favour.

It was not uncommon at this time in Australia, for people to subscribe to English, Canadian and American magazines such as The Illustrated London Times, Harper's Weekly and Illustrated Canadian Times. Lacrosse illustrations and sketches, like the following, appeared occasionally and were helpful in providing a visual appreciation of the sport. The following are from Harper's Weekly in May, 1884 and August, 1886. Action photographs of lacrosse began to appear in newspapers from the late 1890s.

The Stalwarts

By the close of 1884 the VLA had matured into its role of overseeing the annual club competition, setting playing rules, organizing an annual dinner and conducting special events designed to expand the sport. As an organization, it was not overtly assertive and relied on a democratic governance structure in which each member club was entitled to have a say through two appointed representatives. A small group of dedicated 'stalwart' pioneers, recruited originally in 1876 as young men by Lambton Mount, did most of the organizing work for the Association and their clubs. Mount was absent overseas from October, 1872 until April, 1873 but, despite his growing business commitments, he maintained a close presence in the VLA. As a delegator, however, Mount was happy to hand over the President role and have other trusted stalwarts looking after the key administrative functions. Each of these trusted men developed successful business careers and became influential community figures outside of lacrosse. Principally, these stalwarts included the following:

George Beech

George Beech - resident in Emerald Hill when he started lacrosse in 1876 as a 17-year-old. Beech played with Melbourne and served as Club secretary and VLA delegate, VLA Treasurer, coach of the newly established Collingwood club in 1881 and was instrumental in the formation of the Kew Lacrosse Club. Employed as a Manager in a printing inks firm and transferred to Sydney in 1883 to set up a branch. Was a founder of lacrosse in New South Wales and remained active in the sport in administration, promotion and refereeing after returning to Victoria. As Lambton Mount's first 'recruit', Beech is regarded as the "Australian father of lacrosse".

Bill Lyons – 19 years old and resident in Emerald Hill when he started playing in 1876. Became a key player, captain and driver in the Fitzroy club. Trained and employed as an Accountant and later became principal in his Melbourne -based business firm. Served as VLA Secretary for 9 years, 1876-1885.

Jim Barclay – 18 years old when he started playing in 1876. Captained the Carlton and Bohemian clubs and served on the club committees and as a delegate to the VLA. Appointed as the inaugural Treasurer of the VLA, and continued in the position for eight years.

Joel Fox

Joel Fox –born in Fitzroy to English parents in 1855. Attended the Old Model School in Melbourne and became a law clerk in his uncle's firm before serving as Managing Law Clerk in several firms and graduating as a Solicitor. Lived at Emerald Hill when he started lacrosse in 1876, aged 20 years. Appointed as General Manager of Equity Trustees, Executors and Agencies Company and held the role for almost 50 years before retiring in 1933. Prominent in the Commercial Traveler's Association and Rotary. In lacrosse, served as Captain of the Melbourne club, Secretary of the VLA and subsequently VLA President for twenty-one years commencing in 1916. Keen bridge player along with his brother Len J Fox who was a Bridge authority and also played lacrosse. Another brother, Dr David. H Fox also played lacrosse and served the VLA. His most famous brother was Emanuel Phillips Fox, the eminent and prolific Australian painter linked to the famed Australian Impressionist School

Phillip Shappere - Phil was one of the "Reds v Blues" players when lacrosse started in Melbourne. He later played with South Melbourne when the VLA started and travelled as a member of the South

4 – REDS VERSUS BLUES AND THE VLA

Melbourne team to Adelaide in 1887, the forerunner of inter-colonial contests. Subsequently, he held the office of VLA President for twenty-one years, 1895-1915 and was always a keen spectator at interstate matches. A manufacturing jeweller by profession, Phil made numerous generous donations of trophies and premiership medallions to assist the growth of the game. Later, his son, Phillip H. Shappere continued the family contribution to lacrosse with a five-year term as VLA President, 1964-68.

Phil Shappere

Bill Fookes - started lacrosse in 1876, aged 22 years. Outstanding defence player and Committee member with South Melbourne club. Trained as a solicitor and became a partner in the firm of Hedderwick, Fookes and Alston. Became a Director of leading companies, President of the Law Institute, Alfred Hospital, Grand Registrar of the Masonic Lodge and Treasurer of the Yoric Club. Served in lacrosse and was also involved in swimming and hunting.

Amos C. Norcott - along with George Beech, Amos "Amo" Norcott was one of the first young men to respond to the lacrosse opportunity offered by Lambton Mount. He was born in Bendigo in 1856, the son of an English military man who had migrated to the goldfields and a nephew of Mount's great athletics rival, H.C Harrison. His grandfather, Major General Sir Amos Norcott C.D K.C.P. had served with the English military under the Duke of Wellington at the Battle of Waterloo. Amos played lacrosse for a few years and assisted in administration, but his passion was Australian Rules Football and he was appointed as the Secretary of the Melbourne Football Club between 1898-1906.

Walter B. House – born in Sandridge (Bendigo) Active in Rowing and lacrosse and later lawn bowls. Employed as a Civil Servant in the Titles and Taxation Office and later became the curator of intestate estates. Early President of Malvern Lacrosse Club and wrote a weekly column on lacrosse for the Leader newspaper for some years. Started Playing 1880's and played in the 1892 Victorian team against South Australia.

Walter House

Bill Heale – a native of Jersey who arrived in Melbourne as a 14-year-old in 1872. Founder and Managing Director of William Heale & Co., Shipping Agents in Collins Street, Melbourne for the Australia-Italia Line and later Secretary of the Commonwealth Shipping Board.

Dr. David H.Fox – brother of Joel Fox, aged 18 when he started lacrosse in 1879 and was also a skilled and avid cricketer and cricket administrator. Served the VLA as a club delegate, Secretary and Association Auditor, and later was a key mover in the formation of the Caulfield Lacrosse Club in 1893, before transferring to the MCC club.

Of all these men, Joel Fox, Phil Shappere and George Beech stand out as the three of Mount's pioneers who gave long service as volunteers and had the most impact on the subsequent shaping of the sport.

In 1885, Victoria entered its tenth year of lacrosse, all played internally within a small, but keen, metropolitan club competition bolstered by a handful of regional clubs and overseen by the VLA.

The hoped-for expansion of the game to other Australian colonies had not occurred but that was about to change.

Meanwhile, news came through of an important breakthrough in New South Wales. The Sydney Lacrosse Club had been formed on July 19, 1885 and practice sessions had commenced using the 'Reds versus Blues" competition format followed in the early days in Victoria.

Notes

1. Weekly accounts in the Leader (Melbourne) newspaper, April- October 1876-1878
2. Leader (Melbourne) 15/09/1877 p.2
3. Illustrated Australian News 4/09/1876 p.136
4. The Age (Melbourne) 9/07/1872 p.3
5. The Australasian (Melbourne) 7/06/1879 p.31
6. The Age (Melbourne) 23/09/1878 p.4
7. Leader (Melbourne) 7/12/1878 p.3
8. The Age (Melbourne) 28/03/1879 p.3
9. Leader (Melbourne) 26/04/1879 p.13
10. Leader (Melbourne) 26/04/1879 p.13
11. Leader (Melbourne) 4/10/1879 p.12
12. The Argus (Melbourne) 6/08/1879 p.3
13. The Age (Melbourne) 10/04/1880 p.6
14. The Australasian Sketcher with Pen & Pencil (Melbourne) 3.07/1880 p.157
15. The Age (Melbourne) 24/04/1880 p.6
16. The Age (Melbourne) 23/05/1881 p.3
17. The Ballarat Star 24/04/1882 p.3
18. The Ballarat Star 17/04/1882 p.3
19. The Argus (Melbourne) 26/04/1883 p.10
20. The Telegraph, St Kilda, Prahran & South Yarra Guardian 12/05/1885 p.5
21. The Australasian (Melbourne) 11/07/1931 p.9
22. The Age (Melbourne) 28/05/1883 p.1
23. Bendigo Advertiser 23/05/1883 p.1
24. Bendigo Advertiser 23/08/1883 p.3
25. Sportsman (Melbourne) 26/03/1884 p.4

SECTION THREE
ACROSS COLONIAL BORDERS

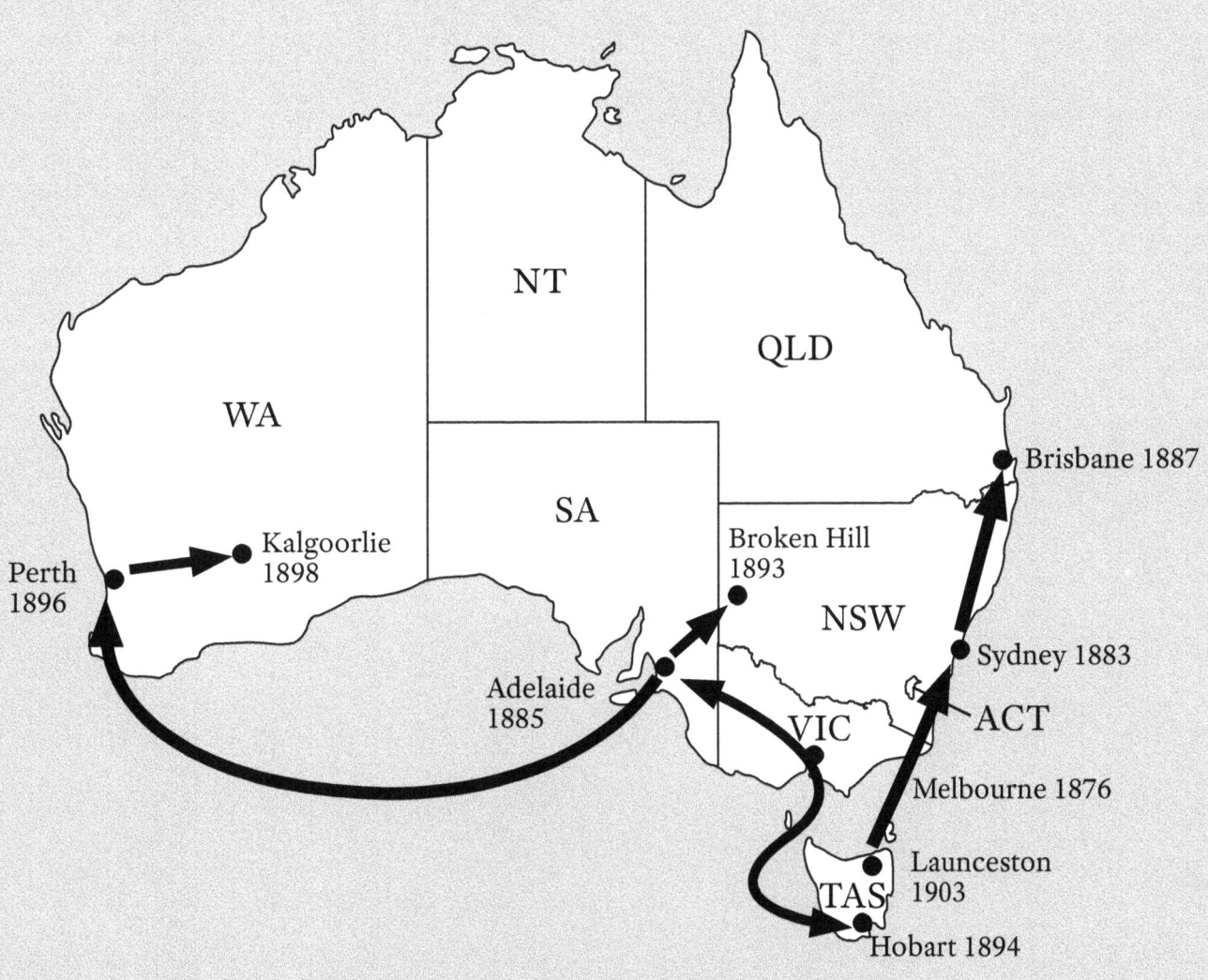

The Expansion of Lacrosse in Colonial Australia

New South Wales

In 1883 New South Wales became the second Australian colony to actively take up lacrosse.

It could easily have been the first, almost twenty years earlier, if the local population had responded to an entertaining display of the Canadian game which was staged at Sydney's Crystal Palace on November 24, 1867. The occasion was the Sydney Flower and Fruit Show with lacrosse included as part of the ancillary entertainments.

In an article published in the Sydney Morning Herald under the nom de plume of "Peter Possum", an enthusiastic report was given on the 'New Game – La Crosse' and the journalist judged it as the "Best Game Out". 'Peter Possum' was the renowned English-born journalist and writer, Richard Rowe, who was famed for his lively sketches of colonial life during many years spent in Australia.

Peter Possum's account notes that the appearance of eighteen Indian natives from Canada at Sydney's Crystal Palace was, in itself, and exciting curiosity. His report, which is reproduced in part below, contains what is possibly the most insightful description and evaluation ever written on the unique appeal of lacrosse. The subsequent lacrosse game on the cricket field provided a display of a kind never before witnessed in Australia. It was described as follows:[1]

> "Nine were dressed in blue caps, blue baggy breeches, with a fringe of red, grey jerseys, white stockings and moccasins; and nine in red caps, red baggy breeches with a fringe of blue, and jerseys &c like their rivals. The first to show were the flag-bearing goal-keepers, who at opposite sides of the field pitched and mounted guard over a brace of flags a piece, some few feet apart – red watching over blue flags, and blue over red.

Then the next of the players marched into the middle of the ground, all peeled off their monkey-jackets, the La Crosse ball was thrown up and the exciting game began. It is played with a bat that is kind of a cross between a battledore and a hockey stick - a stout painted stick with its end brought round in a tightly tied curve and between the bent end and straight stick, a net of cord. The object of each party is to drive the ball between its own foe-blockaded flags. A Red man, say, catches the ball or spoons it up: Off like a hare he runs with it towards his own goal, his white legs lifted in such twinkling alternation that, thaumatrope-like, they both seem to be on the ground. After him races a blue man. Red doubles like a hare; blue turns with him far sharper than a greyhound. Red is foiled and flings the ball with a huge swing to his comrade nearest to their goal. It is caught with marvelous dexterity, but a Blue the next moment has it out of Red's net. With clashing clubs and jostling shoulders, a close fight is kept up for it for a minute between rapidly succeeding pairs of combatants; a red man thinks he has made sure of it but as his club rattles on Blue's, the ball flies out of Blue's net into another Blue's and Red is as far off as ever from the victory. The ball gets near a goal and the adverse keeper rushes forth to bar its entrance. Perhaps he succeeds, and sends it far over the confused crowd of strugglers towards his own goal. Perhaps he fails; the ball shoots between the staves, and a roar of congratulation from the on-lookers proclaims that a goal is won.

In my humble opinion, La Crosse is the "best game out".

Bystanders can understand it at once. and take an intense interest in its ever-varying fortunes. It is as exciting as football, without football's rough-and-tumble brutality. It gives scope for "drives" as splendid as any at golf, without golf's sleepy walks after the balls, and finnicky peddling around the holes. Unlike cricket it keeps all the players on both sides constantly employed – except the goalkeeper, and they too ever and anon, have to rush to the rescue like Achilles, and must always be on the most vigilant look-out. Bowler and batsman do not monopolize the lion's share of interest at La Crosse: it does not keep fielders shivering with palms planted on their knees; each player becomes in very rapid turn bowler, batsman and fielder. For making the eye quick, the breath good, the leg swift and the arm strong, for giving exciting entertainment to non-experts, and for sharing chances of display impartially amongst the players, La Crosse, I repeat, appears to be unrivalled amongst games. In a picturesque point of view, too, it beats any I know: the rival uniforms now in-rushing and now radiating, constantly forming kaleidoscopic combinations on the green sward".

The timing of this lacrosse exhibition in Sydney in 1867 is extraordinary. A few months earlier in June 1867, Dr George Beers formulated in Canada the first uniform code of playing rules for lacrosse. Shortly after, the new Dominion of Canada passed an Act of Parliament on July 1, 1867 making lacrosse the national game of Canada. Organized lacrosse was in its infancy and Sydney, unknowingly, was the recipient of one of the earliest displays of the sport given outside of Canada.

Regrettably, Peter Possum's 1867 account did not inspire a start on lacrosse in Sydney. Within all aspects of human endeavor, the geographic spread of new ideas and activities requires both an active source and a rationale. The active source was present in the remarkable Crystal Palace exhibition but the rationale to start the sport was not.

Apart from direct people-to-people communication, information exchange at this time came mainly from the newspapers. Lacrosse was not a beneficiary of newspaper coverage in Sydney during the six years which followed the start of lacrosse in Melbourne in 1876. Not one single article on the sport was published by the leading Sydney newspapers.

The only references to lacrosse were a two-line report in the Evening News in 1881 about lacrosse players from Canada intending to tour and play exhibition games in England and Ireland[2] and a 'scientific' piece on performance enhancement in sport which turned up in the *Riverine Grazier* and the *Sydney Mail* in 1882. The story was that players from the Toronto Lacrosse Club were drinking a concoction made from cocoa leaves to prevent them from getting fatigued during games.[3]

A number of things are surprising about this almost total lack of commentary about lacrosse in Sydney. The sport had been growing in Melbourne since 1876 and had eight clubs, a parent Association, an inter-club competition and regular newspaper coverage. Also, the sport was making headlines in other parts of the British Empire with stories of substantial growth and Royal patronage.

Maybe the Sydney establishment and the press were reflecting the mutual jealousy that existed from early times between Sydney and Melbourne. Maybe they were treating lacrosse, like Australian football, as a 'Melbourne thing'. It is clear that there were men in Sydney who had played lacrosse in Melbourne, or other parts of the world, and had relocated to New South Wales. None had put up their hand to initiate lacrosse until George Beech arrived in Sydney from Melbourne in 1883 as a twenty-four-year-old on an employment transfer with F.T Wimble & Co, a printing inks supply firm. Beech had been Lambton Mount's first recruit to lacrosse in Melbourne and the first Australian-born person to take up the game. He played in the opening three years of the 'Reds v Blues' scrimmages in Albert Park in Melbourne and continued with the Melbourne Lacrosse Club when the VLA competition commenced in 1879. Later, he left the Melbourne Club to help establish and coach a club at Collingwood. He was a passionate advocate for the sport and wasted no time in seeking to introduce it in his new home city.

Sydney Lacrosse Club

Early in July of 1883 the *Sydney Mail & New South Wales Advertiser* reported that lacrosse was becoming popular in England and Ireland and that Melbourne had a dozen or so clubs. By way of explanation about the sport, it reported that[4]....

> *"the crosse is nothing more than an enlarged tennis bat with a long lance-wood or hickory handle to give it plenty of spring to propel the ball"*

Shortly after, the *Sydney Daily Telegraph* ran a short piece on lacrosse, advising that a number of leading members of lacrosse clubs from Victoria had taken up abode in Sydney and were endeavoring to start the game. The paper included a positive description of the qualities of the sport, advising that[5]....

> *"Accurate slinging, speed and long wind were the principal qualifications needed for the game and players of all weights can take part in it: checking, which means the displacing of the ball from an opponent's stick or crosse, being the only aggressive action allowed."*

This was the perfect opening for George Beech. In company with John Millett, Beech organized a public meeting of "gentlemen favorable to introducing lacrosse". This meeting, held at Ramford's Cambridge Club Hotel on Friday, July 19, 1883, attracted some thirty people and passed a resolution to form the Sydney Lacrosse Club.[6]

John Millett

A follow-up meeting was held a week later which set the member subscription at five shillings, made arrangements for the printing of playing rules, and settled on a uniform of dark blue stockings, knickerbockers and cap with a white jersey. George Beech was elected as Captain, Secretary and Treasurer and John Millett as Vice-Captain with Messrs. Alfred (Fred) R Gregory, W. (Bill) Howe and T. Moloney joining them to form a committee.[7] This was the founding group of lacrosse in New South Wales. The Secretary was instructed to find a suitable playing facility and to write to influential citizens seeking a Patron, President and Vice-Presidents for the new club. John Millett, who later became one of the most distinguished bankers in New South Wales, announced that he would provide a trophy valued at two guineas for the most promising novice player. Fred Gregory was an estate agent and mining broker.

Finding a playing venue proved to be tricky but a field was sourced at Mount Rennie in Moore Park, five miles south of central Sydney. This was a short distance beyond the site of the current Sydney Cricket Ground and close to Federation Valley where sixty thousand people later gathered on New Year's Day in 1901 to celebrate the reading of a proclamation from Queen Victoria which unified the six formerly independent colonies into one Commonwealth of Australia.

The area assigned for lacrosse in Moore Park was neither a good playing nor promotional venue for the sport. The surface was often wet and marshy and the location was in a quiet area of the park away from public view, described by one newspaper as an "out of the way nook". Practice sessions for the newly formed Sydney Lacrosse Club commenced at Moore Park on the 3rd of August, 1883 with Beech captaining the "Reds" and defeating Millett's "Blues" by 5 goals to 2.[8] For Beech, the occasion would have brought back strong memories of his first involvement in Albert Park in Melbourne in 1876. Weekly scrimmages continued on Saturday afternoons at Moore Park for the next two months before going into recess for 1883.

During March of 1884 a revealing report on a census taken of sports in Canada was published in Sydney newspapers. The census revealed an estimated 10.000-15,000 lacrosse players in Canada, 5000 curlers, 4000 snow-shoers, 3000-4000 cricketers, 2000 footballers, 1000 rowers, 1000 baseballers and 1000 cyclists.[9] The size of lacrosse as the dominant team sport in Canada was not lost on advocates for the sport in Australia.

In April of 1884 the first Annual General Meeting of the Sydney Lacrosse Club was held.[10] Beech was re-elected as Secretary/Treasurer and H.M Stephen became President, with T. Moloney (Captain), F. Morris (Vice-Captain) and Messrs. Charlie L. Montague, Cox and Bill Howe appointed to the

5 – NEW SOUTH WALES

Committee. Arrangements were made for weekly practice matches at Moore Park while the Club explored ways of promoting the sport to encourage new teams. An Exhibition game was conducted at the nearby suburb of Waverley with the hope of stimulating a new club. The match was well-attended but no new club emerged. At the end of winter in 1884, lacrosse in New South Wales still comprised just one club.

A similar "Reds v Blues" program was conducted during 1885 and further exhibition games were arranged before an unexpected ally came in September from the Oaklands College at Mittagong, 100 miles southwest from Sydney. Here, Mr J.T Fischer, a teacher who had been a former player and founding member at the Fireflies Lacrosse Club in England, had started a lacrosse program for students. The student team was invited to Sydney and played at Moore Park on Saturday, September 12, 1885, in what was the first bona fide lacrosse match between opposing teams in New South Wales.[11]

New South Wales Lacrosse Association

The Sydney Lacrosse Club members understood that a single club would not sustain the sport. It needed to extend its role as the founder and parent of lacrosse in New South Wales. It was clear that extra competition was needed to add appeal to the sport. Without competition, there was a danger that the repetition and potential monotony of the 'Reds v Blues' format would ultimately be the source of the club's own demise.

A boosted strategy of 'Exhibition Matches', along the lines of the game played at Waverley in 1884, was started early in 1885 to expose the sport in new parts of the city. In addition to the exhibition games, it was agreed that onlookers interested in trying the sport be invited to join the weekly scrimmages at Moore Park. The objective was simple; spread lacrosse in Sydney and spawn new clubs.

Three special exhibition games were arranged during 1885, one at Balmain, one at Redfern, and one at North Shore.[12] The Saturday afternoon practice matches of the parent club continued at Moore Park but they now had a changed purpose. They were no longer an end in themselves. Instead, they became purposeful recruiting and nurturing sessions to accommodate a growing band of aspiring new players. A watch was on for the opportunity and best timing for Sydney Lacrosse Club to split itself and start new clubs. The Havilland brothers, Cecil and Charlie, were designated to form a new club at Redfern. At Balmain, the task was assigned to Messrs. A.W McDonald, George Banks and Frank Sim. This proved to be a successful strategy as new clubs were formed at Redfern (late in 1885), and Balmain (February,1886).[13] The Balmain club commenced with a playing uniform of navy blue and white and updated this slightly in 1887 to navy blue with blue and white stockings.

 Now, with three city-based clubs plus the Oaklands School, it was time for a coordinating body. A meeting was held at Rainsford's Hotel on Friday, April 16,, 1886 to form the New South Wales Lacrosse Association (NSWLA).[14] The Hon. G.H Read MLA, was appointed as President, Mr A. Gregory as Secretary and J.S Scott as Treasurer. As distance prevented the Oaklands School from participating regularly in Sydney, a weekly inter-club match program was arranged for the Sydney clubs with separate dates allocated for games with Oaklands. As the season progressed, the Sydney Club went a step further and encouraged some of its own members to hive off and form the Iroquois Lacrosse Club late in 1886. The Iroquois started their campaign in a uniform of white flannel shirt, blue knickers, cardinal cap and stockings, and a light blue sash.

This was the first official year of inter-club lacrosse organized by the NSWLA. The clubs played each other four times with Balmain remaining unbeaten to claim both the 1886 premiership and gold medals for the players that were put up by the Association. The first premiership trophy in NSW commenced in 1887 when Mr S.J Hyam, the Balmain President, donated five guineas for trophies and the club purchased a fine silver cup which it passed to the NSWLA. The new trophy was designated to be awarded to the premier team in 1887 and was won by Balmain.

A Curious Event

Additionally, during 1886, New South Wales took a surprising jump on the other colonies when, on Wednesday the 16th of June, a team from Deniliquin in country New South Wales travelled forty miles to the Murray River inland port town of Echuca. There, they crossed the border to play a match against a team from Sandhurst (Bendigo) in Victoria.

The local newspaper carried the following account of the occasion[15] ...

> *"Yesterday afternoon teams representing the Sandhurst and Deniliquin La Crosse Clubs played an intercolonial match on the Park oval. The game attracted about 300 visitors to the Park, and was witnessed with satisfaction. The Sandhurst team, which comprised some of the best players out of Melbourne, displayed considerable science during the play, and made some good runs with the ball, they having the best of the game throughout. After half time the Deniliquin players rallied up and appeared in much better form, and by smart play prevented their opponents from scoring a number of goals. The game resulted in a victory for the Sandhurst club by three goals to nil. The Sandhurst men returned home by the 4.30pm train after giving cheers for their opponents and the Park Football Club for the use of the oval."*

Little is known regarding how this match came about. It was not an event organized or sanctioned by the NSWLA or the VLA. Sandhurst was an established and functioning club in country Victoria, formed in 1883. Nothing is known of the team from New South Wales except that a meeting had been held at the Royal Hotel in Deniliquin in March 1886 to organize a lacrosse team. Maybe there was one or more players living in Deniliquin who had played previously in Melbourne or Sydney. Maybe the match was arranged for the sole purpose of making history. For Deniliquin, apart from its participation in this match, there is no evidence of a lacrosse club existing in the town, before or after this time.

Whatever its origins. this curious match, and the Royal Hotel in Deniliquin in 1886, take their place in Australian lacrosse history for their roles in the first-ever, across-borders lacrosse contest to be played in Australia. Another year would pass before the South Melbourne Club from Victoria played matches in Adelaide and the Queensland Association invited the NSWLA to send a representative team to Brisbane for inter-colonial contests.

Royal Hotel, Deniliquin, New South Wales 1886

Expansion and Inter-Colonial Contests

Early in 1887, further exhibition matches were conducted at St Leonard's, Parramatta, Newington College at Stanmore and one was planned for Richmond but abandoned due to extreme weather. Subsequently, St Leonard's Lacrosse Club was formed in March and joined the NSWLA.[16] The club had secured the St Leonard's Reserve on the North Shore as its home ground and adopted a uniform of white jersey and knickers with blue cap and chocolate stockings. Great interest was aroused when the club announced that its appointed captain was W.A (Bill) Lyons, a former Melbourne star player. Before moving to Sydney, Lyons had played with Lambton Mount and George Beech from the beginnings of lacrosse in Melbourne and left the Melbourne Lacrosse Club to become a founder and captain of the Fitzroy club when the VLA was formed in 1879. He was identified as the first player in Australia to have won a medal for lacrosse.

Trophy matches commenced in May between the five metropolitan clubs with a separate schedule added for games between them and the Oaklands School. At the March meeting of the NSWLA, David Fox from the Melbourne Lacrosse Club attended as a guest with news from Victoria that the VLA was keen to send a representative team to Sydney for inter-colonial matches during Easter.[17] As the New South Wales season would not have commenced by Easter, the proposal was declined. Instead, it was agreed to pursue the concept for later in the year, but nothing eventuated.

When the inter-club season of 1887 ended during August, Balmain had beaten St Leonard's to take the premiership and the Hyam Cup. Two important pinnacle events were yet to come.

The first took place when the newly formed Queensland Lacrosse Association invited a representative team from New South Wales to play inter-colonial matches in Brisbane. The New South Wales team, missing some of the best players in the colony who were unavailable, travelled on a steamer by sea to Brisbane in September.

The first-ever, intercolonial match played in Australia with representative teams, was staged at the Albert Ground in Brisbane on Saturday 24th of September and, according to the *Sydney Morning Herald*,

New South Wales Intercolonial Lacrosse Team 1887
Standing: J.C. Silly, G. Noake, Geo. Banks, A.L. Silly (Capt.), W.M. Bligh, E. Broughton, C.J. Grice, S. Ball, A.O. Stevens
Kneeling: G.W. Petitt, Jas. Banks, J. Mathews, W. Howe

attracted 10,000-12,000 spectators.[18] The New South Wales team turned out in a white flannel uniform relieved by a cap and sash of light blue, the colors of the colony. They won by two goals to one, with Alf Silly becoming the first player in Australia to score a goal for a colonial team in a representative match. The visitors lost to Queensland in a return match played at Ipswich two days later.

The Tournament

In a further significant breakthrough for lacrosse in 1887, the NSWLA was assisted by the father of Federation, Sir Henry Parkes, to gain access to the Domain Cricket Ground in Sydney for the purpose of conducting a grand finale tournament to wind up the Sydney season. Until this time, cricket had defended its almost exclusive use of the Domain. The Tournament took place on Saturday, 27th of August and attracted 6000-7000 spectators.[19] It was presented in grand style with invited guests seated in a special marquee and the Naval Artillery Band adding music and color to the proceedings. The format for the six participating clubs was four heats of half-hour matches followed by a final. The inaugural tournament proved to be a great showcase for the sport in Sydney and a great success, with

5 – NEW SOUTH WALES

Balmain triumphing again over the other clubs to win the trophy of goal-post flags put up by the NSWLA. Subsequently, this event became an annual fixture in the NSWLA program.

Promoting lacrosse before the advent of action photographs presented a challenge to both the followers of the sport and to journalists. For public exposure, lacrosse had to rely on written descriptions and explanations or hand-drawn artistic illustrations. The written descriptions were often clumsy or trite and, while the cost for making and publishing lithographic illustrations was limiting, the drawings had great impact when they occasionally appeared. Fortunately for lacrosse, the Illustrated News in Sydney devoted an entire page to reporting on the Sydney Lacrosse Tournament and accompanied its report with the following characterful sketches.[20]

By 1888, lacrosse in New South Wales had established a sound structure. With six clubs in place, some two hundred players and a parent Association operating effectively, the colony now had a solid base. Included in its program were club premiership matches, a Gala Tournament, an Awards Night function and Inter-colonial matches. By this time, the supply chain also seemed to be working well with Sydney merchant stores stocking and advertising lacrosse clothing and equipment. David Jones & Co were selling lacrosse pants in navy blue and white flannel, Thompson & Giles were advertising lacrosse jerseys and hose for sale, and Burroughs & Watts were promoting a stock of fine lacrosse sticks.

Optimism, Decay and a New Association

There was good reason for optimism when the season started for 1888. New clubs at Granville and Kirribilli joined the Association, both having been nurtured by players from the existing Sydney clubs and by the local interest raised through newspaper promotions by the NSWLA of exhibition games and a Tournament on the Domain to open the season on the 26th of May.[21]

> I'M going to the LACROSSE TOURNA-
> MENT. Domain Cricket Ground, SATURDAY,
> 26th. Admission free.

The push to start a team at Granville/Parramatta was led by J. Matthews from the Redfern club. The club was formed at a meeting held at the Granville Royal Hotel on April 25, 1888 with twenty members enrolled.[22] It adopted the name, Mohicans Lacrosse Club, and selected a uniform of white serge shirt and pants, navy stockings, a red, white and blue cap and a cardinal sash around the waist. Two members, Messrs. Pass and Merton, showed what lengths they were prepared to go to in promoting the club when they turned out at the Granville Fancy Dress Carnival, held at the Rosehill Skating Pavilion, and took to the ice dressed in their lacrosse regalia.

Kirribilli was formed through the efforts of Alf Silly, a former St Leonard's player and Captain of the first Intercolonial team which played in Brisbane in 1887. The new club was admitted to the Association in April, 1888 and proved to be the unexpected star team of the competition, beating its more experienced opponents and going on to annex the premiership in its first year.[23]

Paddington Lacrosse Club commenced in the following year under the guidance of C.W Taylor, a former Iroquois member. The inter-club season finished with Kirribilli defeating the Mohicans to capture the premiership and was followed by the second staging of a Tournament in the

5 – NEW SOUTH WALES

Domain. This event was successful and attracted a detailed and illustrated report on lacrosse in the Illustrated Australian News.

In order to lift the recognition given to the premiership and tournament winners, the NSWLA instituted a Presentation Night in the form of a Theatrical and Musical Concert. This was held on Friday, September 21, in 1888 at the YMCA Hall and included musical items, recitations and trophy presentations. As can be seen from the proudly advertised program for this night, the content of nineteenth century colonial occasions of this type, differed markedly from what might be expected by today's young people:[24]

> *Part I: Pianoforte solo, "Marche Hongroise," Miss Evans; trio: "The Wealth," Messrs. S. Perryman, Burrough, and Parker; song, "Toreador's Song", (Carmen), Mr. Oscar Akhurst; song (selected), Mrs. Mollier; recitation (selected), Mr. J. Watson: song; "The Gallants of England", Mr. A.W Green; song, "No Tongue can Tell", Mr. Sydney Parryman; song, "Goodbye", Miss Perryman; song, "Big Ben," Mr. S.H Parker.*

> *Part II: Piano solo, "Symphony on American Airs", Miss Evans; song: "Queen of the Earth", Mr Oscar Akhurst; song: (selected), Miss Paisley; recitation and Aria, "Scenes that are Brightest", Miss Perryman: song: "In Tiefan Kellar Sitz ich Hier", Mr J. H Parker; song, "Welcome Pretty Primrose"", Mrs Moller; song, "Good Night Beloved", Mr. Sydney Perryman.*

The next grand occasion for the NSWLA came in August of 1889 when the Domain was the venue for the first-ever inter-colonial lacrosse match played in Sydney.[25] Some 1200 spectators watched New South Wales defeat Queensland by 11 goals to nil in the opening contest on Saturday, 24th of August. Queensland fared better and secured two drawn games in three subsequent matches played against combined club teams but suffered a loss, 6 goals to nil in the return representative match at Moore Park on the 31st of August. In addition to the five matches, elaborate preparations had been made to provide hospitality and entertainment for the visitors during their seven-day stay. This included a welcoming dinner, a harbor cruise and a concluding Smoke Night.

The New South Wales team comprised: Messrs. J Fischer, W Howe, A Silly, Davis, Barrie, B Clarke, E. Broughton, H. Jefferson, G. Banks, C Montague, B Marsh, James Silly and John Silly.

Sydney Grammar School and the London Chartered Bank started as new clubs in 1890 and lacrosse in New South Wales gave the appearance of being in a major upswing. Regrettably, both clubs lasted only one year. Following the lead given by the Iroquois and Mohican clubs, it became trendy in these years to adopt generic Indian Tribe names for new or re-formed clubs. Redfern disbanded in 1890 to re-form under the name of Delaware, Granville re-formed as the Sioux and Paddington later changed its name to the Dacotahs.

However, the emergence of new clubs in this era was not entirely positive. In some cases, what appeared to be growth, was actually a re-arrangement or re-building of former clubs that were declining or had been disbanded. Balmain and St Leonard's had merged in 1889 and continued the under the name of Balmain, but dropped out in the following year. Sydney, the colony's oldest club, found itself struggling for players for some games in 1889 and the Iroquois failed to keep an engagement with Redfern. Lacrosse was experiencing the beginnings of what proved to be a severe economic downturn and crippling depression which descended across Australia in the 1890's. Before the worst of this had passed in 1894, three quarters of Australia's banks had been forced to shut their doors, thousands of businesses were lost and hundreds of thousands of Australians found themselves without a job and in need of government support for food and shelter. In Melbourne and Sydney, the impact was particularly severe as the speculative land boom of the 1880's came to an abrupt halt and banks stopped lending money. In 1891, the Sydney Lacrosse Club removed itself from membership of the NSWLA as it felt that the Association was not doing enough to foster the sport. Subsequently, The Dacotahs sent a letter to all clubs calling for a new association to be formed with the club secretaries as the single delegates. The matter was bandied around but nothing happened until 1894 when a joint meeting of clubs declared the Association defunct and formed a new NSWLA with a restructure to two delegates per club.[26]

Colonel Lassetter

The new Association moved quickly to reconnect the lacrosse clubs to their local communities. Clubs which had adopted generic names for their teams were requested to rename them to reflect the suburbs and localities in which they were based. This led Delaware to rename as Glebe Lacrosse Club and the Dacotahs to rename as the Montrose Lacrosse Club. Glebe became a powerhouse within the competition but Montrose lasted only one year. Balmain, which had not taken the field since 1889, was revived and formed again as a new club in 1892, but managed only two seasons before going into recess.

Lassetter Trophy

Heading the re-structured NSWLA as President, was Major Harry Lassetter (soon to become Colonel), a highly respected career military man, who founded and built the New South Wales Mounted Rifles Regiment and served for a time in England with Queen Victoria's 60th Jubilee Regiment. Upon assuming the lacrosse role, Lassetter presented the NSWLA with a fine sterling silver trophy, topped with an exquisite figurine of a lacrosse player.[27] The Lassetter Trophy was to be presented each year for the premiership in the inter-club competition and retained permanently by any club which won it twice in succession or twice within three years.

By 1894, Lassetter had retired from his military career and taken over management of his family's, Lassetter & Co., merchandising business in Sydney. Staff from the company formed the Lassetters Lacrosse Club and entered the 1894 competition along with a new Granville club. The NSWLA now had eight teams and played a fourteen-week season with

5 – NEW SOUTH WALES

each club playing all other clubs twice. In 1895 the Iroquois "B" team re-established itself as Newtown Lacrosse Club.

During the mid-1890s, the quantity of newspaper reports on lacrosse in New South Wales declined. It seemed that the newspaper editors had sensed a lack of dynamism in the sport and responded with decreased coverage. The Sydney Morning Herald, Sydney's leading daily, largely dropped lacrosse at this time. Disappointingly, the original parent club, Sydney Lacrosse Club, became defunct and disappeared from the competitions in 1896. During 1897 and 1898 the established format of an inter-club competition, an Annual Tournament and occasional exhibition games continued. Other clubs disbanded or were re-formed under different names when they began to struggle for viability. An Adult Deaf-Mute club started in 1897 but the Lassetters club disbanded. The Adult Deaf team lasted only one season. In 1896 the pricing of lacrosse sticks entered new territory when Mick Simmon's store in Oxford Street advertised sticks at three different quality levels; 10 shillings, 15 shillings and 21 shillings.[28]

New South Wales Intercolonial Lacrosse Team 1897
Back Row L to R: L.L. Higgs, T.J. Redhead, P. Hundt, E.J. Robardss, A. Hopkins, W. Nicholson, H. Simpson
Middle Row: W. McLeod (Vice Captain), W. Morrison (Captain), S.B. Jago (Hon. Sec), A.P. Bradley
Sitting: P.L. Boswell

Among the most positive news of this period was the formation of the North Sydney club in 1896, drawing on a number of the former Sydney club players. This club established itself quickly and was joined by a University of Sydney club in 1898 and the Burwood Lacrosse Club in 1899. Perhaps spurred by this growth, or the prospect of the new millennium, a group of past members of the Sydney Lacrosse Club got together in 1900 and re-established the club.

Unquestionably, the most-anticipated highlight of the later years of the 1890s was the visit of a New South Wales team to Melbourne during July, 1897 to take on the might of the two premier lacrosse colonies. The team held high hopes of making a good showing but found itself outclassed, losing 17 to nil against Victoria and 13 to nil against South Australia.[29]

Victoria visited Sydney in the following year with a strong team and defeated the light blues by 16 to 3, but the showing from the New South Welshmen was an improvement and made them determined to continue with inter-colonial contests. Further cross-border exchanges occurred in 1899 when New South Wales played in Melbourne and then travelled to Adelaide for matches against South Australia. The contests were both lost but the skills gap had been narrowed with a 12 to 3 margin against Victoria and a 9 to 3 result with South Australia.

As the new millennium approached, the NSWLA was working actively to juggle the often-competing tasks of dealing with practical issues and keeping the profile high. Among the everyday matters were issues such as player insurances, catering for clubs with second teams and dealing with occasional reports of rough play. In addition, attention was needed to lifting the profile and publicizing the sport as a pathway to growth. The NSWLA was not averse to innovating. To open the 1900 season, the usual Tournament was replaced with an Athletics Carnival Day, run during April in conjunction with the Amateur Athletics Association. An afternoon program with eight lacrosse and four athletic events was devised and well attended. The competitions for the lacrosse players included novel, but testing, speed events that incorporated scooping, passing and throwing skills. A month earlier, the NSWLA had participated in a Patriotic Sports Day in Sydney to acknowledge and farewell a unit of young soldiers who were departing for active Boer War service in South Africa. Lacrosse players participated in the Mardi Gras style procession that paraded from the central city to the Royal Agricultural Showgrounds, cheered by 25,000 spectators.

By the turn of the millennium lacrosse in New South Wales had weathered its foundation years and built valuable know-how and public respect. However, despite the best endeavours of many hard-working administrators, the sport had not reached a point where it could be described as vibrant or secure.

Star Players and Officials

Not surprisingly, skilled players in sports clubs are commonly the key to maintaining morale and attracting new players. In lacrosse during the colonial era in New South Wales, the star players were often also the key club administrators. The most dedicated of them served for many years and contributed in multiple roles, often within the NSWLA and in various clubs.

5 – NEW SOUTH WALES

The stand-out players of New South Wales lacrosse during the colonial period had their talents rewarded with selection in inter-colonial teams. The best of them included:

Goalkeepers:	John Fischer (Sydney), Bill McLeod (North Sydney)
Defenders:	Alf Silly (Kirribilli), Bill Morrison (Glebe), S. B Jago (North Sydney)
Midfielders:	George Pettit (Iroquois), Ern Broughton (Face-off, Balmain), Alan R. Hopkins (North Sydney), Bill Howe (Sydney)
Attacks:	James Silly (Kirribilli), John Silly (Kirribilli), John Banks (Balmain), P.L Boswell (Glebe), W. Nicholson (Glebe)

As administrators, John Byrne, Frank Sim, Bill McLeod, George Noake, Bill Morrison, Fred Gregory, Charlie Montague and John S. Scott all stood out. Apart from his roles in New South Wales, Bill Morrison worked hard to bring some international involvement for the sport. As Secretary of NSWLA, he communicated on an ongoing basis with Canada in seeking to encourage the Dominion to send a team to Australia. This mission became a regular item on the agenda at conferences of the State Associations once Australian Federation had been achieved.

Bill Morrison

Bill Morrison was also instrumental in re-sparking lacrosse interest in Queensland which had faded out in 1895. He travelled frequently for business and, on a trip to Brisbane during 1899, made a point of catching up with some of the former players from the defunct Queensland association. He urged them to re-start the sport and offered to convene a meeting for that purpose on his next visit north.

Lacrosse in Broken Hill

Lacrosse in the far-western country town of Broken Hill was instigated in March of 1893 by Fred Inman, a former resident of Jamestown, South Australia, where he first experienced the sport.

For an isolated town in a harsh environment with a population of just 20,000, Broken Hill did well to build and maintain its own Association with four to five clubs and an ongoing winter competition. Its only interaction with the outside lacrosse world was via Adelaide teams and the northern country clubs of South Australia.

Due to its eleven hundred kilometers of separation from Sydney, Broken Hill had no direct involvement with Sydney lacrosse or the NSWLA. Broken Hill's affiliation was more naturally with South Australia and its lacrosse story is told in Chapter 6.

Notes

1. ydney Morning Herald 29/11/1867 p.3
2. Evening News (Sydney) 20/04/1881 p.3
3. The Sydney Mail & New South Wales Advertiser 2/03/1878 p.8
4. The Sydney Mail & New South Wales Advertiser 14/07/1883 p.76
5. Sydney Daily Telegraph 14/07/1883 p.7
6. The Sydney Morning Herald 20/07/1883 p.6
7. The Sydney Mail & New South Wales Advertiser 28/07/1883 p.173
8. Evening News (Sydney) 3/08/1883 p.3
9. The Maitland Mercury and Hunter River General Advertiser 29/03/1884 p.12
10. The Daily Telegraph (Sydney) 10/04/1884 p.6
11. The Daily Telegraph (Sydney) 15/09/1885 p.6
12. The Sydney Mail & New South Wales Advertiser 5/09/1885 p.522
13. Sydney Morning Herald 25/02/1886 p.7
14. The Sydney Mail & New South Wales Advertiser 17/04/1886 p.813
15. Echuca & Moama Advertiser 17/06/1886
16. The Daily Telegraph (Sydney) 5/05/1887 p.3
17. The Sydney Morning Herald 12/03/1887 p.12
18. The Sydney Morning Herald 27/09/1887 p.5
19. Evening News (Sydney) 27/08/1887 p.5
20. Illustrated Sydney News 27/09/1888 p.13
21. Daily Telegraph (Sydney) 23/05/1888 p.1
22. The Cumberland Mercury (Parramatta) 28/04/1888 p.2
23. Referee (Sydney) 19/04/1888 p.9
24. The Australian Star (Sydney) 21/09/1888 p.7
25. The Australian Star (Sydney) 26/08/1889 p.7
26. The Daily Telegraph (Sydney) 13/04/1894 p.3
27. Evening News (Sydney) 8/12/1894 p.6
28. The Australian Star (Sydney) 13/03/1896 p.8
29. Australian Town & Country Journal (Sydney) 17/07/1897/Lacrosse

South Australia

When Lambton Mount started lacrosse in Melbourne in 1876, he fully expected the sport to quickly capture the imagination of young men and spread across the borders to other Australian colonies. It took almost ten years before his dream began to be realized, much longer than Mount might have hoped.

In 1885 South Australia became the second of the colonies outside of Victoria to take up the sport. Two clubs were quickly formed but Mount could hardly have imagined that a further two years would pass before a young Jack Wainwright would pedal his penny-farthing bicycle across seventeen miles of poorly-formed tracks from Noarlunga to Adelaide to attend a meeting to establish the South Australian Lacrosse Association.[1] Wainwright was representing the Noarlunga Lacrosse Club, the second club to be established in South Australia.

Wainwright holds claim as the founder of the South Australian Lacrosse Association, but he was not the father of lacrosse in South Australia. That honor is vested with Alf Wilkinson, a young businessman in Adelaide, and came only after an initial stumble and some persistence.

Lacrosse Profile

It could not be claimed that lacrosse had a high profile among the 105,000 residents of Adelaide in the early 1880's. The sport received occasional newspaper stories that focused on its North American indigenous origins or reported briefly on its activities and growth in Victoria.

Given the predominance of English and Irish free settlers in the South Australian population at this time, it is likely that the reports on lacrosse which attracted most attention were the accounts of tours across England, Scotland and Ireland by teams from Canada. When a team of Caughnawaga Indians visited the British Isles in 1876, large spectator crowds turned out to watch and the sport attracted Royal patronage when an exhibition match was played before Queen Victoria at Windsor Castle.[2] The response was similar when Canada's father of modern lacrosse, George Beers, organized an exhibition lacrosse tour in Europe in 1883.[3] By then, the sport had been established and was spreading in the British Isles with club competitions underway and international contests in planning.

Adelaide was open to new sports but, compared with other Australian colonies, its less diverse population composition meant that it was the least likely to experience emigrants from exotic lands seeking to transplant the pastimes and recreations of their homelands.

'Lacrosse' Wood Engraving by Alfred Martin Ebsworth, 1882

6 – SOUTH AUSTRALIA

In July, 1882, The Australasian Sketcher (Adelaide Edition) published a wood engraving depicting lacrosse with a brief accompanying commentary[4]...

> "The game of lacrosse, the latest new sport added to the programme of outdoor amusements, is now a popular game in Melbourne and suburbs. Several clubs now exist, and the matches, which take place every Saturday in the season, are supported with great spirit, and attract a good deal of interest. As a manly, active game, free from the violence and rough usage of football, the game forms an excellent diversion for the winter months, and is likely to grow in popularity".

This favourable publicity was not, however, enough to spark the locals to make a start on lacrosse in South Australia. Instead, the impetus for that came through an encounter which nineteen-year-old, Alf Wilkinson had in Melbourne in 1882.

The Founders

Alfred (Alf) Wilkinson was the first person to pioneer lacrosse in South Australia.

Wilkinson was born at Norwood in Adelaide in January, 1863. His father had migrated to South Australia from Jersey as a free settler and married in Adelaide in 1859. After his education in Adelaide at Young's School, Wilkinson worked for a time with the Bank of Adelaide before deciding in 1882 to open his own groceries importing business under the name Wilkinson & Co.[5] The business succeeded and grew rapidly but his small store in the Marlborough Chambers building was soon inadequate and he re-located twice in subsequent years until building a 45,000 square feet warehouse in Grenfell Street. His company established the famed 'Vanguard' brand for tea imported from Ceylon and the 'Arab' brand for a wide range of flours, coffee, herbs and other groceries. The company's distribution network extended throughout South Australia, western Victoria and southern New South Wales.

Alf Wilkinson

Wilkinson became one of the most successful, well-known and respected citizens of Adelaide. He gave generously of his time to community groups and, in later years, served as a director and Chairman on significant corporate boards. In addition to his business management skills, Wilkinson was a gifted athlete and eager to try his hand at sports.

As a cricketing allrounder with North Adelaide Cricket Club, his skills were recognized with multiple selections to represent South Australia in inter-colonial contests between 1884-1888, plus a place in the team which played the touring All-England team on the Adelaide Oval in October-November, 1886.[6] In 1889 he was a member of the South Australian lacrosse team that defeated Victoria in Adelaide.

How Wilkinson came into contact with lacrosse, and fell in love with the sport, seems to have been a story of chance. During mid-1882 he went on a short holiday to Melbourne and stayed with the Gordon family who were friends of his parents. The Gordons had five sons who had taken up lacrosse with the South Melbourne Lacrosse Club and were participating in the inter-club competition organized by the VLA. Wilkinson apparently witnessed a club match or practice session, handled a lacrosse stick, and ventured into Albert Park with the Gordon boys to enjoy some lacrosse catch and throw. This experience was captivating and compelling. Wilkinson's own account was recorded by Arch Fowler, Secretary of the Victorian Lacrosse Association, in an unpublished article on lacrosse written some years later.[7]

> "They (the five Gordon brothers) used to throw the ball from one side of a swamp to the other, but would not let me try for fear I lodged the ball in the water. I took a fancy to the game and on my return to Adelaide, I induced several others to take it up, including L. Prince, G. Boundy, and R.W Tribe. I sent to Melbourne for half a dozen sticks, but could only get the colonial made article, and that was not very satisfactory. Half a dozen of us used to play in a paddock near Mitcham, but mainly through the paucity of the sticks we were unable to get the game thoroughly on its legs, and lacrosse died early. To W.T Paterson largely belongs the credit of having revived it."

A separate account, published for The Gadfly, described Wilkinson's early contact in Melbourne as follows:[8]

> "It was there he observed a number of reportedly sane men rushing about with elongated tennis racquets, chasing a ridiculously small rubber ball. It was a weird, mystifying game at first sight, neither tennis, football, nor hockey; but apparently a little bit of each. Wilkinson became interested. He had the game explained to him and he became more interested. He borrowed a crosse, and had a few throws himself, and became deeply interested, and eventually he came back to South Australia, a suddenly-recruited but ardent lacrosse enthusiast".

Wilkinson may not have realized at the time that he had landed in the geographic and spiritual heartland of lacrosse in Melbourne. His hosts, the Gordon brothers, were the hottest young lacrosse players in Victoria at the time. Their home in Park Street, Emerald Hill (now South Melbourne) was a short distance from the lacrosse field in Albert Park and a short distance from Lambton Mount's residence in St Vincent's Place. The members of the premier club team of the day, South Melbourne Lacrosse Club, mostly lived close by and many were also keen cricketers.

Lloyd Prince

Excited by this new sporting contact, Wilkinson returned home to Adelaide keen to start lacrosse. Whether he had met Lambton Mount and discussed strategy is unknown but the steps he took had a familiarity with the beginnings in Melbourne. During the later months of 1882, Wilkinson obtained some crosses from Melbourne and enthused a small group of friends and colleagues to practice with him at a local paddock in Mitcham. Among his supporters were his elder brother C.H (Charles) Wilkinson and Lloyd Prince, a close friend who became a business colleague at Wilkinson & Co.

6 – SOUTH AUSTRALIA

The group spent time recruiting interested young men and organized a public meeting on April 6, 1883 at the Prince Alfred Hotel to consider the advisability of introducing lacrosse into the colony.[9] John (Jack) W Colton, proprietor of J. Colton & Co, Saddlers, Ironmongers and General Importers of Currie Street, chaired the meeting. The Adelaide Lacrosse Club was formed and thirty-five young men were enrolled with promises of more to come. Among them was William T. (Bill) Paterson, a Scottish emigrant who had arrived in Adelaide two years earlier with prior lacrosse experience in Scotland. A provisional committee was formed comprising J. W Colton, Charles W Mudie, Lloyd Prince, F. Adams, Reg Tribe and Alf Wilkinson. One week later an application was submitted to the Adelaide City Council seeking a playing area for lacrosse on the parklands fronting North Terrace between Porter and George Streets.[10] It seemed that lacrosse was underway in South Australia.

In retrospect, however, this bid to start lacrosse in Adelaide was premature. The group did not have sufficient lacrosse sticks and they were in short supply in Melbourne. Mount's colonial-made sticks were unsatisfactory and a time lag of some months was needed to import sticks directly from Canada. Interest waned and there is no record of the Adelaide Lacrosse Club doing anything further until new energy came in 1885.

Getting Underway

The pioneer group which had initially attempted to start lacrosse in Adelaide took a more cautious approach when they decided to try again. According to Wilkinson, it was Bill Paterson who this time took the running.[12] A meeting of interested people was advertised for Thursday evening June 25, 1885 at the Prince Alfred Hotel, plus a practice session for Saturday 27th of June, to be held on the South Park Lands near Chance's Corner, Unley.[13]

The meeting was a positive one and resolved to re-form the Adelaide Lacrosse Club but agreed to adjourn for a period to see the outcome of the Saturday practice session before making any further arrangements.[14] With short notice and rainy weather, just twelve men turned out for the first practice. Most were novices. They split into two teams and played enthusiastically in a six-per-side format using the football goal-posts at the ground. The following week, twenty-four players participated in the practice session.

Chas Wilkinson chaired the adjourned meeting on Thursday 9th July when rules for the club were adopted, office-bearers elected and the member entrance fee and annual subscription dues were set at five shillings each. Sixteen members were admitted and a further fourteen nominations were received. The elected office-bearers were: Bill Paterson (Captain), Alf Wilkinson (Vice-Captain), Harry Conigrave (Secretary), Lloyd Prince (Treasurer) and Doug J. Byard, Fred Cornish, W. R (Reg) Tribe, Frank Goode and George P. Boundy as Committee members. Conigrave was the proprietor of the Macclesfield Brewery in Kent Town, and a former journalist with the Advertiser Newspaper. Byard had recently returned from studies at Oxford University and was soon to take up a role as Headmaster at Hahndorf College, a position which he occupied until 1916.

The club costume was agreed as navy-blue jersey and hose, white knickers and navy cap with a gold stripe and the club monogram in gold on the left breast of the jersey. The meeting considered correspondence from the Victorian Lacrosse Association for a representative team to visit Adelaide and the committee was instructed, if possible, to seek to arrange this during August on the Adelaide Oval. Correspondence was also noted from Noarlunga asking for information with a view to forming a club in that district.

Lacrosse in South Australia was officially underway and the prospect of club competitions and intercolonial contests was now already on the agenda.

Little time had passed before news came through that a public meeting had been held in the schoolroom at Noarlunga on Thursday July, 16 1885 and a new club had been formed with fourteen members.[15] The playing uniform was to be white knickers with cardinal jersey, hose and cap. Soon afterwards the newspapers announced that a match between the two clubs in South Australia had been arranged and was to be played at Noarlunga.

Jack Wainwright

The driving force and founder at Noarlunga was Jack S. Wainwright who later was to become a joint founder of the South Australian Lacrosse Association when he made his epic penny-farthing bicycle ride to Adelaide. Wainwright was born in Devon, England in 1859 and became an apprentice mid-shipman for three years before leaving sea at Port Adelaide. He worked for a time on barges on the Murray River and then on the wharf at Echuca and as a bullock driver. In 1884 he joined the Bank of Adelaide as a clerk at the North Adelaide branch, later becoming a bank accountant and long-serving manager.[16]

Transferred for a time to Noarlunga, he was an active citizen; starting a gun club, coaching rowing and starting the lacrosse club. Joining Wainwright as the pioneers of the Noarlunga club were John (Jack) C. Dungey, George C. Fead, Charlie B. Canham and P. Port.[17] Dungey was a storekeeper and farmer at Noarlunga and also publican of the local Horseshoe Hotel. Fead was a teacher at the local school and Charlie Canham was the proprietor of the general store and Post Office at nearby Hackham. Wainwright, affectionately known as "Phoenix", later started clubs at Port Augusta (1888) and Angaston (1898).

The first-ever match between clubs in South Australia was played on Saturday, August 1, 1885 at Noarlunga.[18] The Australian Sketcher (Adelaide Edition) acknowledged the occasion by re-publishing its earlier lithograph depiction of the sport.

At noon on that day, a special horse-drawn coach carrying the Adelaide Lacrosse Club team departed from the central Post Office for the two-hour trip to Noarlunga. The Adelaide team had been practicing each Saturday since the formation of their club in April. At Noarlunga, the newly formed club had only two weeks to prepare but felt privileged to be hosting the inaugural lacrosse contest in South

6 – SOUTH AUSTRALIA

Horseshoe Hotel, Noarlunga, South Australia

Australia. A large crowd of residents from throughout the local district turned out to welcome the visitors, waving flags and cheering their arrival. The match was played on the attractive recreation ground at Horseshoe with Jack Wainwright captaining the local team and Bill Paterson leading the Adelaides. Harry Conigrave served as umpire.

It was a colorful scene with Adelaide dressed in white and navy and Noarlunga resplendent in scarlet and white. Noarlunga thrilled its local supporters with the first goal and led at the half-time break. Adelaide struck back with a goal in the second half and the game finished as a draw.[19] The game was keenly contested but the skills were limited by the brief time the Noarlunga men had experienced the sport.

A report in *The South Australian Register* captured the spirit of the occasion as follows[20]...

> *"Some of the players became strongly excited; one old footballer so much so that at a critical time he dropped his crosse and began to kick the ball. In this way and in others- especially in the direction of shintying and batting – there were on Saturday several departures from the strict rules of the game, particularly on the part of the Noarlunga men, none of whom had seen it played before they began to play it themselves. Nevertheless, the greatest good feeling prevailed. At half past five the players plastered up their skinned knuckles and mollified their smarting wounds. At six o'clock most of them enjoyed a cold plunge in the river. At seven they were seated at a dinner provided by the local club. Songs were*

sung, speeches were made, and toasts were given. The visitors drew up in Adelaide at ten o'clock, having thoroughly enjoyed themselves".

The venue for the dinner referred to in the newspaper report was the Horseshoe Hotel, owned by Jack Dungey, a member and committeeman of the Noarlunga club. This establishment and its hospitality became famed among lacrosse teams hosted in Noarlunga in subsequent years.

In August, the teams played a return match at the Kensington Oval in Adelaide, this time with the city team taking the honors. There was marked improvement in the lacrosse skills among both groups. The players in the second match played on the Kensington Oval on 29th of May were:[21]

Adelaide: G.P Boundy, F. J Cornish, S. A. Davenport, C. Elliot, R. Evans, F. Giles, F. Goode, S.H Goode, S. Impitt, W. Paterson (Captain), L. Prince, R. Tribe, A. Wilkinson and C.H Wilkinson.

Noarlunga: C.B Canham, J.C Dungey, G.C Fead, H.C Fletcher, F. Frler. W. Holman, R. Malpas, O.R Milway, A. Perry, P. Port, H.S Radford, C. Stephenson, J.S Wainwright (Captain)

In May, it was announced that a South Melbourne club team from Victoria would be visiting Adelaide to play matches during October.[22] This visit did not eventuate, however, and it would be two years before an inter-colonial visit was successfully organized in Adelaide.

Growth and Governance

When the 1885 season concluded there was still only two lacrosse clubs in South Australia. Without a coordinating Association, it was not surprising that the main focus of the existing clubs was on their own circumstances despite some efforts being made to seek broader publicity and expansion.

Shortage of lacrosse sticks continued to be an issue. It had been reported during July that a gentleman had been commissioned in Melbourne to purchase sticks for use in Adelaide. Later in the year, advertisements appeared in the *South Australian Register* for "Just Unpacked – Lacrosse Bats and Balls" at Cunningham's store in Rundle Street. The price for a stick at the time was between 12 shillings and fifteen shillings.[23]

In August, Professor Boulger of the Adelaide University attended a general meeting of the Adelaide Lacrosse Club along with twelve masters connected with the St Peters, Prince Alfred and Winham Colleges.[24] This display of interest among the city's most prestigious educational institutions was to prove an important signal of acceptance for the sport.

As the 1886 season got underway, it was clear that lacrosse in South Australia was in need of expansion. The two existing clubs were separated by two hours of awkward travel, making it difficult to sustain a viable competition. The clubs had to rely for competition on what became known as 'color matches.' These were scrimmages among their own players similar to the 'Reds versus Blues' contests played

6 – SOUTH AUSTRALIA

during the initial three years when the sport was initiated in Albert Park, Melbourne. By contrast with South Australia, the early club growth in Victoria had occurred with a favorable geography. Clubs in Melbourne were located in close suburban clusters and linked by quick, convenient train and tram services.

In March of 1886, the South Australian Register published a Letter to the Editor which laid out the case for expansion and for young men to take up lacrosse rather than football.[25] Around the same time, the *RMS Rome* arrived at Port Adelaide from London, bringing Professor William H. Bragg, a decorated scholar and sportsman from Cambridge University. Bragg had come to take up a professorial position as a Lecturer in mathematics and physics at Adelaide University.[26] He was just 23 years of age and a fine cricketer and lacrosse player. Within weeks of his arrival, he attended the Annual General Meeting of the Adelaide Lacrosse Club and was elected to the club Committee along with Sydney Talbot Smith, a Burnside-born solicitor who undertook his boyhood schooling in England and took out Law and Arts degrees at Cambridge University.[27] Despite both playing lacrosse at Cambridge, Smith and Bragg were in different years and had not previously met. Smith had played in the founding year of lacrosse at Cambridge and in 1883 had participated in a match against a visiting team of native Indians which George Beers had brought from Canada.

The experience led Talbot Smith to reflect many years later[28]…

> *"Perhaps I am the only man in Australia who has played against Red Indians"*

Both men were later to become well-known figures in South Australia and both continued to support lacrosse. Bragg enjoyed a distinguished career at the University before returning to England and winning the Nobel Prize for physics in 1915, jointly with his son. Smith practiced as a solicitor and barrister but was also a well-regarded journalist and literary critic with the Advertiser, The Register and the Bulletin.

In later years he was a long-serving Vice President of the East Torrens Lacrosse Club.

Professor William Bragg

When no new clubs eventuated in 1886, Noarlunga and Adelaide continued with their own color matches but expanded their interclub contests to five matches, two in Adelaide and two at Noarlunga, plus a promotional game at Clarendon where interest was being shown in forming a club. Adelaide won four contests and Noarlunga one.

During this period, the two clubs featured in the earliest known team photographs of lacrosse in Australia, taken in 1886 at the Old Racecourse ground in the East Parklands. These historic photographs include a number of the key people who helped start and grow the sport in South Australia.

The expansion and new clubs which South Australia craved, came eventually in 1887 and 1888.

Adelaide Lacrosse Club 1886
*Standing L to R: Frank Giles, R. Evans, William Bragg, Alf Wilkinson, S.H. Goode,
Lloyd Prince, C.H. Wilkinson, W. Paterson, S. Davenport
Sitting: William Boundey, A.H. Roberts, S. Talbot Smith, G. Codd*

Noarlunga Lacrosse Club 1886
*Standing L to R: J.C. Dungey, E. Perry, C. Holman, W.H. Sayers, O.R. Milway,
F. Furler, C. Symonds, C. Symonds jnr., J. Wainwright (Captain)
Front: H.S. Radford, W. Clark, R. Malpas, W. Holmes*

Firstly, the North Adelaide Lacrosse Club was formed at a meeting held in the Prince Alfred Hotel on March 12, 1887.[29] The initiators were Francis Belt and H. Davenport with assistance from Adelaide club members who had agreed to hive off and help start the new club. Among the Adelaide members who re-located to North Adelaide was Professor Bragg, soon regarded as the best player in the colony. Reluctantly, but in the interests of the game, Adelaide also released four other experienced players to the new club - Alf Davenport, Fred Bonnin, J.B Cavenagh and Gow. Sixteen players were soon enrolled and the club adopted a predominantly white playing uniform. The club, which continues to exist as South Australia's oldest continuing club, played initially on the north parklands.

Alf Davenport

In June, the Knightsbridge Lacrosse Club was formed at a meeting held on June 13, 1887 at the Marryatville Hotel.[30] Fourteen players were enrolled, the meeting adopted the rules of the Adelaide Lacrosse Club and a provisional committee was appointed. The impetus for Knightsbridge came from W.D (Doug) Henderson and George H. Cossins with J.W Reed, J.G Douglas, Sydney M. Turner, and W. Burnett Maclaren also prominent.

The advent of new clubs in Adelaide sparked an elevated public interest in lacrosse but it remained to be seen how competitive they would be as both had a high proportion of novice players and only a limited time to prepare. North Adelaide was the first to take the field. Its inaugural match, watched by a good turnout of spectators, took place against Adelaide on Saturday, the 28th May, 1887 and resulted in a drawn game.[31] At a return match two weeks later, Adelaide asserted its authority with a win, six goals to one.

George Cossins

Reports at this time in The Advertiser Newspaper by 'Facer', the 'nom de plume' used by the newspaper's lacrosse reporter, had often made clear his view that the formation of an Association to coordinate the sport was overdue and would bring many benefits.[32] A meeting to consider this was mooted for late in 1887 but, in the interim, the club administrators had the more pressing matter of some inter-colonial contests to deal with. Following an invitation issued by the Adelaide Lacrosse Club, a team from the South Melbourne Lacrosse Club, a leading club in Victoria, arrived in Adelaide by rail on the 21st of June. The Intercolonial Express commenced running between Adelaide and Melbourne in January, 1887. The visit had been eagerly awaited and the opening match made history as the first-ever Intercolonial lacrosse match played in Australia. This contest and three subsequent matches provided the first opportunity for South Australian teams to test themselves against an outsider. The match results from the seven-day visit were as follows:

June 22nd at the Adelaide Oval - Adelaide 2 drew with South Melbourne 2

June 25th at Noarlunga   - South Melbourne defeated Noarlunga 6 goals to 1

June 27th at the Adelaide Oval - Combined South Australian team defeated South Melbourne 4 - 2

June 28th at the Adelaide Oval - South Melbourne defeated North Adelaide 7 goals to 2

The South Melbourne visit whetted the appetite for further intercolonial contests and Victoria was quick to issue an invitation for South Australia to send a representative team to Melbourne in 1888.

When the inter-club competition of 1887 resumed, North Adelaide was still looking for its first win. That came when the Norths travelled to Noarlunga on the 2nd of July and returned home with a one to nil victory.[33] On the same day, an attempt was made to arrange a match for Knightsbridge against a combined Adelaide-North Adelaide team of juniors but insufficient juniors were available and Knightsbridge had to wait another two weeks before making its debut. A third match between Adelaide and North Adelaide intervened on the 9th of July and resulted in a decisive five to one win for the Norths.

Knightsbridge Lacrosse Club circa 1889

The Knightsbridge team had its first game on July 23, 1887 when it met North Adelaide and was outclassed by eleven goals to nil. This crushing start for the new club was to be further compounded on the 6th of August when their team was over-powered by Noarlunga with a record score of thirteen goals to nil. The season concluded on the 3rd of September when Adelaide blitzed Knightsbridge by

6 – SOUTH AUSTRALIA

11 to nil, with Alf Wilkinson scoring nine times. Surprisingly, the new club, North Adelaide, finished at the head of the table.

The advent of intercolonial competition, and the general progress of the sport during 1887, prompted the South Australian clubs to proceed with a joint meeting on the 13th of September to form the South Australian Lacrosse Association (SALA)[34] The meeting was called by Jack Wainwright and the following were appointed as officials: His Excellency, The Governor as Patron, The Mayor of Adelaide as President, Mr. F.E Grundy, Chairman and David Fowler, secretary/treasurer with each club to provide two delegates as their representatives.

Country Lacrosse

Despite the varied playing strength of teams, the expanded club competition in 1887 was a big step forward for the sport. Before the start of the 1888 season, news came through of two new country-based clubs.

Sydney Turner

Jamestown Lacrosse Club was formed at a public meeting on April 17, 1888 and chose a navy playing uniform with a light blue diagonal hoop.[35] Less than a fortnight later, on the 26th of April, the Port Augusta Lacrosse Club was established. Its colours were white jersey with a blue waist sash and a striped cap. Jack Wainwright was the driving force and initiator at Port Augusta. True to his word, Wainwright had been quick to promote lacrosse when he was re-located from Noarlunga to Port Augusta as a Branch Manager for the Bank of Adelaide. At Jamestown, the pioneers were Syd Turner, Hilary Boucaut and C.J Reade.[36] Turner was a 21-year-old law clerk, and later solicitor and Town Clerk at Jamestown. A year earlier, he had been a founding player and captain with Knightsbridge. Boucaut was a principal in the law firm where Turner was employed.

Lacrosse in South Australia had suddenly swelled to six clubs. The geography issue had not been solved as there were now three country clubs based at considerable distances from Adelaide and others were being mooted at Port Germein, Riverton, Strathalbyn and Wallaroo. Port Augusta was a 190 miles trip north-west of Adelaide and Jamestown was 130 miles to the north of the capital. Jamestown, a developing agricultural center with a population of one thousand, had been connected by railroad to Adelaide via Port Pirie in 1878. Port Augusta was growing as an important outlet for exports of wool, grain and copper. Its rail connection with Adelaide was made in 1882. It seems that young men were looking for things to do during their non-work time in the country centres. Rather than choosing between sports, as most of the city men did, many of the names that appeared in the country lacrosse teams were also in football, cricket, athletics and other recreations. In part, this was due to the limited opportunity they got to play against other teams because of their isolation. Matches between country teams, or against city teams, became an occasion rather than just a game as they entailed travel and being available for a full day or more. After-match hospitality for the teams was common, often conducted as formal dinners with speeches, toasts and entertainment.

The excitement of starting a new sport in relatively remote areas was tempered greatly for Jamestown and Port Augusta by the difficulties of securing competition and maintaining morale. In both centers, the majority of their matches were the home-grown, Reds v Blues or Captains v Vice-Captain teams, the so-called 'colour matches'.

Jamestown was the first to break beyond the home cocoon when North Adelaide agreed to travel north to the midway town of Riverton for a match on Wednesday, June 20, 1888.[37] This was the first lacrosse match played in the northern country. Horrific weather almost caused the cancellation of this historic match, but it went ahead after a delay and resulted in a 3 to 1 goal victory for North Adelaide. As part of the Jamestown team on that occasion, there were names that would later emerge as among the best players in Australia. The Jamestown team comprised: C.J Reade (Captain), S.M Turner, J. Burton, A. Burton, G.A Clark, S.E Evans, H. Kruger, Longson, McFeat, Naismith, W.K Thomson, Webb, R. Humphris, J. Humphris and J.J Clarke.[38] Such was the impression which the match made in Riverton, that a club was soon formed in the town.

Jamestown followed this experience with a visit to Adelaide and played three matches on the 4th, 5th and 7th of August, beating Noarlunga, drawing with Knightsbridge and losing to Adelaide on the Adelaide Oval.[39] "Facer", writing for the Adelaide Observer, proclaimed the Jamestown trip as ...'the beginning of a new era in the history of the game'. Jamestown's fleetness and running power impressed the locals and they were judged likely to become a real force once their passing and catching skills improved.

For Port Augusta, the only competition with outsiders during 1888 came when their team took a 50-mile trip in a specially chartered mail coach to play at Nectar Brook against Port Germein, a newly-formed club.[40] Jack Wainwright had been active in acquiring thirty crosses for Port Augusta. They were all soon taken up and he ordered twenty-four more as the player numbers expanded quickly to two teams. Calls for a team to visit Port Augusta from Adelaide went unfulfilled and a planned match against Jamestown for the 1st September did not eventuate. This pattern of home-based scratch matches, interspersed with occasional special trips, persisted throughout the colonial years as the competition norm for these northern country teams in South Australia. Port Augusta undertook some clever planning in 1889 and organized a trip to Adelaide to coincide with the visit of the Victorian team for the intercolonial match against South Australia. During the five-day visit, the Port Augusta team managed four matches, three against Adelaide clubs and one where it joined forces with Victoria to defeat a combined Adelaide clubs' team.[41]

The issue of difficulty getting competition continued to plague the country teams. A plaintiff letter from the Jamestown club to the newspapers in June, 1898 summed up the situation, noting that their club had played a total of 40 games in their history, of which only 15 had been at home. They had travelled 2968 miles by rail, 120 miles by water and 10 by road. Eventually a cluster of new clubs formed in the hinterland around Jamestown; Yongala (1900), Caltowie (1899), Belalie (1899) Petersburg (1900),

Baderloo (1902) and Laura (1902). In 1901 a club was founded at Port Pirie and the basis of a Northern Areas Lacrosse Association had been set.

In the south, Noarlunga was battling to survive. The Evening Journal highlighted the issues when it published the following amusing account of a quintessential Aussie country match during September 1898:[42]

> *"A score of members of the East Adelaide Lacrosse Club and friends journeyed to Noarlunga on Saturday to play the local team. They arrived shortly before 4 o'clock, and found the ground over a mile out of the township. The Noarlungas did not have a full team. They say that owing to the few visits they receive from city clubs it is hard to keep the game alive. Once they played good lacrosse, but they have degenerated. The match was absurdly one-sided, and ended in a win for East Adelaide by 8 goals to nil. The score was larger than that, but the umpire had evidently left his spectacles on the piano. There were no goal nets and the face-off mark was indicated by the position of a sheep's skeleton. The game came to an unusual ending by one of the Noarlungas taking the ball on his crosse and running out of sight. He was last seen going down the hill in the direction of the Onkaparinga. A thunder and lightning storm did not prevent the visitors from having a swim in the fine river, although it drove the fishermen home without any bream. A dance came at night in the hall, but it was scarcely what the East Adelaides, well-known as the ballroom team, were used to. A sounding smack of the hands on the part of the M.C. denoted the start of each dance, and was followed by a burst of music as contained in an accordion, violin and piano combined and indifferently played. The ladies were in a great minority, and a local man was right when he said to some of the visitors. "If you want a girl you've got to rush it". The consequence was that most of the East Adelaides had to dance among themselves, and the proceedings became rather rough. During an interval, the hat was sent around by a Noarlunga gentleman for a lighting and general expenses rate, and the kerosene offertory having been taken up the accordion opened out alone.".*

In 1900, a new country cluster of lacrosse clubs sprang to life on the Yorke Peninsula, 100 miles north-east of Adelaide on the coast of Spencer Gulf. Here, at Moonta, the largest copper mining activity in the Southern Hemisphere was supporting the largest population centre outside of Adelaide. Lacrosse clubs were established at Moonta and Kadina in 1900 and Wallaroo (1907) and the Yorke's Peninsula Lacrosse Association was later established to co-ordinate a local competition.

South Australia versus Victoria

The most talked about lacrosse event in South Australia during 1888 was the intercolonial match against Victoria. Speculation and argumentation went on over team selection during the two months of lead-up to the event which was played in Melbourne during September. SALA was keen to show South Australian lacrosse at its best and the Victorians were determined to exert their perceived superiority following the less than convincing visit to Adelaide by the South Melbourne club in the previous year.

The members of the first-ever representative South Australian team were:[43]

> Alf Davenport (Captain), Doug Henderson, Ern Phillipson, Gordon Cavenagh-Mainwaring, Dashwood Connor, Seymour Smith, Arthur Rowley, David Fowler, Dick Evans, Harry Adamson, Pam Heath, Frank Belt, Rowley J Hill.

A group photograph of the South Australian and Victorian teams is included in Chapter 10 page 165. The team departed Adelaide by rail on Wednesday, 29th of August and stopped on the way at Ballarat in Victoria where it played a match against the local club, winning comfortably in atrocious weather. The much-anticipated contest against Victoria took place on Saturday, September 1, 1888 on the East Melbourne Cricket Ground and was witnessed by 5000 spectators.[44] Victoria triumphed by 5 goals to 1, but the experience was enough to confirm to the visitors that their skills were a match for the Victorians and that pinnacle contests of this type were valuable for the promotion and enjoyment of the game. At a lavish dinner held on the evening following the match, Victoria confirmed its intent to visit Adelaide in the following year. The great rivalry of lacrosse contests between South Australia and Victoria had commenced, and persists to the present.

For players, the opportunity of intercolonial representation was enticing and interest in the sport increased in Adelaide during the period 1889-90. The Adelaide University was formed in 1889 and the Iroquois Lacrosse Club followed in 1890.[45] The pioneer members of the Iroquois team were mainly novices but four experienced 'old' players in David Fowler (Adelaide), Reg Hill (North Adelaide), Herb Hill (North Adelaide) and Seymour Smith (North Adelaide) joined the team to help in the expansion of the sport. The club playing colours were navy and light blue. The Iroquois, or "Squaws" as they were dubbed by their opponents, advanced quickly and became a leading club over the next decade.

Gordon Cavenagh-Mainwaring

University joined the SALA in 1889 following a well-attended meeting of undergraduates on Thursday, 4th of April.[46] The entry of the University club resulted in a five-team format for the metropolitan competition. Its playing uniform was a black jersey with white hoops, white knickerbockers and black socks. The key drivers in the club's formation were experienced players J. Gordon Cavenagh, Professor Bragg, W. Margarey, R.B Andrews, Percy E.R Whitby and Jack E.H Winnall. All of the other players in its inaugural year were novices. The club's playing ground was on the North Parklands at Medindie, opposite the Zoological Gardens.

Both of the new clubs soon made their mark on lacrosse in South Australia, dominating the inter-club competition and winning the next eleven of the thirteen premierships leading up to end of the colonial era. The North Adelaide club took out premiership for 1889 and was presented by SALA with a newly established trophy donated by "Facer", the lacrosse correspondent for the Adelaide Advertiser. The trophy was a decorative satin flag. This was the first official recognition for the premier team in South Australia.[47]

6 – SOUTH AUSTRALIA

Adelaide University Lacrosse Team – SALA 1896 Premiers
Back Row l. to r.: W. Stewart, J.G Cavenagh-Mainwaring, A.W Campbell, F.G Ayers, E.J Stucky, F.J Douglas, J. Ayers, Dr A.J.E Russell
Middle Row: P.M Newland (Captain), J.F Downer (Vice Captain)
Front Row: T. Ward, H.H.E Russell, T.M Drew
Courtesy of State Library of South Australia

The Victorian team made its promised return visit to Adelaide in 1889, giving South Australia its first opportunity to play on home soil. The South Australian team was drawn from six clubs as follows:

S.A Davenport, A. Wilkinson (Captain), R. Evans (Adelaide), D. Fowler, S.D Smith (Iroquois), D. Connor, E. Phillipson, R.J Hill, (North Adelaide), H. Adamson, G.H Cossins (Knightsbridge), J.C Cavanagh (University) and J.S Wainwright (Port Augusta).[48]

They won in style, beating the Victorians by 9 goals to 2, with Hill scoring 3, Wilkinson 2, Evans, Cossins and Wainwright 1 each. At the post game dinner, the Victorian Captain, John Parnell, complimented the South Australians as … "the best team he had ever seen on a lacrosse field".

The Nineties and the SALA

By 1890, the organizational structure of lacrosse in South Australia was well-established and maturing. The South Australian Lacrosse Association (SALA) was presiding over a collection of eight clubs and some 180 players, including a significant spread into country towns. Five of the clubs, North Adelaide (1887), Adelaide University (1889), East Torrens (1898), Woodville (1899) and Sturt (1899) have continued in existence to the present day.

The format and arrangements for inter-club competitions overseen by the SALA had been set, a Junior Association had been formed, a representative team had visited Victoria and the Association had subsequently hosted a return visit to Adelaide.

David Fowler

Regular newspaper reporting, and the sizeable crowds that turned out in Adelaide to watch Intercolonial matches, had lifted the visibility and acceptance of the sport. There was now a solid and growing body of skilled players and experienced administrators and the future looked rosy.

SALA was managed primarily by its Secretary, David Fowler, a pioneer player with the Adelaide club who was a respected businessman as the proprietor of D & J Fowler, Wholesale Grocers in Adelaide. He was an accomplished player, passionate about the development of the sport, and a member of the South Australian teams for the inaugural Intercolonial match against Victoria in 1888 and the return match in 1889. Fowler had left the Adelaide club in 1898 to help advance the sport as a founder of the Iroquois club. In 1899 he resigned as secretary of SALA and departed Australia to live in England.

Despite the positive outlook in Adelaide, the nineties proved to be difficult years for lacrosse in Australia. The sport took a hit as the land boom in the eastern colonies came to a sudden end and a severe economic depression spread across Australia. The circumstances were compounded in Queensland when the Great Floods of 1893 brought lacrosse to a virtual standstill and eventually to decline and halt. South Australia was the least affected, its solid agricultural base and lesser involvement in reckless property speculation, giving it something of a protective shield. The sport stagnated and dwindled in Victoria, New South Wales and Tasmania as the worst of the economic depression took hold. By contrast, In South Australia, each successive SALA Annual Report throughout the 1890's carried glowing commentaries on the advancement and healthy state of the game.

It is a truism, however, that community sporting clubs live in a constantly changing world and need to adapt to survive. To get started, they need pioneers with vision and passion. To remain viable, they need dedicated members, ongoing promotion and responsive officials. Lacrosse in South Australia during the decade of the 1890's illustrates this point.

Thirteen new clubs were formed in the 1890's in South Australia, eight in metropolitan Adelaide and five in country areas. Most did not survive for more than a season or so. Two of the SALA original clubs were disbanded and lost; Adelaide in 1896 and Knightsbridge in 1899.

The new clubs formed during this decade were Port Pirie (1890), Crystal Brook (1890), Salisbury 1891, Heathpool (1892), Kapunda (1899), Belalie (1899), Yongala (1900), Holdfast Bay (1895), Old Boy's Institute (I897), later identified as the Vikings (1898), Gawler (1897), Angaston (1897), East Adelaide

6 – SOUTH AUSTRALIA

East Adelaide Lacrosse Club 1898

(1896), Woodville (1899), Semaphore (1899), and Sturt (1899). YMCA followed in 1900 along with country clubs at Belalie (1889), Caltowie (1899), Kadina (1900), Petersburg (1900), Yongala (1900) and Moonta (1900).

Three of these clubs, formed during the 1890's, provided the underpinnings of the East Torrens-Payneham, Woodville and Sturt clubs which are today, long-standing member clubs within the SALA. Each of them had unstable early years, either disbanding, re-naming or merging before being re-formed in later years. The East Torrens club played for two seasons before merging with the Iroquois club in 1901. Woodville and Semaphore played two seasons before merging in 1901 under a new name as the Port Adelaide Lacrosse Club. Sturt and YMCA merged in 1901 under the name Adelaide Lacrosse Club. The other new clubs of the 1890's and 1900 did not last, only Holdfast Bay at Glenelg and Gawler managing to field teams for more than a few seasons. The East Adelaide club was something of an aberation. The team failed to win a game in its inaugural year, won the "B" premiership in its second year and disbanded in 1899 after forfeiting many of its matches due to a shortage of players. It was not the direct catalyst for the re-start of the East Torrens club a few years later, but some of its players joined the new club.

Similarly, the Holdfast Bay club which played on the Glenelg Oval, was not the direct forerunner of the Glenelg club which exists today. It grew out of an amalgamation of two local Glenelg-based clubs during the 1930's.

The role of SALA was becoming increasingly complex by this time. Early in the 1890's, SALA was grappling with a three-pronged issue affecting the club competition. New clubs were likely to be overwhelmed if forced to start against the strength of the established clubs; weaker teams in the established competition had to endure morale-sapping beatings year after year; and some of the established clubs had grown so large that they were not always able to give all members a game.

In order to fix these issues, Gordon Cavenagh-Mainwaring and Reg Sholl set to work to establish the South Australian Junior Lacrosse Association. (SAJLA) in 1894.[49] The criterion for participation was not age-based, as in the current understanding of 'junior'. The association was designed so that existing clubs could retain members by having second and third teams and new clubs could have a more sympathetic point of entry. The Junior Association was constituted separately from the SALA and clubs were required to affiliate, pay membership fees and appoint delegates. Cavenagh-Mainwaring was appointed to the chair and J.K Wright as secretary to manage the new association and arrange fixtures. The Junior Association grew steadily and eventually was forced to establish "A" and "B" sections and institute a player permit system to maintain the integrity of the separate competitions by controlling player movements between SALA and SAJLA. Cecil Wright, from the North Adelaide club was a keen supporter of the SALJA before his departure for Western Australia in 1896, where he became one of the founders of lacrosse in the West.

In another attempt to encourage an even competition and control the growth of the power clubs, an "Electorate" system was introduced after 1900.[50] This followed the system used in football and cricket and provided for players to play with clubs within the locality in which they resided. With the exception of the University club, players were prevented from leaving their electorate clubs to move to a stronger club. It was not well received by the Iroquois club which had styled itself with a generic name. Match referees were provided during these years by teams with a bye and by retired players. Referees were allocated to matches by the Associations as no formal Referees Association existed in South Australia until former Port Adelaide Captain, Harry Hocking, recruited other past players and formed an association in 1931.

Generally, reports of unseemly play were few and far between but W. Nordmann took exception to the behaviour of players in a University versus Iroquois match which he refereed on Saturday July 16, 1898. He wrote to the newspapers to report:[51]

> *"culpable savagery, a little in excess of what is technically known as 'willing play". I saw enough to convince me that this uncalled-for roughness constitutes for lacrosse an insidious but deadly disease, which, if not taken in hand firmly, will ultimately wreck the game here, as it has done before in other localities. The multiplicity of scars which almost any player can show, together with public opinion, regarding a game which entails such souvenirs, are significant of the situation"*

During this period, the Association also represented its clubs in dealings with the other Australian colonies on matters of changes to playing rules, inter-colonial fixtures and a proposal to bring a team to Australia from Canada. Generally, the playing rule changes proved to be controversial and included:

the size of the goal crease; the introduction of goal nets; inclusion of a "free position" when a player was fouled, rather than a face-off; and the re-structuring of game times from two halves to four quarters.

After 1889, the award for the club winning the SALA premiership became a satin banner which had been donated by the Victorian intercolonial team. The Observer reported it as a "pretty championship flag" and described it in the following terms:[52]

> *"The flag or bannerette is of black satin, suspended on a walnut crossbar, which in turn is sustained by cords from a long walnut pole. In each of the top corners radiating crosses, worked in filoselle, serve somewhat to illustrate the letters 'SALA', which are worked between them. Below the words 'Championship Flag' in teutonic lettering of ruby and gold filoselle appear, and 'won by' and 'season' are traced in the same colours, space being left for the winners year to year to get their names recorded."*

Under the rules established for the award, any team winning the premiership for a third time could retain the banner permanently. University achieved this in 1894 and the banner was replaced by a polished timber shield with silver plates for engraving, donated by Mr. J Bonython, proprietor of the Advertiser Newspaper. It became known as the "Advertiser Shield" and remained as the SALA premiership award for the senior club competition. When the end of the century came, the premiership record stood as follows:

	Premiers	Runners-Up
1888	North Adelaide	Adelaide
1889	North Adelaide	Adelaide
1890	University	Adelaide
1891	University	Iroquois
1892	Iroquois	University
1893	Iroquois	University
1894	University	North Adelaide
1895	University	North Adelaide
1896	University	North Adelaide
1897	North Adelaide	Iroquois
1898	University	North Adelaide
1899	Iroquois	University
1900	Iroquois	University

Table 1: SALA Premiership Table 1888-1900

Promising signs of a breakthrough to establish lacrosse in schools and colleges came in May of 1891, when a match between the old scholars of St Peters College and Prince Alfred College was played.[53] Both schools had many past students who were playing lacrosse and, while the exhibition game was well-received, it did not result in lacrosse being added to the programs of either school. Further

Victorian Lacrosse Team 1896

attempts were made in later years. In June, 1895 the headmaster at St Peters requested a scratch match between past scholars of Prince Alfred, St Peters and Winham schools with a view to starting a club connected to St Peters. The Association was also active in occasional ventures to put lacrosse forward more broadly to the public. It partnered local Athletic clubs and Cycling clubs by promoting their community sports days, suspending fixtures and conducting innovative lacrosse events for these occasions.

In 1890, as lacrosse in Victoria took a severe downturn related to the prevailing economic stress, Intercolonial lacrosse stalled and was not resumed for two years.

When the intercolonial fixture was revived in Melbourne in 1892, South Australia put forward a proposal that New South Wales and Queensland also send teams to Melbourne for a "grand tournament".[54] This was not taken up but South Australia went ahead and visited Melbourne, defeating Victoria by 6 goals to 3 on the 14th, August at the Richmond Cricket Ground. Intercolonial matches then went into another recess until 1896 when a re-constituted VLA sent an under-manned Victorian team to Adelaide. The Victorians were humiliated by a 13 to nil loss. As part of the generous hospitality, the visitors were transported in a four horse drag on a day trip picnic to Mount Lofty.[55] The suited photograph of the Victorians on that day displayed a formality in keeping with the times.

6 – SOUTH AUSTRALIA

Victorian and South Australian Teams at the MCG 1897

This visit re-started a cycle of annual intercolonial contests which then continued unbroken through to Federation and beyond.

In the following year, 1897, South Australia travelled to Melbourne and played matches against Victoria and New South Wales. A significant Intercolonial Conference was held to develop a roster of future games and plan for the unification of the playing rules. The SALA representatives at this first-ever intercolonial conference were Reg Sholl, George Auld and Charlie Cornish.

During the late 1890's, Bob Morrison, the energetic secretary of the NSWLA, raised the sights of lacrosse in Australia when he commenced liaison with lacrosse officials in Canada. Morrison communicated with the other colonies, expressing his view that a visiting team from Canada could be supported financially to tour Australia and that such a tour would be immensely valuable in elevating the sport in Australia.[56] "Facer", writing for the Adelaide Observer had first promoted the idea of a Canadian visit as early as in 1889. Communications and negotiations on this matter continued for more than a decade before the idea was consummated in 1907.

While South Australian lacrosse largely avoided the worst effects of the World Depression, it was the hardest hit colony when Australia went to war in 1899 to support Britain in the fight against the Boers in South Africa. Many clubs lost players for a period and some lacrosse men from South Australia were killed in action. The North Adelaide club alone had some thirty active members in South Africa.

As the century came to a close, lacrosse in SA was in a stable position but had not grown to the same extent as some other team sports. The tally was 24 teams and approximately 310 players. By comparison with the other colonies, South Australia had quickly reached pre-eminence in representative contests and had achieved a substantial non-metropolitan following. The latter was both a plus and a disadvantage as it left SALA fractured by travel distance and it left the country teams isolated and vulnerable. None of the fifteen country-based clubs which existed in colonial South Australia have survived to the present.

South Australia had solved the issue of the need for opportunity for young and new players or new clubs by splitting itself into Senior and Junior Associations. The downside of this strategic move was that under-strength clubs, not wanting to drop out of the Senior Association, faced season after season of beatings at the hands of the more powerful clubs, causing them to lose impetus and face disbandment.

Lacrosse in Broken Hill

The most unlikely lacrosse development in colonial Australia occurred in March of 1894 in the isolated, hot and arid, desert township of Broken Hill, located 700 miles from Sydney in south-western New South Wales. The township of Broken Hill did not exist until 1883 when a boundary rider on a remote pastoral property discovered what turned out to be the richest body of silver, lead and zinc ore in the world. The Broken Hill Proprietary Company (BHP) was formed to mine the ore and the township grew quickly to a population of 20,000 and became known as the "Silver City". Broken Hill is situated in New South Wales but its lacrosse origins, support base and unofficial affiliation was always with South Australia.

The instigator of a move to start lacrosse in Broken Hill was Frederick (Fred) De Couray Inman, a 20-year-old. Nothing is known of his motivation except that he was born in Jamestown, South Australia where lacrosse enjoyed a prominent profile following its establishment in 1888. Inman inserted an advertisement in the *Barrier Miner* inviting "persons desirous of forming a lacrosse club" to attend a meeting at 8pm on March 28, 1893 at Mrs. Timms Terminus Hotel.[57] There is no record of how many attended this meeting and Inman did not succeed in forming a lacrosse club at that time. Another year passed before his objective was realized. He was joined at this time by Charlie Nicolls, also from Jamestown. The Broken Hill Lacrosse Association was established in April, 1894 with thirty or so young men and two clubs named Willyama and Broken Hill. The North Broken Hill Lacrosse Club was added shortly afterwards and a three-club competition was played in the opening season, with Willyama taking the premiership. Inman and Nicolls were both attached to the Willyamas, Inman in attack and as a goal-keeper, and Nicolls as face-off.

Lacrosse proved to be a novel new source of athletic recreation for the predominantly young male population of Broken Hill. The Banks club joined the competition in 1895 and the local Association now had a four-team competition. Matches were played on the Central Oval and the Gaol Oval. The club competition was something of a year-by-year proposition. When it was struggling in 1898, the Broken Hill Lacrosse Association made a radical change to its structure to preserve a four-team

6 – SOUTH AUSTRALIA

format. All players were pooled and a Selection Committee divided them up into four teams with generic names replacing the former club names as Wallaroos, Sturts, Borers and Barrier United.

The lacrosse initiatives in Broken Hill did not come from Sydney and the NSWLA never had any governance involvement with the Broken Hill Lacrosse Association. Isolation and limited opportunity for outside competition was always the biggest challenge for Broken Hill. It looked for support to Adelaide and the SALA, three hundred miles south and linked by rail. SALA encouraged its affiliated country-based clubs of Jamestown, Port Augusta, Port Germein, Crystal Brook and Port Pirie to assist Broken Hill. Somehow, the Broken Hill Association managed to maintain a continuing but somewhat shaky local competition, supplemented with occasional trips to, and visits from, the South Australian clubs. As a mining center, it suffered from the transient nature of its population but made useful contributions to lacrosse in other parts, especially to the formation and development of the sport on the Western Australian goldfields.

Always in search of outside competition, the Broken Hill Association arranged an 'intercolonial' visit in 1895 when it travelled south to play matches against Jamestown and Crystal Brook. Despite being beaten solidly by Jamestown, this trip helped to boost morale in Broken Hill.[58]

Leading Colonial Players and Administrators

Newspaper coverage of lacrosse in South Australia was substantial during the colonial years. Generally, the lacrosse reports were contributed for publication under *nom de plumes* and syndicated between the newspapers by a small group of lacrosse supporters who were directly connected to the clubs.

Publication	Reports by
Adelaide Observer	"Facer"
Evening Journal	"Right Attack" & "Face-Off"
Evening News	
Express and Telegraph	"Crosse" & "Darnoc"
South Australian Register	"Facer"
The Critic	"Attack"
The Chronicle	"Facer" & "Canadia"
Port Augusta Dispatch, Newcastle & Flinders Chronicle	"Leading String"
Broken Hill Miner	
Port Pirie Standard	
Other nom de plumes used were	"First Home" and "Referee"

The leading players of the period were generally rewarded with selection in the representative South Australian teams which played between 1888 and 1900. Others, who were the mainstay players for their clubs, missed out on representative teams due to being unavailable to travel or due to the disruption to matches which occurred during the first half of the 1890s. By the time of Australian Federation, the founding 'old players' had been displaced from representative teams and most had retired from club lacrosse.

Among the colonial star players in the founding years up to 1890, Alf Wilkinson, Dick Evans, Lloyd Prince, Reg Hill and Frank Belt stood out among the forwards. At the defensive end, Jack Wainwright, Dashwood Connor, Doug Henderson, George Cossins, Alf Davenport and Herb Hill were the standouts with goal-keeper Julian Ayers. The most effective midfield players were Ern Phillipson, David Fowler, Seymour Smith, Bill Paterson, and William Bragg. Many of these players were members of the first two years of intercolonial teams.

Ageing, and a flush of new young talent in the late 1880s, brought a changing of the guard in representative ranks and the star players from the increasingly dominant University and Iroquois teams took over as South Australia's finest during the 1890s.

The dominant players of the period were:

- **Dr Fred Russell**, an impassable point man who captained the University team for a number of years and played only a single year in a South Australian team in 1896 owing to the cessation of intercolonial contests before that time.

Phil Newland

- **Phil Newland**, a highly skilled, key attack player from University, who topped the SALA goal-scoring for six consecutive years from 1895 with a 35-goal average and played in every South Australian representative team from 1896 onwards. Newland also played football with Norwood and was a star representative in South Australian State cricket teams and the Australian Cricket Team.

- **Lou Humphris**, a tough and powerful Left Home specialist who came to the Iroquois club in 1896 from Jamestown and quickly asserted himself as an indispensable part of South Australian teams for a decade.

- **Julian Ayers**, a brilliant goalkeeper from University whose stopping and accurate long-throwing were legendary and whose reign continued for more than a decade after 1896.

- **Charlie Cornish**, from the Iroquois club, who succeeded Fred Russell as the point player and organizer of the South Australian defense.

- **Fred Kell**, a tireless runner and dashing centre player from the Iroquois club who was also effective in attack.

- **Charlie Fotheringham**, an elusive outside attack player from North Adelaide who combined perfectly with Newland and Humphris in representative games.

- **Gordon Cavenagh-Mainwaring**, a midfielder who came to prominence in the powerful University teams of the mid 1890's, did not appear with a South Australian team as he left Australia for England in 1898 to take up a substantial family inheritance of money and property.

South Australia dominated intercolonial lacrosse up to and beyond Federation, establishing itself as the un-disputed leader among the Australian colonies and winning seven of its nine contests played during this period. The match records were:

1888 – Victoria 5 defeated South Australia 3 in Melbourne

1889 – South Australia 9 defeated Victoria 2 in Adelaide

1892 – South Australia 6 defeated Victoria 3 in Melbourne

1896 – South Australia 13 defeated Victoria 0 in Adelaide

1897 – South Australia 8 defeated Victoria 1 in Melbourne

1897 – South Australia 13 defeated New South Wales 0 in Melbourne

1898 – Victoria 9 defeated South Australia 5 in Melbourne

1899 – South Australia 10 defeated Victoria 3 in Adelaide

1900 – South Australia 8 defeated Victoria 3 in Melbourne

The shining lights of lacrosse promotion and administration during the early colonial period were:

Alf Wilkinson, Jack Wainwright, Alf Davenport, Doug Henderson, David Fowler, Fred Grundy, Gordon Cavenagh-Mainwaring, Arthur Rosman and Reg Sholl.

When the close of the century came, only two of the founding clubs from the 1880's remained, North Adelaide and University. Both have survived to the present day. Holdfast Bay continued at Glenelg well into the new century, and eventually was replaced in the area by the present-day Glenelg Lacrosse Club.

Three other clubs established before Federation have also survived to be currently operating clubs within Lacrosse South Australia, the present-day parent association for men's and women's lacrosse.

These clubs are Woodville, Sturt and East Torrens (now East Torrens-Payneham). In addition to these pre-Federation clubs many of the country-based clubs had teams for a few years before disbanding and Gawler Lacrosse Club fielded teams well beyond Federation. Jamestown, once the strongest of

North Adelaide Lacrosse Club – SALA Premiers 1897
Back: D.E. Hay, A. Rosman, G. Acraman, L.Jones, R. Evans, H.R. Young, A.C. Thomas, F. Acraman (Vice-Capt)
Middle: C.H.T. Conor (Patron), C.C. Cornish (President), A.S. Fotheringham (Vice President)
Front: C. Fotheringham, R.E. Cussen (Captain), H. Hay, F. Joyner, S.M.B. King

6 – SOUTH AUSTRALIA

Woodville Lacrosse Club- A Grade Premiers 1900
Back: S. Stokes, J. Fletcher, C.W. Ive (Vice President), N. Stokes (Vice Captain), C. Ive
Middle: L. Liston, H.E.H. Liston, A. Connoly (Captain), W.S. Hughes (Secretary), F.E. Stapleton, F. Goldney
Front: N.C. Stapleton, F. G. Walker, J.N. Stapleton

the country clubs, disbanded in the 1920's while Port Pirie remained vibrant beyond the colonial years and maintained a local Association.

Notes

1. South Australian Register 10/09/1887 p.7
2. Weyand A.M. & Roberts M.R. The Lacrosse Story H & A Herman, Baltimore 1965 p.31
3. Weyand A.M. & Roberts M.R. The Lacrosse Story H & A Herman, Baltimore 1965 p.105
4. Australasian Sketcher (Adelaide Edition) 1/8/1885 p.140
5. Journal (Adelaide) 24/1/1922 p.1
6. South Australian Register (Adelaide) 3/11/1886 p.6
7. Fowler, Arch. Lacrosse in Australia, Unpublished VLA Paper 1933 p.5
8. Gadfly (Adelaide) 31/7/1907 p.16
9. Advertiser (Adelaide) 14/04/1883 p.1
10. Advertiser (Adelaide)17/04/1883 p.6
11. Fowler, Arch. - Unpublished VLA Paper 1933 p.6
12. Register (Adelaide) 27/06/1885 p.14
13. Observer (Adelaide) 14/07/1885 p. 19
14. Observer (Adelaide) 4/07/1885 p.25
15. Advertiser (Adelaide) 18/07/1885 p.4
16. Chronicle (Adelaide) 27/07/1950 p.2
17. South Australian Register 18/07/1885 p.7
18. South Australian Register (Adelaide)3/08/1885 p.3
19. Chronicle (Adelaide)18/07/1885 p.22
20. South Australian Register (Adelaide)3/08/1885 p.3
21. South Australian Register (Adelaide) 31/05/1885 p.7
22. Chronicle (Adelaide) 29/08/1885 p.15
23. South Australian Register (Adelaide)28/11/15 p.2
24. Advertiser (Adelaide) 5/08/1935 p.17
25. South Australian Register (Adelaide)23/04/1886 p.6
26. Express & Telegraph (Adelaide)27/02/1886 p.2
27. Chronicle (Adelaide) 10/04/1886
28. Advertiser (Adelaide) 5/09/1949 p.21
29. Chronicle (Adelaide) 26/03/1887 p.15
30. South Australian Register (Adelaide) 15/06/1887 p.7
31. Evening Journal (Adelaide) 30/05/1887 p.4
32. Observer (Adelaide) 13/08/1887 p.18
33. Observer (Adelaide) 9/07/1887 p.14
34. South Australian Register (Adelaide) 10/09/1887 p.7
35. Evening Journal (Adelaide) 17/04/1888 p.4
36. Port Augusta Dispatch 1/05/1888 p.3
37. Adelaide Observer 23/06/1888 p.19
38. South Australian Register (Adelaide) 20/06/1888 p.
39. South Australian Register (Adelaide) 8/08/1888 p.7
40. The Port Augusta Dispatch, Newcastle & Flinders Chronicle 7/09/1888 p.2
41. The Port Augusta Dispatch, Newcastle & Flinders Chronicle 13/09/1888 p.4
42. Evening Journal 5/09/1898 p.3
43. Adelaide Observer 1/09/1888 p.18
44. South Australian Register (Adelaide) 5/09/1888 p.3
45. Adelaide Observer 24/05/1890 p.18
46. Chronicle (Adelaide) 13/04/1889 p.15
47. Adelaide Observer 28/09/1889 p.19
48. The Express & Telegraph (Adelaide) 19/08/1899
49. South Australian Chronicle 5/05/1884 p.15
50. The Express & Telegraph (Adelaide) 11/03/1902 p.3
51. South Australian Register (Adelaide) 16/07/1898 p.5
52. Adelaide Observer 24/08/1899 p.19
53. Quiz and Lantern (Adelaide) 8/05/1891 p.12
54. Adelaide Observer 20/08/1892 p.20
55. The Advertiser 11/08/1896 p.5
56. Evening Journal (Adelaide) 10/07/1897 p.6
57. Barrier Miner 22/05/1893 p.1
58. Barrier Miner 25/06/1895 p.3

Queensland

By 1887 the "lacrossing" of the Australian colonies was progressing with promise. Victoria had celebrated a decade of activity and had multiple clubs engaged in regular club competition in Melbourne plus regional footholds emerging in Ballarat and Bendigo. South Australia and New South Wales had both taken to the sport with gusto and also had metropolitan and regional clubs in organized competitions.

The young colony of Queensland came comparatively late to the sport but moved rapidly once things got underway. Within a year of the first club being formed in Brisbane in May of 1887. Queensland was able to boast:

- four clubs taking part in competition with a total of 120 members and further new clubs expected.
- one club based in the regional town of Ipswich, more than an hour's train journey from Brisbane.
- hosting of the first-ever Inter-Colonial lacrosse competition against New South Wales in September, 1887.
- formation of the Queensland Lacrosse Union as the coordinating body.
- an invitation accepted to send a representative team to play in Sydney.
- some cheeky newspaper commentary suggesting that Queensland might be ready to match it with Victoria and South Australia.

The Pioneers

The impetus for the start of lacrosse in Queensland was the fortuitous coming together in 1887 of a number of individuals in Brisbane who each had prior involvement with the sport. Between them they formed a small working group and placed advertisements in newspapers to call a public meeting. The plan was to form a club in Brisbane and commence a program of weekly scrimmages similar to those in the model established by Lambton Mount in Victoria and subsequently used to get the sport underway in other colonies.

The following advertisement was placed in the Brisbane Courier and The Brisbane Telegraph on Thursday, April 28, 1887:[1]

The founding fathers of lacrosse in Queensland were the four men who attached their names to and funded these initial newspaper advertisements.

> A MEETING is called for MONDAY NEXT, the 2nd May, at 8 p.m., in the Y.M.C.A. Rooms, of all who are interested in the formation of a Lacrosse Club in Brisbane.
> JOHN CRAIG GIBSON
> C. R. FINLAY
> Dr D. H. WAUGH
> R. W. BALL.

Among this founding group was Charlie Finlay, a 27-year-old accountant/clerk and former inaugural player with the Fitzroy Club when the Victorian Lacrosse Association was formed and a club competition started in 1879 in Melbourne. Finlay was a skilled player and had enjoyed eight seasons of lacrosse in Melbourne as a goalkeeper/attack before being transferred in employment to Queensland. He was not about to have his passion for the sport dented by his re-location and it was not long before he found some like-minded colleagues in Brisbane.

Walker Ball

Finlay was joined by Robert Walker Ball, a 26-year-old Canadian born of Irish descent who had some lacrosse background in Canada before arriving in New South Wales. He had played two seasons with the Sydney Lacrosse Club before being transferred to Brisbane in 1887 as a bank accountant. Further Canadian lacrosse heritage was added by Dr David Waugh, a physician practicing in Brisbane.

Jack Gibson, the fourth member of the group, curiously had no documented lacrosse experience. He was a 29-year-old accountant who had moved from Melbourne to Brisbane in 1878 to help set up an office for the Robert Harper & Company group. In Melbourne he had resided at Emerald Hill, the key locality where Lambton Mount lived and recruited the majority of the earliest Australian exponents of the sport. Before arriving in Brisbane, Gibson was a prominent sportsman with the South Melbourne Cricket Club and the South Melbourne Football Club. Whilst not recorded in any of Mount's "Reds versus Blues" scrimmages, Gibson had likely handled a lacrosse stick as a young man with his Emerald Hill friends and sporting colleagues.

An equally significant pioneer of lacrosse in Queensland was 27- year-old, Adelaide-born, Percy Robin. He was a student at Prince Alfred College in Adelaide before the commencement of lacrosse in South Australia. His introduction to the sport came at Cambridge University where he gained a "Lacrosse Blue" while studying in England on a government scholarship between 1883-1886.[2] Having completed a Bachelor of Arts degree at Cambridge and subsequently a Master's Degree in Classics at London University, Robin returned home to South Australia late in 1886 to find that lacrosse was growing in Adelaide. Shortly after, he took up a role in Queensland as a schoolmaster at the Ipswich Grammar School. Here he was vocal in espousing the qualities and benefits of lacrosse and quickly emerged as a keen enthusiast for starting the sport in Queensland.

As these five pioneers pushed forward to test the prospects for starting lacrosse in Queensland, a few other men with prior experience of the sport emerged, each becoming important contributors in the early years.

Among them were Edward. H (Ted) Macartney, Havilland le Messieur (Lem) Chepmell and Sam H. Adams. Macartney was 24 years of age and had come to Queensland in 1883 from Ireland where he had some contact with lacrosse. As a "new chum" he went outback, jackarooing for a while, and then made home in Brisbane where he commenced employment in banking and later took articles as a solicitor. He keenly embraced lacrosse as a player with the Brisbane Lacrosse Club, but also gave willingly of his time as an organizer. In later years he emerged as one of the most prominent figures in legal and political circles in Queensland, serving terms in Parliament and as Leader of the Opposition. Following his political career, he served many years as a director and Chairman of a number of major companies and as Agent-General for Queensland before receiving a knighthood for his outstanding services within the community.

Sir Edward Macartney

The Newspapers

In the years leading up to the first club being formed, occasional brief reports on lacrosse had been published in Queensland newspapers. The reports contained news on the progress of lacrosse in the other Australian colonies, its participant strength as the largest sport in Canada, and its spread in England. One report noted that Ireland had beaten England in a match played at Lords in London.

In general, however, lacrosse was treated as a curiosity rather than a serious contender for a place on the local calendar. Some articles expressed overtly partisan views that lacrosse would never be a match for the favorite sports of cricket, football and horse racing that prevailed at the time in Queensland.

Others gave accounts of the indigenous origins of the sport and acknowledged that it was an exciting and highly skillful athletic pursuit. One account of a lacrosse match between the Montreal Lacrosse Club and the Shamrocks, described the action as...

> *"Men running and striving, with cunning of hand and fleetness of foot, in a game whose mastery needs the feet of Achilles, the hand of Diomedes and the craft of Odysseus"*[3]

Lacrosse Clubs Formed and Competition Begins

The public meeting held at the YMCA rooms in Brisbane on May 2, 1887 attracted a total of sixteen men. Before enthusiastically passing a resolution to form the Brisbane Lacrosse Club,[4] they listened while Walker Ball and Charlie Finlay gave an account of how lacrosse was played in Canada and Australia. The meeting appointed a small Committee to develop a Constitution and Rules, research possible playing grounds and report back to the newly-formed club.

When a second meeting was held a week later on the 9th of May at the Imperial Hotel in Brisbane, the club already had twenty-five listed players. The meeting adopted the draft code of rules, elected officials and agreed on a striking playing uniform of navy-blue knickerbockers and cap, white jersey with a red sash and red stockings.[5] Disappointment was expressed that the facilities in the Albert Park would not be available as the primary playing venue for the club but playing space was assured nearby at the Toowong Sports Ground. To further publicize the sport, the group had also secured arrangements to have an innovative "lacrosse race" included as an event in the sports program of the Union Athletic Club to be held in Queens Park, Brisbane on Saturday 28th of May.[6] The format was a 120-yard dash in playing uniform with each competitor required to carry a lacrosse stick, scoop up a ball twenty yards from the start and carry it without dropping to the finish line.

The inaugural Committee comprised Patron: His Excellency Sir A. Musgrave, President: Sir T McIlwraith, Secretary: E.H. McCartney, Treasurer: J.C Gibson, Committee: Dr Waugh, Dr Kesterven, P. Robin, F. McMullen, Captain: R.W Ball and Vice-Captains H. Chepmell and C.R Finlay.

As the Brisbane Club quickly set about arranging some 'Reds v Whites' practice sessions, Percy Robin wrote a letter to the Queensland Times & Ipswich Herald on the 14th of May outlining plans for a second club to be formed in Ipswich. No time was lost and a public meeting held on the 19th of May unanimously decided to form the Ipswich Lacrosse Club.[7] Percy Robin, Bob Stainton and E Swan were appointed as a provisional Committee to draw up rules and purchase sticks and other equipment. Entrance fees and annual subscriptions of 5 shillings each were agreed and the club uniform was set as white jersey with red sash, white knickerbockers and red stockings and cap. Twenty-three members joined the new club and fourteen attended the first practice session on Saturday, 28th of May.[8] Robin was the only participant with any previous lacrosse playing experience. On the same day Jack Gibson won the first-ever Lacrosse Race at the Union Athletic Sports meet, edging out Fred Mc Mullen who was also a new player at the Brisbane Lacrosse Club.[9]

7 – QUEENSLAND

The Brisbane menswear supplier, Messrs. Pike Bros in Queen Street, was authorized to supply playing uniforms for the clubs and practice sessions were beefed up until the day came for the first-ever lacrosse match played in Queensland. This took place between Brisbane and Ipswich at the Ipswich North Reserve on Saturday, July 15, 1887 and resulted in a win for Brisbane by 2 goals to nil.[10] The teams comprised:

Brisbane: R. W Ball (Captain), J.C Gibson, E.H Macartney, J. Chalk, W. A Coxen, H. le Messurier Chepmell, C.R Finlay, F.M Mullen, M.T Stanley, W.N Wilson, G. Sutherland and S.H Adams.

Ipswich: P.A Robin (Captain), A.E Hardaker, L. Rowlands, L. Heiner, H.E Bray, F.A Whitehead. E. Walker, R.K Stainton, V. Tozer, T.R Drake, C. Hegarty and G. Vowles.

In a return match played at Toowong Sports Ground in Brisbane on Saturday, 6th of August,[11] a large spectator audience attended, including many females, and the Headquarters Band added music to the event. The Ipswich team showed considerable improvement and pushed Brisbane to a 3-all drawn game.

The Start of Intercolonial Lacrosse

By late July of 1887, the Queensland founders had every reason to feel satisfied with their rapid progress. After just three months they had two clubs formed, a domestic competition established and indications of interest for further clubs to be started. They chose not to rest on their laurels and boldly sent off an invitation to the New South Wales Association to send a team to play matches in Brisbane during September. The invitation was quickly accepted and dates for two matches were set for Saturday, 24th of September in Brisbane and Monday 27th of September at Ipswich. This was to be a further boost to the promotion of the sport in Queensland but the prestige of hosting the first-ever inter-colonial lacrosse in Australia was clearly part of the incentive. Interest in inter-colonial sporting contests was growing in Australia at this time with cricket and football already operating and other sports dabbling.

The Queensland v New South Wales match-up would not be the first lacrosse played across colonial borders in Australia but it was historically significant as the first-ever competition between two colonies.

Curiously, bragging rights for the first cross-border lacrosse match had been taken during July 1887 by a match played at the Murray River town of Echuca on the Victoria-New South Wales border. The competing teams were Sandhurst, a fledgling club from Victoria based in Bendigo, and Deniliquin, a team that seems to have been cobbled together for the occasion with some locals and players brought from Sydney. Sandhurst won the match by 5 goals to nil but there was no subsequent mention of lacrosse ever being played in Deniliquin.

When the Queenslanders issued their invitation to New South Wales, they were aware that a team from the South Melbourne Lacrosse Club had visited Adelaide during June for matches against other clubs in the South Australian colony. This was a highly successful tour involving four separate matches but it was not colony versus colony.

Preparations for the Queensland versus New South Wales matches included selection practices between the Probables v Possibles, negotiations to secure suitable venues, invitations to local dignitaries and special tram and bus arrangements for public transport. The Queensland Figaro & Punch newspaper ran an illustrated feature on how lacrosse was played, supported with illustrations showing the key techniques and urging spectators to attend with "admission only a paltry bob".[12]

Facing the Ball.

Despite careful preparations for the event, drama struck unexpectedly when the steamer *Cintra,* which was carrying the New South Wales players from Sydney on the day before the first match, ran aground in the Brisbane

Throw

"A Throw for Goal"

River. This caused a delay to the Mayoral reception which had been organized for the visitors, but the reception proceeded a few hours late after the Organizing Committee managed to charter another steamer to transfer the New South Wales team into the city. [13]

The participants in the first Intercolonial Match on Saturday, 24th of September at the Albert Sports Ground in Brisbane were:[14]

Queensland: R.W Ball (Captain), S.H Adams, J.C Gibson, M.T Stanley, E.H Macartney, J. Chalk, W.N Wilson, R.K Stainton, P.A Robin, R. Swan, L. Heiner and C.R Finlay

New South Wales: A. L Silly (Captain), W. Howe, G. W Pettit, W.M Bligh, G. Noake, E. Broughton, Geo. Banks, J. Banks, J. G Silly, A. Stevens, J. Matthews, G. J Grice and S. Ball.

The Queensland team comprised eight players from the Brisbane Club and four from Ipswich. Six clubs were represented in the New South Wales team. Six hundred spectators turned up to see the action. New South Wales won by 1 goal to nil after the game was tied without score at half time but the fortunes were reversed two days later at Ipswich when Queensland were victors by 3 goals to 1. The newspapers carried detailed descriptions of the games.

New Clubs and the Queensland Lacrosse Union

The first lacrosse season of 1887 had ended on an enthusiastic high and it was not far into the new year when further positive steps were taken. The pioneering group understood that a coordinating body was needed to manage future promotions and growth and ensure co-operation between clubs. Advertisements were placed in Queensland newspapers during February, 1888 for a meeting to be held to consider forming the Queensland Lacrosse Union.[15]

Twenty men attended the 14th of February meeting and resolved to form the Union and have draft rules prepared. The following were subsequently elected as office-bearers:[16]

Patron: His Excellency the Governor

President: Sir Thomas McIlwraith

Secretary: Fred A. McMullen

Treasurer: Ed. H Macartney.

Charlie Finlay was appointed as the Field Captain of the Union.

Within a matter of weeks, two new clubs were established and added to the Union. The Savages Lacrosse Club, was formed on 22nd of February and based in Fortitude Valley with James. F (Jim) Maxwell appointed as Secretary/Treasurer, Lem Chepmell elected as Captain and Jack Chalk and Maxwell as Vice-Captains.[17] The chosen playing uniform was dark blue with a light blue silk waistband.

Six weeks later the South Brisbane Club[18] was formed on April 10, 1888 with a list of 26 intending players and Charlie Finlay appointed as Captain. The club playing uniform was blue singlet, red sash, white trousers, navy stockings and navy cap with a Maltese cross.

With four clubs now participating, the Queensland Lacrosse Union (QLU) drew up and distributed an inter-club competition fixture for the season, starting in June and culminating with a finale Tournament Day in September. A pair of attractive Championship Flags were commissioned for presentation to the premier team. These measured 2 feet 6 inches by 2 feet, fashioned in green silk edged with gold bullion and embroidered with crossed sticks and the words "Queensland Lacrosse Union 1888". The flags were much admired when they went on display for a few weeks at the clothing supplier store of Finley, Isles & Co, Brisbane.[19] With participant numbers expanding quickly, supply of lacrosse sticks was always an issue. There were many months of turnaround time when importing crosses from Canada and significant funds were needed to hold supplies. The QLU solved this problem by entering into an arrangement with the Queensland Sports Depot.[20]

CAMPBELL'S QUEENSLAND SPORTS DEPOT, 29 QUEEN STREET.

Under the patronage of the Cricket (junior and senior), Lacrosse, Northern Rugby Union, Queensland Football, and Lawn Tennis Associations.

The Leading House in Queensland for all kinds of ATHLETIC REQUISITES.

Special attention directed to our supply of Winter Games, Lacrosse, Lawn Tennis, Football, Lawn Bowls (silver-mounted for presentation), and other sporting goods by the first makers.

Our prices are consistent with quality, and our study is the interest and convenience of those who support us.

Queensland's first formal inter-club competition opened in June of 1888 with each club scheduled to play nine home and away matches plus the culminating tournament. The Brisbane Club took out competition and also won the handsome Championship Flags, but not without some stiff competition and a few defeats. The inaugural Tournament was coordinated and refereed by Fred McMullen. It took place at Queens Park in Brisbane on September 29, 1888, attracting a good body of spectators.[21]

By season's end the QLU had indications that the Brisbane Lacrosse Club was providing help for a new club soon to be formed at Toowong. Prospects for a further new club at New Farm were also being discussed. Disaster struck unexpectedly in November with the news of the untimely death of Charlie Finlay in a tragic work accident.[22] Finlay was descending in an open lift in the building of his employer when he leaned out and had his head trapped between the lift and an external beam. His death was a

7 – QUEENSLAND

Queensland Intercolonial Team 1889

major blow for the South Brisbane club and for the game in Queensland. A Fund was established for a special memorial to recognize Finlay's contribution and a huge entourage attended the funeral.

When preparations got underway for the 1889 season, lacrosse in Queensland seemed to be firmly implanted on the sporting calendar and ready to reach greater heights. Lacrosse was impacting the social scene in Brisbane with frequent reports of attendees at Fancy Dress Parties and Balls coming dressed as lacrosse players in club colors. It did not go un-noticed that the sport had entertained large crowds and received a Royal audience when a team from Canada toured and played exhibition matches in England.

On February 14, 1889 The Toowong Lacrosse Club was formed with Ed Macartney as Secretary, Jack Gibson as Captain and a few other players also from the Brisbane club.[23] Toowong adopted a uniform of white singlet and knickers, black cap, black sash and stockings and soon became known as "The Magpies". On the downside, some of the experienced players of the Ipswich club had decided not to continue playing and the club was struggling to replace them. When the Annual meeting for the Ipswich club was called in April only seven club members turned up. The QLU tried to help, organizing special recruiting promotions and urging clubs to assist. These efforts failed and the Ipswich Club struggled through a few matches before dropping out of the competition during 1889.

In other news, Percy Robin was appointed by the Union to the position of "Field Captain of Queensland". His role was to spearhead skills development for players in the colony and, at the end of the domestic season, to lead Queensland on a visit to Sydney for intercolonial contests. These were good signs from an emerging sport.

The Savages club proved to be the powerhouse team for 1889, prevailing in the Championship final with a 3 to 1 goal victory over Brisbane.

The end-of-season inter-colonial trip to Sydney during August resulted in two goal victory for Queensland against a combined Redfern/Mohicans club team and then a defeat at the hands of New South Wales by 7 goals to nil.[24] During this visit, a conference on playing rules was held with a view to achieving standardization between the two colonies. Despite the disappointment of the sound beating which the Queensland team had suffered in Sydney, the 1889 season ended on an optimistic note.

Malaise, Economic Downturn and the Great Flood

Unhappily the green shoots of growth were disguising a malaise which was already emerging to threaten the progress. Flooding in Brisbane early in 1890 made it difficult for lacrosse to find good playing surfaces and Queens Park became unusable. Entries for the 'lacrosse race' events at community sports meetings dried up and the event disappeared from most programs. To make matters worse some experienced players in the colony had left Brisbane or dropped out and the clubs began struggling to get player numbers.

The established format of club games and a year-end Tournament continued unchanged in 1890 with four clubs participating and The Savages winning their second premiership. During the year the QLU received a set of proposed uniform playing rules which had been drafted by the New South Wales Association for consideration by all Australian colonies. The QLU adopted the draft but insisted on the inclusion of a rule to prohibit the kicking of the ball.

Additionally, the New South Wales Association had announced that it proposed to hold a tournament in Sydney in 1891 and have a team from each colony participating. Had this come to pass it would have been the commencement of the Australian Carnival concept which, ultimately, was not achieved until 1910.

When the new season came, the Brisbane Lacrosse Club shocked the QLU by announcing that it was unable to continue to field a team. Hasty efforts were made to help and the loss of the founding club was averted when enough new members and a reorganization came to save the club in time for the 1891 playing season. With the prospect of a new club being formed at Sandgate, the lacrosse community turned out to support an exhibition game and the QLU discussed similar promotions in Toowoomba, Warwick and Ipswich. All was to no avail as the Sandgate promotion was unsuccessful. In August, the Savages took out their third consecutive premiership before making a stunning announcement in December that the club had decided to disband in order to spread its players and help strengthen the other clubs.[25]

7 – QUEENSLAND

Between 1890-96, Australia came under the grip of a severe economic depression which followed the crash of the speculative land boom in Melbourne and, to a lesser extent, Sydney. The impact spread Australia-wide as investment and offshore capital dried up, banks and building societies closed, unemployment rose quickly, and many families found themselves impoverished and relying upon food hand-outs. These were not helpful circumstances for lacrosse which was already struggling. When the 1892 season got underway, the QLU found itself back to just three clubs; Brisbane, Toowong and South Brisbane. A competition season was conducted with each club bolstered by the addition of players from the disbanded Savages. Toowong succeeded in taking out its first premiership.

Based on newspaper coverage, the key lacrosse feature of 1892 was the intercolonial matches which took place between 20th of August and 1st of September when a representative New South Wales team visited Brisbane.[26] Four matches were played and the visitors were hosted in style with a Mayoral Reception, a Smoke Concert and a picnic day trip to St Helena Island. The QLU ran a subscriber ticket offer for spectators priced at one guinea to cover admittance to all games for one gentleman and two ladies. Prior to the final match, a long-throw competition was conducted with H. Ewart recording the winning throw of 116 yards, 1 foot and 9 inches. This was well short of the 145 yards record previously recorded in Melbourne.

Disappointing crowds turned out to see the matches but the results confirmed that Queensland was still holding its own, despite the dwindling lacrosse base. The Queensland team was presented in a uniform of navy-blue singlet, cap, knickers and stockings with a light blue belt. The team for the final game comprised:[27]

> T.J Brown (Goal), E.H Macartney (Home), T.P Strickland (Second Home), T. Neilson (Third Home), Wm Maxwell (Left Attack), E.H Decker (Right Attack), E.W Stanley (Centre), F. Trumble (Left Defense), J.F Chalk (Right Defense), Talbot Stanley (Third Man), W.J Ewart (Cover Point), M. Stanley (Point & Captain).

The match results were:

> August 20 - NSW 6 defeated Queensland 5
>
> August 23 - NSW def Combined South Brisbane/Toowong 3 goals to 1.
>
> August 25 - Brisbane 1 drew with NSW 1
>
> August 27 - Queensland 1 drew with NSW 1

Following the close of season, the QLU reported at its Annual General Meeting in October that it had earlier received correspondence from the South Australian Lacrosse Association encouraging it to send a team to Melbourne for a tournament between all colonies.[28] This had not been taken up.

Prospects for lacrosse had not improved when the 1893 season came. The QLU met with the clubs seeking some re-energization and the South Brisbane club was renamed as the Mohicans Lacrosse Club. Ed Macartney, now the QLU President, stressed the need for players to put aside club loyalties and be prepared to play wherever it would help the sport to get three evenly matched teams. As part

Queensland Intercolonial Team 1892

of the survival efforts, two junior lacrosse clubs were formed, the 'Verona' at Indooroopilly and the 'Miowera'. These junior teams played a few matches against each other during 1893 and a Seniors versus Juniors day was organized by the QLU to stimulate interest.

The ravages of the economic depression were compounded in March of 1893 when unprecedented cyclonic rains hit Brisbane, resulting in months of widespread flooding. Sport was severely disrupted across the city and homes and businesses were flooded and became inaccessible. Lacrosse made do with weakened clubs, poor playing conditions and a reduction of matches with Brisbane taking out the premiership. The sport had reached a low ebb in Queensland. It would stumble on for one more season but the signs were imminent that the Great Floods of 1893 had triggered the end.

Elsewhere in Australia, lacrosse was rolling along with optimism and eyeing off new frontiers. The Victorian Lacrosse Association invited Queensland to send two representatives to Melbourne for a conference in November to consider the concept of sending an Australian team to play in the Pan Britannia games in London in 1894. The prospect of involvement in international competition was enticing but the QLU lacked the finance needed to attend the Melbourne conference. It ran an appeal to raise the funds but received little interest and resolved to decline the invitation.

7 - QUEENSLAND

In 1894, with equipment in short supply and a dearth of new players taking up the sport, many of the existing Queensland players lost interest and the sport faded towards extinction. The QLU was hanging on and sent to Canada for a shipment of crosses. When the South Brisbane Club disbanded, the inter-club competition was no longer functioning and matches soon regressed to 'Whites versus Blues'. After 1894, reports of lacrosse matches disappeared in the colony of Queensland. It seems that the QLU was discontinued by mutual consent without any formal winding up as there is no public record of its closure. It was not until after Australian Federation that lacrosse activity resumed in Queensland.

Notes

1. The Brisbane Courier 28/04/1887
2. The Telegraph (Brisbane) 29/06/1937 p.17
3. The Brisbane Courier 17/10/1884 p.3
4. The Telegraph (Brisbane) 3/05/1887 p.4
5. The Queenslander (Brisbane) 14/05/1887 p.776
6. The Queenslander (Brisbane) 14/08/1887 p.776
7. Queensland Times, Ipswich Herald & General Advertiser 14/05/1887 p.3
8. The Telegraph (Brisbane) 29/05/1887 p.2
9. The Telegraph (Brisbane) 6/06/1887 p.4
10. The Telegraph (Brisbane) 18/07/1887 p.5
11. Queensland Figaro & Punch (Brisbane) 6/08/1887 p.18
12. Queensland Figaro & Punch (Brisbane) 24/09/1887 p.19
13. The Brisbane Courier 24/09/1887 p.5
14. The Brisbane Courier 26/09/1887 p.7
15. The Telegraph (Brisbane) 11/02/1888 p.1
16. The Brisbane Courier 15/02/1888 p.5
17. Queensland Times, Ipswich Herald & General Advertiser 25/02/1888 p.7
18. The Brisbane Courier 11/04/1888 p.4
19. The Brisbane Courier 20/09/1888 p.5
20. Queensland Figaro & Punch 1/10/1888 p.1
21. The Telegraph (Brisbane) 1/10/1888 p.2
22. The Brisbane Courier 3/08/1888 p.5
23. Queensland Figaro & Punch 23/02/1889 p.16
24. The Queenslander (Brisbane) 7/09/1889 p.455
25. The Telegraph (Brisbane) 8/12/1891 p.6
26. The Week (Brisbane) 2/09/1892 p.15
27. The Week (Brisbane) 12/08/1892 p.19
28. The Brisbane Courier 29/10/1892 p.69

Tasmania

History shows that Tasmania was a late-comer to lacrosse in Australia. Its first club was formed in 1895, a decade after the sport had crossed the colonial border from Victoria into South Australia. Tasmania's small population and the geographical disadvantage of being separated by a sea crossing from mainland Australia were major inhibiting factors.

There is, however, a fascinating and previously untold lacrosse story about the island colony.

In March, 1863, thirteen years before Lambton Mount initiated lacrosse in Melbourne, the Cornwall Chronicle newspaper in Launceston published a long article titled "A Rival to Cricket" that it reprinted from the Chambers Journal of Popular Literature, Science and Art, an English weekly magazine.[1] The article gave a detailed description of the Canadian sport of lacrosse and presented a case for lacrosse as a better sport than cricket, arguing that fielding was boring and batting left most players sitting around idle for long periods of time with nothing to do but 'stare at the grass'.

Had this call been taken up then Tasmania would have been years ahead of other colonies as the founder of lacrosse in Australia.

A subsequent opportunity for Tasmania to become the second colony to pioneer lacrosse in Australia came twenty years later.

Geo B. Gordon

LACROSSE IN AUSTRALIA

In June of 1883, George B. Gordon wrote a letter to the editor of the 'Tasmanian' newspaper in Launceston, indicating that he had been seeking to introduce lacrosse into Tasmania.[2]

Sir – Before leaving Launceston I wish to inform your readers that I am very sorry that I have not been able to introduce them to a winter's game, and which I am glad to say is slowly but surely running football to earth – that game being lacrosse, which was started in Victoria about six years ago by a few gentlemen (including a Canadian, in whose country the game originated with such success that there are now ten clubs in full swing.

An order for three hundred lacrosses was sent to Canada by the Victorian Lacrosse Association just before I left Melbourne, but their supply had run short, owing to a great demand for them coming from England and Ireland, where the game has already taken a great hold. Through this I was unable to try and start it here.

Last season I read in a London paper an account of the match England v Ireland, which was played in England, unfortunately on a wet day, but in the presence of about 5000 people. This shows how the game of lacrosse is appreciated in the old country, where football has been for many years one of the leading games.

How it has grown in favor in Victoria is shown by the fact that on last Queen's Birthday a number of players journeyed from Melbourne to Sandhurst to give an exhibition or opening match there, and although it rained the whole day about 1000 spectators witnessed it.

The length of the ground for playing is about 299 yards by about 100 yards in width, while the goal posts must be 6ft high and 6ft apart; through these the ball must be put. Whether it touches the players or not it is a goal; if it goes higher than the posts it is no goal, but the ball is still in play, although behind. (If played on cricket grounds or reserves arrangements must be made for behinds).

The game is not started in the same manner as football, as before the ball is put into action the players take their different positions. The ball used is not quite as large as a cricket ball, and is made of india-rubber, with a small hole in it which makes it bounce more than an ordinary india-rubber cricket ball.

In conclusion, I hope to hear of a club being formed here next season, and I shall be most happy to give any assistance that lays in my power to do so.

Besides being a healthy pastime, it must be understood that the accidents that occur in football are impossible to happen when playing lacrosse.

Thanking you for allowing me the above space in your valuable paper.

Yours, etc.,

GEO. B. GORDON

Care Messrs., Boyle and Scott, Melbourne

Launceston, June .9

This letter was written two weeks before the first club was initiated in South Australia by Alf Wilkinson. The author, George Gordon, was a champion player from the South Melbourne Lacrosse Club, and

one of the brothers who had hosted Wilkinson as a guest at their home in Melbourne during 1882 and inspired him to start lacrosse in Adelaide. Gordon was on a business stay in Launceston during the first half of 1883, but returned home in June and threw six goals in South Melbourne's win over University to take out the VLA premiership. As his letter shows, but for a lack of being able to get lacrosse sticks at the time, Tasmania might well have been the second colony to take up the sport in Australia. Gordon's letter was marked care of Messrs. Boyle and Scott, Melbourne. Harry Boyle was the proprietor of a sports supply store in Melbourne and a star Australian Cricketer from South Melbourne Cricket Club, where Gordon also played cricket. Lambton Mount recruited Boyle to his organizing committee in 1876 when he started lacrosse In Melbourne.

Gordon, who had arrived in Launceston from Melbourne on the 27th February aboard the SS H. Clinch, was also a good cricketer. While in Launceston, he played for the Launceston Cricket Club and was selected for Northern Tasmania in the North v South cricket contest in March, 1883.

Regrettably, no-one in Launceston at that time took up George Gordon's call to lacrosse.

The only occasion when lacrosse came to public notice occurred in November, 1885 when Miss Kitty Winter was awarded first prize for the Most Original Character at the Owl Club Ball, a prominent event on the Hobart social calendar. Her gown carried a sports theme and was embroidered all over with action scenes and images of celebrity sportspeople from every sport. Lacrosse earned a spot on the underside of one sleeve.[3]

A Faltering Start is Made

Eight years passed with hardly a mention of lacrosse until, on the 13th of September, 1893, advertisements were placed in the Tasmanian News and Mercury dailies in Hobart for a public meeting of persons interested in forming a Tasmanian Lacrosse Association.[4]

> THERE will be a meeting of all interested in Lacrosse held at Tramway Works THIS DAY, 8 o'clock p.m. sharp, for the purpose of forming a Tasmanian Lacrosse Association.
> NOEL L. MURRAY.

The initiator on this occasion was Noel Lathrop Murray, a twenty-two-year-old engineer and established lacrosse and cricket player from Melbourne. Murray had come to Tasmania to manage the design and installation of a tramway system for Hobart. He later became Chief Engineer of the Hobart Tramways and the over-seer of a hydro-electric scheme in Launceston. He was a keen lacrosse player in Melbourne, commencing as a founding member of the Caulfield Lacrosse Club in 1893, and transferring to the MCC Lacrosse Club on his return to Melbourne in 1896. He represented Victoria in four Intercolonial teams against South Australia and New South Wales between 1897 and 1900.[5]

Noel Murray

Murray was passionate about lacrosse and aware that calls to start the sport in Tasmania had been made many years earlier. Like Lambton Mount, he faced uncharted territory in deciding to initiate a new sport without others around him who had previously played the game.

When his newspaper advertisements failed to produce a groundswell for starting lacrosse, Murray used his association with cricket and had the matter raised at the Annual General Meeting of the Southern Tasmania Cricket Association on the 22nd of September 1893. He proposed opening up the game of lacrosse as a winter sport for the cricketers.[6] The matter was referred to the incoming committee but was not taken up.

Undeterred, Murray let some time pass while he encouraged friends and tramway work colleagues to join his quest. In the new year he again advertised a meeting, this time with the purpose of forming a Tramways Lacrosse Club. The meeting was held on the 16th April, 1894, at Eady's Federal Hotel in Liverpool Street, and the Hobart Mercury reported as follows:[7]

> *"There was a fair attendance of employees of the Hobart Tramway Company at Eady's Hotel last evening to consider the possibility of forming a lacrosse club among themselves. Mr. Noel Murray first thoroughly explained the principles of the old Canadian pastime, after which a conversational discussion on several matters appertaining to the game took place when it was decided to play a scratch game on Wednesday afternoon for the benefit of those intending members who have not witnessed the sport. Another meeting is to be held shortly when the club expected to be inaugurated and the game set going".*

The advertised practice game, held at the New Town showgrounds, must have had some success as Murray organized a follow-up meeting on the 25th of April to formalize a club and elect office-bearers. He understood that his chances of succeeding would be greater if at least two clubs existed to provide competition, so he pushed on and quickly advertised a further public meeting for the 27th, April with the purpose of forming Hobart Lacrosse Club as a second club.

There was no follow-up account of how this meeting went, whether a club was formed, or whether the Tramways group continued with their practice games. Once again, lacrosse went silent and another year passed before anything further appeared in newspapers. The next mention came on April 17, 1895, when a meeting was called at the Carlton Club Hotel for members and interested members of the Hobart Lacrosse Club.[8] One month later, the Mercury reported that the Hobart Lacrosse Club was established and had played a practice game on Saturday the 25th of May at the New Town Show ground with the teams distinguished by red and white sashes.[9]

A roster of inter-club matches was organized for July through September on Saturday afternoons.

A week before this announcement, letters to the editors of the Launceston newspapers were published under the *nom de plumes of "Meteor"* and "Right Attack", each singing the praises of lacrosse and calling for the local sports community to take up the sport. Noel Murray was clearly the author. He had persisted with his quest to start lacrosse but his time in Tasmania was to come to a close before he could enjoy the eventual accomplishment. Murray was not included among the players named when the next match in Tasmania was played between the 'Reds v Whites' of the Hobart Lacrosse Club at

8 – TASMANIA

the New Town ground in Hobart on Saturday the 22nd of June 1895. The teams were selected from the following:

Reds: Walker, Burn, Peech, Byfield, Askey, Harper, Deegan, Grimacy, Sangwell, Tottenham, Belbin, Toby and others.

Whites: Anderson, Swan, Wallace, Humphreys, Emerson, Harper, J. Brownwell, Keogh, J. O'Brien, and others

Saturday matches continued until the end of August 1895 but did not resume in Hobart in 1896, or in the subsequent years before Australian Federation. It seemed that lacrosse, after a brief flurry of one year in Hobart, had died. By this time, Noel Murray, the key driver for lacrosse, had returned to Melbourne.

A Second Beginning

Almost a decade, and the coming of Australian Federation, passed before the lacrosse spark was re-ignited in Tasmania.

A few of the pioneer Hobart men retained interest in the sport and re-emerged as players and officials when the sport was revived in 1903, earning their badge alongside Noel Murray as founders of lacrosse in Tasmania. Included among these was John R. Byfield, a Tramways employee recruited by Murray, who became an active player again and helped to establish the Southern Tasmanian Lacrosse Association.

In sparsely populated Tasmania, sport from its earliest beginnings had always been split by geography into two primary clusters. Separate Northern and Southern Associations had been established for cricket, football and other sports and a co-operative but robust rivalry existed whenever North versus South competitions took place.   Clearly, this model would benefit lacrosse if clubs were able to be established in both parts.

Curiously, when an announcement came in April, 1903 of a meeting to establish a lacrosse club in Launceston, it was presented as a first for Tasmania and the prior heritage of colonial lacrosse in Hobart went unmentioned.

When the Launceston Lacrosse Club was formed at a well-attended meeting on Friday, April 3, 1903 at the Brisbane Hotel, the Examiner reported...

> *"The first steps were taken at a meeting at the Brisbane Hotel last night to introduce to Tasmania the winter game of lacrosse, a field sport which many years ago was imported from Canada to Australia, and has of late displayed a marked tendency with great vigor in southern soil. Numerous associated clubs exist in the states of South Australia, Victoria and New South Wales and the pennant matches excite increasing interest each succeeding season, bidding fair at no very far distant date to rival football amongst a large section of the followers and admirers of athletic sports".*

Examiner (Launceston) Saturday 4 April 1903, p 3

The new club received a welcoming letter from the Victorian Lacrosse Association and resolved to go into active practice immediately. Playing facilities were secured at Inveresk and a follow-up meeting was held at the Mechanics Institute in early May to adopt rules and elect officials.

The first office-bearers of the Launceston Club were: S. Spurling jun. (President), S.T Wood (Captain), R. J Marshall (Vice-Captain), R.T Woods (Secretary), W. Fordyce jun. (Treasurer) and M. Cato, N. Nisbet, R. Freeby, A.G Smith and W. Pierce (Committee members). Within two weeks the club had more than thirty members at practice sessions, a set of new lacrosse nets and a body of interested athletes watching the new game.

Sam Ward

Sam T. Ward, a commercial traveler for the drapery and general importing firm of Paterson, Laing & Bruce in Launceston, is credited as the person responsible for the movement to start lacrosse in northern Tasmania. It is unclear whether he had prior lacrosse experience or where his interest came from. He became an avid player and inaugural Captain of the Launceston club and later captained the North in the 1905 North v South contest.

When the news of lacrosse in Launceston reached Hobart, a few of the original pioneers of the sport in Tasmania were spiked into action and responded quickly by convening a meeting for the re-formation of the defunct Hobart Lacrosse Club. This meeting took place on the 23rd of May, 1903 at the Eildon Chambers. Twenty members enrolled and passed a resolution to re-start the Hobart lacrosse Club and commence practice on the 30th of May. John Byfield from the 1895 team was appointed to the Committee and news was received of an attempt being mounted to form a YMCA team. This was successful and another new team followed on the 19th of June when the University team was formed with twenty players led by Leonard (Len) Neil Morrison, R Seager and C. Sprent. Len Morrison, a master at the Hutchins School and a skilled athlete, soon became a leading player in Tasmania and captained the South team in 1904. Unfortunately, his energy as a player and promoter of lacrosse was lost in September of 1904 when he departed for Oxford University as the first-ever person to be awarded as a Rhodes Scholar in Tasmania.

A new YMCA Lacrosse Club joined the action during 1903, comprised almost totally with beginner players. Among them was a young Bob Coldstream, drawn into lacrosse by friends to fill a team shortage. Coldstream was born in Hobart and worked in a family retail haberdashery and clothing business. He was a successful harrier and took quickly to lacrosse, progressing to be club captain and later becoming President of the Southern Tasmania Lacrosse Association. Eventually he moved to Melbourne and became a long-serving player, coach and official with the Malvern Lacrosse Club, progressing from Club President to VLA President (1957-63) and Australian Lacrosse Council President (1959-62).

The new teams in Hobart were almost totally made up of "raw talent" with just a few "old hands" to provide instruction. They set about practice in preparation for the season and, on the 24th of

June, conducted a joint meeting to form the Southern Tasmanian Lacrosse Association and make arrangements for a weekly local competition and a match against the North. Mr. H.J.H Ford was appointed as Honorary Secretary.

In July, the following images from a scratch match between the Hobart and University teams were published in the Weekly Courier.

Hobart Lacrosse Club 1903

University versus Hobart 1903

University Lacrosse Team 1903

Meanwhile, things were progressing well in Launceston. The Launceston club realized that additional clubs were needed for a viable competition in the North and, at a meeting of members on the 11th of July, discussed the desirability of some members leaving the club in order to form a second club. This plan proceeded and the Esk Lacrosse Club was born at a meeting on the 22nd of July with E.M Law as President, M. Cato appointed Secretary, and Stephen E. (Ted) Spurling jun. and F. Stephens being named as Captain and Vice-Captain respectively. The new club fixed the member fees at five shillings and chose a playing uniform of dark blue with a red stripe on knickers and jersey, topped with a red cap. The Launceston club uniform was predominantly white.

Stephen Spurling

Spurling, the Captain, was the son of like-named Stephen Spurling sen. who was a highly acclaimed and innovative photographer. Between them, they operated a photographic supplies and photography business in Launceston which Spurling senior had established in 1879. Both men became players and administrators with the Esk Lacrosse Club and, fortuitously for lacrosse, brought much more to the sport than their athletic skills. Their firm, Spurling & Son, was retained to provide photographic images to the Examiner newspaper and the Weekly Courier. Between them, the Spurlings used this connection to ensure that high-quality photographs of lacrosse teams and games were featured prominently in the news for the following three decades.

Just prior to the formation of the Esk Lacrosse Club, another new club was formed at a meeting held in the YMCA rooms on the 18th of July under the name of Tamar Lacrosse Club. The names of these two clubs were derived from Launceston's Esk and Tamar rivers. The Tamar club adopted a uniform of dark blue with a white cap and appointed Mr P O. Fysch as President, J. Scott as Secretary, A. Marshall as Captain J. Simpson, Vice-Captain and Messrs D. Facy, A. Clarke. M. McKinlay. H.C Pilbeam, S. Frost and H. T. Bourke to the Committee. The meeting instructed its officials to approach the other Launceston clubs with the view of forming an Association. This was achieved on the evening of the 25th of July, when the Northern Tasmanian Lacrosse Association came into existence. Earlier on that day, an exhibition lacrosse match with teams chosen from the combined clubs was staged on the Launceston Cricket Ground as a curtain-raiser to the day's football. Lacrosse was well received and attracted a good deal of attention from the large crowd of spectators. The participants in this first official lacrosse encounter in Launceston were:

White Uniforms	Position	Red and White
Perrin	Goalkeeper	R. Friebe
Stevens	Point	Barnard
Burke	Cover Point	Scott
Lithgow	Third man	Baker
McKinley	Left Defence	Spurling
Brain	Centre	Simpson
Ward	Right Defense	Smith
Marshall	Right Attack	Cato
Hunt	Left Attack	Senior
Fordyce	Third Home	Pearce
Wikinson	Second Home	Boag
Coulter	Home	O. Friebe

Following this game, interclub matches were played each weekend until the end of August with Launceston coming out on top with wins over the other clubs and Tamar defeating Esk.

Launceston Lacrosse Team 1903

Tamar Lacrosse Team 1903

Esk Lacrosse Team 1903

Commencement of Representative Lacrosse

In Hobart, the season concluded with University as 'premiers' with five wins ahead of Hobart with four wins and YMCA unable to secure a victory. Lacrosse was now represented in both the north and south of the island and the appeal of intra-state competition in the form of a North v South game was being savoured. The inaugural contest was played in Launceston at the Old Showgrounds at Inveresk on Saturday 3rd of October, commencing at 2.45 pm. A large crowd watched the contest and a Ladies Committee provided afternoon tea.

The competing players in the first-ever North v South match were:

North: W (Bill). Fordyce (Captain), Herb. Pilbeam (Vice-Captain), O. Friebe, Brain, Simson, Love, Stephens (2), Perrin, Frost, McKinlay, Scott.

South: Gardiner (Captain), Len Morrison (Vice-Captain), Ford, Williams, Ife, Wise, Green, Seager, Burgess, Masterson, Clemons, Smith

The North team played in blue uniforms with a gold sash and the South wore white sweaters, navy trousers and maroon stockings. Mr. C. Coulter served as referee. The Northerners over-powered the visitors by 8 goals to 4 to become the State Champions, bringing an eventful 1903 lacrosse season in Tasmania to a close.

8 – TASMANIA

Southern Tasmania Lacrosse Association Team 1903

Northern Tasmania Lacrosse Association Team 1903

In the space of six months in Tasmania, the isolated minnows of lacrosse in Australia had progressed rapidly. Six clubs supported by Southern and Northern Associations had been established and both Associations had conducted successful inter-club competitions, culminating in an intra-state championship. For the first time in Tasmania, there was a sense of appeal and permanence about the sport.

The foundation stones of an ongoing structure were in place and lacrosse in the Apple Isle was set to advance further in the Federation years and test itself against the mainland states.

Notes

1. Cornwall Chronicle (Launceston) 18/03/1863 p.2 (Reproduced in this book as Appendix 2)
2. Tasmanian (Launceston)16/06/1883 p.651
3. The Mercury (Hobart) 27/03/1883 p.3
4. Tasmanian News (Hobart) 13/09/1893 p.1
5. Sportsman (Melbourne) 4/08/1891 p.6
6. Tasmanian News (Hobart) 23/09/1893 p.3
7. The Mercury (Hobart) 17/04/1894 p.2
8. The Mercury (Hobart) 17/04/1895 p.2
9. The Mercury (Hobart) 27/05/1895 p.2
10. The Mercury (Hobart) 15/06/1895 p.3
11. The Tasmanian (Launceston) 08/06/1895 p.38
12. The Mercury (Hobart) 22/06/1895 p.3
13. Tasmanian News (Hobart) 16/11/1885 p.3
14. Examiner (Launceston) 04/04/1903 p.3
15. Examiner (Launceston) 11/05/1903 p.2
16. The Mercury (Hobart) 26/05/1903 p.5
17. The Mercury (Hobart) 23/06/1903 p.4
18. The Mercury (Hobart) 06/08/1904 p.6
19. The Mercury (Hobart) 26/06/1903 p.5
20. Examiner (Launceston) 13/07/1903 p.3
21. Daily Telegraph (Launceston) 23/07/1903 p.3
22. Daily Telegraph (Launceston) 20/07/1903 p.3
23. Daily Telegraph (Launceston) 27/07/1903 p.3
24. Daily Telegraph (Launceston) 27/07/1903 p.3
25. Examiner (Launceston) 03/10/1903 p.3

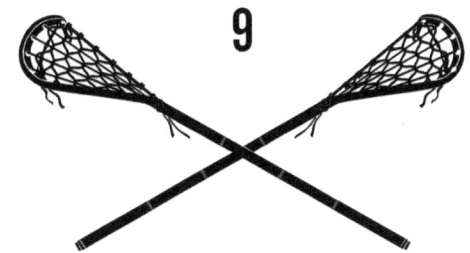

Western Australia

Australian lacrosse is fortunate to have the fine compilation published by Ian Toy in 2016, titled " A History of the Western Australian Lacrosse Association, 1896-2010". The author was restricted by the dictates of space and balance from giving more than an overview of the colonial years of lacrosse in Western Australia, which are the subject of this chapter.

It is hardly surprising that Western Australia was the last of the Australian colonies to join the adventure of lacrosse.

The sheer isolation of colonial Perth had a lot to do with the late start. Two thousand, eight hundred kilometres of desert, and a sea voyage of seven or more days, separated the former Swan River Colony from the eastern population centres. Perth's population of just 8,400 in 1891, was four times smaller than Hobart's, and the city had no electrification or transport service apart from the rail to the port at Fremantle.

Significant change came quickly after 1893 when discoveries of major gold resources were made at Coolgardie, and then Kalgoorlie, inland five hundred kilometers east of Perth. A 'gold rush' followed, different in kind from the halcyon days of alluvial mining at Ballarat and Bendigo, but similar in its impact in growing and transforming the population. In order to win the Western Australian gold, mine shafts and mining infrastructure were required, not miners with shovels and panning dishes. Building and hardware supplies, food supplies and the full range of community services were needed as the populations swelled rapidly on the goldfields and at Perth. Engineers and architects, bankers and lawyers, doctors and nurses, construction and hospitality workers, road builders and the full range of ancillary employments, all joined the miners in the stampede. It quickly became apparent that a rail link between the goldfields and the coast was required to ferry people and supplies. That came in 1896 as the population of Perth almost quadrupled and 20,000 settlers poured into Kalgoolie and Coolgardie.[1]

Until this time, lacrosse had never been a subject of consideration or public exposure in Western Australia. One of the first newspaper acknowledgements of the sport came in 1895 when the *West Australian* ran an article to inform readers about the sport and supported it with the expansive, but somewhat bizarre, set of illustrations which are reproduced below.[2]

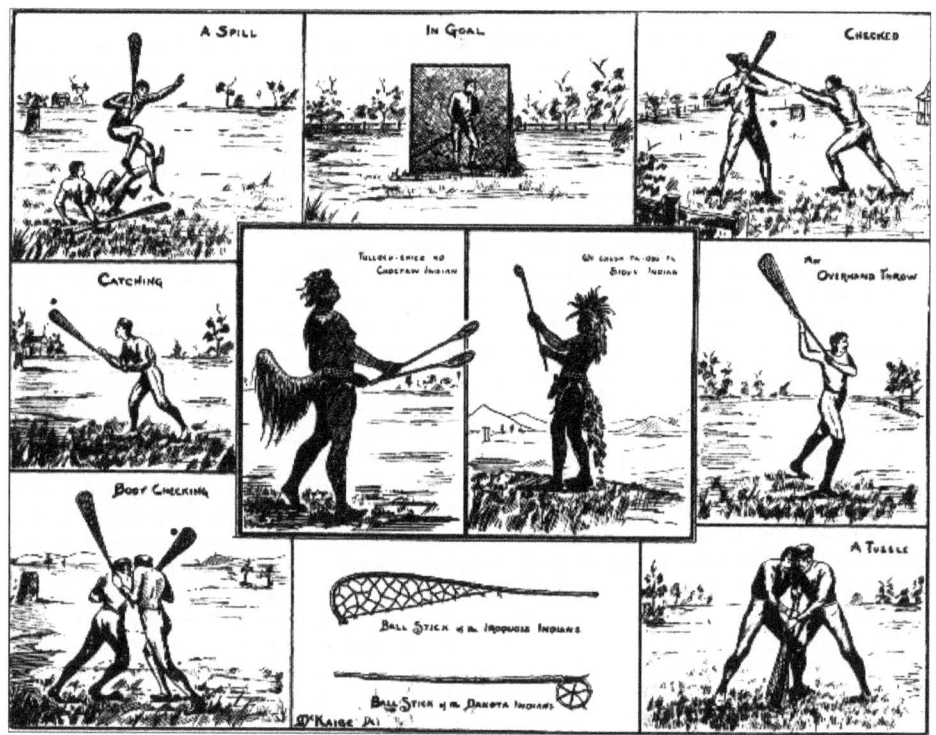

Depiction of Lacrosse in West Australian Newspaper, Perth 1895

When the time came for a start on lacrosse, Western Australia enjoyed an advantage that had not been available in the other Australian colonies.

By 1896 the economic ills which had earlier hampered the development of lacrosse in the eastern colonies had passed. The rapid population growth that came with the gold discoveries brought people from the east who were looking for work or had been transferred to Western Australia in their employment. Many had prior lacrosse experience and some were highly skilled players. Having a nucleus of quality players who were already committed to the sport, made the early days of newly formed clubs much easier than experienced in other colonies. In Perth alone, rather than starting with novices, there were at least thirty experienced players and others were resident on the goldfields.

9 – WESTERN AUSTRALIA

The Founding Four

Among the newcomers who arrived in the West in the mid-1890s, were four men from the eastern colonies who were especially enthusiastic about and directly involved in starting lacrosse. This group included Frederick (Winnie) C. Wingrove, Edward C. (Charlie) Atkins, Frederick (Freddie) C. Parsons and Cecil (Bonner) F. Wright. They did not act alone, but they were the key pioneers and founders of Western Australian lacrosse.

- **Frederick (Winnie) Charles Wingrove** was a 24-year-old when he arrived in Perth from Victoria in 1895. He had been the leading schoolboy athlete at Scotch College and was a founding member of the Melbourne University Lacrosse Club in 1883, where he played three seasons as a fast, athletic defender. He had also served as club Secretary. Following his University studies, he worked for a time in Victoria as a representative of the wholesaling and importing firm of Robert Harper & Co, before being transferred with the firm to Perth. In addition to becoming a founding member of Perth Lacrosse Club and the Fremantle Lacrosse Club, he was later a founding member and Secretary of the Western Australian Lacrosse Association and the East Fremantle Lacrosse Club. At the time of his death in 1933, he was President of the Nedlands Lacrosse Club, Vice-President of the Western Australian Lacrosse Association and an active referee.[3]

    Fred C. Wingrove

    Wingrove, along with nine brothers and sisters, was born at Eltham in Victoria. His father was employed as the local government Manager of Public Works, and had moved to Eltham after initially migrating from England to the Ballarat Goldfields in 1853. One younger brother, Robert (Bob) Wingrove, followed Fred into lacrosse at the University. Bob had been a champion schoolboy athlete at Kew High School and later won the Quarter-Mile Championship of Victoria. Not long after taking up lacrosse, Bob emerged as one of Victoria's finest-ever players, representing Victoria over a period of eight years. The family home at Eltham was Wingrove Cottage, built in 1856 and today preserved as a heritage building. Curiously, the cottage is located in Wingrove Park, just one kilometer from the present home base of the Eltham Lacrosse Club.

- **Edward Charles (Charlie) Atkins** was born in Adelaide in 1874. He was not a lacrosse player but watched with interest as a number of his school colleagues at Prince Alfred College gravitated to the sport. Atkins was an accomplished athlete and had his own claim to sporting fame as a star winger for the Norwood Football Club. He came to Perth early in 1896 and, in company with his friend and business partner, George C. Peters, opened the Perth Sports Depot in Barrack Street. His interest in lacrosse was largely commercial and his sports store was advertising lacrosse equipment before the game got started. His partner, Peters, was a keen road cyclist and had served as Secretary of the North Adelaide Bicycle Club where he knew a number of the lacrosse men who had also found their way to Perth.

Charlie Atkins

Atkins was a charismatic fellow who had an extraordinary upbringing. His father, Charles Atkins senior, arrived in Adelaide from Cheshire in 1871 as a penniless adventurer. Through frugal living, enterprising business and successful investing by buying every share he could afford in Broken Hill Propriety Ltd; he steadily built some wealth and reached a point where he could afford to educate his two sons at Prince Alfred College.[4] Mining investments in Broken Hill led to pastoral investments and, in 1904, Charles sen. joined Charlie in Western Australia. Between them they formed Atkins & Co. and purchased Murgoo Station, a 500,000-acre sheep farming property near Geraldton. Their company grew and became known world-wide for its prime merino wool and merino stud breeding. In Perth, the company also operated a large engineering and general supplies business. Further purchases of Mt Narrya Station and Tibraddon Station lifted the land holdings of Atkins & Co beyond one million acres and their enterprise was shearing more than fifty thousand merinos per year.[5] Charlie, who became known as the Squire of Murgoo, travelled between the country properties and a home in Perth, where he and his ageing father had adjoining houses at Applecross for some years. Charlie died in 1954, aged 92 years.

It was Atkins who initiated the first meeting in Perth of people interested in starting lacrosse. His motivation was commercial rather than based on a desire to play, but it seems that he advanced his credentials by taking part in some early practice sessions when the sport got underway. Bonner Wright, in a letter published in the Adelaide Observer on the 8th of July 1896, expressed his delight that lacrosse had started and proclaimed[6]...

> "Westralia is on the straight road to civilization as lacrosse is fairly under way now. Several late Adelaide players, with the assistance of others, have worked up an interest in lacrosse. We have lured footballers. Charlie Atkins and Tommy Coombes (also a former Norwood star footballer) have decided to give up leather for India rubber hunting".

Apart from his role in calling the initial meeting and providing a commercial service of lacrosse equipment for sale through his sports store, there is no evidence of Atkins having continued involvement in promoting lacrosse.

- **Frederick (Freddie) Charles Parsons** was born in Adelaide in July, 1868. He played lacrosse as a skillful and canny attackman with the North Adelaide club, participating in tours to South Australia's northern country clubs and serving time as Club Secretary and delegate to the SALA. He arrived in Perth during August, 1895 on an employment transfer with the National Bank. After one year he transferred to the accountant's branch of the Public Works Department and later established F. Parsons & Co., his own accountancy and land agent business.

Fred Parsons

Later he was appointed as an auditor of the city of Perth. He had been a highly valued player and administrator with the North Adelaide club and, on his departure, received a special presentation of a leather dressing case bearing an inscribed silver plate. Parsons went on playing lacrosse and contributing to the promotion and administration of the sport up until his premature death in May,1901 when, at just 33 years of age, he succumbed to typhoid and complications from an appendicitis operation.[7]

- **Cecil "Bonner" Frederick O'Halloran Wright** was the fourth person in the pioneer group. He was aged 21 years when he came to Perth in July, 1896, also from the North Adelaide Lacrosse Club. There, he had been a solid utility player and a keen contributor to the club in administration roles. He was also involved with SALA and was a leader in the establishment of the South Australian Junior Lacrosse Association. His transfer to Western Australia in June, 1896, was to take up a role with the West Australian Bank on the goldfields. As the timing coincided with the meetings to form lacrosse in Perth, he enthusiastically joined the action before leaving for Coolgardie. As the Secretary of the newly-formed Perth Lacrosse Club, Wright played in the inaugural match in Perth and scored the first-ever competition goal in Western Australia.

After a period in Coolgardie where he unsuccessfully sought to establish a lacrosse club, Wright returned briefly to Perth and later joined an Australian army contingent for the Boer War campaign in Transvaal, South Africa.[8] Cecil came from a family with a long and distinguished military history and joined his brother, Allan O'Halloran Wright who was the youngest person to enlist in the Second South Australian Contingent at 14 years of age. During his time in South Africa, Wright remained active in lacrosse, re-starting the defunct Durban Lacrosse Club and serving as Treasurer for the Transvaal Association. After service in South Africa, Cecil returned to Adelaide in 1905, established his own business and took over a part-time diplomatic role as Consular Agent for Italy. He died in tragic circumstances in Adelaide in 1921, when a factory millstone fell on him, crushing his skull and lacerating his brain.

There is good reason to accept that each of this "founding four" should be regarded as the pioneers of lacrosse in Western Australia. Who the key initiator was is a matter of conjecture but an analysis of their roles, and the timing of their contributions, indicates that Freddie Parsons was the key driver. Obituary accounts at the time of Parson's death credit him as the founder of Western Australian lacrosse.

That said, there was clearly a team effort at the time. Wingrove and Wright helped Parsons to make contact with known lacrosse players in Perth and Atkins is recorded as having initiated the meeting that got things moving. Clearly, communications had been occurring during the lead-up to the inaugural meeting, as evidenced by Fred Wingrove's letter to the Evening Journal in Adelaide in July, 1896, requesting the names and contacts of any known South Australian lacrosseurs who had moved to the West.

Wingrove had been in Perth longer than Parsons and, while he may have had a wish to start lacrosse during this time, there is no evidence of him trying and he had not made it happen. Wright was a willing helper but not the instigator of the idea, as he was headed for employment on the goldfields and had only arrived in the colony a fortnight before the initial lacrosse gathering. Wright did send a letter to the Adelaide newspapers a few weeks after the start had been made, claiming that he had helped his friend Fred Parsons to start lacrosse in the West. His letter also named ten experienced lacrosse players in the start-up group who had come from outside of Western Australia, including five who were from his own former club, North Adelaide.

Experienced Player Pool

Prior to the first public move to start lacrosse in Western Australia, the 'founding four' had successfully made contact with a number of lacrosse players who were known to be resident in Perth. They were referred to as 'old players' by the newspapers, not because of their age, but in reference to their prior lacrosse experience. Some of these 'old players' became involved from the outset and others emerged as the news spread in Perth about the possible commencement of lacrosse. The majority were from South Australia and had learned their lacrosse in Adelaide. A number also came from the New South Wales mining settlements at Broken Hill. Others were from Victoria and other colonies and some came from England, Ireland and Canada. In addition to the 'founding four', they brought a wealth of both playing and administration talent to the beginnings of Western Australian lacrosse, as is evidenced in the pen-pictures which follow. When the first two clubs were formed in Perth in 1896, the 'old players' aligned themselves as shown, although switching between clubs was common.

Perth Lacrosse Club

- **Albert (Bert) Edwin Thurston** – (North Adelaide L.C), 28 years, a merchant businessman and later Managing Director of Bettell & Thurston, General Importers and Hardware, Tools and Building Supplies of William Street. In Adelaide he had been a cyclist and held the record for the South Australia One Hundred Miles Road Race. His administration experience included a term as Secretary of the North Adelaide Lacrosse

Club. He continued his cycling interests in Perth and served as Captain of the Fremantle Cycling Club and Handicapper for the League of Western Australian Wheelmen.

- **Fred W Hankinson** – (South Yarra and South Melbourne L.C), 33 years, an artesian bore contractor with Davies, Hankinson & Co. Played as an attackman and was a player in the South Melbourne premiership team in 1884. He had also served on the Committee of the South Yarra club in Melbourne.

- **Alfred (Alf) Ernest Joyner** - (North Adelaide L.C), 24 years. In addition to lacrosse, he had been a leading rower with the Adelaide Rowing Club and moved to Perth as the local representative of the London firm of D &W Murray's, Importers and Warehousing, in Gawler Place. Later he became a director of *Bon Marche*, a major fashion clothing and tailoring establishment in Perth.

- **Charles (Charlie) Henry Nicholls** - (Port Augusta and Willyama L.C), a midfielder who had been cited by the Adelaide press as "a centre player of great promise" when he played in Adelaide with the visiting Port Augusta team in August, 1889. Later he represented Broken Hill in a representative inter-colonial match against Jamestown in South Australia.

- **Jack W. Scott** – (Fitzroy L.C.), 30-year-old defender. Before moving west had been employed as a glass cutter in Melbourne in 1894, possibly by Lambton Mount's Glass Works business.

- **Wilfred "Wilfie" Stow** – (North Adelaide L.C & Knightsbridge L.C), 26-year-old accountant, Played lacrosse as a defender. Served on the Perth club Committee and also as Secretary of the WALA

- **Harold (Harry) Richard Gordon** – (Knightsbridge L.C), 21-year-old, born in Geelong, Victoria of Irish heritage. Played as defender.

- **Gerald Tracey Gordon** – (Knightsbridge L.C) – 23 years, brother of Harry Gordon. Attackman.

- **Guy Thurmall Berling** –, 21-Year-old from Adelaide. Classed himself as a metallurgist and mining engineer. Worked with Hollmans Ltd, Hardware Goods Supplier. Amazed the chess fraternity when he won the Sommer Chess Championship soon after arriving in Perth in 1896. Served on Committee and as Secretary for the Perth L.C in 1896.

Fremantle Lacrosse Club

- **John (Jack) Woodforde O'Halloran** (North Adelaide L.C) – 19-year-old, Employed as a clerk with the Railways Locomotive Branch after a period in Coolgardie during which he represented the Goldfields in a match against the Combined Coastal Team in 1898.

- **Thomas (Tom) Francis Deason** – (Snaresbrook L.C, England), 24-year-old Englishman who came to Australia to take up a role with the London-based firm, McBean & Deason, mercantile, shipping & estate agents. Played lacrosse as a key defender.
- **William Douglas (Doug) Henderson** – (Knightsbridge L.C), born in Adelaide and an excellent defense player. Had served as Secretary for his club and as Delegate and Treasurer with SALA.
- **Rupert Barker – (North Adelaide L.C)**, 26 -year-old, skilled attack player. Served as Fremantle club secretary before departing to Victoria in late 1897.
- **Guy T Falkener – (Knightsbridge L.C.)**
- **Harold (Harry) Falkener (Knightsbridge L.C)**
- **Arthur B. (Dickie) Dickinson** – (North Adelaide L.C) 21 year-old who had been developing as a promising player in Adelaide. -
- **James Burton** – (Jamestown L.C), Goalkeeper who arrived in Perth in June 1895
- **John S.Scott** –
- **Matthew .J.** Moody - 29 year-old accountant who worked as Paymaster at the Customs Department.
- **William J Woods**
- **B. F Conigrave** (North Adelaide L.C)
- **Les Wilke** – (North Adelaide L.C), Attack player who became identified as the best forward in the colony
- **John (Jack) C. Angel** (Port Pirie)
- **Thomas J. Brown** - (Savages L.C – Queensland)), Goalkeeper and attack. Founding club member for the Savages and played 1888-1892 including two premiership teams and Queensland team of 1892 for intercolonial matches against New South Wales in Sydney.
- **F.W O'Halloran (North Adelaide)**
- **Lewis Hayes Wicksteed (Noarlunga L.C)** 31-year-old when he arrived in Western Australia in 1895. Played on the goldfields and in Perth. Served in various administration roles and a founder of East Fremantle L.C with Fred Wingrove.

Formation of Clubs

The founding four were all participants when the initial meeting to start lacrosse was called by Charlie Atkins. The meeting took place on Friday July 17, 1896 at the United Service Hotel in St Georges Terrace and was attended by about a dozen men.[9]

9 – WESTERN AUSTRALIA

A sub-committee was formed to draft rules, pursue other arrangements for a club and report to a subsequent meeting. This group comprised Messrs. Parsons, Wright, Atkins, and three others, Rupert Barker, Guy Berling and S. F Wright. all from Adelaide. Twenty-five intending players attended the follow-up meeting, held one week later on the 24th of July. This meeting resolved to form the Perth Lacrosse Club, noting that a number of the attendees lived at Fremantle and moves were also being made to form a club at the Port.[10] The rules of the SALA were adopted for the club and the first practice was arranged for 27th of July with Harry Gordon as practice Captain. The club chose a playing uniform of white jersey, white knickers and black stockings.

The following were appointed to the Perth Committee:

President: George Parker

Secretary: Cecil Wright

Committee: Fred Parsons, Alf Joyner, Harry Gordon and Guy Berling.

On Friday, 31st of July the *West Australian* newspaper advertised a meeting to be held at Fremantle as follows:

> *"All persons interested in the game of lacrosse at Fremantle are requested to attend a meeting which will be held at O'Beirne's Club Hotel this evening for the purpose of forming a club at the Port. There are several old lacrosse players in Fremantle who are desirous of forming a club at the Port, and as Fremantle has always been a keen competitor with Perth in anything appertaining to sport, no doubt a strong team will be put together with the view to trying conclusions with the Perth Club before the season closes".*[11]

The meeting was well attended and the Fremantle Lacrosse Club was formed that night with a committee comprising Harry Falkener, John Scott, Doug Henderson and Rupert Barker with Fred Wingrove as interim Secretary. The club started with twenty-four players on its list and selected a playing uniform of black and white hooped jerseys, white knickers and black stockings.

As the winter sports season was drawing to a close, the Committees wasted no time in conducting practice sessions and also set out a timetable for some scratch matches between the two clubs. For the Perth club, practice took place on weekdays immediately after working hours on the Esplanade grounds adjoining the city centre. This attracted interest and drew recruits of young men from other sports. For Fremantle, finding a suitable playing field late in the winter sport's season was challenging, but space was secured at Plympton Oval and Fred Wingrove submitted an application to use Fremantle Park for the following year.

Both clubs soon had approximately thirty members with a good mix of experienced and novice players.

On Friday 14th of August, the *Western Australian* reported that...

> *"Good practice is being indulged in almost every evening by the members of the newly-formed Perth Lacrosse Club, and the beginners at the game – local athletes who, previous to the introduction of the*

game here, had never played it, and are therefore not proficient in throwing, dodging and passing tactics as it is essential they should be to ensure their selection for match games – are fast becoming expert with the crosse. Fremantle players are also practising when the opportunity offers and the first club match, Perth v Fremantle is to be played on the Lacrosse Ground (late Polo ground) next Saturday, promises to be very evenly contested.".[12]

Three scratch matches were held before the winter season came to a close. The first took place on Saturday, 8th of August at Towton's Paddock in East Perth and resulted in a 7-all draw with Wingrove captaining the Fremantle team and Harry Gordon captaining Perth.[13] The goal-scorers for this first recorded match were; Wingrove 3, Wright 2 and Faulkener 1 for Fremantle and H. Gordon 2, Parsons 2, Berling 2 and G. Gordon 1 for Perth. On the following day, Cec Wright departed Perth for Coolgardie and Guy Berling took over as the Perth club Secretary. For the second practice match at Fremantle on 15th of August, the Perth players were requested to meet at the railway station to catch the 2.30 pm train to Fremantle for a 4 pm start. Insufficient players to form a team made the journey and Fremantle was also short-handed, so two evenly matched sides were chosen and an enjoyable game resulted in a win for Fremantle, 7 goals to 3. In the final match, played in Perth on the 22nd of August, the result was in favour of the city team by 3 goals to 1. This brought an end to the first 'season' of lacrosse. It was a brief and hasty start, but the build-up to these early matches established a robust rivalry between the Perth and Fremantle teams.

Despite efforts to encourage more clubs in 1897, the new year brought no result and the competition remained as two teams. Apart from the contests between the Perth and Fremantle clubs, no other lacrosse was played in Western Australia in 1896 and 1897. Despite this, enthusiasm remained high and a good many of the 'old players' continued to play in 1898. The two clubs built their special rivalry in these years which played out as 'Test Matches' whenever they met on the field.

At the final 'Test Match' played between Perth and Fremantle on 29th August 1897, a combined photograph of the teams was taken, which is reproduced opposite.[14] It reveals a high level of retention of the 'old players' who had pioneered the sport in these two clubs in 1896.

On March 24, 1898, the Western Australian Lacrosse Association (WALA), was formed at a large gathering held at the Criterion Hotel in Perth. Will Stow, Cec Wright, Fred Parsons, Tom Deason and Fred Wingrove all spoke in support of the proposal and moved a set of motions to form the Association. George Parker was elected as President, Doug Henderson as Chairman and Wingrove was appointed as interim Secretary.[15] George Parker was a 46-year-old employed in the Government Printing Office and a well-known man in business and sport circles in Perth. As a noted cricketer, he had been one of the founders of the sport in Western Australia and earned fame as the first ever century maker in the colony. He continued to serve the WALA as President in future years.

Two new clubs were added early in 1898, the first being the Mercantile Lacrosse Club, which was initiated on the 30th of March at a meeting held at the Criterion Hotel.[16] The membership came from old and new players connected with the business houses of Perth, with help from players splitting off from the Perth club. Les Wilke and Jack Angel were appointed to represent the club as delegates to

9 – WESTERN AUSTRALIA

Perth and Fremantle Teams 1898
Standing L to R: Hughes, Supporter, Scott, Edwards, Supporter, Johnson, Hankinson, Manning, Wood, Supporter, Turner, A. Gordon, Wicksteed, Hooper, Supporter, Wilke
Middle Row Kneeling: Walker, McClure, Gardiner, Dickinson, Howard, Jury, Henderson, Barker, T. Brown
Sitting: H. Gordon, Colin, Wingrove, Parsons, O'Mahoney
Front: Angel, Deason

the WALA. The club chose a uniform of white guernseys with black trim and a black diagonal sash, white knickers and black socks. It started with a number of skilled 'old players' in Dickinson, Wilke, Angel and Hughes and drew to its ranks Harry D 'Grip' Johnson, a star footballer with the Rovers in the Western Australian Football League. Johnson famously completed a lacrosse match on one afternoon and then stripped again to take to the football field when his old club was short of players. The Mercantile club joined the Perth club in conducting its practices and matches on the Esplanade grounds and played its first competition match on Saturday 4th of June, going down to Perth by 8 goals to 1.

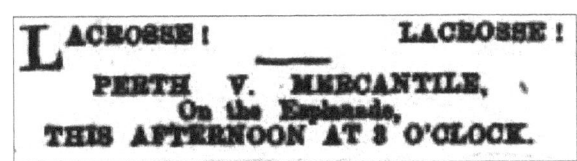

A second new club was established at Cottesloe under the guidance of Tom Deason, Matthew Moody and Harry Gordon. The team was often short-handed and battled hard but failed to record a single victory before dropping out of the WALA after one season. Otherwise, the inter-club competition in Perth during 1898 was hotly contested with a fixtured program of weekly matches on Saturday afternoons spanning the months from June through until late September. Mercantile stepped over the

Mercantile Lacrosse Club – Premiers 1898
Back Row: F.C. Bishop, A.W. Manning, A. Turner, L. Wilke, O.G. Weston, H.H. Hunter
Sitting: H.N. Venn, J.H. Inverarity, J.C. Angel, A.B. Dickenson (Captain), H. Johnson, R. St John Hughes, H.A. Crase
Front Row: R.P. Edwards, E. Blackburn

founder clubs and defeated Fremantle in a final play-off game to win the first-ever club premiership in Western Australia. The players in this premier team are listed in the photograph.

Before the inter-club competition had concluded in Perth, a Combined team selected from the coastal clubs, took the train to the goldfields and played a series of matches during the period July 26-27, 1898. The team met stronger than expected opposition and lost two of its three matches.[17]

The Goldfields

When Cec Wright left Perth in July, 1986, to take up employment in Coolgardie, he was intent on starting a lacrosse club and getting the sport adopted on the goldfields. His early reports back to Perth were not encouraging. Despite the presence of a number of 'old players' scattered through the goldfield towns, his efforts to raise interest were not successful. Sports were played on Saturdays and football already had a strong hold on the local young men. He made further unsuccessful attempts during 1897 but his time at Coolgardie came to a close and he returned to Perth, not having achieved his aim.

Things changed early in 1898. By this time, the sport was advancing well in Perth and reports kept coming of the growing profile of lacrosse in the eastern colonies, including the expansion of Inter-colonial contests. The first move on the goldfields came on the 28th of February when the Mines

9 – WESTERN AUSTRALIA

Lacrosse Club was formed at a meeting held at Lake View Consols at the southern end of the Kalgoorlie field.[18] Mr. W.H Mortimer was appointed as secretary pro tem and reported that interest was being shown in teams being formed in Kalgoorlie among the Banks, the Post & Telegraph Department and possibly at Bonnievale, Kanowna and Boulder. The Mines chose a playing uniform of black & white jersey and cap, with white knickers and black stockings.

The local media responded to the news of lacrosse starting with an amusing article in the Coolgardie Miner on the 7th, April...

> *"Lacrosse seems to be catching on with the public of the goldfields. We don't pretend to know too much about the fine parts of the game ourselves; we know it is less exciting and not so dangerous to life and limb as shinty, but the latter game is the favorite pastime of the 'foine ould Oirish gintleman' who loves to have a 3-inch toe plate of railway iron on his shoe when out for a quiet bit of fun. Lacrosse gives the pretty girl with the pretty ankle, a number one chance to score off the maid with the beefy underpinning. It also allows the refined youth who has two silk shirts in his wardrobe to get a dead lead on the plebian who wears a dicky and a couple of paper cuffs, and for that purpose, if for no other, we hope to see the sport, or science, or pastime, or whatever its votaries call it boom, because now we are a member of the Salvage Corps it will go hard with us if we are not in a position to ruffle it with the bravest of them all after the next fire. We rather fancy that the goldfields ought to turn out a few champion lacrosse teams, because lacrosse demands its votaries be active and fleet, and most people up this way are in good training just now, and well may they be, for there is nothing like dodging one's creditors to keep the human animal, male or female, sound in wind and limb. It was hard times in NSW which brought out the legion of champion runners. Few men know how fast they can travel on a pinch until they are chased by an officer of the court".[19]*

On the 2nd of May, 1898 the *Coolgardie Miner* reported that several former lacrosse players from England, Canada, South Australia and Broken Hill were showing interest in starting lacrosse.[20] It was clear that coordinated discussions had taken place between groups in Coolgardie and Kalgoorlie.

In Coolgardie, two older men who were lacrosse-aware, Messrs. Horace V. Rounsevell and John (Jack) L. Ochiltree, had been actively supporting a move to establish lacrosse along with Arthur V. Kewney, an English businessman who was a keen lacrosse player.

This group of well-educated, influential men were experienced in getting things done. Rounsevell was a practicing solicitor from Adelaide and had been captain of football at Prince Alfred College around the time of the appearance of lacrosse. Ochiltree, also from Adelaide, was an architect and a former lacrosse player. Kewney was especially active in working for the formation of a lacrosse club. He was employed as the representative of a number of British mining companies and later pursued a very successful thirty-five-year career

Arthur Kewney

in the racing industry, serving as Secretary of the Kalgoorlie Racing Club, the South Australian Jockey Club at Morphetville, and then the Victoria Racing Club in Melbourne.

A well-attended meeting was held at the Australia Hotel in Coolgardie on Thursday, March 24, 1898 at which the Coolgardie Lacrosse Club was formed with W. Richardson, appointed as secretary.[21] Two weeks later it was reported that Coolgardie had enrolled sufficient numbers of active players to form two teams. At the same time, news came of the formation of the Kalgoolie Lacrosse Club at a meeting held at Brennan's Commercial Hotel on Friday, 3rd of May.[22] Frank Hosking, an ex-Broken Hill lacrosseur, was a prime mover and was appointed as secretary. Four days later, on Saturday 7th of May, the Kalgoorlie team played against the Mines team on the Kalgoorlie Recreation Reserve, in what was the first-ever interclub match played on the goldfields. A return match was arranged for the following Saturday with Kalgoorlie travelling the 30 miles to Boulder by the 2.30pm train.

At Coolgardie, the organizing group moved quickly and met to adopt rules for their club and arrange matches with the newly-formed Kalgoorlie and Mines clubs. Rounsevell accepted a role as Patron for Coolgardie and a committee of eight was appointed which included Messrs. Richardson, Kewney, Basham, Hird, Webster, Whitby, Anderson and Sabine. The club was granted use of Reserve 1086 for its games, a piece of the parklands situated between Jobson and Moran Streets in Coolgardie, and Saturday 21st May was set down for the first practice game between two Coolgardie teams.[23] The first inter-district match in Coolgardie followed on Tuesday, 24th of May when a combined Kalgoorlie team went down to the locals by 3 goals to 2.

By June there were five teams playing on the goldfields: Kalgoorlie, Mines and Banks under the auspice of the Kalgoorlie District Association and Coolgardie and Coolgardie Commercials affiliated with the Coolgardie District Association. A vibrant program of inter-club matches operated in each district and was interspersed with inter-district contests with teams travelling by train between Kalgoolie, Coolgardie and Lake View. By seasons end in August, the Banks team from Kalgoorlie headed the table for the Goldfields Lacrosse Association, unbeaten with three wins and a draw. The Mines club finished in second place ahead of Kalgoorlie and Commercials.

The highlight of this first season of lacrosse on the Western Australian goldfields was the visit in August by a combined Coastal team of Perth and Fremantle players. Three matches and a busy social and touring program were arranged for the visitors, commencing on Thursday 25th of August when the players were met at Coolgardie Railway Station and taken by four-horse drag to the Royal Hotel for a reception. An afternoon match followed in which the combined Coolgardie Association surprised the Coastal team with the quality of their play, winning by 4 goals to nil.[24]

On the following day, the visitors played their second match on the Kalgoorlie Recreation Reserve against a combined Kalgoorlie-Boulder team, this time recording a win 2 goals to nil. The final and most important match of the tour between the Combined Goldfields and the Perth/Fremantle combination took place on the Recreation Ground in Coolgardie on Saturday 27th of August and was watched by a large and enthusiastic crowd who cheered the locals to a 4 goal to nil victory. The teams for this first-ever, Combined Goldfields versus WALA match were:[25]

9 – WESTERN AUSTRALIA

WALA: F.C Wingrove (Capt), J.W Scott, Turner, Young, Dickenson, Trathan, Johnson, Gardiner, Parsons, Jones, Brown, Howard.

Combined Goldfields: Andrews (Capt), P. Scott, Mortimer, Richardson, Webster, Plummer, Sargeant, Hannah, Myhill, Crock, Carter, O'Halloran

With a structure in place and the experience of a season behind them, the teams and governing associations on the goldfields conducted a similar program of inter-club and inter-district competitions in the years leading up to Federation. A Combined Goldfields team first visited Perth in 1899 for matches. On this occasion, the locals had the satisfaction of avenging the defeats which the Goldfieldites had unexpectedly inflicted on them a year earlier in Coolgardie and Kalgoorlie. The fixture was repeated in 1900 with a combined Perth team visiting the goldfields and this time asserting its superiority.

A new club was formed at Boulder in 1900 and joined the Kalgoorlie District Association. The club uniform was white jersey with a diagonal blue sash, white knickers and black stockings. A. S Parkin was appointed Captain and T. Brown as Vice-Captain with A.J Greenwood as secretary/treasurer. The club secured a playing ground adjacent to the Launceston Hotel in Boulder and set up a mutually beneficial partnership with the publican, Patrick Daly. In return for the team's patronage of his hotel, Daly presented one gold medal and eleven silver medals as an incentive for the team which won the most contests between Boulder and Kalgoorlie during the 1900 club season. Kalgoorlie took the prize.

Combined Coolgardie Lacrosse Team 1898

Approaching Federation

Despite considerable optimism that lacrosse was about to take off and challenge football as the sport of choice in Western Australia, the game remained largely static during the three years leading up to Australian Federation. When the Fremantle club had grown beyond its capacity to have all members participate in matches, it was decided that a second club should be formed in Fremantle. The East Fremantle Lacrosse Club was formed at a meeting held on April, 11, 1899 at the Federal Hotel in Fremantle with the prime movers being Fred Wingrove and Lew Wicksteed.[26] Wingrove was appointed Captain and Wicksteed became secretary/treasurer, supported by a committee of A.G Acraman, W.F Gardiner and J. Murray. The preliminaries which led to the establishment of the East Fremantle club were remarkably pragmatic and amiable. Fremantle's Umpire newspaper reported as follows on Saturday, April 8, 1899:[27]

> *"Last night the lacrossites of the Port commenced operations for the forthcoming season by holding the annual meeting of the Fremantle Lacrosse Club in the Federal Hotel, where a good number of members (presided over by Mr. Thomas of the South Australian cricket team) had mustered. For some time past the idea had been entertained that the old Fremantle club, which was the only one at the seaside, would be too strong to allow of the three clubs (into which the players of the Perth had been split up) having a fair chance against it in the Association matches, while it could not afford its own members a sufficient opportunity of obtaining a game. It was, therefore, proposed to establish a second club, and last night this idea was carried into effect, for after consideration it was decided that an East Fremantle Club be formed. In arriving at this decision, a perfectly friendly spirit between all members was manifested.*
>
> *A division of the players on an electoral basis was made, the parties being divided under the headings – East Fremantle and South Fremantle- High Street being, as in cricket, regarded as the dividing line. The Fremantle Club is to consist of all members residing to the south of High Street, and the East Fremantle Club of those residing on the other side of that thoroughfare. The division showed that the lists of probable players of the two clubs will be as follows: East Fremantle – Wingrove, Gardiner, Linton, Byers, Robinson, Anouis, Lane, Murray (2), Scott, McClure and Hammond (2): Fremantle – Howard, Lowe, Harvey, Wright, 'Jonah' Birtlil, Wilson, Stapleton, Rickards, Smiley, Duckett and Tickell. From the foregoing it will be observed that the East Fremantle club will be the much stronger of the two bodies so far as the playing talent is concerned, but the Fremantle Club (which is properly South Fremantle) has a big field to choose from, and it should be able to make a fair stand. Perth will have, it is said, three clubs, so that one club will have a bye each Saturday. This bye is, however, considered to be an advantage to the Lacrosse Association in consequence of its giving an opportunity of obtaining from the team, which is idle for the day, experienced umpires for the matches set down each Saturday. In the past, it is said, the game has suffered through the lack of competent umpires, and with an idle team on hand each Saturday this matter should be easily coped with"*

A subsequent meeting of the new East Fremantle club to formalize these arrangements was held at the Federal Hotel on Tuesday 11th of April. The club chose a playing uniform of navy blue guernsey, stockings and cap with broad orange braid and white knickerbockers. The following committee was elected for the season: F.C Wingrove (Captain), L.H Wickstead (Secretary and Treasurer), A.G Acraman, W.F Gardiner and J. Murray.[28]

9 – WESTERN AUSTRALIA

The Cottlesloe club was discontinued in this year and changed its name to Banks Lacrosse Club, adjusting the uniform to maroon jerseys and socks with black knickers. The WALA now had a five-team club competition which continued without change up to Federation. This was matched with a five-club fixture on the goldfields. Perth won its first premiership in 1899 but Banks Lacrosse Club annexed the premiership in 1900 when Perth failed to turn up for its final game. Fred Wingrove (East Fremantle) was named Best All-Round Player for 1900 and Les Wilke (Fremantle) led the competition goal-scorers with 24 goals.

The rivalry 'Test' matches between Perth and Fremantle continued to be a highlight of the season, irrespective of whether their teams were competitive within the WALA club competition. By 1900, the player composition within each club had changed markedly from the pioneer groups, as is evidenced in the team photographs. Only a handful of the 'old players' remained; among them Parsons, Angel and Hughes with Perth and Wingrove and with Fremantle.

Fremantle Lacrosse Team 1900
Back Row: Mortimer, Wilson, Hammond, Ferguson
Middle Row: Harry, Rogers, Wingrove (Captain), Byers, Mathieson
Front: Levine, Nicol, Absent – Jones

Perth Lacrosse Team 1900
Back Row: W.M. Nairn, R. Crawford, A.E. Joyner
Standing: E.A. Mackintosh, J.C. Cavenagh, W.D. Henderson, F. Nadebaun, Hy B. Lynch
Seated: Jno. F. Burkett (Vice Captain), W. Stow (Captain), Fred C. Parsons
Front: J.R. Max Law, C. O'Mahony

The premiership record for clubs in the colonial Western Australian Lacrosse Association stood as follows when the century came to a close.

1898 Mercantile

1899 Perth

1900 Banks

Western Australian lacrosse still remained relatively isolated at this time, but the appetite for outside experience was whetted by reports of 5000 spectators attending an Intercolonial match between Victoria and South Australia and plans to entice a team from Canada.

Quality players continued to arrive from the eastern colonies, among them Fred and Gerry Acraman and Herb Hill from Adelaide and Basil Murray from Melbourne. Some, like Max Law and Frank Meares were drawn to lacrosse from other sports. Law was the 100 yards sprint champion of Western Australia and Meares was a star young cricketer with the Perth Cricket Club. Against the flow, however, was the loss of a number of players who enlisted in the military contingents heading to South Africa to support Britain in the Boer War.

Key Players and Administrators

All of the 'old' and new men who played and took the extra step of contributing via leadership and administrative roles in clubs and the WALA, deserve recognition for the part they played in establishing lacrosse in Western Australia.

Some stand out for their ongoing contributions. Among these, Fred Wingrove, or "Winnie" as he was fondly known, stands head and shoulders above any other person (as he does as the Fremantle Captain in the adjoining photograph) in the early development of lacrosse in Western Australia. He was one of the founding group rather than the originator, but he surely deserves the title of 'father' of Western Australian lacrosse for all that he did both on and off the field over many years.

Had Freddie Parsons lived longer, he would likely stand alongside Wingrove. Others of particular note were Wilf Stow, Lew Wicksteed, Harry Gordon, Doug Henderson, George Parker. Bill Mortimer, Jack Scott and Fred Hoskins.

The stars on the playing field included Wingrove, Hughes, Wilke, Dickinson, H. Gordon, Scott, Parsons, Brown, Howard and Gardiner.

Fred Wingrove as Referee

As the photograph shows, the WALA showed foresight in giving early consideration to the importance of having competent umpires and including recognition for them as essential to the game. Sitting on the left next to Wingrove is Wilf Stow, the umpire for the day. On the right is the Perth captain, Jack Straw.

Among the founding clubs of the colonial years, only Fremantle and East Fremantle have survived until the present, both still operating as vibrant and successful clubs with impressive histories. Both have experienced some volatility along the way, dropping out of competition in a few years before re-surfacing. The Fremantle club adopted the new name of Phoenix Lacrosse Club in 2009 in a strategic move to improve its playing facilities and connection to its local community.

As the curtain came down on the century, lacrosse in Western Australia was soundly established but remained small and untested outside of its own environs. That was to come in the form of Interstate and International competition in the Federation years.

Notes

1. Australian Bureau of Statistics
2. The Western Mail (Perth) 23/09/1898 p.32
3. New Call (Perth) 7/09/1933 P.21
4. West Australian 12/06/1896 p.8
5. Sunday Times (Perth) 18/02/1934 p.2
6. Adelaide Observer 08/07/1896 p.13
7. Western Mail (Perth) 01/06/1901 p.71
8. The Daily News (Perth) 10/08/1904 p.9
9. Inquirer and Commercial News 24/07/1896 p.4
10. West Australian 24/07/1896 p.3
11. West Australian 31/07/1896
12. Western Australian 14/08/1896 p. 6
13. Daily News 10/08/1896 p.3
14. Western Mail 27/08/1897 p.29
15. The West Australian 25/03/1898 p.7
16. Umpire (Fremantle) 02/04/1898 p. 2
17. Coolgardie Miner 26/08/1898 p.6
18. Kalgoorlie Miner 03/03/1898 p.4
19. Coolgardie Miner 07/04/1898 p.5
20. Coolgardie Miner 02/05/1898 p.3
21. The Golden Age 24/03/1898 p.3
22. Kalgoorlie and Boulder Standard 04/05/1898 p.3
23. The Golden Age 23/05/1898 p.3
24. Coolgardie Miner 25/08/1898 p.6
25. The Goldfields Morning Chronicle 29/05/1898 p.3
26. Western Mail 21/04/1899 p.41
27. Umpire (Fremantle) 08/04/1899 p.2
28. The Umpire (Fremantle) 15/04/1899 p.3

10

New Frontiers, Decay and Revival in Victoria

By the time that lacrosse commenced its expansion across colonial borders in 1883, Victoria had a well-established governing Association, the VLA, and a total of eight clubs participating in inter-club competition.

The period up until the late 1880s was one of great prosperity in Australia, especially in Victoria where enormous wealth continued to be generated from gold and wool. These were heady days of urban expansion in Melbourne with fortunes being made in property speculation. It seemed that lacrosse could happily sail along on the coat-tails of this largesse.

Having a well-founded competition in Victoria was an accomplishment, but it fell well short of Lambton Mount's original vision. Mount wanted, and expected, lacrosse to be embraced throughout Australia. Seven years had passed since the first gathering of players in Albert Park and still the sport was confined to Melbourne and two regional centres in Victoria.

The breakthrough came in 1883 when circumstances, and the efforts of a few individuals, resulted in the introduction of the sport into New South Wales and an attempt to start in South Australia. This migration across the colonial borders was gratifying for Victoria and set the scene for a fully Australian sport with cross-border competitions. Unfortunately, things stalled in South Australia but a successful start was made in 1885 and Queensland embraced the sport in 1886. Tasmania and Western Australia

VLA Premiership Medallion 1884

followed later. Accounts of this cross-border expansion, and the people who pioneered it, are contained in previous chapters.

Buoyed by the growing expansion in other colonies, the VLA looked set to break into its own new era of growth. The 1884 season had been claimed as the best ever with nine teams, approximately 160 participants, some exciting young players and moves afoot for the start-up of additional clubs in Melbourne at Kew and Essendon. South Melbourne won the 1884 club premiership and the winning team members each received a silver medal in the shape of a Maltese Cross presented by the VLA President.

On May 15, 1885, the North Melbourne Advertiser boldly proclaimed the ascent of the newly named Bohemians club:[1]

"A club has been formed from the inhabitants of Carlton, Brunswick and surrounding districts which plays immediately at the rear of the Zoological Gardens. This club, styled the Bohemians, bids fair to become premier for season '85".

It was not to be. The Bohemians won nine of their eighteen matches in 1885 despite having a number of the best players from the formerly powerful Carlton club. A number of the 'old players' had left the colony or dropped out with the result that, early in the 1886 season, the Bohemians were struggling to get a team into the field. Part way through the season they disbanded and merged with Fitzroy.[2]

Collingwood took out the Premier Cup in 1885 with an unbeaten run of sixteen wins and two drawn matches. The table at season's end showed only six clubs, South Melbourne having withdrawn from the Association during July due to a dispute over player eligibility.

	Played	Won	Drawn	Lost
Collingwood	18	16	2	0
Fitzroy	18	13	2	3
Melbourne	18	11	4	3
South Yarra	18	11	3	4
Bohemians	18	9	0	9
University	18	7	1	10

Following the pattern established from previous years two Tournaments were played during 1885. The first, at the East Melbourne Cricket Ground on 23rd of May, was won by South Melbourne, and the second was won by Collingwood at the South Melbourne Cricket Ground on the 6th of August.[3]

The tournaments were supported by extensive newspaper advertising with an entrance fee of sixpence and a further sixpence for a seat in the grandstand, but they failed to draw sizeable crowds.

10 – NEW FRONTIERS, DECAY AND REVIVAL IN VICTORIA

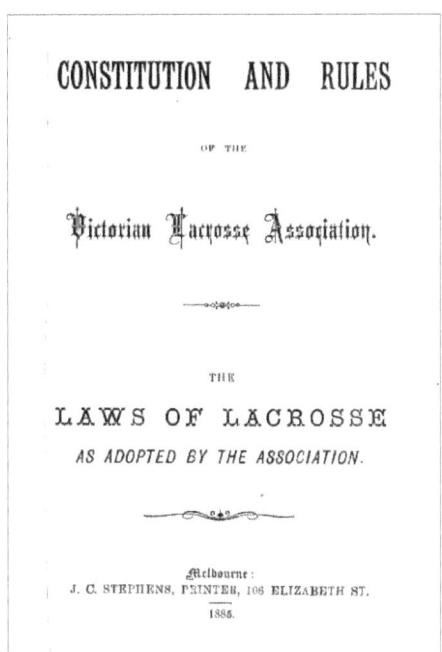

Also, during 1885 the Association arranged for the printing of an updated version of the VLA Constitution and Playing Rules in booklet format. This was distributed among clubs and players and the playing rules were those adopted by the other colonies. The contents of the booklet are reproduced in full in Appendix 1 in this publication.

Inter-Colonial Lacrosse

When Queensland entered the lacrosse family during 1886, the sport now had participation in four of Australia's six colonies. The circumstances were right for the new frontier of intercolonial competition.

During 1886, the VLA Executive Committee investigated the concept of sending a team to Sydney for intercolonial matches with the players to be responsible for their own expenses. When insufficient players indicated their availability, the matter was put aside.

On April 23, 1886, the VLA received news via the local Echuca newspaper of the following unexpected, and somewhat cheeky, letter from the Riverina town of Deniliquin in southern New South Wales.......

> *"In your issue of the 9th inst. I see a paragraph from the hon. sec. NSW Lacrosse Club. For the information of those interested in the game I might state that we have succeeded in forming a club in Deniliquin, called the Deniliquin Lacrosse Club, and that so far we have met with good support, have about 20 members, great interest is taken in the game, and the club are to meet the Sandhurst Lacrosse Club at an early date, so that match will, I think, be the first intercolonial match played in the colony. There being no association in New South Wales at the time the club was formed, it was decided to adopt the Victorian Lacrosse Association rules and to play under the same. The match is to be played at Echuca. – I am, etc., yours &s.,"*
>
> W.S. Clark. Hon. Sec, Deniliquin Lacrosse Club, Deniliquin, N.S.W.

The match was played at the Park Oval in Echuca on Wednesday, 16th of June with some 300 spectators enjoying the spectacle. Sandhurst won the contest by 3 goals to nil and became the first lacrosse club in Australia to win an across-borders match.

Little is known regarding how this match came about. It was not an event organized or sanctioned by the NSWLA or the VLA. Sandhurst was a newly established and functioning club in country Victoria, formed in 1883. Nothing is known of the team from New South Wales except that a meeting had been held at the Royal Hotel in Deniliquin in March 1886 to organize a lacrosse team. There seems little doubt that the match was arranged for the sole purpose of making history. For Deniliquin, apart from its participation in this match, there is no evidence of a lacrosse club existing in the town, before or after this time.

A full year would pass before inter-colonial lacrosse would feature again. In June of 1887, the South Australian Lacrosse Association issued an invitation to the South Melbourne Lacrosse Club to send a team to Adelaide.[7] Clearly, Alf Wilkinson's connections with the Gordon family and the South Melbourne club were at work. While not all of the best of South Melbourne's players were available to make the trip, thirteen players and two officials travelled by train to Adelaide in August and participated in four matches. This visit received limited reporting in the Melbourne newspapers but the occasion and the four matches were extensively covered by the South Australian media and the visitors were showered with hospitality. South Melbourne won two matches, drew one and lost to a combined team from the Adelaide clubs.

South Melbourne Lacrosse Club Team in Adelaide 1887
Back Row: P. Shappere, Cornish, Lucas, A. Anderson, Billsborrow, Miche, Henderson, Fraser, Billsborrow
Middle Row: House, Moore, Evans
Front Row: Davie, Knight (Captain)

10 – NEW FRONTIERS, DECAY AND REVIVAL IN VICTORIA

Victorian and South Australian Teams – Inaugural Intercolonial Match, 1st September 1888
Victoria in dark color uniforms, South Australia in white
Back: E. McHaige, Robin, Ross (Referee), J. Robertson, J. Cuddy, C. Gordon, S.A. Davenport, F.W. Best,
D. Fowler, R. Evans, J.G. Cavenagh-Mainwaring
Middle: A. Gordon, W. Gordon, C. Murray, J. Michie, D.C. Connor, E. Phillipson, R.J. Hill, S.D. Smith, H.R. Anderson
Front: H. Hutchinson, A. Anderson, G. Batchelor, A. McHarg, W.D. Henderson, P. Heath, Amos Rowley

Lacrosse had now recorded two experiences of cross-border competition. The participating teams were club based rather than representatives selected as the best of their colony. The first intercolonial representative contests came about in Brisbane, one month after the Adelaide event, when Queensland invited New South Wales to Brisbane for two contests.[8]

Soon after the successful visit of the South Melbourne club to Adelaide in 1887, the South Australian Lacrosse Association was formed and the VLA encouraged the new association to send a team to Melbourne for a representative match between the two southern colonies. This came about in September 1888 amid great speculation as to the likely outcome. As the founder and long-standing 'parent' of lacrosse in Australia, the Victorians assumed that their playing skills were superior. The build up to the contest was significant in both Melbourne and Adelaide, and attracted greater interest in the sport than had previously been generated. The importance of the occasion was highlighted by player selection trials, newspaper evaluations and accounts of the plans for the program of matches and civic hospitality.

The South Australian team left Adelaide on Thursday 30th of August and stopped along the way at Ballarat to play a warm-up match against the recently established Ballarat Lacrosse Club. The Ballarat team for this first contest by Victorians against a visiting Intercolonial team comprised Messrs. Bradley (captain), Robertson, Rushbrook, Cocking, Fanning, Sleep, McKay, Adair, P. Robertson, Smith, Hardie, Eddie, Drury; and emergencies, Willaton, Rickey, and Thompson.[9] This was a colorful affair, played at the Eastern Oval and watched by 2000 spectators, despite rainy weather. The South Australians were dominant and took the match by 5 goals to nil. After a dinner at the Buck's Head Hotel the visitors proceeded to Melbourne by the 7.10 pm train and were hosted the next morning at a welcoming ceremony at the Town Hall by the Lord Mayor of Melbourne.

The East Melbourne Cricket Ground had been specially reserved for the occasion of the Inter-colonial contest on Saturday 1st of September but, unhappily, something went astray in communications with the ground managers. The Australasian Newspaper reported:[10]

> *"Considerable disappointment was experienced by the players and admirers of the game on arriving at the cricket ground to find that the authorities of the club had marked off a playing space for the match which was altogether too small for lacrosse. Requests were made to the authorities that additional playing space should be given, but the request could not be complied with, as the additional portion of the ground required had been top-dressed, with a view to making it in good order for the coming cricketing season, and it was considered that it would be spoiled if the lacrosse players carried on their game over it.*

This impediment of a narrow and shortened field was annoying for the players and limited their opportunity to display the skills of the game, but it did not deter the enjoyment of the spectacle for the 2000 spectators who turned out to witness lacrosse.

Victoria had the better of the game and won by 5 goals to 1 with Anderson (2) and McHarg, W. Gordon and Michie scoring for Victoria and Evans for South Australia. A combined photograph was taken of the two teams for this historic match. At a celebratory dinner in the evening, the VLA announced that it would send a team to Adelaide in the following year. So began the rivalry matches between Victoria and South Australia which have continued almost annually ever since. The South Australian team played two further matches in Melbourne before returning to Adelaide, securing a 3-all draw against Melbourne University and losing to South Melbourne by 4 goals to nil.

Decay in Club Lacrosse in Victoria

Maintaining community sporting clubs, and the associations which coordinate them, is always a challenge and carries no guarantees. It demands energetic and wise leadership and a willingness to adjust to constantly changing external circumstances.

During the second half of the 1880s, the club scene in Victorian lacrosse began to show signs of malaise. After a decade in the sport, many of the original players had dropped out or were becoming too old to continue. Squabbles between clubs and dissatisfaction with the Association began to emerge. In July of 1885, the South Melbourne club dropped a mid-season bombshell by withdrawing from the Association due to a dispute over an Association ruling on player eligibility.[11] For the first time, the VLA found itself involved in awkward, and potentially destructive, arbitration. Almost a year passed before South Melbourne was admitted back into membership and there were other signs that the Association was grappling with a new era of increased, and sometimes annoying, workload. Walkovers, disputation with umpire decisions, games abandoned due to weather and fighting between players were issues that demanded attention.

On the positive side, the build up to the first intercolonial contest between Victoria and South Australia brought a new dimension and excitement to the sport. So also did some visionary thinking displayed by Joel Fox and George Gordon at the VLA Committee on June 2, 1885, when they proposed that the Association write to the Secretary of the Canadian Lacrosse Association and seek to induce the Canadians to send a team to play in Australia.[12] Their view was that it would not be difficult to attract enough men of means in Canadian lacrosse to assemble a team and pay their own costs. Ultimately, it took a further twenty-two years before the Canadian tour was achieved and international lacrosse came to Australia.

Attempts to expand the game were still prominent in the minds of the administrators. The VLA maintained annual tournaments to showcase the sport and used the Easter break to arrange team visits to selected regional towns. During mid-1885 an attempt was made to introduce lacrosse into independent secondary schools. Xavier College in Kew played a match against Melbourne University but this failed to materialize into a schools' program or a new club.[13] The recently formed Bohemians Lacrosse Club (formerly Carlton) was struggling for players.

Moves to establish a new club at Williamstown during 1886 evaporated after the South Williamstown Football Club put up a spirited fight to convince the Williamstown Borough Council to keep lacrosse from the playing fields at the Gardens Reserve. The Williamstown Chronicle published a sarcastic report on Saturday, April 3, 1886, as follows:[14]

> *"Lovers of the graceful and picturesque will be delighted to hear that an attempt is being made to form a lacrosse club in Williamstown. Lacrosse, the national game of French Canada, must be played in costume – the game itself is not up to much – and the costume is a cross between a harlequin's and that of an Italian nobleman. At important matches bell-toppers and 14-button gloves are worn. The club desire to play in the Gardens, but we think if a little friendly pressure was brought to bear upon the members, they would consent to perform on the reclaimed piece of land fronting Nelson Place, on Saturdays. This would prove a great boon to persons travelling to and from the Gem Pier, and to such of the residents of the Front, as cannot spare time to go to the gardens. If the club were to do this, and to throw in a band and a few swinging boats – Aunt Sally would be out of place – the entertainment would be very popular during the winter months. Anyone wishing to join the lacrosse club can receive full particulars from Mr. Walter Clarke (president) or Mr. John Robertson (secretary)."*

When the Williamstown Council met to decide on the issue on Thursday 1st of April, it resolved to refuse the lacrosse club application in favor of football, on the grounds that the lacrosse club was an embryo club and not yet formed.[15] The decision was loudly applauded by a number of young footballers who were present in the council chambers. More than a decade would pass before lacrosse re-appeared in Williamstown and the Williamstown Lacrosse Club was formed.

The VLA kept its promise to send a representative team to Adelaide in 1889 for a return match against South Australia. It struggled, however, to get all of the best players to participate, perhaps due to the deteriorating state of the economy as the property boom collapsed and the nation stepped towards economic depression. The Victorian team was beaten soundly and no further contests took place for the two ensuing years.

Even the staunchest of the pioneers of the sport were showing signs of declining time and interest for lacrosse. Bill Heale did not seek re-election as Secretary after 1887 and Jim Barclay's long service as Treasurer came to an end in 1889.

On the playing field, the club competition suffered as team entries declined. The formation and affiliation of the Essendon Lacrosse Club in 1889 came as a lonely bright spark within the growing decay. The Essendon club chose colours of white flannel shirt with a red and black sash, white knickerbockers and dark blue hose and cap. It competed with gusto, finishing its first season in third place.

By 1889, club lacrosse in Victoria had declined to just five clubs and six teams. Fitzroy and South Melbourne had discontinued and a drop in morale had infested the remaining clubs. A club competition was conducted in 1890 with just five clubs participating. The pages of the minute book of the VLA for the 1890 year are blank, with not a single record kept of any meeting, a poignant reflection on the level to which the energy in managing the sport had declined. The VLA, it seemed, had ground to a halt and might not survive.

Revival

A changing of the guard occurred in 1891 when a meeting of lacrosse players was arranged on the 18th of May at the Young & Jackson's Hotel in Swanston Street, Melbourne. Representatives from six clubs attended the meeting: Essendon, Melbourne, Collingwood, University, and new clubs Tortoise and Caulfield. With them came a bunch of new club representatives and a resolution to reform the Association.[16] What followed was a refreshment rather than a revolution but it was clear that many players were unhappy with the state of the game. W J. (Bill) Mountain MLA was elected as President and Cecil L (Cis) Murray was appointed as Secretary/Treasurer. Amendments to the VLA Constitution and Rules were passed to revamp the Association's ailing financial structure and update the playing rules. The "throw up" of the ball to start a game, or after a goal, was replaced with a "face-off" with the ball placed on the ground between opponent's sticks. Team size was altered from 13 to 12 players.

Bill Mountain was an Emerald Hill resident and Mayor, and son of the South Melbourne Mayor at the time when Lambton Mount started lacrosse. His name does not appear as a player but he was sympathetic to the sport, an experienced administrator, and friends with a number of the players and supporters of the sport. He served the South Melbourne Club as Vice-President and President during the years 1880 -1888 and was also President of the South Melbourne Cricket Club. Murray, from the University, and later, Caulfield clubs, was the emerging star player of the colony with a genuine love for the game and desire to see it spread.

In 1891, as these leaders took up the challenge of re-vitalizing the VLA, two others were emerging who were destined to become even more influential. They were Phil Shappere, already a steady contributor, and Dan White, a young man with seemingly endless drive and energy. Dan White later succeeded Murray as the VLA Secretary and wrote in The Victorian Sporting Record about the disastrous Victorian team visit to Adelaide in 1889[17]...

> *"Whilst rapid strides were being made in South Australia, the game, for want of proper management and support, was fast declining in Victoria, and though several good players undertook the journey, the team had to be completed with absolute novices. The result was South Australia 9 goals, Victoria 2 goals. For a few years from this date lacrosse almost fizzled out in Victoria, but the visit of a South Australian team in 1892 gave a new fillip to the game, and though the visitors again won by 6 goals to 3, the seed was sown for the up-shooting of a new generation of lacrosse players in Melbourne".*

The changes which came in 1891 marked a shift in the VLA from a governance structure with a figurehead President and Vice-Presidents who had been recruited on the basis of their positions in the community rather than their interest in the sport. Now the leader was to be a hands-on, working President who would chair delegate meetings and work closely with the Secretary on the management of the game.

Among the clubs, the lacrosse section of the Tortoise Club was formed with great hopes in 1891 but it had a short lifespan. If the name itself seemed inappropriate for a team of lacrosse players, the main activities of the club seemed even less appropriate. The Tortoise Club had similar objectives to the Bohemians, providing members with a unique, experimental mix of literary, artistic, social and sporting activities. The Melbourne Herald ran a short feature on the club's first anniversary function, noting that it had been formed in 1890 on Shakespeare's Day, the 23rd of April, with subsequent meetings held every Wednesday and Saturday:[18]

> *"All of Shakespeare dramatic works had been read on the Wednesday nights, while the Saturdays had been devoted to the more social pastimes of games and tourneys in chess, euchre, whist, draughts, etc. A cricket team, formed in connection with the club, had passed creditably through the season. Musical and dramatic evenings had been held monthly and had been successful......A lacrosse club was then formed so that members would be provided with a suitable outdoor winter game.*
>
> *On Thursday night (Shakespeare's Day), Hamlet was read by members, and the principal dialogues in the play were given by the members to whom the parts in them had been cast for the reading. It was announced that Goethe's Faust and the plays of Goldsmith would be among the first takes of the new year.*
>
> *The anniversary proceedings were brought to a conclusion on Saturday night, when a banquet, to which 50 Tortoises sat down, was held in the rooms, a dish of hare appropriately forming the chief item in the menu. The first toast honoured was that of the Queen, coupled with the Commonwealth of Australasia.*

Toasts to The Club and, the Retiring Vox were also honoured A bust of Shakespeare draped in the club colours, and a tortoise enclosed in the club's motto, "Silently. Slowly, Surely, Straightly", adorned the centre of the table. During the evening topical and other songs were rendered...The evening terminated with the singing of the Tortoise Anthem, with the following refrain sung to the tune of Choir Boys Cheer: -

> *Tortoises be always true and trusty*
> *Tortoises step silent, sure and slow*
> *Cheer your hearts with renders loud and husky*
> *Singing of hopes as onward straight ye go"*

The Tortoises failed to win a game in the 1891 season and did not continue.

The Caulfield Lacrosse Club, on the other hand, started well in its first full season. It finished in third place in 1891 behind Collingwood and University, winning more than half of its matches. It quickly established itself as a leading club within the VLA, winning consecutive premierships in 1892, 93 and 94. Its pioneers were the athletically talented and energetic Murray brothers; Cecil, Hugh, Noel and Basil, with support from Dave Fox, Tom Handfield and a bunch of new players. Cecil had played the 1890 season with Melbourne University where he was an engineering student, but transferred briefly to St Kilda and then to Caulfield to play with his brothers and help start the new club at a time when lacrosse was struggling.

Cecil Murray

Three of the Murray family, Hugh, Cecil and Noel, commenced lacrosse as students at Melbourne University. Together, they were a formidable combination but were unable to stay together as their studies and professional careers took them along differing paths. Cecil, Noel and Basil played in attack and Hugh, who graduated as a physician, was an outstanding goalkeeper. Noel trained as an engineer and left Victoria in 1895 for two years of employment in Tasmania where he was successful in starting lacrosse in Hobart. Basil also left Victoria but picked up lacrosse in Perth during the formation years of Western Australian lacrosse. In 1896, Cecil left the Caulfield club and used his administration and playing skills as one of the founders of the MCC Lacrosse Club. Here, he had a long and decorated playing career at club and Victorian team levels and was widely recognized as the star attack player in Victoria. In 1897 he was joined at MCC, and in the Victorian team, by his brother Noel who was returning from employment in Tasmania and his other brothers. Caulfield was struggling to find twelve players to put into the field and decided on a year of recess. The Caulfield name did not re-emerge until 1909 when a 'new' club was established.

In 1892, the Auburn and Civil Services clubs were affiliated but Melbourne disbanded in 1893 and the core group from the former Bohemians re-affiliated as Hawthorn Lacrosse Club. With the worst of the economic depression waning, further growth came in 1894 when South Melbourne re-established and Caulfield, Essendon and Hawthorn each entered second teams into the competition. A new club at Flemington was added in 1895 and a flurry of newcomers swelled the VLA in 1896: Brighton, Auburn, Moonee Ponds, Glenferrie and Albert Park. To a degree, this club growth was false as some were

10 – NEW FRONTIERS, DECAY AND REVIVAL IN VICTORIA

second teams from existing clubs. Moonee Ponds was part of Essendon, Glenferrie was the second team from Auburn and Albert Park was linked with South Melbourne. A Port Melbourne club was added in 1897, also an offshoot of South Melbourne. In 1898, South Melbourne changed its name to St Kilda, Glenferrie became Kew and then merged with Hawthorn in 1899.

The most important growth of new clubs in the late 1890s came with the MCC lacrosse section in 1897 and the addition of Williamstown one year later.

Success on the playing field during the 1880s and 1890s came to the clubs which each won the Premier Cup and, after 1891, were presented with silver or gold medals for the players donated by the Vice-President (and later President), Phil Shappere. The Premiers and Runners-Up are shown in Table 1.

Year	Premiers	Runners-Up
1879	Carlton	
1880	Fitzroy	Melbourne
1881	Melbourne	
1882	Fitzroy	Carlton
1883	South Melbourne	Collingwood
1884	South Melbourne	Melbourne
1885	Collingwood	Fitzroy
1886	University	South Melbourne
1887	University	South Melbourne
1888	South Melbourne	University
1889	University	
1890	Essendon	
1891	Collingwood	University
1892	Caulfield	Collingwood
1893	Caulfield	Collingwood
1894	Caulfield	Essendon
1895	University	Essendon
1896	Essendon	MCC
1897	University	MCC
1898	MCC	University
1899	University	MCC
1900	University	Essendon

Table 1. Victorian Lacrosse Association
"A" Section Premier and Runner-Up Teams 1880-1900

A key new direction in the revival of lacrosse in Victoria came in 1894 when the VLA Annual General Meeting was asked to consider a restructured constitution for a new Association. Wally House, who had taken over as Secretary from Cecil Graham, spoke to the proposal saying[19]....

> "The old association had arrived at the conclusion that its constitution was unsatisfactory and did not give the general body of players sufficient interest in its management, and in order to meet the defect had decided to disband and ask the players to adopt a constitution drawn up by the speaker and Mr. C.L Murray and approved by the old association."

The new structure was approved unanimously and, in 1895, Bill Mountain finished his term as President and was replaced by Phil Shappere, with Dan White elected as the new Association secretary. This pair presided together over VLA affairs for a further eight years. The years leading up to Federation were especially significant for their formative role in developing regular lacrosse contests between the separate colonies and adding both structure and stature to the events. The Melbourne Cricket Ground played an integral part in these developments.

The MCC Lacrosse Club and the MCG

The best-preserved lacrosse club history in Victoria is that of the MCC club which is fortunate to have the resources of the Melbourne Cricket Club Library, the premier sports library in Australia. In 2017, Trevor Ruddell, a research librarian at the MCC, published a detailed, illustrated history of MCC lacrosse in an article in The Yorker, the Journal of the MCC Library.[20] This history covers lacrosse at the Cricket Ground and the story of the commencement, growth and achievements of the MCC Lacrosse Club.

Ruddell points out that the MCC club was not, as is often assumed, the same entity known as the Melbourne Lacrosse Club, which Lambton Mount had formed in 1876. That club had ceased to exist in 1893 and the MCC club started as a separate new entity in 1896, formed when Harry Graham, an MCC member who had played lacrosse in England and later at Caulfield and Hawthorn, approached the MCC Committee about having a lacrosse club. He had earlier been successful, as the VLA Assistant-Secretary, in gaining the support of the MCC Committee to fixture some lacrosse matches on the MCG. The first inter-club lacrosse match played on the MCG took part on June 8, 1895 between Caulfield and South Melbourne as a curtain-raiser to a Victorian Football League game.[21] Curtain-raiser games continued at the MCG during 1895 and 1896 and the MCC Committee became increasingly interested in lacrosse. When, in 1896, Graham approached the Committee about starting a club, he had the support of four other established players, and fellow MCC members, in Cecil Murray, Theo Handfield (from Caulfield), Dan White (from South Melbourne) and F. Holmes (from University). Dan White was well-known within the junior cricketers at the MCC club and had no difficulty in attracting some to join lacrosse as novices. When the new club played its first match on the MCG on Saturday, May 2, 1896, its team contained seven 'old' players and 5 new recruits. The match was played as a curtain-raiser to the Melbourne v Essendon football and finished in a 1-all draw with Cec Murray scoring for MCC.

10 – NEW FRONTIERS, DECAY AND REVIVAL IN VICTORIA

The inaugural MCC team comprised:[22]

    Experienced players: H. Graham, C. Murray, T. Handfield, D. White, F. Holmes, C. Eccles, A Mayne.

    Novice Players: Messrs. Jacobs, Phillips, Simson, Willmott and Thomas.

From the outset, with Murray and White, the club was blessed with having two leaders who were among the most influential and hard-working administrators in Victorian lacrosse.

The club playing uniform consisted of white flannel jersey, navy knickerbockers, navy stockings and navy cap with white and red trimmings. Its home ground alternated between the mighty Melbourne Cricket Ground and the Warehouseman's Oval in St Kilda Road, Albert Park, (later renamed as the Albert Ground). After a successful first year in which MCC claimed third place on the premiership list behind Melbourne University and Essendon, other established players transferred to the club and MCC powered its way to the VLA premiership in 1898.

MCC Lacrosse Team – Victorian Premiers 1898
Photograph courtesy of the MCC Museum Collection M10

This was the era of the beginnings of action photographs in newspapers and magazines which brought lacrosse and other sports to the public with a new vibrancy. In addition to team photographs, lacrosse could now be seen in action shots from on-field incidents and images depicting player skills for coaching. The Melbourne Cricket Ground and MCC lacrosse featured strongly in this new visibility and became especially prominent as the home of Intercolonial and future Interstate and International matches.

Basil Murray
Photograph courtesy of the
Melbourne Cricket Club Library

Dan White
Photograph courtesy
of the Melbourne
Cricket Club Library

Lacrosse Action

Action photographs first appeared in newspaper coverage of Inter-colonial contests in 1897.

The Australasian and the Weekly Times both ran features on the games played at the Melbourne Cricket Ground during the 3rd-10th of July, 1897 with both South Australia and New South Wales participating against Victoria.[23] Although the images lack clarity and sharpness, they did bring a new public awareness to lacrosse. Further action photographs came from the Intercolonial contests played in Melbourne at the MCG in 1898 and 1899.

In these Intercolonial contests, South Australia continued its dominance, winning by 13 goals to nil when Dan White insisted on taking a clearly sub-standard team to Adelaide in 1896 in order to re-establish the contests which had lapsed since 1892.

Dickenson (NSW) facing off against Dan White (Victoria) in 1899

The South Australian supremacy was surprisingly broken at the MCG in 1898 when Victoria accounted for the visitors in a 9 to 5 victory with Goss, Cis and Basil Murray and White as Victoria's goal-scorers. New South Wales first entered the fray against the southern colonies in 1897 when it ventured to Melbourne and was

10 – NEW FRONTIERS, DECAY AND REVIVAL IN VICTORIA

Simson scoring for Victoria against NSW in 1899 at the Melbourne Cricket Ground
Photograph courtesy of the Melbourne Cricket Club Library

beaten by Victoria by 17 goals at the South Melbourne Cricket Ground on Saturday, 10th of July. The Sydneysiders closed the gap in the following year with a 16-3 result on the Sydney Cricket Ground[24] and improved further in the two subsequent years, going down 10-3 in Melbourne in 1899 and 12-2 in Sydney in 1900. South Australia regained its position as the top colonial team with victories over both Victoria and New South Wales in the two years leading to Federation.

The 1898 Victorian team pictured below contained three Murray brothers and was captained by Dan White. Its playing uniform in this year included red and blue bands on the white guernsey.

Victorian Lacrosse Team – 1898 in Sydney
Back Row: S. Simson, B. Murray, E. Kent, F. Bainbridge, R. Pyke, C. Handfield, F. Sampson, N. Murray
Middle Row: F. Delves, D. White (Capt), E. Doney, W. Tait
Front Row: W. Walsh, E. Jacobs, P. Kent

The Williamstown Lacrosse Club

The lacrosse season of 1898 was notable for the continued expansion of the game and the beginnings of a new club at Williamstown, located across Port Philip Bay from Melbourne.

Efforts to initiate lacrosse in the Melbourne suburb of Williamstown had failed in 1886 when the Williamstown Borough Council refused an application for use of the Gardens Reserve, in Victoria Street. More than a decade passed before a second, and this time successful, request was made for a playing venue.[25]

Harry Radford, a 20-year-old attackman who had played with both the Flemington and Essendon Lacrosse clubs, started the interest at Williamstown during 1898, perhaps inadvertently. In a note to the editor of the VLA Newsletter in May, 1960, Harry recalled the beginnings of the Williamstown club[26]...

> "During 1898, I was in Williamstown and some lads of my age became interested in my crosse. I borrowed some racquets and gave them some practice on Market Square, open ground near the State School. That, I think, was the beginning of the Williamstown Club, formed soon after in 1898. The names of some of those beginners: F & B Arthurs, G. Westcott, Arthur Whitney, Charles Scott, two Hicks brothers and McKenzie".

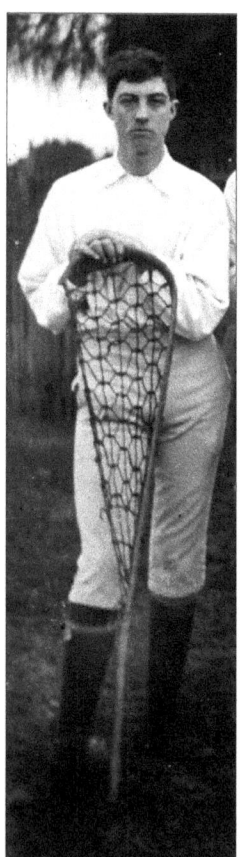

Harry Radford

On Saturday April 30, 1898, the Williamstown Chronicle carried a brief news report that practice for lacrosse had started and was continuing at Hannan's Farm.[27]

Arthur Whitney was the son of the Minister at the Williamstown Baptist Church and it was there in the Sunday School Hall on Tuesday, August 23, 1898 that a meeting to form a lacrosse club was held.[28] Harry Radford chaired the meeting and John Waycott moved that ...." those present unite under the name of the Williamstown Lacrosse Club". The motion was passed unanimously and a playing uniform was chosen of blue guernsey, yellow band across the right shoulder and under the left arm, white knickers and blue stockings. Radford was elected pro tem as Captain and Whitney as Vice-Captain. Fred Scott was appointed as the Secretary.

Following the formation of the club, arrangements were made for a team from the Essendon club to come and play a scratch match with the new players and let the public see lacrosse. Bill Strickland, the Essendon Captain agreed to play and brought with him a team which included Victorian representative stars, George Gay and Alan Dean. The match took place at the Williamstown Cricket Ground on Saturday, September 10, 1898.[29] Dean and Gay volunteered to play with the Williamstown team and scored two goals each to help the locals win their first-ever match by 6 goals to 2. B. Arthurs scored the other two goals for Williamstown. The inaugural Williamstown team comprised the following:

10 – NEW FRONTIERS, DECAY AND REVIVAL IN VICTORIA

Williamstown Lacrosse Premier Team 1899
Photograph courtesy of Williamstown Lacrosse Club

B. Arthurs (Home), G. Arthurs (Right Attack), A. Hick (Left Home), W. Waycott (Right Attack), F. Arthurs (Left Attack), F. Scott (Centre), C. Scott (Left Defense), T. Golding (Right Defense), B. Davis (Third Man), E. Parkes (Cover Point), A. Whitney (Point), H. Radford (Goalkeeper)

Following this match, the club continued to practice at Hannan's Farm, adjoining the rifle butts, and travelled to Hawthorn to play a second practice match against the Auburn Lacrosse Club. Now with a viable playing group, the club needed a home playing venue and Fred Scott wrote to the Williamstown Council in October requesting permission to use the Gardens Reserve and have the Bandstand Rotunda moved to another location.[30] When Councillor Schutt opposed the request on grounds that 'if permission was granted, all of the reserves in the town would be monopolized by clubs" it seemed that a start on lacrosse in Williamstown was set to be blocked a second time. The matter received discussion at two subsequent Council meetings before being referred to the Gardens Committee for review and recommendation.[31]

The recommendation finally came to Council on Monday, March 6, 1899, stating that …."The Lacrosse Club be granted the use of the Gardens Reserve for two years, the club to remove the bandstand at their own cost to a site to be fixed by the Committee, the practice or games of the club not to be fixed so as to interfere with any other entertainment in the reserve".[32] A further recommendation was that ...." tenders be invited for the construction of a latrine and W.C. at the Garden's Reserve". Not all Councillors were happy with the recommendations and the matter was again held over.

While waiting on a final determination from Council, the club held a full meeting on Monday 20th of March at the Mechanics Institute and resolved to join the VLA and enter a team in "B" section for 1899 with the expectation that nine to ten of its matches would be fixtured to play locally.[33] Ultimately, the club prevailed with its request for playing space, but it came not at the Gardens Reserve, but nearby at the Williamstown Cricket Ground at Point Gellibrand. In 1910, the club moved to Gardens Reserve (now named Fearon Reserve) and began a tenancy which has continued since that time to the present.

In its first year of operation, Williamstown succeeded in taking out the VLA "B" Grade premiership, so commencing a long and decorated playing history which has ever-since marked it as one of the powerhouse clubs in Victorian lacrosse. The club soon earned the confidence of the Williamstown Council and today is highly respected for its outstanding recreation contributions for both male and female residents as one of the leading community sporting clubs in the municipality.

Snapshot of 1900

In 1895, Phil Shappere took over as Association President, commencing a stellar period at the helm which lasted 25 years until 1914. At his side was Dan White as VLA Secretary, later claimed by the media, as the most influential operator in lacrosse. Between them, they presided over a period of stability and consolidation in Victorian lacrosse, encouraging new clubs and innovation.

Dan White shone as a leader, both on and off the field, putting himself on the line to Captain a young Victorian team visit to Adelaide in 1896 to once again revive Intercolonial lacrosse which had lapsed for a second time after 1892. White knew that the Victorians were in for a beating but understood the bigger picture of the promotional power of cross-border competitions. Writing in 1903 he observed[34].....

> "In August 1896, sixteen or seventeen players entrained for South Australia to try conclusions with what were then by far the most expert wielders of the hickory that Australia had yet produced. The little band of pilgrims were unmindful of the "drubbing" which they knew to be in store for them. Their object was the establishment, if possible, of regular interstate contests. South Australia won easily, by 13 goals to nil, but what of that? A return visit from the representatives from the City of Churches in 1897 was assured"

Shappere, White and Walter House were enthusiastic supporters of any moves to establish new clubs. Under their watch the VLA added multiple new teams and a junior competition commencing in 1895 which was initially styled as "B" Grade and later extended to "B" and "C" grades.

A decade after the sport had almost collapsed in Victoria, the prospects looked much brighter as the colony approached Australian Federation.

10 – NEW FRONTIERS, DECAY AND REVIVAL IN VICTORIA

A snapshot of the 1900 season in Victoria reveals that the sport had matured but still retained much of the flavour of its birth years. The VLA had an established pattern of operating with 7 to 8 Committee meetings spread throughout the playing season and an Annual Meeting conducted in April in conjunction with a 'Smoke Social' at which medals and trophies were presented to the premier teams of the preceding year. The Committee Meetings, held at the Amateur Sports Club, comprised the appointed VLA Officers and six club delegates elected on a rotating retirement basis for a three-year term.

In 1900, at the Annual General Meeting on the 18th of April, the President, Phillip Shappere, was in the Chair. The meeting received correspondence from the South Australian and New South Wales associations seeking to finalize dates for Intercolonial matches and for a Conference to consider a proposed invitation for Canada to send a team for international competition in Australia.[35] After adopting the Annual Report and Financial Statements, the following office-bearers were elected:

Patron:	Sir John Madden, Lieutenant-Governor of Victoria
President:	Mr Phillip Shappere
Vice-Presidents:	Messrs., Batchelor, J. Fox, W.J Fookes, W. B House, C.L Murray, K.S Murray, Professor Laurie, P. Jager, and Major B.T Wardill.
Treasurer:	Mr E. Doney
Secretary:	Mr D. White
Committee:	Messrs. Hamblett and Wettenhall.

Following the usual vote of thanks to the Chair, the Annual Meeting closed and was followed with musical items and speeches and the presentation of medals for the 1899 season. It was the appointed Patron of the Association, Sir John Madden, who famously labelled lacrosse as "the sport for thoroughbreds" when he spoke at a dinner following his viewing of the Victoria versus New South Wales match at the MCG on July 22, 1899.[36]

The 1900 VLA club competition had 8 teams entered in 'A' Section and 10 teams in 'B' section. Part way into the season, a late entry was accepted into the "B" section from a re-formed club at South Yarra. In order to promote the sport, the Association determined that the Treasurer should place an advertisement each week in the Age, Herald and Argus newspapers to publicize selected matches and their venues. Additionally, a sub-committee was empowered to make arrangements for two teams from Melbourne to be sent to play an exhibition match at Camperdown during July.

Among the eight clubs in the 'A' Section were three, and arguably four, that have lasted until the present. Each have enjoyed periods as the powerhouse club within the VLA. – University, MCC and Williamstown. Today's Caulfield Lacrosse Club, which records its formative year as 1909, was preceded by the triple premier Caulfield club that competed in the VLA competition between 1890 and 1896.

The emergence of a number of talented younger players continued during 1900, many of them excelling in the VLA club competition and joining the established star players in the Victorian team for intercolonial contests. Among the best which Victoria had to offer at this time were the Murray brothers and Dan White (MCC), Stuart Simson (MCC), Charlie Handfield (MCC) and a younger breed which included George Gay (Essendon), Will Bryning (Hawthorn), Frank Bainbridge (Hawthorn), Francis Bonnin (University), Bob Wingrove (University), Alf Rudd (University), Bill Waters (University), Fred Delves (St Kilda), Bill Furneaux (St Kilda), John Latham (University) and Bill Walsh (MCC).

The playing season opened in May with a 16- week schedule and a break for two weekends at the end of July for intercolonial matches, one at the MCG and one at the Sydney Cricket Ground. The University club quickly established itself as the team to beat with first round victories over all other clubs in the "A" section. The students went on to take out the premiership with an unbeaten match record and the highest total goal tally ever achieved in a single season. The merged Hawthorn/Kew combination won the 'B' grade following a close battle with St Kilda and Brighton. The club standings at the conclusion of the 1900 playing season are shown below.

A Grade	B Grade
University	Hawthorn/Kew
Essendon	St Kilda
St Kilda	Brighton
MCC	Williamstown
Hawthorn/Kew	University
Collegians (University)	MCC
Collingwood	Essendon
Auburn	Melbournians
	Auburn
	Collingwood

Lacrosse came temporarily to the western district of Victoria in August, 1900, when the regional town of Camperdown hosted two teams from Melbourne.[37] Dan White sent twelve carefully selected lacrosse sticks to Camperdown from the VLA and the locals took to the sport eagerly. A local club was formed and practised assiduously over a six-week period leading up to the visit and two locals, J McDonald and J. Henderson were included in the exhibition match.

During July, the fifth Annual Ball conducted by the Auburn Lacrosse Club was successfully held in the Hawthorn Town Hall, decorated for the occasion in club colours and lacrosse regalia. This event had been established in 1896 as a joint venture between the Auburn and Hawthorn clubs. Over four hundred people attended the inaugural year and the event became a key social event on the lacrosse calendar. It provided an opportunity for lacrosse to interact with local and State dignitaries and was

10 – NEW FRONTIERS, DECAY AND REVIVAL IN VICTORIA

well-received by the wives and girl-friends of players. The newspapers of the day carried detailed descriptions of the ladies' gowns and full listings of the attendees.

The Intercolonial matches in 1900 commenced with a clash against South Australia at the MCG on Saturday, 21st of July.[38] The ongoing dominance of South Australia was again to the fore and the result finished 6 goals to 3 in their favour. A week later at the Sydney Cricket Ground, Victoria held their winning record over New South Wales by a margin of 12 goals to 2.

The prospect of International lacrosse was high on the agenda in 1900, spurred by the urgings of the NSW Secretary, Bill Morrison. A Conference on this subject between three states was held in Sydney in conjunction with the Intercolonial Matches. Ultimately, the VLA agreed to approaches being made for Canada to send a team to Australia on the basis that the gate entry takings from matches would be used to defray the costs of the Canada team and any travelling costs of the local players. Expectations of this visit taking place in 1901 were high after Canadian, Richard Garland, visited Sydney during October and confirmed that he was confident of being able to assemble a team if the Australian colonies were supportive.[39] Garland was later to become a resident in Australia and well-known in lacrosse as

Victorian and South Australian Teams at the MCG in 1900

the part donor in 1910 of the superb Garland-McHarg Cup which later became the permanent trophy for the national championships played between states.

As the 1900 playing season came to a close, and the time drew near for Australia to become a federated nation, lacrosse in Victoria had been revitalized after some shaky years. In the main, the recovery was due to the skilled leadership and attentive management provided by four key leaders within the VLA – Bill Mountain, Cecil Murray, Phil Shappere and Dan White, with special help from Ninian Batchelor, Walter House and Joel Fox. This transformation positioned the VLA to move into the Federation years with confidence.

Notes

1. North Melbourne Advertiser 15/05/1885 p.3
2. Sportsman (Melbourne) 26/05/1886 p.8
3. The Age 25/05/1885 p.6
4. The Sydney Mail & New South Wales Advertiser 29/05/1886 p.1137
5. The Echuca & Moama Advertiser 17/06/1886
6. Correspondence from Deniliquin Historical Society
7. Adelaide Observer 16/07/1887 p.19
8. The Queenslander (Brisbane) 1/10/1887 p535
9. The Ballarat Star 1/09/1888 p.4
10. Australasian (Melbourne) 8/09/1888 p.30
11. VLA Committee Minutes 4/05/1886 p.3
12. VLA Committee Minutes 2/06/1885 p.2
13. The Argus 27/04/1885 p.9
14. Williamstown Chronicle 3/04/1886 p.2
15. Williamstown Chronicle 3/04/1886 p.2
16. The Age 18/03/1891 p.7
17. The Victorian Sporting Record 1903, McCarron, Bird & Co, Melbourne. P.238
18. The Herald (Melbourne) 27/04/1891 p.4
19. VLA Annual General Meeting Minutes 1894
20. The Yorker: Journal of the Melbourne Cricket Club Library Issue 62 Autumn 2017 pp 18-27
21. VLA Committee Minutes 14/04/1896 p.1
22. The Age (Melbourne) 4/05/1896 p.3
23. Australasian (Melbourne) 10/07/1897 p.25
24. Australasia (Melbourne) 29/07/1899 p.30
25. Williamstown Chronicle 3/04/1886 p.2
26. VLA Lacrosse Newsletter, May, 1960
27. Williamstown Chronicle 30/04/1898 p.3
28. Williamstown Chronicle 27/08/1898 p.2
29. Williamstown Chronicle 10/09/1898 p.3
30. Williamstown Chronicle 22/10/1898 p.2
31. Williamstown Chronicle 22/10/1898 p.2
32. Williamstown Chronicle 11/03/1899 p.2
33. Williamstown Chronicle 25/03/1899 p.2
34. The Victorian Sporting Record 1903, McCarron, Bird & Co, Melbourne. P.239
35. VLA Annual General Meeting Minutes 1900
36. The Herald (Melbourne) 12/07/1901 p.6
37. The Age 4/08/1900 p.11
38. The Herald (Melbourne) 20/07/1900 p.3
39. VLA Committee Minutes 21/08/1900 p.1

SECTION FOUR

LACROSSE IN POST-FEDERATION AUSTRALIA

Garland McHarg Trophy

The Early Years of Federation

When a new year of lacrosse opened in 1901, the formerly independent colonies were now federated as states of the Commonwealth of Australia. This brought new possibilities, opportunities and challenges.

Australian lacrosse had already experienced some years of interstate competition, backed by structured club competitions in every State, and overseen by elected governing State associations. What it did not have was a coordinating National Association, International competition or lacrosse for girls and women. Each of these missing elements would be satisfied during the Federation Years.

The biggest disappointment during the closing years of the approach to Federation was the loss of Queensland and Tasmania where lacrosse had lapsed in the mid to late 1890s. A renewed pioneering effort was needed in both states and it soon came.

As a measure of where the sport was at when Federation came in 1901, the lacrosse clubs and teams operating in each State in 1901 are listed on the next page in Table 1.

LACROSSE IN AUSTRALIA

NSW	Qld	South. Aust	Tasmania	Victoria	West. Aust
13 clubs, 17 teams	*Nil*	*14 clubs, 24 teams*	*Nil*	*9 clubs, 19 teams*	*11 clubs, 15 teams*
Glebe		Iroquois		MCC	Fremantle
North Sydney		University		Collegians	Perth
Balmain		Nth Adelaide		St. Kilda	Mercantile
Wentworth		Woodville		Essendon	Banks
Newtown		"B"		University	East Perth
University		Holdfast Bay		Collingwood	
Mohicans		University B		"B"	"Junior"
"B"		YMCA		Auburn	Fremantle
Burwood		East Torrens B		Kew	East Fremantle
St Stephens		North Adelaide B		Elsternwick	Perth
Balmain B		Sturt A		Williamstown	Merc-Banks
North Sydney B		Woodville B		"C"	"Goldfields"
Glebe B		"C"		Essendon B	Mercantile
Newtown B		Holdfast Bay B		St Kilda	Mines
Broken Hill		University C		MCC	Kalgoolie
Norths		East Torrens B		Auburn	Banks
Souths		North Adelaide C		Collingwood	Coolgardie
Wests		E Torrens-Iroquois		University	Boulder
Centrals		Sturt B		Essendon C	
		E Torrens-Iroquois B			
		Country			
		Kadina			
		Moonta			
		Jamestown			
		Port Pirie			
		Petersburg			
		Caltowie			

Table 1. Lacrosse Clubs and Teams in Australia, 1901

In total, there were 47 lacrosse clubs with 75 teams and 1125 players participating in Australia in 1901. These statistics provide a baseline for determining how successful the sport was in achieving its expansion and growth objectives, and in capitalizing on its opportunities through international competition and nationally coordinated governance.

Revival in Queensland and Tasmania

When the sport faded to a halt in Brisbane in the mid 1890s, Bill Morrison, the energetic NSWLA Secretary and an Intercolonial representative player for New South Wales, expressed his desire to help. Years later he arranged a meeting in 1899 with former Queensland lacrosse officials during a business trip to Brisbane and offered his support to get lacrosse re-started in Queensland.

Four further years passed without any indication of a rebirth, but Morrison became an active advocate after relocating to live in Queensland. Queensland newspapers carried occasional reports on Intercolonial lacrosse contests between the southern colonies and snippets from England and Canada. In 1902 a match played at the Lords Cricket Ground in London caught public attention when the King and Queen attended as spectators.[1] In the following year a combined team from Oxford and Cambridge Universities toured the USA and Canada and played a series of games, famously beating Harvard University by 5 goals to 4 during July.[2]

By this time, the lacrosse drums were beating again in Brisbane and elsewhere in Queensland. On March 4, 1903 a meeting of local lacrosse enthusiasts was held in Rockhampton, a coastal town 500 miles north of Brisbane. They formed a temporary committee and decided to call a public meeting for the 19th of March 1903 at the Criterion Hotel to try and form a lacrosse club. The meeting was well-attended and proceeded to form the Rockhampton Lacrosse Club.[3] The instigator, Gerry Fetherston, was elected as Club Captain, a Committee was appointed and an order was sent to Melbourne for the purchase of 23 lacrosse sticks. Practice commenced as soon as the lacrosse sticks arrived and the Rockhampton Cricket Ground was booked for a scratch match for the 14th of May. Bill Morrison, the ex-NSW player, now resident in Queensland, refereed the game, which resulted in a 2-all draw.[4]

The news from Rockhampton appeared to strike a chord in Brisbane. Clearly, a group of past players had been communicating between themselves about their latent desire to play again. A meeting was convened at the Royal Queensland Yacht Club on Monday, May 18, 1903 to consider the idea of restarting lacrosse.[5] The main driver was Frank Hambridge who was supported by four others in Fred Jacobs, Harry Hooper, Jack Arthur and Ted Stanley. Hambridge, a former defenseman with the Iroquois Club in Adelaide and an active citizen in community affairs in Glenelg, South Australia, had come to Brisbane in August 1900. The group came armed with the knowledge that some forty men had already indicated their willingness to play. A general meeting of interested players was called for the 22nd of May at the Grand Hotel in Mary Street, Brisbane with Norman Turnbull serving as Chairman.[6] Among the attendees were several men who had been well known as players in the QLA competition before the sport died out. The meeting was informed that indications had been received of at least three clubs being formed if a decision was made to re-commence lacrosse in Brisbane. A motion to form the Queensland Lacrosse Association was passed enthusiastically and Trevor Nielson, secretary of the old QLA commented that he would endeavour to find the old minute book for future guidance. Fred Jacobs was elected as Secretary, the names and contact details of intending players were recorded, and a committee of four was established to draft a constitution and seek to form four clubs. Bill Morrison was part of this committee.

Within seven days three clubs had been formed: Iroquois, Indooropilly and Delaware. The Mohicans Lacrosse Club in South Brisbane followed a few days later and suddenly Queensland had a governing association and four clubs ready to participate in competition. In preparation for a start on 5 July, practice matches were played between Iroquois and Indooropilly at Chelmer on the 20th of June and between Iroquois and Mohicans at Albion on the 27th of June. A successful season followed and the Queensland premiership for 1903 was taken out by the Iroquois club. In addition, a promotional tournament was played on the Wolloongabba Oval with Indooropilly and Mohicans playing a drawn game in the final.

Queensland lacrosse had been brought back to life and the scene was set for further growth as new clubs joined in the following years. In 1904, the North Brisbane Harriers Lacrosse Club joined the ranks and the following year brought the Buffalo Lacrosse Club and the Young Men's Christian Association (YMCA). In 1906, a club was established in the regional town of Toowoomba, 100 miles inland from Brisbane. Along with its club competition, the QLA was active and successful in seeking Interstate competition during these years of rebuilding. At the QLA Annual General Meeting in 1905, Ted Macartney MLA, one of the original pioneer players and a stalwart of Queensland lacrosse, returned as Association President.[7] Sadly, for Queensland during 1906, Jack Gibson, another of the original founding fathers, passed away prematurely.

The revival in Queensland brought a spate of talented new players who quickly graduated to the Queensland State Team and brought unexpected success against their more highly fancied opponents. Among them were Roy Darvall, Jim Thorpe and Ossie Thorpe.

In Tasmania, a similar revival occurred in 1903 in Hobart, and the sport expanded to the north of the Island State in the same year with the establishment of teams in Launceston and the formation of the Northern Tasmanian Lacrosse Association. These developments are documented in Chapter 8. Growth occurred steadily in the North and, despite only having three clubs, a representative team visited Melbourne in June, 1906 and played against the MCC, Hawksburn and Melbourne University clubs.[8] This was the first ever Interstate experience for Tasmania, its primary purpose being to improve the standard of play and bring home new techniques. The Tasmanians were beaten 20-6 by MCC on the Melbourne Cricket Ground on the 1st of June, 13-2 by Hawksburn on the 3rd of June and 11-2 by University on the 5th of June.

Following this visit, the MCC club sent a team from Victoria to Tasmania in August, 1906. Their match at the Launceston Cricket Ground on 2nd August was billed at the time as the most important event in the history of Tasmanian lacrosse. MCC won the match by 13 goals to 7.[9]

11 – THE EARLY YEARS OF FEDERATION

Northern Tasmania goalkeeper, Fred Green, makes a save in the match against MCC, 1906

Northern Tasmanian Lacrosse Team – Melbourne Cricket Ground, 1906
Back Row: H.C Pilbeam, H. Williams, S.B Reid, J.A Huston, W. Maloney
Front: H. Stewart, W.G Dawson, J.L Murphy, W.J Stephens (Capt), H.T Batty, F. Green, R. Whitfold

Clubs and Competitions

The progress of lacrosse in other Australian States can be gauged by a comparison of the relative strength of clubs in Tables 1 and 2. In 1906 there were 61 clubs, 89 teams and 1335 players in lacrosse club competitions in Australia. This was an increase of 14 clubs, 14 teams and 210 players over the five years.

In New South Wales, the Glebe, Wentworth, University and Mohicans clubs were lost during the span of years from 1901 to 1906, but new clubs at Petersham and Mosman entered the competition in 1906. Lacrosse in Broken Hill remained stable with a four-club competition but a re-arrangement of team names.

In South Australia, the metropolitan competition remained relatively stable with the Iroquois club no longer competing, the YMCA and Adult Deaf starting up as new clubs, and Woodville making a name change to Port Adelaide.

NSW	Qld	South. Aust	Tasmania	Victoria	West. Aust
10 clubs, 11 teams	*8 clubs, 8 teams*	*13 clubs, 22 teams*	*6 clubs, 6 teams*	*11 clubs, 23 teams*	*13 clubs, 19 teams*
North Sydney	Buffalo	Sturt	**North**	Essendon	Fremantle
Balmain 1	Delaware	North Adelaide	Tamar	Malvern	East Fremantle
Burwood	Iroquois	East Torrens	Esk	Hawksburn	Iroquois
Petersham	Mohicans	University	Launceston	University	Swan
Balmain 2	Indooroopilly	Port Adelaide	**South**	MCC	Perth
Mosman	Iroquois	**Junior "A"**	Moonah	Kew	Banks
Marrackville	YMCA	Holdfast Bay	Hobart	Auburn	North Perth
Broken Hill	Toowomba	University B	YMCA	**"B"**	**Junior**
Norths		North Adelaide B		MCC B	Swan
Commercials		Sturt B		Kew B	North Perth
Proprietory		Port Adelaide B		Essendon B	Claremont
Wests		Deaf Adults		Williamstown	Banks
		East Torrens B		University B	Iroquois
		Junior "B"		South Yarra	Fremantle
		Holdfast Bay B		Coburg	Perth
		Sturt C		Malvern B	East Perth
		North Adelaide C		Auburn B	**"Goldfields"**
		Port Adelaide C		Elsternwick	Kalgoolie
		University C		**"C"**	Boulder

11 – THE EARLY YEARS OF FEDERATION

NSW	Qld	South. Aust	Tasmania	Victoria	West. Aust
		Country		Essendon C	Banks
		Jamestown		University C	Iroquois
		Petersburg		Kew C	
		Mount Gambier		Hawksburn C	
		Port Pirie		South Yarra B	
		Kadina		Hawksburn D	
		Caltowie			

Table 2. Lacrosse Clubs and Teams in Australia, 1906

The significant growth that had occurred in Western Australia is revealed in Table 2. The number of clubs and teams grew in Perth in the five years up to 1906. The Claremont, Swan, Iroquois and North Perth clubs were added to the WALA competition and the East Fremantle club advanced into the "A" Grade and strengthened, showing its hand as one of the future powerhouse clubs in the West. Perth,

Perth Lacrosse Club in 1904

the original parent club in Western Australia, continued as a force and followed its runner-up success in 1904 with premierships in 1905, 06, 08 and 1913.

Among its number in the 1904 Perth team photograph was Ike Taylor who is standing in the back row, second from the right. Taylor played with Perth from 1902 – 1927 and was State goalkeeper from 1905-1925. He served as Club Secretary-Treasurer before taking over as WALA Secretary/Treasurer in 1915 and holding that office until 1932. When the Australian Lacrosse Council was formed in 1932, Ike was appointed as Secretary and held office with the national Association until 1957. Taylor was the consummate administrator and, for more than thirty years, was the most active, visionary and influential person in Australian lacrosse. In 1932 he left Western Australia on employment transfer and spent two years in Tasmania and then moved to Victoria, continuing his involvement with the ALC and serving on the VLA Executive Committee 1936-56, including 20 years as Chairman until ill-health forced him to retire. A two-page tribute to Ike Taylor is given in Ian Toy's, *History of the Western Australian Lacrosse Association*.[10]

In Victoria, the number of clubs grew from 9 to 11 between 1901-06, despite the loss of the Collingwood club. Among the new clubs were Coburg and Malvern, plus Hawksburn which changed name from St Kilda to improve its playing venue. Team numbers swelled from 19 to 23 along with registered player numbers increasing by 60.

The Coburg club was formed at a well-attended meeting on 31st January, 1905[11] and commenced a highly successful period in the VLA competition which included the 1930 senior premiership and lasted for 90 years until it was disbanded in 1994. The undoubted star addition to VLA ranks during this period was the Malvern Lacrosse Club, formed in 1903.

During this era, the administration of club lacrosse competitions relied upon printed fixture booklets, rule books, handbooks and programs. Samples of the items produced by the Associations and clubs are reproduced below along with a Melbourne Sports Depot advertisement showing the prices for lacrosse equipment.

 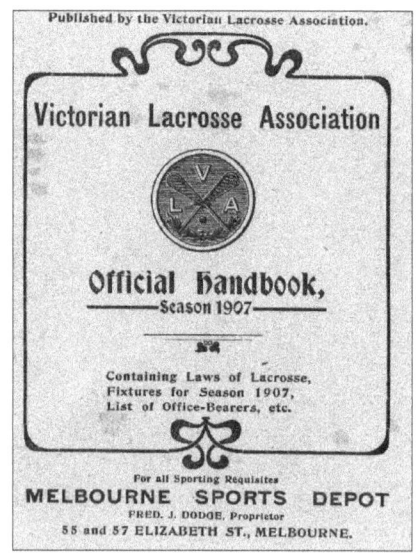

11 – THE EARLY YEARS OF FEDERATION

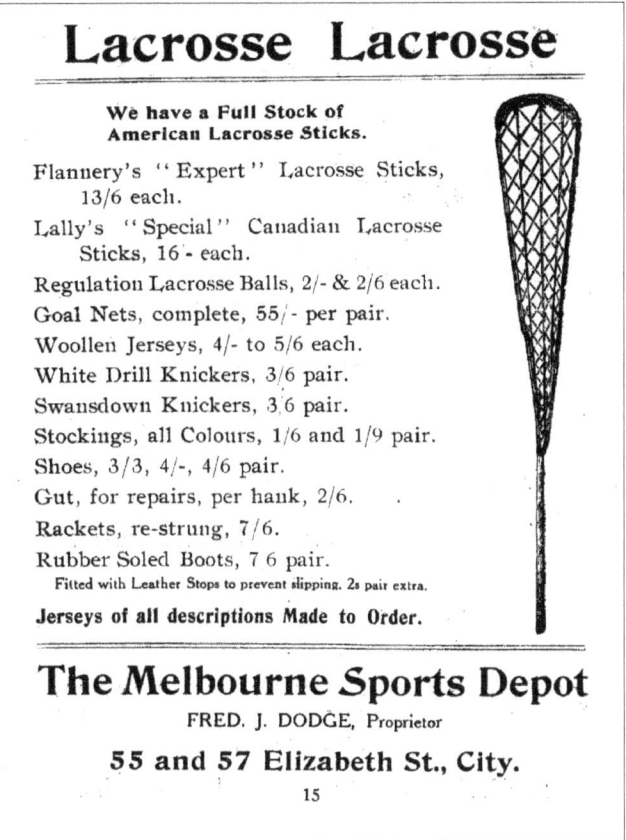

Malvern Lacrosse Club

The year of 1903 was an important one for Victorian lacrosse. This was the embryo year for the Malvern Lacrosse Club which came into existence in a partnership arrangement with the St Kilda club. Included within the playing membership at St Kilda were Jack Schafe, Reverend Thomas Redhead, and Phil Appleby, all experienced players of some years standing. These three attended a meeting at the St George's Church schoolroom on the 18th February, and, with Redhead in the Chair, the meeting resolved to form a new club.[12] Each had an expansionary zeal to see the sport grow and spread, although it is not clear that this was the rationale for the establishment of Malvern in a partnership club format. Maybe St Kilda was seeking to build a feeder club for itself. Maybe St Kilda had a surplus of players. Maybe the key was the growing residential appeal of Malvern as a desirable Melbourne suburb, well-served by public transport and expansive parks.

The club's first season of VLA competition was played in the "C" Grade in 1903 as a combination team under the name of St Kilda-Malvern with its home ground split between the Malvern and St Kilda Cricket Grounds. However, relations became strained between Malvern and St Kilda midway through the first playing season when the VLA awarded two matches against the St Kilda-Malvern team for playing unregistered players. Malvern blamed St Kilda for the breach of rules and determined that the club would stand alone as Malvern in the next season.[13] Noel Murray, the ex-Interstate player and founder of lacrosse in Tasmania, left the MCC club to join Malvern, and, along with Schafe and

Malvern Lacrosse Club in 1904
*Back Row: A.M. Scott, W. Stillman, J. Barrie, Mr. E. Byrne (Umpire), M.H. Rogers, J. Schafe, E. Edwards jnr
Middle Row: N. Murray (Captain), Mr. Ed. Edwards (President), J. Poyett, P. Wilson, H. Fripp
Front Row: A. Locke, H. I. Byrne, P. N. Appleby, A. Paton*

Appleby from St Kilda, became players and mentors of the new club which was comprised mainly of beginners. Redhead, who was the pastor at the Holy Advent Church, Malvern from 1902, contributed as a mentor but continued to play at St Kilda and was selected to play for Victoria in 1904. Malvern fielded two teams in 1904 and resoundingly announced its independence with the No. 2 team defeating St Kilda on 28 May by an Australian record 41 goals to nil. Phil Appleby scored 18 goals and H. Byrne 16 goals.[14]

Jack Schafe

Jack Schafe, who was appointed as club Secretary, threw his energy into the fledgling Malvern club and contributed greatly, despite his somewhat fiery personality. He was a prominent personality in professional foot-running circles where he earned the knick-name of "Sherlock Holmes" for his dogged investigative work as Handicapper and Stipendiary Steward for the Victorian Athletic League.[15] On the lacrosse field he was a strident and tough competitor, famously being rubbed out for four weeks for unduly rough play and abusive language in a match against Fitzroy in 1909.

Whilst it took some years to build playing strength, the Malvern club was destined to become Australia's most successful, powerful and respected club. After two seasons in "B" Grade, the club's senior team was promoted to "A" Grade in 1906 where it was unable to secure a win, finishing last on the premiership list.

The 1907 season brought improvement and the senior team finished in 6th position after recording 2 wins and a draw. In this year the club commenced a recruiting initiative in local schools which was later to propel it to the top levels of the VLA competition, a position which it has occupied in most years since that time. The club Secretary, Jack Schafe, with support from Noel Murray, Ron Fripp and Jim Barrie, organized the first-ever lacrosse match between teams from the local Spring Road and Tooronga Road Schools.[16] The match took place on the Malvern Cricket Ground on Saturday the 14th of September and was won by Spring Road by 5 goals to 2. The first goal in the game was scored by 13-year-old, Master Jack Beattie, a fitting beginning for a player who was later to become Victoria's greatest ever attack player and State Captain.

Jack Beattie

Jack Beattie joined the Malvern club as a junior player in 1909 and was assigned the no. 91 jersey, a number which he famously carried on his back for many years of his illustrious playing career. Almost two decades after he commenced playing, the Malvern Club membership booklet shows the official player numbers with Jack Beattie at 91, the very last position on the list. His elder brother, Jim, was already a member and his three other brothers, Ivo, Hugh and Mel, joined in following years. Each of the Beatties subsequently played Interstate lacrosse and served Malvern with great distinction for many years. Mel was killed during the War in 1915. Many other famous Malvern players have followed the Beatties down the pathway from local schools to the Malvern club in subsequent years.

The Malvern Annual Report for the 1907 year, which is shown opposite, illustrates the costs of running a club in this era. The total club income of £14.5.3 is derived from member fees and a donation of £1.1.0. With a playing list of 40 members in 1907, the membership fee equates to an average of 6 shillings per member, or 60 cents in today's money. The simple Balance Sheet records costs of just over £13, with most of this relating to ground rental of the Malvern and Caulfield Cricket Grounds and small amounts for purchase of balls and goal nets and for printing. As the President points out in the body of the report, the club was unable to pay an amount of £4.7.6 owing to the VLA for player registration fees and a levy towards subsidizing costs for the visiting team from Canada.

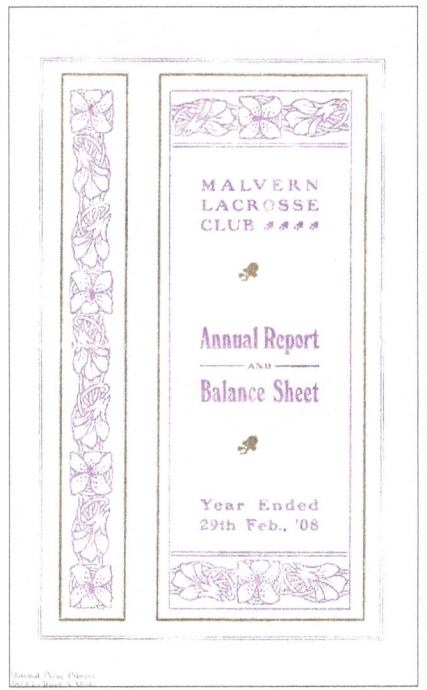

The Malvern club's printing at this time was handled by the Secretary/Treasurer, Jack Schafe, who owned a printing business located in the Melbourne CBD.

At this time, Malvern commenced the annual publication of miniature "Members Books" like the 1908 version shown below. The booklets contained lists of club officials, match fixtures and player lists.

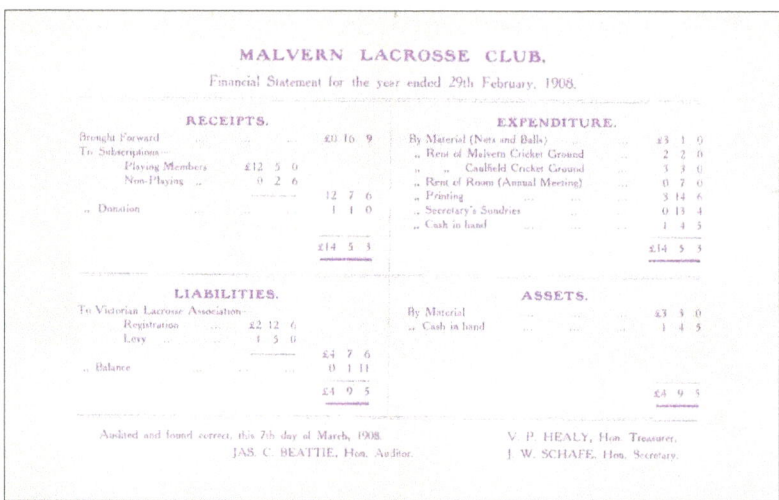

Malvern's first senior premierships came in 1917 and 1918 in a VLA competition weakened by the loss of players and teams due to the World War. When it broke through again to win the 1924 "A" Grade premiership, Malvern started an unbroken run of 45 years during which it was either premiers or runner-up at the top level. This run included thirty-one "A" Grade premierships and two sets of ten consecutive "A" grade premierships during the 1930s and 50s, emphatically confirming the elite status which Malvern continues to enjoy today.

That record stands as a seemingly unassailable challenge to all other clubs in Australia. The famous Malvern black jerseys with the horizontal red hoop are always respected by opponent teams.

Australian Lacrosse Union

In the years prior to Federation, there were two issues that frustrated the administrators in the separate colonies and became increasing points of discussion when cross-border competitions were played.

The first was the lack of uniformity in playing rules, where, despite the differences being minor, each Association reserved the right to make their own adjustments. The second issue was the costs involved for players travelling outside of their home colony to play inter-colonial games. Gate receipts from the inter-colonial matches were a potential source of subsidizing travel costs but there was no agreement between colonies.

Following Federation, it was these two issues which led to a call for a national governing body. When New South Wales, Victoria and South Australia came together in Adelaide for Interstate matches in in 1903, a conference of representatives resolved to recommend the following to all states:[17]

11 - THE EARLY YEARS OF FEDERATION

1. *"That a scheme be set up in the most suitable manner for setting aside 75% of the net receipts from Interstate matches for the purpose of defraying the expenses of team journeys from one State to another.*

2. *That an Australian Union be formed, consisting of three delegates from each State, which shall have entire control of the laws of lacrosse, and all the States joining the Union shall be under its jurisdiction. Such Union shall have the entire control of all finance, as provided for above".*

Subject to the approval of the State Associations, it was recommended that these resolutions should become operational on January 1, 1904. Mr. H.F Wyly from SALA was elected as Secretary pro tem to advance these recommendations.

All States expressed willingness to join the Union but the VLA was not satisfied on account of there being no rules laid out to guide the running of the new body. It drafted some governance rules and distributed them to all States. After a lapse of 7-8 months the other States notified agreement to some, but not all, of the VLA suggestions. The VLA modified the contentious points and re-distributed them but the Secretary did not respond and instead sent out a request for subscriptions to be paid. The VLA ignored the request for payment and the SALA then advised that the VLA proposals were unacceptable.

It was a bumpy start for the proposed national governing body and the matter remained unresolved. When, in 1906, agreement was reached by the States to support a tour of Australia by a team from Canada, neither the SALA or VLA wanted the arrangements to be handled by the non-functioning Australian Union. Ultimately, in 1908, the media in South Australia was particularly vocal about the ineffectiveness of the Union. "Canadia", writing in the Evening News in 1908, stated:[18]

"The organization has existed only on paper since it was formed in 1904, and it did absolutely nothing for the game"

Soon after, in September 1908, a meeting of representatives of the States decided on the fate of the Union and resolved:

"It was decided that, as the Union's control of the game had proved unwieldy, the organization should be wound up forthwith".

Amazingly, a further 24 years would pass before the Australian Lacrosse Council was founded in 1932 to coordinate the sport on a national basis.

The International Quest

As far back as July 1885, the concept of enticing a team from Canada to tour Australia on a promotional visit had been pushed by George Gordon and agreed by the VLA. Later, Dan White and Gordon Cavanagh-Mainwaring established separate connections in Canada in efforts to secure a team visit. During the late 1890s, Bill Morrison, the then Secretary of the NSWLA, established communications with lacrosse officials in Vancouver and urged the Australian colonies to support a lacrosse tour of Australia from Canada.

In April 1902 reports came through that the Prince of Wales (soon to be coronated as King Edward V11 following the death of Queen Victoria) and the Princess of Wales and other members of the Royal Family had attended the Lord's Cricket Oval to witness an international lacrosse match between a visiting team from Canada and a Scottish team assembled by the Duke of Argyll.[19]

The Prince and Princess of Wales watching Lacrosse at Lord's Oval, London 1902

Royal recognition of this kind was exciting for lacrosse in a young nation which valued highly its place within the British Empire and calls for a visit from a team from Canada were intensified. During the early years of Australian Federation, the Canada quest became almost an obsession and was regarded as the holy grail that would lift the sport to new heights. Despite these numerous attempts, the matter never seemed to advance.

Ultimately, it was Richard Garland who put the quest on a positive pathway. Garland, a former President of the Toronto Lacrosse Club, was Irish born but had lived a large part of his life and conducted business in Canada. When he came to Australia in 1900 to establish the Dunlop Pneumatic Rubber Tyre Company, he was impressed to see lacrosse flourishing and keenly began to provide support. His advice was that Australia should deal with Canada's key officials in Toronto, Ottawa

11 – THE EARLY YEARS OF FEDERATION

and Montreal, not the Vancouver officials on the west coast. He offered to raise the concept during a business trip in 1905, and expressed the view that, if Australia was able to put up funds to subsidize a team from Canada, he felt confident that the right people in Canada would make it a reality.[20]

The idea of an international touring team received universal support around Australia but there were issues of funding, timing, and amateurism versus professionalism to be sorted. The dream finally came to pass in 1907 when a Canadian team landed in Brisbane during July and spent three months touring most of Australia. This tour is the subject of Chapter 12.

Programme for the American Fleet Visit in 1908

Also, in 1908, it seemed that Australia would play its first international match against a team from the United States of America. A USA naval fleet visited Melbourne in August- September and lacrosse and football matches were arranged for the crew. Arrangements for the match were made between the VLA and the Commonwealth Government, but, unhappily, it did not proceed as the Americans decided that they did not have sufficient lacrosse players of quality among their number.[21]

Other ideas and approaches for international competition, both within and outside of Australia, came in the Federation years. In 1907, the VLA received contact from the English Lacrosse Union to convey an invitation for Australia to take a team to London for the 1908 Olympic Games.

Further, in 1908, the Melbourne University Sports Union received contact from Oxford University with a proposal, subject to a guarantee of £1,500 for team expenses, to bring a combined Oxford-Cambridge team to play in Melbourne and Adelaide in 1909. Regrettably, neither of these opportunities were taken up and war came to intervene before further international visits eventuated.

Interstate Competition

In the years before international competition came to Australia in 1907, the pinnacle opportunities for lacrosse players were the growing and strengthening contests which were arranged between the State Associations.

The Interstate lacrosse records reveal the predominance of South Australia over Victoria in contests which became an annual affair after 1896. It is likely that NSW v Queensland matches would also have been annual but for the years in the 1890s and early 1900s when the QLA was defunct. Owing to their geographical disadvantages, Western Australia and Tasmania had the least interstate opportunities during these years.

11 – THE EARLY YEARS OF FEDERATION

Western Australian State Team in Adelaide 1905
Back Row: C. Glover, F. Jackman, H. Bromfield, F. Harvey (Manager), F. McDonnell, R. M. Wilson, W. Tickell, C.G. Clifton
Middle Row: A.W. Hughes, G. Clarke (Captain), L. Kell, L.B. Bolton, R. Eagle
Reclining: A. Mather, J. Kaye

Western Australia had its first Interstate experience when South Australia sent a team by ship to Perth in August, 1903. Although it was not the strongest team that South Australia could field, it did contain Les Jones, Will Noblett, Lou Humphris, Cec Hughes and Alan Presgrave, all talented players who would later gain selection in the Australian teams which competed against Canada in 1907. The South Australians defeated the locals 10 goals to 5, watched by a large crowd at the Western Australian Cricket Association Ground on Saturday 22nd August, 1903.[22] Heartened by their performance, Western Australia sent a team to Adelaide in August, 1905 where they played matches against Victoria, South Australia, the local champion club team, Sturt, and a South Australian second team. The Western Australians lost all matches but gained valuable Interstate experience.

Tasmania's first Interstate experience took place in Melbourne in 1906, when the Northern Tasmanian Association played matches against three Victorian club teams.[23] Later in that year the MCC club paid a visit to Tasmania and played matches in Hobart and Launceston.

Commencing in 1903, the Interstate fixtures sometimes brought more than two States together in the one location. South Australia and New South Wales journeyed to Melbourne in June, 1903 and played matches at the Melbourne Cricket Ground.

Despite the poor quality of the image, the photograph below of the 1903 Victorian team is especially historic. Included in the photograph were a number of the pioneers of lacrosse in Australia together with key administrators who had been invited to watch the game. Lambton Mount, who had returned from England on a trip, is seated in the middle row, fourth from the left. With him were George Beech, the first Australian player in 1876, and other inaugural players, Joel Fox, Phil Shappere and Wally House. Seated to the right of Lambton Mount is the Lieutenant Governor of Australia, Sir John Madden who was responsible for publicly declaring lacrosse to be "The Game for Thoroughbreds". Others in the group, along with the Victorian players, were Major Wardill, Secretary of the Melbourne Cricket Club, Walter Forster, the VLA Secretary, Richard Garland, the Canadian emigrant who made many contributions to Australian lacrosse, and player Jack Latham, who in later years was knighted and served in the Australian Government as Attorney-General, Chief Justice and Deputy Prime Minister.

Victorian Lacrosse Team 1903
Back Row: Dr F. Bonnin, G. Gay, F. Bainbridge, J. Latham, Major Wardill, W.J. Forster (Hon Sec), B. Bryning, J. Morris
Middle Row: W. Moulton, W.B. House (Vice Pres), P. Shappere (President), L.L. Mount, Sir John Madden (Patron),
J. Fox (Vice pres), A. Rudd
Front Row: W. Walsh, John Davine, F. Dunn, James Davine

Interstate contests were usually organized around a format that included, in addition to the games, one or two practice matches for the travelling teams, a civic welcoming function, a rest day with a picnic or special place visit and a closing dinner for presentations and speeches. Generally, printed programs listing the teams were produced to assist spectators to identify the players and sometimes tickets were added for admission to the ground or grandstand. A copy of the handbill program for the 1904 Interstate contests in Sydney is reproduced opposite, together with some action photographs from the games on the following page. By this time, action photography of sport, had become increasingly common and had advanced in quality.

LACROSSE
Interstate Matches, 1904

July 13, South Australia v. N. S. Wales

July 20, Victoria v. N. S. Wales

on New Sports Ground, Moore Park, at 3 o'clock

July 16, South Australia v. Victoria

on Agricultural Ground, at 2 o'clock

TEAMS

South Australia
Colors—Black and White Bars

1	Goal	F. Clare
2	Point	A. G. Pritchard
3	Cover Point	C. V. Hughes
4	Third Man	L. Jones
5	Defence Wing	F. Goode
6	Do.	G. Graham
7	Centre	F. Kell
8	Attack Wing	A. Newman
9	Do.	M. J. Naughton
10	Left Home	C. Gepp
11	Right Home	L. Humphris
12	Home	W. Noblett

Victoria
Colors—Blue, with White Facings

1	Goal	F. T. Delves
2	Point	F. Bainbridge
3	Cover Point	W. Walsh
4	Third Man	C. Graham
5	Defence Wing	V. Charlwood
6	Do.	H. E. Jones
7	Centre	C. Maidment
8	Attack Wing	W. Furneaux
9	Do.	V. Rainsford
10	Left Home	P. Pennefather
11	Right Home	H. Henty
12	Home	W. Bryning
13	..	Rev. T. J. Redhead

New South Wales
Colors—White, with Blue Facings

1	Goal	W. G. Watson
2	Point	H. Barry
3	Cover Point	O. Robards
4	Third Man	R. Fitzhardinge
5	Defence Wing	Rup. C. Ward
6	Do.	W. King
7	Centre	P. M. Loutit
8	Attack Wing	L. Reynolds
9	Do.	A. L. Jones
10	Left Home	W. Loutit
11	Right Home	R. J. Morison
12	Home	R. Higgs

Referee—
Mr. G. M. NOAKE

CLYDE U. B. GURNETT
Hon. Sec., N.S.W.L.A.
c/o Town Hall, Sydney

W. E. Smith, Sydney

Action in the Victoria versus South Australia Match in Sydney, 1904

Victoria scores a goal against South Australia in Sydney, 1904

It was through these Interstate contests that Australia's best players were showcased and hardened for the international matches which came against Canada in 1907. Each State had its own star players but a total of only sixteen players gained selection in the first-ever representative Australian teams which earned the privilege of playing in the four test matches against Canada. These players are featured in Chapter 12.

11 – THE EARLY YEARS OF FEDERATION

Summary

The hope in 1901 was that the coming of Australian Federation would of itself result in a major spurt of growth for lacrosse. The prospect of an Australian Lacrosse Union (ALU), established to coordinate promotions, Interstate and International matches, was also something to be savoured.

Regrettably, the ALU made a stumbling start and had no influence in growing the sport. Despite this, there was considerable growth in the early years of Federation as shown in Table 2. What remained to be seen, was whether the long-hoped for visit to Australia of an international team would accelerate the growth of the sport. This came in the form of a Canadian team touring in 1907, and is the subject of the following chapter.

Notes

1. The Week (Brisbane) 2/05/1902 p.30
2. Morning Bulletin (Rockhampton) 31/07/1903 P.3
3. Morning Bulletin (Rockhampton) 20/03/1903 p.6
4. Morning Bulletin (Rockhampton) 15/05/1903 p.7
5. Brisbane Courier 11/05/1903 p.6
6. The Brisbane Courier 23/05/1903 p.2
7. Brisbane Courier 5/04/1905 p.7
8. Daily Telegraph (Launceston) 4/06/1906 p.7
9. Examiner (Launceston) 9/08/1906 p.2
10. Toy, Ian A History of the West Australian Lacrosse Association 1896-2010 pp.23-24
11. The Coburg Leader (Victoria) 11/02/1905 p.1
12. Punch (Melbourne) 19/03/1903 p.24
13. Leader (Melbourne) 26/09/1903 p.19
14. Weekly Times (Melbourne) 18/06/1904 p.14
15. Sporting Globe (Melbourne) 13/09/1947 p.6
16. The Herald (Melbourne) 14/09/1907 p.6
17. Chronicle (Adelaide) 4/07/1903 p.21
18. Evening Journal (Adelaide) 29/08/1908 p.8
19. The Week (Brisbane) 2/05/1902 p.30
20. Chronicle (Adelaide) 28/01/1905 p.16
21. Table Talk (Melbourne) 27/08/1908 p.28
22. The Daily News (Perth) 22/08/1903 p.1
23. Examiner (Launceston) 9/08/1906 p.2

12

The Canadian Lacrosse Tour of Australia, 1907

The Canadian lacrosse visit to Australia in 1907 must surely rate as one of the most remarkable team tours in the history of world sport.

From the outset it was an ambitious and speculative project and a stop-and-start affair. It came at a time when Australia had not long become a nation and when travel and communications were slow and costly. To have brought together such a venture, speaks volumes for the vision and persistence of our pioneers.

For the fifteen Canadians who were enticed to our shores, the tour was both exciting and arduous. By necessity of cost, their team size was restricted to a minimum. Even so, they committed to play games in every mainland State at a rate of a match every two to three days. Their total journey lasted a little over three months and included fifty days at sea, five thousand six hundred miles of rail travel and countless trips in horse-drawn drags. Motor cars were a rarity in 1907. In Australia, they played in places where lacrosse no longer exists. They played on grounds lacrosse can no longer aspire to. They were warmly greeted and lavishly entertained wherever they went. Large spectator crowds turned out to watch them play. Their deft and flamboyant lacrosse skills were universally admired and they educated Australian lacrosseurs in new ways of thinking and playing. At times they infuriated their audiences and the media with what were claimed to be "roughhouse", even unfair, tactics. Dubbed variously by the media as the "snowmen", "mooselanders", "lumbermen", "Canucks" and "maple leafers", they made news wherever they travelled.

They were welcomed by the Prime Minister and feted by State Governors, State Premiers, Lord Mayors and the leading citizens of the day. For the first and only time ever in Australia, lacrosse was elevated into the limelight among governments, community leaders, media and the general public.

The tour injected new energy into the promotion of the sport in Australia. It inspired growth and led to changes in playing rules and equipment. It gave impetus to the introduction of the first Australian Lacrosse Carnival held in Adelaide in 1910, the beginning for the regular national championships which have been enjoyed ever since. Those who have had the good fortune to experience interstate or international lacrosse will have much to smile at when reading this account. They will recognize the source of many of the customs and curiosities, and that unique blend of fun, friendship and serious endeavour, which still define our sport.

To the pioneers must go the accolades!

The International Dream

The concept of bringing a Canadian lacrosse team to Australia had been mooted and negotiated for eight years before it became reality. From the beginning, the idea was to have the Canadians demonstrate and teach lacrosse as it was played in its home of origin.

Correspondence occurred between the New South Wales Lacrosse Association and Vancouver Lacrosse Club as early as 1899 and "Left Attack", writing in The Australasian newspaper, commented that[1] ...

> "perhaps the day when Australia might take part in an international contest was not far distant".

In 1900, the New South Wales Association began active dialogue with lacrosse officials in British Columbia. The aim was to get a Canadian team to Australia in 1901, to coincide with the first year of Federation. It was proposed that matches against a representative inter-colonial team be played in Adelaide, Sydney and Melbourne and that other matches be played against leading club teams. The Canadian authorities were receptive and enthusiastic but indicated that suitable financial arrangements would need to be put in place. A meeting of representatives of the South Australian, New South Wales and Victorian Associations was held during 1900 to discuss the proposal and a decision was made to invite a team from Canada with Australia providing a guarantee of £600 plus the whole of gate-takings from the games. The three State Associations were each to be responsible for one third of the guarantee monies.

When the 1900 season concluded The Australasian carried this promising report[2] ...

> " The season just concluded has seen a great improvement in Lacrosse in the three colonies, Victoria, South Australia and New South Wales, where the game has been firmly established. The prospect of a Canadian visit next year augurs well for the success of the game in 1901, and there seems no doubt that lacrosse has come to stay, and to be a popular sport. Till next season, crosses and mits are all stowed away,

12 – THE CANADIAN LACROSSE TOUR OF AUSTRALIA, 1907

strings have been loosened, and lacrossists are seen no more about the streets, but if, during the summer months, men may be seen tightening out the string and having a throw occasionally, be it known that these are enthusiasts, making ready for the Canadians, and hoping thereby to gain a place in the Federated Australia team against the Dominion of Canada in 1901."

Despite this enthusiasm nothing transpired in 1901 and the New South Wales Secretary, W. Morrison, reported in July that the negotiations were stalled. As the Canadian season took place over summer months and the inter-provincial championships were so keenly contested, no clubs would release their players before August or September. By this time the Australian season would be over and grounds would be undergoing top-dressing for cricket. Also, a division had arisen within Canadian lacrosse between rival amateur and professional groups who were vying for control.

Interest in the Canadian visit was rekindled during 1902 when news came through that a Toronto Lacrosse Club team was touring England. Contact with the Toronto team was made in London via the Australian Cricket Team. Advice was received that a Canadian tour of Australia would be more likely to be achieved if the Australian authorities dealt with authorities in Montreal, Ottawa and Toronto where the sport was strongest.

At a dinner prior to the Interstate match between South Australia and Victoria in Adelaide on 26th June 1903, the South Australian President stated that it would never be possible to see a completely representative Canadian team in Australia. The clash of playing seasons would prevent professional players getting away and Australia's "White Australia" immigration laws would debar some of Canada's best players, who were native Red Indians.[3] During 1905, unsuccessful attempts were made to form an Australian Lacrosse Union to coordinate playing rules and foster interstate and international competition. The prospect of an international visit was still being discussed with Canadian authorities although concerns existed about rough play brought about by the professional elements of the game in Canada. During 1906, the South Australian Association continued active negotiations with the Canadian Lacrosse Association and a financial plan was constructed. It was not until May 1907 that the Australian authorities finally reported that the visit had been secured.

Under the agreed financial plan, a guarantee of £1,500 was required for the visitors' expenses. It was a bold and ambitious plan and there were many skeptics. The guarantee was achieved through commitments as follows:

Melbourne Cricket Club	£250
Victorian Lacrosse Association	£300
South Australian Cricket Association	£250
South Australian Lacrosse Association	£300
Western Australian Lacrosse Association	£300
Queensland Lacrosse Association	£100

The agreement provided for the pooling of the nett gate receipts from all matches. In the event of a shortage of funds, the guarantors agreed to contribute proportionally. In the event of a surplus, profits were to be distributed on a proportionate basis to the guarantors. The positive support of both the South Australian Cricket Association and the Melbourne Cricket Club were vital to the project proceeding. None of the State Associations had significant assets and they each had to call upon their clubs for support. Typical of this process was the attendance of the VLA Secretary, W.J. Forster at the Annual General Meeting of the Malvern Lacrosse Club held on the 15th April, 1907. The minutes of the meeting record that Forster outlined the programme for the Canadian team and the VLA's position in relation to the guarantee of funds and that ...... "A subscription list was opened in the room in connection with this matter and the sum of £10-17-6 was raised."[4]

The first £800 of the guarantee funds were required to be cabled to Canada by the 10th of May to cover sea passenger fares. On the 25th of May, "Left Home", writing in The Leader newspaper, reported with concern that the arrangements for the tour were very nearly brought to a sudden termination. The South Australian authorities, who had been entrusted to forward the guarantee monies, had decided to offer an initial £750. The offer was quickly rejected by the Canadians who advised that the tour would not proceed unless £950 was advanced. After some harsh words between the Victorian and South Australian associations, this requirement was quickly met.

Arrangements for the schedule of matches, travel and hosting and the selection of Australian teams were placed in the hands of a co-ordinating Board of Control which met occasionally in Adelaide. Its composition included South Australian and Victorian representatives plus individuals from Adelaide who were appointed to represent the other State Associations.

A program was agreed upon, with matches commencing on the 20th of July in Brisbane and concluding in Perth during early September. The programme was to include three test matches between Australia and Canada, one in Melbourne on the 27th of July and the others in Adelaide on the 3rd and 24th of August. Somehow, without the knowledge or agreement of the Canadians, this schedule was adjusted by the time of the visitors' arrival to include a total of eighteen matches extending up to 21st September.

The planned match schedule was as follows:

20th July	v	Queensland in Brisbane
22nd July	v	New South Wales in Sydney
27th July	v	Australia in Melbourne
3rd August	v	Australia in Adelaide
7th August	v	South Australia in Adelaide
9th August	v	Victoria Twelve in Ballarat
10th August	v	Victoria in Melbourne
14th August	v	Victoria Twelve in Bendigo

17th August	v	Victoria in Melbourne
24th August	v	Australia in Adelaide
26th August	v	Jamestown Lacrosse Club in Adelaide
28th August	v	South Australian Premiers in Adelaide
4th September	v	Fremantle Lacrosse Club in Fremantle
7th September	v	Western Australia in Perth
11th September	v	Western Australia in Perth
14th September	v	Combined Goldfields in Kalgoolie
18th September	v	Goldfields Premiers in Kalgoolie
21st September	v	Western Australia in Fremantle

The Canadian Team

Few modern-day coaches would contemplate a twenty-five-match international tour with just two reserve players on their team. The 1907 Canadian team members were either foolhardy, uncommonly tough or simply optimistic when they chose to embark on an arduous tour with only fourteen players and a team manager. Lacrosse in 1907 was a twelve per side game so, even with a maximum rotation of players, the Canadian players had to expect to take the field in Australia every two to three days throughout the tour. As it was some played every match.

The reality was that the size of the team was fixed by the limitations of finance, the Australian authorities having agreed to pay all travel, accommodation and living costs. Certainly, there was no shortage in Canada of lacrosse men eager to offer themselves for selection to come Downunder.

The team was assembled under the auspice of the Canadian Lacrosse Association, by Team Manager, Mr. John C. Miller. Miller was a member of the Orilla Lacrosse Club and Past President of the Canadian Association. His fourteen players were all accomplished amateur players, selected from clubs within the province of Ontario.

They were a well-presented and well-educated lot, most of them qualified or working in professional careers and five currently attending university. With three doctors, a dentist, two barristers and a journalist in their ranks they were well prepared for any eventuality, on or off the field.

From the moment they set foot on Australian soil they impressed the locals. Their dress, their bearing and their speech-making were noticed along with their obvious athleticism. Strangely, it is not possible to introduce them all on first name terms. Such was the formality of the times that surnames and first-name initials were the norm in media reports and printed programmes.

Canadian Team for 1907 Tour of Australia
Back Row: W. Attow, A. Rose, R.J. Arens, T. Hanley, E.V. Graham, Dr. Campbell
Second Row: H. Camplin, W.D. Ramore, W.J. Hanley (Captain), J.C. Miller (Manager), J.M. Kearns, G.A. Macdonald, R. Gilbert
Front Row: F.J. Grace, F.E. Combs

Here is how the team presented:[5]

Rudy J. Arens (goalkeeper), 23 years, 6 feet 3 inches, 12 stone 1 lb.
Chemistry student from Toronto University team and Orilla Lacrosse Club.
Played in three Ontario Association Championship wins and two Canadian Lacrosse Championship wins.

Dr. H.L. Campbell, M.D. (point) 40 years, 5 feet 10 ½ inches, 10 stone 10 lbs.
A physician, described as the Grand old Man of Canadian lacrosse.
Played for Bradford and has been in more championship teams than any other player in Canada.

J.M. Kearns, B.A. (coverpoint) 29 years, 5 feet 10 inches, 11 stone 9 lbs.
A barrister and Senior Vice-President of the Canadian Lacrosse Association.
Played with Bangville and Arthur clubs with three national championship titles

Thomas Hanley (third man) 22 years, 6 feet, 11 stone 8 lbs.
Medical student. Played with Orilla and Midland clubs.
Participated in two Championship wins.
An all-round sportsman who is also an expert in football and ice-hockey.

12 – THE CANADIAN LACROSSE TOUR OF AUSTRALIA, 1907

Alex Rose (right defense) 23 years, 5 feet 9 inches, 10 stone 8 lbs.
Journalist with Toronto News. Orilla Lacrosse Club Member.
All-rounder who has played in every field position in Championship games.

William J. Hanley, B.A. (left defence) 27 years, 6 feet, 11 stone 1 lb.
Barrister and Captain of the team. Formerly Toronto University player, now with Stratford.
Has played in seven Championship teams. Visited England in 1902 with Toronto University team.
All-round sportsman who also excels in ice-hockey and canoeing.

Frank Grace (centre) 27 years, 5 feet 9 inches, 11 stone 1 lb.
Electrician. A cousin of famous English cricketer, W.G. Grace.
Formerly with Chatham Club, now with Arnprior.

Fred Coombs, B.A. (right attack) 26 years, 5 feet 6 inches, 9 stone 11 lbs.
Student. Plays for Toronto University and Bradford.
Member of four championship teams.

Robert Gilbert (left attack) 19 years, 5 feet 7 inches, 10 stone.
Electrical railway officer. Baby of the team.
Plays with Toronto Junction Shamrocks, the current CLA Champions.

Gordon Macdonald (left home) 28 years, 5 feet 8 inches, 12 stone 8 lbs.
Lumber merchant. Plays with Port Arthur club.
All-round Sportsman prominent also in cricket, rowing, football and boxing.

W.D. Ranmore (right home) 24 years, 5 feet 9 inches, 10 stone 5 lbs.
Dentist. Plays with Fergus club and formerly Toronto University.
Three times winner in Ontario Championship teams.

E.V. (Vic) Graham (home) 23 years, 5 feet 11 inches, 11 stone 9 lbs.
Medical student. Bradford and Toronto University player.

Harry Camplin (emergency defense) 24 years, 5 feet 11 inches, 11 stone 1 lb.
Toronto Junction Shamrocks player, CLA Champions.

Walter Atton (emergency goalkeeper and home field) 19 years, 5 feet 9 inches, 10 stone 5 lbs.
Student at Toronto University.

John C. Miller (Team Manager) Past President of Canadian Lacrosse Association.

Prior to sailing from Vancouver on the 21st of June, the Canadian team had travelled some 2000 miles by rail across Canada from Toronto. Departing on the 2nd of June they travelled without sleeping berths and on the way played matches against Orilla, Port Arthur, Winnipeg, Regina, Moose Jaw, Calgary, New Westminster, Vancouver and Victoria (British Columbia). They won all but two of these encounters but were thrashed 17 to 0 by New Westminster, one of Canada's best professional teams.

News of this massive loss reached Australia and led sections of the Australian press to cast doubt about their quality. That, as their Team Manager and Captain were often to declare, was far from the truth.

William Hanley (Captain) – Left Defense

Rudy Arens – Goalkeeper

Robert Gilbert – Left Attack

Arrival in Australia

One thousand enthusiastic Queenslanders were at Pinkenba wharf in Brisbane to greet the Canadians on their arrival during the afternoon of Saturday, July 13, 1907.[6] They came aboard the Royal Mail steamship Aorangi which had sailed from Vancouver twenty-three days earlier.

A lusty cheer went up from the Queenslanders as the ship berthed. It was answered by the Canadians with a lengthy ringing Indian war cry[7] …

> "The cry was certainly the strangest ever given from a sporting team:
>
> *Toike! Oike! Toike! Oike!*
> *Shagonosh Kawene*
> *Big Injon Nishnobie!*
> *Ah Ge Meshin*
> *Kenna Keena Waugh Waugh!*
> *Kenna Keena Chew!*
> *Canada! Canada!*
> *Hurraw, Hurraw, Hurraw!*

Translated, the meaning of the cry is:

> *What ho! What ho!*
> *White man? What ho!*
> *White man? I guess not*

12 – THE CANADIAN LACROSSE TOUR OF AUSTRALIA, 1907

Real Indian!
Let us join hands and beat them well
Canada Canada
Hurrah, Hurrah, Hurrah

The syllables were sounded short, "Toike" being sounded "Tike!"

The Indian wah or waugh was also prominent."

This battle cry intrigued Australians whenever the Canadians chanted it at matches and functions throughout the tour.

Upon disembarking from their ship, the party were taken to their accommodation at the Gresham Hotel in Brisbane. Sunday morning brought a tour of the Botanic Gardens and was followed by an

Canadian Team Pre-Match War Cry

afternoon concert performed by the Besses and Barns band. On Monday, 15th of July, the team was officially welcomed at a civic function hosted at the Town Hall by the Mayor of Brisbane and attended by various Government officials and other community dignitaries. In his welcome, Alderman W. Thompson, Mayor of Brisbane said,[8]

"Australians looked upon Canadians as brothers; they heard nothing but good of Canada, felt nothing but good for it, and were somewhat envious of it."

The Hon. R. Philip (Leader of the Opposition) added [9]...

"For many years Canada and Queensland had been closely connected by the cable and mail service; Queensland had done everything to make friendly and business relations closer. This visit would increase the friendship. A few years ago, Queenslanders and Canadians had fought side by side in South Africa,

and if occasion arose, they would do so again for the great Empire to which they belonged. He hoped the visitors would teach the Queenslanders a few points of the game, and be rewarded for their long journey by winning."

In the afternoon the team practised at the Exhibition Oval watched by a throng of interested locals. The Queenslanders were immediately struck by the appearance and skills of the visitors[10].

"Their guernsey is a beautiful royal purple with narrow white facings and a broad white collar, while the word 'Canada' is worked in white across the breast. They all wore heavy tan gloves resembling those used by a wicket-keeper. They also donned white caps with a padded brim and a peak which in the event of the crosse striking it comes down and protects the face. White knickers and white shoes completed the uniform, and probably no more prettily garbed team of athletes has ever entered the field in Queensland."

The stick skills of the Canadians were a revelation. They were adept at passing, underhand around their body or backwards across their shoulder, and their quick short exchanges when attacking the goal were breathtaking.

The program for the Canadians first week in Australia involved a mix of sightseeing, practice sessions and rest, designed to let the visitors acclimatize ahead of their demanding schedule. They conducted coaching sessions for the Queensland team and other players in the lead-up to their opening match. The promotional build-up included a tram car ride through the city and suburbs in a special car provided by the Queensland Government.

Opening Games

The opening match of the tour was played in Brisbane at the Exhibition Oval on Monday, 22nd of July. Fine weather, 8,000 spectators and Vice-Royalty in the form of State Governor, Lord Chelmsford and his Lady were present for the occasion.[11]

Under the heading "Picturesque International Struggle – The Snowman Triumphs" the Brisbane Courier published this entertaining account of the setting:

"Canada and Queensland, Empire builders, full and warm- blooded brothers of the same mother both, despite differing climes, met in friendly and picturesque rivalry on the green turf of the Exhibition Oval in the brilliant sunlight of Saturday afternoon. The flower of Queensland's youth was in the arena, the flower of its maidenhood looking on wearing warm silken favours on their breasts; some of them in their ardour clad from head to foot in the rich maroon State colour so suggestive of the luxuriant warmth and wealth of Queensland. It was the first peaceful invasion of our shores by a Canadian team of sportsmen, and in honour of the event Brisbane turned out full 8000 strong to greet the visitors, who, nearly all graduates of the Toronto University, had crossed wide leagues of land and sea, not to ruthlessly scalp Australians, who are in a manner speaking innocents at the Canadian national game, but by precept and example to instruct them in it. Seeing that full forty years ago our brothers of the snows took over the crozier-like gutted crosse from the Red Indian and learnt some of the wiles and cunning of that race of keen sportsmen

12 – THE CANADIAN LACROSSE TOUR OF AUSTRALIA, 1907

it was quite to be expected that the men from the land of the moose would completely envelop Queensland. The scene in the bright Queensland winter sunshine, approximating closely to the Canadian summer heat, was interesting, almost historic. The sweep of the eye around the exterior of the golden-tracked oval revealed a sea of faces and a mass of straw hats. The grand and minor stands were things apart from the main circle, wherein was discovered a very rainbow of graceful feminine costumes mingling and co-mingling in pretty confusion of form and colour. Vice-royalty itself had honoured the event, the State Governor with his gracious lady and party being present to witness a game of international import.

Glimpses of ruddy-coloured jerseys announced the entrance of the Queenslanders into the arena. There was hearty hand-clapping, to be renewed threefold when the royal purple and white of Canada flashed in the sunlight and the snowshoe men stood discovered, a band of twelve sturdy men, somewhat ruddier of face than our own men, and looking broader chested: but the white band running round the shoulders would account for that. The Queenslanders, with accompanying wave of cap, gave three ripping cheers. The Canadians, all dight in royal purple, in more stately manner raised their crosses above head, and chanted the picturesque Canadian-Indian warcry after the manner of Maori firewalkers, in which was incorporated cheers for Queensland.

The Queensland captain J.S. Hutcheon won the toss and, playing in the centre, secured the first face-off. Five minutes after the opening, Thorpe for Queensland pierced the Canadian defence to goal

Queensland Interstate Team 1907
Back Row: E.G. Spence, J.F. Connolly, J. Thorpe, R. Darvall, R. Hartigan, R. Dean
Second Row: A.D. Clarke, W.V. Morley, J.Hiron, J.S. Hutcheon (Captain), R.D. Pyke, E.A. Brighouse, O. Thorpe
Front Row: A.L. Thorpe, E.A. Thorpe

Lou Humphris (Australian Captain) guarding Harry Camplin (Canada)

and set the crowded grandstand ringing with applause. The game was a contrast of styles. On the one hand, the fast, open running and wing play of the Queensland team. On the other, the tight, rugged defence of the Canadians and their skilful rapid passing to retain possession of the ball when attacking.

At three-quarter time the score was level at 3 goals all. The Queensland spectators, who had expected to see their Maroons outclassed, were warming to the prospect of a home town victory.

It was not to be. As the Canadians found their feet, their teamwork, slick passing and feinting skills began to tell, and they finished

New South Wales Representatives 1907
Back Row: J. Farebrother (Referee), C. Booth, A. Rankin, C. Hughes, R. Lane, R. B. Fitzhardinge, H. Whisker
Middle Row: R. A. Cullenward, H. Dawson, P.M. Loutit (Captain), S. Meyer, C.U.B. Gurnett
Front Row: F. Henriques, A. Newman, W. Stillman

the game with a rush of scoring to win by 6 goals to 3. Match details of this, and other games, are presented in the Appendix.

The Canadians were farewelled at a post-game Smoke Concert dinner held at Rowe's Café on the Saturday evening. The Queensland Lacrosse Association President, Mr. E.H. Macartney proposed the health of the Canadian Lacrosse Association and in doing so assured the visitors that no credence was placed on the attack made on them by a section of the Southern Press. The Canadian Team Manager responded warmly, explaining that his team "was really the strongest amateur combination which could be sent from Canada and the game had been played in the presence of the largest and most generous crowd before whom they ever appeared."[12]

The team left Brisbane by the Sunday mail train bearing a letter of introduction to the Governor-General of the Commonwealth from Earl Gray, the Canadian Governor-General. They were farewelled by 100 lacrosseurs. Arriving in Sydney on Monday morning they again experienced an enthusiastic welcome. Despite the long rail journey, they played a match against New South Wales in the afternoon at the Sydney Cricket Ground. They were watched by 2000 spectators and the State Governor.[13] The contest was all in favour of the visitors and the final score was 11 goals to nil. The visitors were entertained after the game and departed by train for Victoria.

Melbourne and the First Test

Following a welcome late on Wednesday morning by the Victorian Lacrosse Association and 400 lacrosseurs at Spencer Street Railway Station, the Canadians were transported by open drag to the Grand Hotel. In the afternoon they went to the Melbourne Town Hall for a Mayoral reception and afterwards to the Melbourne Cricket Ground for a Melbourne Cricket Club welcome. In the evening the visitors and the Australian team players were guests of the Victorian Association at a theatre party to see "Blue Moon" at the Princess Theatre. The following morning, Thursday 25th of July, they were entertained at Parliament House by the Acting Prime Minister of Australia, Sir William Lyne. The Prime Minister, Alfred Deakin, was in ill-health and unable to be present as he had retired to Point Lonsdale for recovery.[14]

In welcoming the visitors, Sir William Lyne commented on the "brotherhood and unity" between Canada and Australia and wished both teams well for the test series. The Canadian Manager, Mr. Miller, responded with thanks and then proceeded in a humorous vein to refer to Australian affairs. Amid roars of laughter, he said that if there were any difficulty about the site for the future Federal capital, his team would undertake to settle it in half an hour and, as Canada had had experience of federation, the team would be happy to settle any other Federal difficulty that might occur."[15] The vexed issue of a location for the Australian capital city had been under review for seven years and took a further six years to be settled by the Australian Parliament.

In the afternoon, the party were afforded a welcome at the rooms of the Australian Natives Association and managed to squeeze in a practice session at the Melbourne Cricket Ground. Friday, the eve of the first test match, brought more practice, a photographic session and entertainment in the evening as dinner guests of the Victorian Association at the Austral Salon.

The Australian preparation for the test match was not without some controversy. Disagreements had occurred over selection issues. The Victorian and South Australian Lacrosse Associations had each appointed one selector, Mr. W.B. House representing Victoria and Mr. L. Humphris representing South Australia. In the event of these two not agreeing as to the merits of two players for a particular position, Victoria wanted the preference to be given to the player of the State in which the game was being played. South Australia favoured adjudication by a third selector, Mr. A.J. Rudd, a former Victorian but now a South Australian player. The impending impasse was resolved by agreement that all three selectors should be present at trial games to be played in Adelaide on 6th of July and Melbourne on 13th of July.[16]

Australian lacrosse in 1907 boasted a total of 84 teams and some 1200 players, sixty percent of whom were from South Australia and Victoria. Regular inter-colonial contests and subsequently inter-state contests had been held between South Australia and Victoria since 1888. New South Wales had competed against Queensland and against Victoria in many years leading up to 1907. The skill superiority clearly rested with South Australia which had won thirteen of sixteen contests against Victoria. When the Australian team was named for the opening test match, it was drawn solely from the two strongest lacrosse states, and contained eight South Australians and four Victorians.

The first-ever Australian team was:

F. Delves	-	Goalkeeper (Victoria)
E.O. Gooden	-	Point (South Australia)
L. Jones	-	Cover Point (South Australia)
C.V. Hughes	-	Third Man (South Australia)
C. Graham	-	Right defense (Victoria)
V. Steet	-	Left defence (Victoria)
F. Kell	-	Centre (South Australia)
W.C. Noblett	-	Right attack (South Australia)
A.S. Mann	-	Left attack (South Australia)
R. Taylor	-	Right Home (South Australia)
L. Humphris	-	Left Home (South Australia)
W. Bryning	-	Home (Victoria)

Of the South Australians, Humphris, Kell, Noblett and Hughes played with the Sturt Lacrosse Club; Jones and Taylor hailed from the North Adelaide Club and Gooden and Mann were East Torrens representatives. Victorian clubs were represented by Steet (MCC), Delves and Graham (Essendon)

12 – THE CANADIAN LACROSSE TOUR OF AUSTRALIA, 1907

Australian Lacrosse Team for the First Test Match
Back Row L to R: C. Graham, E. Gooden, R. Taylor, J. Latham (Referee), F. Kell, L. Jones, W. Bryning
Front Row: V. Steet, C. Hughes, F. Delves, L. Humphris (Captain), W. Noblett, A. Mann

and Bryning (Hawksburn). Most of the team had a number of years of inter-state experience. Physically, they were taller and lighter than the Canadians. They wore none of the armpads, gloves and padded caps which protected the visitors.

On the morning of the first test match, The Argus Newspaper whetted the appetite for a clash of differing playing styles[17] ...

> "Today's game should be one of contrasts. Australians have learned lacrosse after they learned football, and thus football methods are often used. There is more running, more dodging, longer throwing than in Canada. The Australian trusts to his pace, his ability to dodge, and to throw while the Canadian never hurries, if he can help it; but passes the ball quickly to his comrade until, after the centre is passed, the forwards come on like a cloud, passing the ball rapidly backwards and forwards one to another. The Australian dodges till he gets a man clear to pass to; the Canadian always has a man close handy to receive the pass. Australians check their man closer than Canadians, and it remains to be seen whether the visitors, when closely checked, can show that cool, accurate passing they have displayed in other contests. Another point of difference is that the Australian plays with the net of his crosse fairly tightly strung; the Canadians crosse is loose, like a fisherman's landing net."

LACROSSE IN AUSTRALIA

The long-awaited match came on Saturday, 27th of July at the Melbourne Cricket Ground. 'Left Home', writing in The Leader newspaper, summed up the importance of the occasion [18]...

> "To-day will indeed be a red-letter day in the history of lacrosse in Australia for it marks the occasion of the first international game in the Commonwealth.... This team (Canada) is said to be thoroughly representative of amateur lacrosse in Canada, and their opponents, the Australian Team, are likewise regarded as equally representative of lacrosse in Australia. With fine weather, a good exhibition of lacrosse is certain to result, no matter which gains the victory." .

Other sporting bodies in Victoria cancelled their Saturday fixtures in recognition of the international significance of the lacrosse and to help with the promotion of the game. The Victorian Lacrosse Association expressed its gratitude to the Victorian Football League and to the Melbourne Cricket Club for making the premier stadium available for the game. The football authorities co-operated admirably but, when 16,000 spectators turned up and paid £354 to see the game, took the precaution of inserting the advertisement at left alongside the Melbourne Herald's account of the contest.[19]

Though many of the big crowd of spectators were new to lacrosse, they were quick to recognize its best features and to show their appreciation.

Face-off between Kell (Australia) and Grace (Canada)
Ball placed by Phil Shappere, VLA President
Photograph courtesy of the Melbourne Cricket Club Library

12 – THE CANADIAN LACROSSE TOUR OF AUSTRALIA, 1907

The game commenced on time, just after 3pm, when the VLA President, Mr. Phillip Shappere placed the ball between the crosses of the centremen, Grace for Canada and Kell for Australia, and the referee, J.G. Latham, (later Sir John Latham, Chief Justice of the High Court) set the ball in play. The Australian team played in the green and gold colours of the wattle, symbolic of the new Federation.

Spectators at the Melbourne Cricket Ground for the First Test Match

Noblett (Australia) shooting for Goal

Fred Delves (Australian Goalkeeper) defending the goal

Full field view of the MCG during the First Test

The following breezy account of the game was published in 'Table Talk' [20]...

"With a war-whoop as long as a layman's sermon the Canadians invaded the M.C.C. ground on Saturday, and in the presence of a crowd of perhaps 14,000 people – the number might have been doubled if the VLA had pushed and advertised the international and epoch-marking game as it deserved – commenced their first and famous match against Australia. In this country lacrosseurs have cherished a reverence for Canucks as the inventors and perfectors of "the fleetest game played on foot," but our men on Saturday didn't waste a second after the face-off in watching to see what the visiting wonders would do. Lacrosse, of all games, calls for speedy action, so in a flash the Australians found themselves in the thick of a stirring struggle. The face-off itself gave no revelation of Canadian superiority, but the stick play of the visitors was astounding. They put force into the shortest throws, and made their opponents look ridiculous by passing the ball in one direction whilst staring fiercely somewhere else. They flicked the ball to and fro as they jog-trotted in a pretty bunch of purple and white up the centre of the ground, and for a while Australians who dashed in to check their elusive crosses found themselves, to their chagrin, beating the air. Canada secured a goal early in the first quarter, and, evidently pleased with the success of their short passing tactics, tried to do the same thing again. But it was harder next time. The Australians had been collecting ideas as was evident from a sudden rush of play to the wings. Canadians do not trouble about wing play, and were in turn puzzled to find their goal attacked by flying couriers from the green and vacant outfield. They met the attack, and for a time successfully, by bunching in goal, their first defense man taking several shots on the full, and saving the goal-keeper from what would probably have been awkward long hops. But by dint of passing the ball across and across the goal line from wing to wing the Australians tempted their opponents at length to fly out of their phalanx formation; and then came the Australian forwards' chance. They seized it gleefully, and whipped in a succession of fiery shots. Angle snaps at goal are apparently not common in Canada, and soon three got home past the long and wary Arens.

12 – THE CANADIAN LACROSSE TOUR OF AUSTRALIA, 1907

The subsequent parts of the match were but a repetition of these varied and conflicting tactics. The Canadians seemed to perform marvels of jugglery, catching the ball with their crosses upside down, flicking the rubber sideways and backwards, just as readily as forwards, and keeping it well off the ground. In stick play and system, the Australians were utterly outclassed, and yet somehow, they won. Thinking it over, I should ascribe the victory to the superior speed, dash, and endurance of our fellows. The Canadians seemed to hope our men would run themselves to a standstill, but as a matter of fact, after running the Canadians off their legs in three quarters, they simply romped over them in the last, and finished up fresh and frolicsome, whilst the Canucks limped slowly off the field. The score – 5 goals to 3 – is a fair reflex of the honours of the match."

Both teams were loudly cheered as they left the ground, particular attention being given to the Australian goalkeeper Delves and to the solid defense line of Gooden, Jones and Hughes. For Canada, the Hanley brothers. Kearns and Campbell were outstanding and earned the plaudits of the crowd.

Spectators Enjoying the First Test at the MCG

In the evening, a complimentary dinner was given to the visitors at the Vienna Café. It was a night of speech-making, entertainment and sumptuous dining with a Toast List of eight separate speeches plus replies and a total of twelve musical items and recitations. Busy evenings of this kind were common at the many dinners, smoke nights and other functions held throughout the tour in honour of the Canadian team. After a rest day on Sunday, the University Lacrosse Club entertained the visitors and, in the evening, they were guests of the Hawthorn Lacrosse Club at the club's annual ball. On Tuesday, 30th July both the Canadian and Australian teams departed by train for Adelaide to prepare for the Second Test.[21]

Programme for the Complimentary Dinner

Re-arrangement of Schedule and Playing Rules

When the original arrangements were made for the tour, the Canadian contingent had understood that they would arrive in Australia on 14th of July and complete the tour in Perth on the 2nd of September. Five of the team were due back in Toronto for University commitments starting on the 15th of October. The team was surprised to find on their arrival in Brisbane that matches had been arranged up to the 21st of September.

On reaching Melbourne, the Team Manager made the local authorities aware of his problem, declaring that the team had come to Australia under a definite contract which he desired to keep.[22] At first, it seemed that the West Australian section of the tour would have to be curtailed or cancelled. This was unacceptable to the West Australians as they had been as forthcoming as the other states in raising the guarantee monies needed to have the tour proceed. Their representative on the organizing Committee in Adelaide stood firm on their desire to have the Canadians visit the West and the matter caused ill-feeling in Western Australia. Ultimately, Victoria agreed to a shorter stay and the loss of two scheduled matches against Victorian teams in Melbourne in return for the addition of an extra test match in Melbourne. The Western Australian section of the tour was reduced from six matches to four and the second part of the South Australian stay was squeezed to enable the Canadians to depart from Adelaide for Perth immediately following the fourth test on the 24th of August. The re-arranged schedule is reported in the Appendix with full match results.

The playing rules also came in for some review and negotiation. The original intent of the tour was for Australia to learn how the game was played in its home of origin. There had been no contact with Canada since the sport's introduction into Australia in 1876. Even then, the founder, Lambton L. Mount was already a long-established Australian, having migrated from Canada to the Victorian gold-diggings as a sixteen- year-old in 1853. Little wonder that the styles of play and rules of the game which existed in Canada and Australia had diverged. There was, it seems, naivete in the pre-tour arrangements so far as playing rules were concerned. It was as if everyone assumed that lacrosse was lacrosse and, should any differences exist, they would be minor. The Canadians assumed that Australia wanted to learn their game. All would have been fine had it not been for the growing intensity which came when Australia won the first test. Now each nation's honour was at stake.

The opening test match in Melbourne was played with the goals placed 150 yards apart, a major difference from the standard 115 yards played in Canada. The Canadians sought to have this changed for the second test and lodged a letter from their team captain explaining ....

> " If the goals are more than 115 yards apart it will be impossible for us to display the efficacy of combined tactics and stick work. It seems to me that this was the object you had in mind when inviting us to come to Australia and besides you will find the game more exciting and picturesque from the spectacular stand point." [23]

The Australian players were consulted on this issue and were against granting the change. After discussion it was agreed by a 7 to 6 vote to compromise and reduce the distance to 130 yards for the second test. In the first two tests a Canadian ball was used for one half of the game and the lighter Australian ball in the other half. Various other differences over rules were to emerge, often giving rise to accusations that the visitors were employing deliberate tactics in breach of the rules.

Adelaide and the Second Test

By the time the Canadians arrived in Adelaide, their visit had created great expectation in South Australia and public and media interest was beyond anything previously experienced in lacrosse.

A Mayoral reception followed the team's arrival by train on the morning of Wednesday, 31st of July. The function was "crowded with leading citizens and lacrosseurs". The State Premier, the Hon. T. Price, announced that, in order to take part in welcoming the Canadian visitors on behalf of the people of South Australia, he had induced the Governor to cut short the Executive Council meeting that morning.[24]

In the afternoon the South Australian Football League provided a welcome in the League's rooms at the Selborne Hotel. The Chairman, Mr. J.R. Anderson, commented that his "members were happy

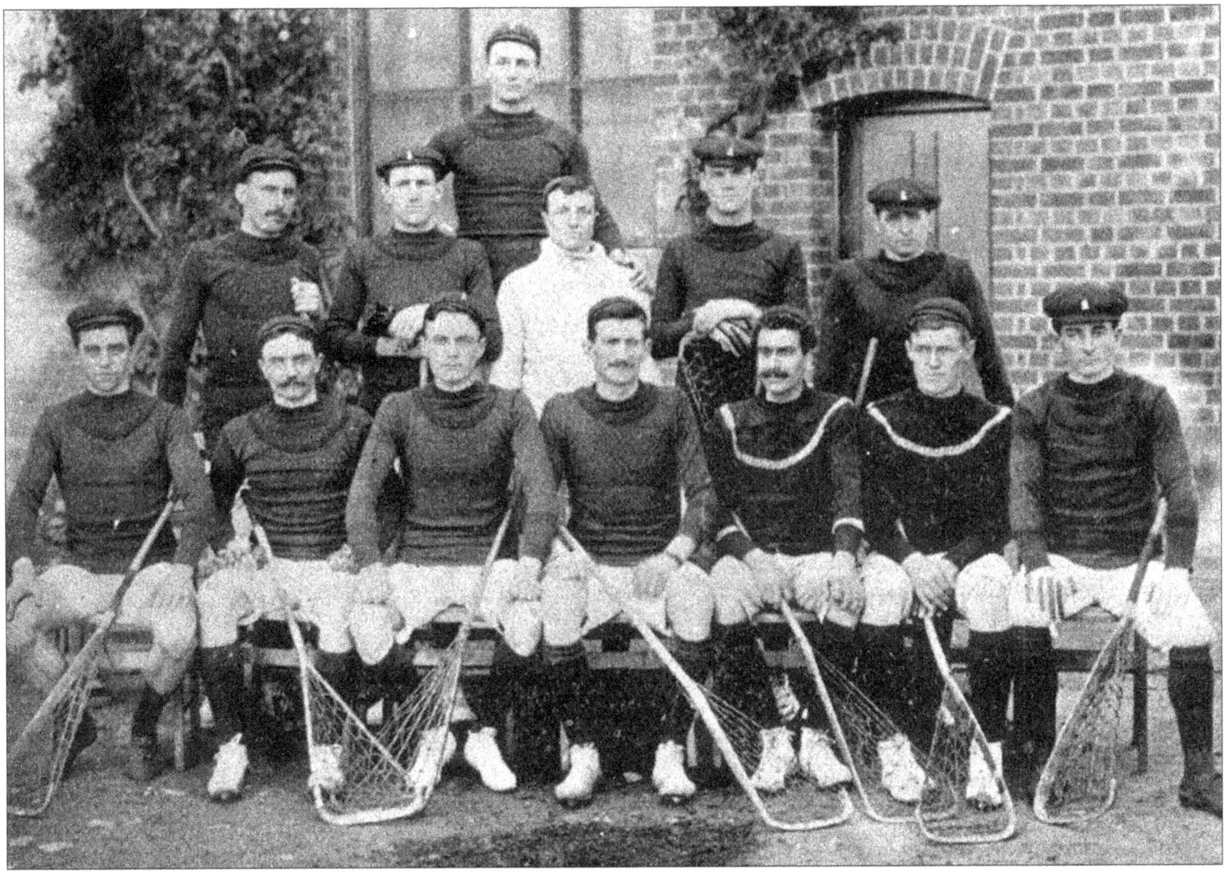

Australian Team for the Second Test in Adelaide
Back Row L to R: E. Gooden
Centre Row: F. Kell, R. Taylor, A.J. Rudd (Referee), L. Jones, A.S. Mann
Front Row: V. Steet, C.V. Hughes, W.C. Noblett, L. Humphris (Captain), A. Presgrave, J. Fletcher, F. Delves

Full Grandstands at the Adelaide Oval for the Second Test

to show their sympathy by keeping the test match dates free from football engagements, so that there might be record crowds at the Adelaide Oval".[25]

The Canadians experienced their first wet weather in Adelaide on the Thursday. Their day had started with an outing in an open drag provided by the Football League. They briefly toured the suburbs and were intrigued to know why every Australian front garden had a fence. Heavy rain disrupted their practice sessions at the Adelaide Oval on both the Thursday and Friday before the Second Test. The bad weather abated on Saturday, 3rd of August for the Second Test which attracted 10,000 spectators to the Adelaide Oval.[26] The gate-takings of £396 were, with the exception of the previous football grand final, the largest for a sporting contest since the last visit of the English Cricket Team.

As Victorians Graham and Bryning were unable to be in Adelaide, they were replaced in the Australian team by South Australians Fletcher (from Port Adelaide) and Presgrave (from Sturt). Camplin replaced Rose in the Canadian team.

Canadian Team and South Australian Lacrosseurs at the Horndale Winery

12 – THE CANADIAN LACROSSE TOUR OF AUSTRALIA, 1907

South Australia Team for the Match against Canada
Back Row: A.Mann, F. Kell, J. Hooper, R. Cockburn (SALA Secretary), J. Fletcher, R. Taylor
Middle Row: W. Noblett, A. Presgrave, L. Humphris (Captain), L. Jones, E. Gooden
Front Row: C. Hughes, J. Larner (Referee), A. Rudd

The South Australian Governor, State Premier, State Treasurer and Chief Justice were among the dignatories present for the game. The Canadians regrouped from their initial loss in Melbourne to take victory by 6 goals to 3 after the scores were even at half time. Again, the play was a contrast of styles, the Canadians teaming in tight defence combinations and restricting their attack to short, sharp passing and possession play.[27] The Canadian's game was more rugged than in the Melbourne encounter and the referee awarded seven "free positions" against them, leading The Register to report [28] …

> "The Dominion players at times did not hesitate to smash at the body, trip, hit, shepherd and lay hands on opponent's crosses"

In the evening the visitors were entertained at a Smoke Social at the Selborne Hotel. The entertainment included musical ditties, animated talking, speeches, a fine vocal program and the inevitable Canadian war cry. The Canadians responded to toasts proposed by the South Australian Lacrosse Association, the South Australian Cricket Association and the South Australian Football League.

The partying continued on the following day when the Canadian team were entertained at the Horndale wine cellars at Happy Valley. Four drag loads of South Australian lacrosseurs accompanied them on the two-hour journey for a cellar tour, luncheon and wine tasting arranged by Ben Basedow, the winery Manager.

After the Horndale visit, the Canadians continued on in the drag to where they had been invited to dine at the private residence "Medindie" of Mr Arthur Ware, C.M.G., a gentleman of high standing in South Australia.

Next morning the party were welcomed at Auldana as guests of Senator Sir Josiah Symon K.C. They enjoyed another winery tour and a champagne tasting before returning to the Adelaide Oval for an afternoon match against the South Australian Second Twelve. Rain spoiled the game which was won by Canada by 10 goals to 3. The evening was spent at the South Australian Hotel as dinner guests of the South Australian Lacrosse Association.

On Wednesday, 7th of August the match program continued at the Adelaide Oval with 7 to 3 victory for the Canadians over the South Australian team. The South Australian players had equipped themselves with padding similar to that worn by the Canadians and some had endeavoured to copy the Canadians protective headgear by obtaining a loan of jockey skull caps from the racing clubs.[29]

Ancillary Games and the Final Two Tests

The Canadians travelled on Thursday, 8th of August by rail from Adelaide to Ballarat in Victoria. There they encountered similar excitement, a Mayoral welcome, a tour of the Sebastopol gold mines and a large crowd to witness their match against a Victorian Twelve on the Friday afternoon. Shops were closed and school students dismissed early to enable the people of Ballarat to witness the spectacle. The game resulted in a 14-0 win for Canada but the spectators found the action riveting and wildly cheered the visitors at the conclusion of the match.[30]

The third test took place at the Melbourne Cricket Ground on the next day, Saturday, 10th August. Two Queenslanders, J. Hutcheon and O. Thorpe and two Victorians, A. Box and B. Bryning were brought into the Australian team. Rainy weather and the counter attractions of League and Association football, reduced the crowd to a still-impressive 11,000 spectators. They were treated to an exciting and skillful game, marred to a degree by tactics from the Canadians which attracted negative comments from the media. The Melbourne Age reported [31]...

> "It was unfortunate that the spirit of fairness which characterised the first game in Melbourne was not so manifest, the Canadians frequently resorting to tripping their opponents who happened to have at the moment bested them. Grace, the Canadian centre, so far forgot himself as to lose his temper on being outplayed by Steet and deliberately struck the latter with his crosse. The Victorian retaliated, and the promptness of the referee stopped what would otherwise have been a disgraceful scene, but not before Camplin, another Canadian, who is usually one of the most gentlemanly and inoffensive members of the team, tripped up the goal umpire, for which he was sent off the ground for five minutes."

12 – THE CANADIAN LACROSSE TOUR OF AUSTRALIA, 1907

Australian Team for the Third Test in Melbourne
Front Row L to R: A. Box, F. Kell, F. Delves, L. Humphris (Captain), W. Bryning, J. Hutcheon, V. Steet
Back Row: B Bryning, C. Graham, A. Rudd, O. Thorpe, W. Noblett

The match finished with a victory for Canada by 4 goals to nil. In the evening, the teams were entertained by the Melbourne Cricket Club at a smoke concert in the MCG pavilion.

On Monday morning, 12th of August, the Canadian team attended the morning call at the Melbourne Stock Exchange and were welcomed by the Exchange Chairman. Afterwards, they visited the Canadian Government offices where they presented lacrosse sticks bearing the signatories of the team to Mr. Richard Garland, a Melbourne businessman and to the Canadian Agent in Melbourne, Mr. D.J. Ross. Garland was an Irish Canadian who had come to Melbourne in 1899 as a Director of the Dunlop Pneumatic Tyre Company. He was an ex-President of the Toronto Lacrosse Association and an enthusiastic supporter of lacrosse in Melbourne. Later, he and Andrew McHarg, a former Victorian state representative and business colleague, donated a fine silver cup that became the perpetual trophy which is still played for at Australian Championships. On the Monday evening the Canadians played an ice hockey exhibition match against Victoria at the Glaciarium, completely outclassing the locals.[32]

Prior to departing Victoria, the Canadians inflicted a 9 to 1 defeat on Victoria, watched by 2000 spectators at the Melbourne Cricket Ground on the afternoon of Monday, 12th of August.[33] This was followed by a morning rail trip to Bendigo for a further match against Victoria on Wednesday, 14th of August. This game, played at the Upper Reserve, attracted 3,000 spectators and resulted in a 16 to 3 goals victory for Canada. The usual Mayoral reception and an after-game dinner were held before the visitors returned to Melbourne by the evening train.

With the schedule completed in Victoria, the Canadians departed on Thursday for Adelaide. There they played and defeated a team from Jamestown on Friday, 16th of August, one day before the final test match.[34] The fourth test on the 17th of August was billed as the "decider". The contest and fine weather brought 8,000 spectators to the Adelaide Oval and Australian expectations were high for a good result. Rudd from South Australia and Hutcheon (Queensland) had been included in the Australian line-up and both teams threw themselves into the game with energy and dash.

Canada opened with a 5 to 1 lead in the first quarter and started the second quarter with 11 men after Camplin had been ordered off for five minutes for rough checking. Using defensive tactics, the Canadians maintained their lead to half time but gave up one goal in the third quarter when Australia added two goals to one. Media reports again focussed on some ugly incidents. The account in The Australasian recorded the following [35]...

> "The crowd resented many of the tactics of the Canadians, who did not hesitate to punish their opponents heavily, even by flagrant breaches of the rules. The Australians naturally retaliated now and again, but seldom stooped to measures which were more than fairly rough. In one scrimmage Camplin laid around him on all sides, but Humphris was his particular victim. He held the Australian skipper tight, and when Humphris attempted to pass to Kell, Camplin smashed at both. Kell replied vigorously with his fists. The referee parted them, but immediately Camplin winded Humphris by jabbing his stick at his ribs. Noblett rushed in and knocked Camplin over. Fisticuffs and a wrestling match ensued until mounted troopers parted them, when Noblett and Camplin were dismissed for the remainder of the play. Subsequently, Canada's tactics of wasting time behind the goal were resented by the crowd, who hooted vigorously."

Canadian and Victorian Teams at the MCG – 12 August 1907
Photograph courtesy of Australian Gallery of Sport and Olympic Museum 1907.1857.6

12 – THE CANADIAN LACROSSE TOUR OF AUSTRALIA, 1907

Australian Team for the Fourth Test in Adelaide
Back Row L to R: C. Graham, C. Hughes, A. Taylor, F. Delves, A. Rudd
Centre Row: F. Kell, J. Hutcheon, L. Humphris (Captain), W. Noblet, E. Gooden,
Front Row: V. Steet, E. Sellars (Referee), W. Bryning

Canada went on to record a 6 to 4 goal victory. Soon after the game the visitors left Adelaide by train for Largs Bay where a launch took them to the steamer Kyarra to sail to Western Australia for the final leg of the tour.

Western Australia

Western Australians had followed with interest the media reports of the Canadian's matches in the eastern states. Their arrival in Fremantle on Thursday, 22nd of August had been approached with expectation and some apprehension.

Experience of lacrosse outside of local club competition was limited for Western Australia to a handful of Interstate contests. Distance is a tough master and the West had remained largely cut off from the intercolonial and interstate fixtures which had become commonplace for the eastern states.

Special selection trials were conducted by the Western Australian Association to assist in deciding which players should represent them against Canada. Public interest was high and one keen lacrosse supporter wrote to the Perth newspapers exhorting local businesses to close their shops and offices on the afternoons of the matches so that people could witness the international events.

Another, fuelled by the eastern state's reports of Canada's rough play, provided his own advice to the selection committee in a letter to the newspaper, published under the nom de plume of "Sioux" [36].........

> *"Our team, especially the forward line, must be composed of "battlers" not afraid of a friendly crack or so .... As the Canadians are evidently brought up to playing the 'strenuous' game, I would suggest that the Association lift the disqualification from the Dyson brothers (Fremantle) and that J. Dyson take the place of Hugall in the back line and D. Dyson take the place of A. Clark in forward. I can assure you, sir, that these two players would make it particularly hot for our Canadian visitors, who seem to invite a good willing game."*

At a welcoming function at the Palace Hotel in Perth the Canadian Team Manager made the following remarks on the press comments of rough tactics used by his team [37]....

> *"The reports of last Saturday's match were irresponsible statements from a diseased mind and had evidently emanated from some schoolboy reporter .... not one man on either side could show a scratch or bruise at its conclusion."* He desired to acknowledge the *"thorough British sportsmanlike spirit which the Australians invariably displayed."* He pointed out that his team had not been brought to Australia to play international test matches, they had come to play exhibition games of lacrosse as it was played in Canada. In Canada they did not have teams picked from states or counties or inter-State teams in any sense of the word. When they got here, they found teams picked from the various States, a circumstance they were quite unused to."

W. Hanley, the Team Captain commented that he had been surprised and impressed at the standard of play in Australia. He noted that differences in playing rules, particularly in relation to body checking and shepherding had been largely responsible for the misunderstandings that had been often commented upon as unfair tactics on the part of his team.

A crowd of 6,000 turned out in fine weather at the Western Australian Cricket Association Ground on the 24th of August to witness the opening encounter.[38] The Western Australians played in white and blue colours with a black swan emblazoned on their chests. Football, rugby and soccer codes had agreed to suspend their fixtures for the day so the turnstiles ran hot as £212 was taken at the gate. This result alone covered most of the £300 guarantee put up by Western Australia towards the visitor's expenses.

Canada won by 17 goals to 4 but the Western Australians showed they were fleet of foot and gave a good account of themselves. Two days later a match was played against a Western Australian Second Twelve, again at the W.A.C.A. ground. Spectators were treated to a one shilling admission to see the Canadians win 17 to 2. After the game the visitors caught the express train for Kalgoolie.

Arriving in Kalgoolie on the morning of Tuesday, 27th of August, the Canadians were entertained at a Town Hall reception. In the afternoon they were taken on a tour over the Tramway Company's lines and the Kalgoolie and Boulder racecourses before an evening social. The following day, their match

12 – THE CANADIAN LACROSSE TOUR OF AUSTRALIA, 1907

Western Australia Team v Canada at Perth, 24 August 1907

against a Combined Goldfields team attracted 4,000 spectators to the Kalgoorlie Recreation Reserve.[39] The result was a 14-0 whitewash but the locals were happy. They had experienced international competition and taken £130 at the gate. In the evening, the Goldfields Lacrosse Association hosted the visitors at a banquet. Prior to their return to the coast the following afternoon, the team enjoyed a tour of the Kalgoolie gold mines.

Back in Fremantle preparations were made for the final match of the tour, this time at the Fremantle Oval. The game, on Saturday, 31st of August, attracted 4,000 supporters.[40] Once again, the Canadians were far superior but Western Australia put up one of the strongest goal-throwing results for the tour, led by left home E. Stokes (Banks Lacrosse Club) who scored 4 goals. The final result was a 14 to 6 win for Canada.

With the contests and the social whirl all finished, the Canadians spent some time resting and sightseeing before departure. They sailed from Fremantle early in the morning of Tuesday, 3rd September on the Orient Mail ship, Ortona. Scores of Western Australian lacrosse friends had travelled to the wharf to farewell them on the Monday evening but the sailing was delayed by many hours. By the time the final farewell came it was the early hours of the morning, so the throng had gone home.

Controversy – The Final Say

Perhaps the only uncomfortable aspect of the entire tour was the constant and vexatious commentary of the Australian press on the subject of playing rules and rough play. It had a positive effect in attracting crowds to the games but it clearly annoyed the Canadians. The Canadian Manager and Captain pointed out on many occasions that the Canadian game, with its cross-checking, shepherding and smaller fields, was fundamentally different to what they experienced in Australia.

To their credit, the Canadians retained their composure in the face of the negative press comments and handled the situation with good grace. It was not until the team had departed Australia that the Canadian Manager, John Miller could no longer restrain himself. He lodged a provocative letter with the Australian media.

This was Canada's final say on the controversy [41].......

> *"Sirs,*
>
> *The members of the Canadian lacrosse team have been greatly amused at your vain endeavours to prejudice public opinion against them and your efforts to create discord between them and their hosts – the Australian Lacrosse Association.*
>
> *Were your criticisms at all fair all sportsmen would welcome them, but your latest effusions are so manifestly unfair and brutal, and display such a low, vulgar and depraved spirit of spite and jealously, that we cannot allow them to pass unnoticed.*
>
> *You refer to us as though we were a group of ruffians and blackguards, who were endeavouring to maim or kill outright the players whom we have met. We feel that the players in particular, and the public generally, are to be deeply sympathised with in having to bear the shame of being championed by writers who in their blind prejudice do more to kill good sport than any gang of convicts could possibly do.*
>
> *It would appear from your writings that we laid out Australian lacrossists at every opportunity and it might surprise you to know, as it will certainly please your depraved dispositions, that in the numerous games we have played the Canadian players have certainly been the greatest sufferers from accidents in the games – if you will allow me to call the blows accidental.*
>
> *We have had in our various games one man with two teeth knocked out, two other men with a tooth a piece knocked out or broken, one man with his arm broken, one man with his eye cut so badly it needed four stitches to close it, one man with his chin cut so that it took two stitches, one man with his toe broken, one man with his finger broken, one man with the muscles of his leg torn so badly, that, even though he is a medical man and should look at things cheerfully, he fears he will never again be able to play the game, besides numerous bruises about the arms and legs of our men.*
>
> *All this in spite of the much-abused armour we wear; and through it all we have yet to see any report in your fair and sportsmanlike endeavours to acquaint your readers with the true facts or any mention of any of them. In justice to the lacrossists I would add that the broken arm and cut eye were received in hockey games on the ice but these games were played under the auspices of the Victorian Lacrosse Association.*

12 – THE CANADIAN LACROSSE TOUR OF AUSTRALIA, 1907

This is the first mention any of us has yet made of any of the above injuries, and were it not for your most ignorant and brutal attack they would have been allowed to pass unnoticed. Will you kindly acquaint your readers with the casualty list on the Australian side, and let them judge whether your attacks are justified?

In 'The Bulletin' mention is made of your intention to ask the governing body of lacrosse in Canada to debar some of our men from taking part in future games, and I would just add that the men who are at the head of the game in Canada have built up the game by the application at all times of the true spirit of British justice, and would certainly not act as you have done in convicting a man without giving him the chance to defend himself.

Neither would they be led astray by the irresponsible vapourings of a diseased mind such as actuated the effusion complained of. We have received, from all over the Commonwealth, letters and wires from numerous of our opponents asking us to kindly take no notice of those articles and we certainly bear no ill-will against any lacrossist we have met.

We leave here in a few days with the most kindly feelings towards Australian lacrossists and the general public, who have given us so much pleasure, and are pleased to know that in the whole Commonwealth there are only two exceptions that prove the rule, that as a whole the Australians are gentlemen of the highest type.

I can only say, that in waiting to the eve of our departure before writing as you did, you have shown that you have much more discretion than your limited supply of brains would lead one to believe.

Were we in your State, it would have given us a great deal of pleasure to try and fill in the vacancy in your head where your brains should be with sand or some other solid matter, so that those rumblings which you mistake for thought would never again be reduced to print.

We have yet to see any report from any of the Australian players in which they try to take advantage of your slanderous and unfair statements to account for their numerous defeats, and they won our admiration by their sportsmanlike conduct on and off the field.

The very fact that a few players on each side temporarily lost their tempers only goes to endear the game to us, and shows that it is a game worth playing. We have never claimed even a distant relationship with archangels.

Neither do we admit any of our players having Indian blood in their veins, although if they had they certainly could claim that truest traditions of the noble North American red man prevent them stabbing a man in the back as you have tried to do.

In conclusion I can only say that the memory of the pleasures we have enjoyed and the true friends we have made will so overshadow the very few little unpleasantnesses that have arisen that we will always hold in our affections the kindliest thoughts for Australia and Australians." – I am yours truly, John C. Miller, Manager Canadian Lacrosse Team."

Retrospect

The tour started out with considerable financial risk hanging over the promoters. Their entrepreneurship was rewarded as the crowds turned out to watch. Success was assured before the Canadians reached Western Australia. Detailed financial records held in the archives of Lacrosse Australia show that all expenses were met and the original guarantors were fully refunded.

The visit achieved the hoped-for effect of challenging Australian lacrosse with new techniques, different patterns of play and new equipment. The local Associations, and those among the media who thought carefully about what they had witnessed, realized that international exchanges were necessary to lead the sport to common playing rules.

With the Canadians departed, the State associations and clubs returned to the completion of their domestic playing seasons. The mood was anti-climactic. Club games seemed commonplace compared with the excitement created by international duels. The visit had fostered ideas and desires for more overseas contact and for a new wave of growth in the sport. Left Home, writing in The Leader, commented as follows [42] ....

> *"In Victoria the influence of the visit is apparent on all sides and next season is certain to see the ranks of the players considerably augmented. Nearly all the clubs have been approached by would-be players, while several have been asked to lend their assistance and advice in forming new clubs. In the provinces, clubs have been formed at Numurkah, Shepparton, Tatura and later at Bendigo. Castlemaine is anxious to follow in the same direction, and Ballarat, though to a lesser degree, is also moving to the same end."*

Despite the perceived benefits of this international boost, more than fifty years passed before another international team visited Australia. World wars and the economic depression of the 1930's intervened. Lacrosse, which seemed headed for a golden future, never quite regained the momentum which 1907 had so much promised.

Match Results

The matches played by the visiting Canadian team in 1907 were of such significance to Australian lacrosse that it became a highly-prized badge of honour for every Australian player who had the good fortune to take the field and compete against them.

In later years, claims by players to have 'played against the Canadians' became commonplace but were not always accurate. The full results of all sixteen matches played by Canada on the 1907 tour are presented opposite in order to put the record straight.

12 – THE CANADIAN LACROSSE TOUR OF AUSTRALIA, 1907

Match: 1 - played Saturday 20th July

Opponent:	Queensland	**Result:**	Canada 6 d. QLD 3
Location:	Brisbane	**Gate Takings:**	£280
Venue:	Exhibition Oval	**Referee:**	W. Bruce
Spectators:	8,000	**Goal Umpires:**	I. Spode, W. Exton

Canada

R.J. Arens, Dr. H.L. Campbell, H. Camplin, W.J. Hanley, J. Kearns, T. Hanley, F. Grace, A. Rose, F. Coombs, R> Gilbert, G. Macdonald, W.D. Ranmore

Queensland

R.D. Pyke, J. Hiron, J.F. Connolly, R. Hartington, W.V. Morley, J.S. Hutcheon (Captain), J. Thorpe, R. Darvall, O. Thorpe, A. Clark, E.A. Brighouse, E.G Spence

Goals:	Macdonald 2, Rose 2, Gilbert, Ranmore	**Goals:**	O. Thorpe 3
Best Players:	Gilbert, Arens, Campbell	**Best Players:**	Hutcheon, Brighouse, Pyke

Match: 2 - played Monday 22nd July

Opponent:	New South Wales	**Result:**	Canada 11 d. NSW 0
Location:	Sydney	**Gate Takings:**	
Venue:	Sydney Cricket Ground	**Referee:**	
Spectators:	2,000	**Goal Umpires:**	

Canada

R.J. Arens, Dr. H.L. Campbell, J.M. Kearns, T. Hanley, A. Rose, W.J. Hanley, F. Grace, F. Coombs, R. Gilbert, G. Macdonald, W.D. Ranmore, E.V. Graham

New South Wales

F. Henriques, H. Dawson, A. Rankin, C.U.B. Gurnett, S. Meyer (Captain), P.M. Loutit, C. Booth, W. Stillman, R. Lane, R.B Fitzhardinge, R.C. Ward

LACROSSE IN AUSTRALIA

Match: 3 - played Saturday 27th July

Opponent:	Australia	**Result:**	Australia 5 d. Canada 3
Location:	Melbourne	**Gate Takings:**	£354
Venue:	Melbourne Cricket Ground	**Referee:**	J.G. Latham
Spectators:	16,000	**Goal Umpires:**	Dr W. Summons, E. Tyrie

Canada

R.J. Arens, Dr. H.L. Campbell, J.M. Kearns, T. Hanley, A. Rose, W.J. Hanley, F. Grace, F. Coombs, R. Gilbert, G. Macdonald, W.D. Ranmore, E.V. Graham

Goals: Grace, Gilbert, T. Hanley

Best Players: Campbell, Kearns, W. Hanley, Grace, Gilbert, Macdonald

Australia

F. Delves, E.O. Gooden, L. Jones, C.V. Hughes, C. Graham, V. Steet, F. Kell, W.C. Noblett, A.S. Mann, L Humphris (Captain), R. Taylor, W. Bryning

Goals: Taylor 2, Humphris 2, Bryning

Best Players: Delves, Gooden, Hughes, Humphris, Bryning, Taylor

---

Match: 4 - played Saturday 3rd August

Opponent:	Australia	**Result:**	Canada 6 d. Australia 3
Location:	Adelaide	**Gate Takings:**	£396
Venue:	Adelaide Oval	**Referee:**	A.J. Rudd
Spectators:	10,000	**Goal Umpires:**	M.J. Naughton, O. Tonkin

Canada

R.J. Arens, Dr. H.L. Campbell, H. Camplin, J.M. Kearns, T. Hanley, W.J. Hanley, F. Grace, F. Coombs, R. Gilbert, G. Macdonald, W.D. Ranmore, E.V. Graham

Goals: Camplin 2, Gilbert, Coombs, Ranmore, Hanley

Best Players:

Australia

F. Delves, E.O. Gooden, L. Jones, C.V. Hughes, V. Steet, J. Fletcher, F. Kell, W.C. Noblett, A.S. Mann, L. Humphris (Captain), R. Taylor, A. Presgrave

Goals: Presgrave 2, Taylor

Best Players: Fletcher, Hughes, Delves, Steet, Kell

12 – THE CANADIAN LACROSSE TOUR OF AUSTRALIA, 1907

Match: 5 - played Monday 5th August

Opponent:	SA Second Twelve	Result:	Canada 10 d. SA Second Twelve 3
Location:	Adelaide	Gate Takings:	£11
Venue:	Adelaide Oval	Referee:	W. Fisk
Spectators:		Goal Umpires:	

Canada

W. Atton, Dr. H.L. Campbell, H. Camplin, J.M. Kearns, R.J. Arens, W.J. Hanley (Captain), F. Grace, A. Rose Gilbert, G. Macdonald, W.D. Ranmore, E.V. Graham

Goals: Gilbert 3, Ranmore 2, Macdonald 2, Rose, Hanley, Graham

SA Second Twelve

T. Horton, L.O. Betts, O. Tonkin, A. Thompson, R. Goode (Captain), R. Neill, I. Ballans, M.J. Naughton, D.M. Steele, R Hopkins, G.K. Thomas B. Healy

Goals: Thomas 2, Naughton

Match: 6 - played Wednesday 7th August

Opponent:	South Australia	Result:	Canada 7 d. SA 3
Location:	Adelaide	Gate Takings:	£54
Venue:	Adelaide Oval	Referee:	J. Larner
Spectators:	2,000	Goal Umpires:	G. Blockey, W. Atton

Canada

R.J. Arens, Dr. H.L. Campbell, J.M. Kearns, T. Hanley, A. Rose, W.J. Hanley, F. Grace, F. Coombs, R. Gilbert, G. Macdonald, W.D. Ranmore, E.V. Graham

Goals:

Best Players:

South Australia

A.J. Rudd, L. Jones, E.O. Gooden, C.V. Hughes, J. Fletcher, J. Hooper, F. Kell, A.S. Mann, W.C. Noblett, L. Humphris, A.R Taylor, A. Presgrave

Goals: Presgrave 2, Humphris

Best Players: Hughes, Jones, Gooden, Fletcher, Hooper

LACROSSE IN AUSTRALIA

Match: 7 - played Friday 9th August

Opponent:	Victorian Twelve	**Result:**	Canada 14 d. Victorian Twelve 0
Location:	Ballarat	**Gate Takings:**	£51
Venue:	City Oval	**Referee:**	
Spectators:	2,000	**Goal Umpires:**	

Canada

W. Atton, R.J. Arens, Dr. H.L. Campbell, H. Camplin, J.M. Kearns, W.J. Hanley (Captain), F. Grace, F. Coombs, W.D. Ranmore, G.Macdonald, E.V. Graham, A. Rose

Victorian Twelve

H.E. Poole, H. Bald (Captain), Dr W. Summons, Jim Beattie, B.Dawson, E. Tyrie, J. Barbour, P. Nieheuson, A. Dean, V. Rawsthorne, A. Loch, A. Lampard

Goals:

Best Players: Campbell, Kearns, Hanley

Goals:

Best Players: Dean

Match: 8 - played Saturday 10th August

Opponent:	Australia	**Result:**	Canada 4 d. Australia 0
Location:	Melbourne	**Gate Takings:**	£205
Venue:	Melbourne Cricket Ground	**Referee:**	W. Lampard
Spectators:	11,000	**Goal Umpires:**	

Canada

R.J. Arens, Dr. H.L. Campbell, J.M. Kearns, H. Camplin, T. Hanley, W.J. Hanley (Captain), F. Grace, F. Coombs, A.Rose, G. Macdonald, W.D. Ranmore, R. Gilbert

Australia

F. Delves, A. Rudd, C. Graham, B. Bryning, V. Steet, J. Hutcheon, F. Kell, W.C. Noblett, A. Box, L. Humphris (Captain), O. Thorpe, W. Bryning

Goals: Ranmore 2, Gilbert, Hit-in

Best Players: Arens, Campbell, Kearns

Goals:

Best Players: Hutcheon, Rudd, Delves, W. Bryning Humphris

12 – THE CANADIAN LACROSSE TOUR OF AUSTRALIA, 1907

Match: 9 - played Monday 12th August

Opponent:	Victoria	**Result:**	Canada 9 d. Victoria 1
Location:	Melbourne	**Gate Takings:**	£19
Venue:	Melbourne Cricket Ground	**Referee:**	
Spectators:	2,000	**Goal Umpires:**	

Canada

R.J. Arens, H. Camplin, J.M. Kearns, T. Hanley, W.J. Hanley (Captain), F. Grace, A. Rose, F. Coombs, R. Gilbert, E.V. Graham, G. Macdonald, W.D. Ranmore

Goals: Ranmore 3, Graham 2, T. Hanley, Macdonald, Coombs, Gilbert

Best Players: Kearns, Ranmore

Victoria

F. Delves, F. Bald, Dr W. Summons, W. Throssell, J. Latham, W. Musgrove, E. Tyrie, A. Dean, F. Dunn, G. Gay, P Pennefather, V. Rawsthorne

Goals: Rawsthorne

Best Players: Delves, Bald, Summons, Throssell

Match: 10 - played Wednesday 14th August

Opponent:	Victoria	**Result:**	Canada 16 d. Victoria 5
Location:	Bendigo	**Gate Takings:**	£69
Venue:	Upper Reserve	**Referee:**	W.J. Lampard
Spectators:	3,000	**Goal Umpires:**	

Canada

Dr. H.L. Campbell, J.M. Kearns, H. Camplin, R. Arens A. Rose, W.J. Hanley (Captain), F. Grace, F. Coombs, R. Gilbert, G. Macdonald, W.D. Ranmore, W. Atton

Goals: Atton 5, Ranmore 3, Macdonald 3, Hanley, Coombs

Best Players: Atton, Ranmore

Victoria

L.B. Gordon, R.J. Latham, H. Jones, B. Dawson, C. Musgrove, H. Winterbottom, E. Tyrie, A. Dean, V., Rawsthorne, G. Gay H. Doyle, W. Bryning

Goals: Doyle 2, Winterbottom, Gay, Rawsthorne

Best Players: Doyle

LACROSSE IN AUSTRALIA

Match 11 - played Friday 16th August

Opponent:	Jamestown	**Result:**	Canada 12 d. Jamestown 0
Location:	Adelaide	**Gate Takings:**	£2
Venue:	Adelaide Oval	**Referee:**	D.M. Steele
Spectators:		**Goal Umpires:**	

Canada

R.J. Arens, J.M. Kearns, H. Camplin, T. Hanley, A. Rose, W.J. Hanley (Captain), F. Grace, F. Coombs, R. Gilbert, G. acdonald, W.D. Ranmore, W. Atton

Goals: Atton 6, Ranmore 3, Gilbert 2, W. Hanley

Best Players: Atton, Ranmore, Gilberton

Jamestown

A.G. Burton, S.J. Noblett, S. Rowe, J. Gordon, O. Gerke, A. Dunstan, H. Parrington, W. Noblett, J. Parrington, N. Moffatt, R. Wilkinson, W. Naismith

Goals:

Best Players: Moffatt

Match: 12 - played Saturday 17th August

Opponent:	Australia	**Result:**	Canada 6 d. Australia 4
Location:	Adelaide	**Gate Takings:**	£146
Venue:	Adelaide Oval	**Referee:**	R.W. Sellars
Spectators:	8,000	**Goal Umpires:**	E.V. Graham, G. Blockey

Canada

R.J. Arens, J.M. Kearns, A. Rose, H. Camplin, T. Hanley, W.J. Hanley, F. Grace, F. Coombs, R. Gilbert, G. Macdonald, W.D. Ranmore, W. Atton

Goals: Gilbert 3, Rose, Macdonald, Ranmore

Best Players: Gilbert, Kearns, Macdonald

Australia

F. Delves, A. Rudd, E.O. Gooden, C.V. Hughes, C. Graham, J. Hutcheon, F. Kell, V. Steet, W. Bryning, W.C. Noblett, L Humphris (Captain), R. Taylor

Goals: Bryning 2, Humphris, Taylor

Best Players: Bryning, Graham, Steet, Delves

12 – THE CANADIAN LACROSSE TOUR OF AUSTRALIA, 1907

Match: 13 - played Saturday 24th August

Opponent:	Western Australia	**Result:**	Canada 17 d. WA. 4
Location:	Perth	**Gate Takings:**	£168
Venue:	W. A. Cricket Ground	**Referee:**	
Spectators:	6,000	**Goal Umpires:**	

Canada

R.J. Arens, Dr. H.L. Campbell, H. Camplin, J.M. Kearns, T. Hanley, W.J. Hanley, F. Grace, F. Coombs, R. Gilbert, G. Macdonald, W.D. Ranmore, A. Rose

Goals:

Best Players: Grace, T. Hanley, W. Hanley, Arens, Macdonald

Western Australia

I. Taylor, T. Goodwin, G. Clarke, E. Harvey (Captain),. R.M Wilson, J. Blyth, W. Kirkby, E. Stokes, J. Ewers, D. Brown, R Eagle, F. McDonnell

Goals: Stokes, Kirkby, Eagle, Brown

Best Players: Kirkby, Goodwin, Clarke, Harvey

Match: 14 - played Monday 26th August

Opponent:	Western Australia Second	**Result:**	Canada 17 d. WA 2
Location:	Perth	**Gate Takings:**	£11
Venue:	W. A. Cricket Ground	**Referee:**	A. Mather
Spectators:		**Goal Umpires:**	H. Taylor, Lennon

Canada

R.J. Arens, J.M. Kearns, H. Camplin, A. Rose, T. Hanley, W.J. Hanley, F. Grace, F. Coombs, R. Gilbert, G. Macdonald, W.D. Ranmore, W. Atton

Goals: Atton 9, Ranmore, Coombs, Gilbert, Macdonald

Best Players: Arens, Kearns, Camplin

Western Australia Second Twelve

F. Wilkie, J. Hugall, H. Earle, G. Cussen, Johnson, W. Tickell, H. Bromfield, Ingleton, C. Hickey, F.C., Wingrove, A. Clark W. Hutchinson

Goals: Bromfield, Wingrove

Best Players:

Match: 15 - played Wednesday 28th August

Opponent:	WA Combined Goldfields	**Result:**	Canada 14 d. WA Goldfields 0
Location:	Kalgoorlie	**Gate Takings:**	£130
Venue:	Kalgoolie Recreation Reserve	**Referee:**	
Spectators:	4,000	**Goal Umpires:**	

Canada

R.J. Arens, Dr. H.L. Campbell, J.M. Kearns, T. Hanley, A. Rose, W.J. Hanley, F. Grace, F. Coombs, R. Gilbert, G. Macdonald, W.D. Ranmore, E.V. Graham,

Goals:

Best Players:

WA Combined Goldfields

Angell, Llewellyn, Banks, Grieve, Laybourne, Smith, Daniels, V Henderson, G. Mettam, B. Mettam, Burkitt, Sands, Harrison,

Goals:

Best Players:

Match: 16 - played Saturday 31st August

Opponent:	Western Australia	**Result:**	Canada 14 d. WA 6
Location:	Perth	**Gate Takings:**	£175
Venue:	Fremantle Oval	**Referee:**	F.C. Wingrove
Spectators:	4,000	**Goal Umpires:**	A. Mather, H. Taylor

Canada

R.J. Arens, Dr. H.L. Campbell, H. Camplin, J.M. Kearns, T.Hanley, W.J. Hanley, F. Grace, F. Coombs, R. Gilbert, Macdonald, W.D. Ranmore, A. Rose.

Goals: Ranmore 5, Coombs 3, Rose 2, Macdonald 2, Grace 2

Best Players: W. Hanley, T. Hanley, Arens, Camplin, Kearns

Western Australia

T. L. Wilkie, J. Goodwin, G. Cussen, E. Harvey, J. Blyth, G. M. Wilson, W. Tickell, W. Kirkby, H. Bromfield, E. Stokes, G Clarke, R. Eagle

Goals: Stokes 4, Kirkby, Bromfield

Best Players: Goodwin, Stokes, Kirkby, Wilkie, Harvey

Notes

1. Australasian (Melbourne) 8/07/1899 p.24
2. Australasian (Melbourne) 29/09/1900 p.23
3. The Advertiser (Adelaide) 29/06/1907 p.5
4. Minutes of Malvern Lacrosse Club Annual General Meeting 15/04/1907
5. The Leader (Melbourne) 27/09/1907 p.21
6. Brisbane Courier 15/07/1907 p.5
7. The Register (Adelaide) 20/07/1907 p.6
8. The Telegraph (Brisbane) 16/07/1907 p.2
9. Brisbane Courier 16/07/1907 p.5
10. Brisbane Courier 16/07/1907 p.5
11. Brisbane Courier 22/07/1907 p.5
12. The Telegraph (Brisbane) 22/07/1907 p.5
13. The Daily Telegraph (Sydney) 23/07/1907 p.5
14. The Herald (Melbourne) 24/07/1907 p.3
15. The Argus (Melbourne) 26/07/1907 p.4
16. The Age (Melbourne) 15/07/1907 p.9
17. The Argus (Melbourne) 27/07/1907 p.17
18. The Leader (Melbourne) 27/07/1907 p.21
19. The Herald (Melbourne) 27/07/1907 p.6
20. Table Talk (Melbourne) 1/08/1907 p.20
21. The Age (Melbourne) 29/07/1907 p.8
22. The Register (Adelaide) 31/07/1907 p.8
23. The Register (Adelaide) 3/08/1907 p.7
24. The Register (Adelaide) 1/08/1907 p.9
25. The Advertiser (Adelaide) 5/08/1907 p.7
26. The Register (Adelaide) 3/08/1907 p.5
27. The Express & Telegraph (Adelaide) 8/08/1907 p.3
28. The Register (Adelaide) 6/08/1907 p.6
29. The Express & Telegraph (Adelaide) 8/08/1907 p.3
30. The Ballarat Star 10/08/1907 p.2
31. The Age (Melbourne) 12/08/1907 p.11
32. The Australasian (Melbourne) 29/11/1919 p.22
33. The Age (Melbourne) 13/08/1907 p.8
34. The Register (Adelaide) 17/08/1907 p.6
35. Australasian (Melbourne) 24/08/1907 p.23
36. The West Australian 17/08/1907 p.14
37. The West Australian 23/08/1907 p.6
38. The West Australian 26/08/1907 p.8
39. Kalgoolie Miner 29/08/1907 p.8
40. The West Australian 2/09/1907 p.2
41. The Observer (Adelaide) 21/09/1907 p.16
42. The Leader (Melbourne) 21/09/1907 p.2

Club Development, Championships and Women's Lacrosse

In June 1908 the Australasian newspaper in Melbourne published one of the most intriguing, and perhaps symbolic, photographs involving lacrosse[1]. It showed a lone lacrosse player occupying a seat on a crowded 'Direct to the Football' cable car. The rest of the throng on the tram were headed to the East Melbourne Oval to watch an Essendon versus South Melbourne football match.

Ruddell[2] suggests that the lacrosse player, dressed in business suit and carrying his lacrosse stick and a Gladstone bag, was likely heading to the Melbourne Cricket Ground to take his place as a participant player in the MCC v Fitzroy lacrosse match fixtured for that day.

Despite hopes for major growth following the success of the Canada tour, the message of the

Off to the Football – Essendon versus South Melbourne, June 20, 1908
Photograph courtesy of the Melbourne Cricket Club Library

photograph seems prophetic for lacrosse. Pitted against the burgeoning spectator appeal of football, lacrosse was facing an uphill battle to win broad public support. Like the photograph, lacrosse had a place as a curiosity, but not as a main player.

After 1907, some club growth occurred in each state and visibility improved as the newspapers seemed to have developed a new respect for lacrosse, grown from the glamour of the international action. However, it was not the opening of floodgates.

New Clubs and Embryo Clubs

During the years after the Canadian Team visit and the onset of the World War, a number of new clubs were formed in each State. Some existing clubs ceased active participation and did not re-appear after hostilities had ended. Others re-formed, only to be lost twenty years later when the world entered a second World War.

New clubs established, and existing clubs lost, in each state during the period following 1907 are recorded in the following table.

	New Clubs	Clubs Lost
New South Wales	Federals, Hurstville, Mosman, Wanderers, YMCA, Moore College, Delaware	Burwood, Waverley, Stanmore North Sydney, City, Manly, Federals, Moore College, YMCA, Wanderers
Queensland	Kangaroo Point, Toowong, Alberta, Dandies, Milton	Past Grammar, Orilla, Delaware, Indoorpilly, Iroquois
South Australia	Strathalbyn, Goodwood, West Torrens (re-formed)	YMCA
Tasmania	Midwood	Mohicans, Iroquois, Launceston, YMCA
Victoria	Elsternwick, Caulfield, Footscray, Box Hill	Fitzroy, South Yarra, Kew, Hawksburn, Hawthorn, Essendon, Elsternwick, Maribyrnong, Carlton Cricketers
Western Australia		Claremont, Banks, Trinity

Table 1: Lacrosse Clubs Established (and lost) in Australia, 1908-1914

Records of actual numbers of registered players for all states are not available for these years, but, where not, can be estimated on the basis of fifteen players per participating team to provide an indicative assessment of the impact of the international tour. On this basis, the total number of lacrosse players in Australia grew from 1299 in 1906 to 1725 in 1908, and to 2192 by the close of 1914 when World War 1 intervened to decimate the sport. As the numbers show, the growth that followed the Canada Tour

13 – CLUB DEVELOPMENT, CHAMPIONSHIPS AND WOMEN'S LACROSSE

was substantial, with almost 500 players added in just two years. However, it had been hoped that the international exposure would catapult lacrosse to much greater heights.

Among the growth that occurred during the post-Canada Tour, pre-war years, were some new clubs which remain an important part of the lacrosse fabric today. Victoria's mighty Caulfield and Footscray Lacrosse Clubs are included in this category.

Caulfield Lacrosse Club

On the 22nd of March of 1909, a meeting was held at Caulfield Town Hall in Melbourne and the Caulfield Lacrosse Club was formed in a partnership with the Caulfield Cricket Club.[3] The club had existed previously and had played in the VLA competition at the Caulfield Cricket Ground between 1891-1896 before a shortage of players caused it to be discontinued. The restart involved new pioneers and the club competed successfully until the World War again caused it to go into recess. It started with the promised support of some prominent local players and an expectation that it would field two or three teams. The new club's first practice session was held on Saturday 27th March at the Caulfield Cricket Ground.[4] The club subsequently entered teams in the VLA 'B' Section and 'C' Section and played its first season with great success to capture the 'B' Section premiership, losing only two matches. Key players included George Browne, Dick Woodman, Keith Looker, Norm Nation, Ivon Bromilow, Garnet Bainbridge, Alan Harrison and Messrs. Purbrick, Kingbolt, Kimber, Florence and Griffiths.

After the war, a decimated Caulfield was re-started with a "B" Grade team in 1919 by a group which included some of the old names. George Browne, a former Captain and now goalkeeper, got the club going again and was helped by Les Brooks, Foster Nutting, Bert Aulder, Joe Aulder, Bill Roy, Bill Furneaux, Cliff White and Ted Michelson. The latter two were professional foot-runners. In 1920, Ken Keogh, Frank Trainor and Ron Gibbs, who had watched the Caulfield team play during 1919, gathered together a bunch of beginners and Caulfield entered a second team in "D" Grade.[5] The 'Green and Gold' colours of Caulfield finally returned to the senior "A" Grade ranks in 1923 and has remained there ever since, winning seven senior premierships, producing many of Victoria's most celebrated players and earning ongoing status as one of the VLA's leading clubs.

Footscray Lacrosse Club

The Footscray Lacrosse Club can boast a long and successful history but the journey has not occurred without a number of lapsed years and multiple re-starts.

The prospect of a lacrosse team being formed at Footscray was talked about during colonial years and an exhibition lacrosse match was played as a curtain-raiser to the Footscray v Essendon VFL football game at the East Melbourne Oval in 1894.[6] The game created public interest but no immediate outcome for lacrosse. In 1898 there was further talk of lacrosse clubs being formed at both Footscray and Williamstown. The Williamstown effort succeeded but nothing came to fruition at Footscray at that time.

It was not until 1914 that the Footscray club was formed.

On May 9th 1914, the Footscray Advertiser reported [7]....

> *"During the last few months there has been a movement on foot to introduce the game of Lacrosse to Footscray. The movement was taken up by a number of local residents, who, during recent years have been compelled to journey to Williamstown in order to take part in lacrosse matches.*
>
> *At a meeting held recently it was decided to form a local club, thereupon an application was made to the Victorian Lacrosse Association for registration as a club. This application was granted and the local club was entered to play in "C" section.*
>
> *The uniform of the Footscray Club is purple jersey with white collar and cuffs and the ground is situate on the east side of the Maribyrnong River between the Hopetoun and Swing bridges.*
>
> *On Saturday last the Lacrosse premiership matches commenced, when the local club met Coburg at Coburg. After a strenuous fight the game resulted in a win for Footscray. The scores were Footscray 5, Coburg 3 goals. Goal-throwers for Footscray were Leonard 2, Critchley, Scott and Brown. This was considered most satisfactory for a new club".*

One week later the Footscray Independent reported that the club had suffered its first defeat at the hands of Carlton, going down by 10 goals to 1. The Footscray team comprised Shepherd (Captain), Burton, Critchley, Miller, Scott, Pitt, Drew, Mason, Davis, Leonard, Stewart and Booth.[8]

The first Annual General Meeting of the club was held in the clubrooms at the Maribyrnong Street ground on Wednesday 10th March, 1915 with a good muster of members.[9] The Secretary, Mr T. Drew, reported on a successful first year and sound financial balance sheet. The club had won five of its sixteen matches and had shown great improvement as the year progressed. W.J McCann was elected as President, with T. Drew as Secretary and C. Critchley as Club Treasurer.

It was noted that some of the previous year's players were now with the Australian Expeditionary Forces in Egypt but that several promising colts would be available for selection. Training was already in full swing on Tuesday and Thursday nights.

Enthusiasm was high for the 1915 season. Footscray's team remained in "C" Section where it won 11 of its 12 matches and took out its first premiership. The 1915 season also included an unexpected highlight during the weekend of June 5-6 when the club responded to a VLA request for teams to travel and play games in Kyneton where efforts were being made to consolidate a club. Footscray obliged and played two matches, one against a Kyneton team and one against a team from Kew Lacrosse Club.[10] The visitors were entertained at an evening dinner and with a Sunday picnic trip after the games.

As for many clubs, the World War was devastating for Footscray. Twelve Footscray players were listed in the VLA Honour Roll as enlisted for active war service in the VLA Annual Report for 1918:

| Harry Brown | Roy Stewart | W.K Scott | H. Parnum | H. Booth | C. Critchley |
| T. Drew | F. Drew | G. Miller | J. Masen | W. Williams | J. Delahey |

13 – CLUB DEVELOPMENT, CHAMPIONSHIPS AND WOMEN'S LACROSSE

The club ceased playing in 1916 and did not enter teams after the war.

It was not until the 1935 season that the Footscray name re-appeared. The VLA Annual Report noted that Footscray Technical School Old Boys had been admitted as a "new club".[11] A team was entered in the junior "E" section competition and entries continued each year until 1939 when World War came again to cause a cessation of lacrosse.

In 1961 the Footscray club was re-formed again with teams entered in the VLA "C' and "E" sections and a team entered in the VWLA Women's competition. Detailed accounts of the history of the club since 1935 are contained on the club's website. The club has continued to operate continuously since that time and has expanded and strengthened over recent years to become a premiership club in both men's and women's lacrosse.

A number of other clubs which were weakened or became direct casualties of the first World War, provided the springboard for the formation of new clubs in the post-war years.

In Victoria, the present-day Camberwell Lacrosse Club was formed in 1927 through a merger of the Canterbury and Kooyong Clubs which had both suffered large losses of players during the war. Both clubs continued on a weakened footing after the war but never fully recovered. The Surrey Park

Tasmania North versus South Teams Played in Launceston, June 1914

Lacrosse Club had its origins in the Box Hill Lacrosse Club that formed in 1912 and later, following the second great war, merged with the Wattle Park club.

In Tasmania, the established separate club competitions conducted by the Northern and Southern Associations continued, with the Moonah club dominating in Hobart and the Tamar club winning the bulk of the Launceston-based premierships. The great rivalry of the annual North versus South game continued as the pinnacle domestic event in the lacrosse year, drawing strong spectator support.

The club competition in New South Wales was volatile during this period with eight new clubs formed between 1908-14, offset by a loss of ten clubs which discontinued or re-named. Honours for the leading club in this period were shared between Petersham with 5 premierships and Balmain with 4.

In Western Australia, Fremantle, with 4 premierships and Perth with 3, were the best-performed clubs in the early Federation years. After 1908, North Perth and the Iroquois club emerged and were among five different clubs which took premiership honours prior to the World War.

In Victoria, Essendon was the stand-out club with 8 senior premierships before 1911, including six in succession. South Yarra emerged with 3 consecutive titles leading up to the commencement of war.

After its 1903 resurrection, the Queensland Lacrosse Association went from strength to strength with the Iroquois club taking out 4 premier cups between 1903-07 and the Buffalo club capturing five premierships, mainly in the period leading into the wartime break.

Buffalo Lacrosse Team- Queensland Premiers 1909

13 – CLUB DEVELOPMENT, CHAMPIONSHIPS AND WOMEN'S LACROSSE

1912 South Australia Premiership – Sturt 12 defeated Port Adelaide 7

In South Australia, the Sturt Lacrosse Club drew a bunch of skilled players from Jamestown, the leading country-based club, and added some of its own to become the most successful club. Sturt won eleven premierships during a 13- year period from 1901-1920, including 1912 when it beat Port Adelaide and featured in the novel newspaper presentation above.[12]

Interstate Contests

The popularity of interstate competition continued after the Canada Tour with Tasmania and Western Australia increasingly enticed into participation. For Western Australia, the massive disadvantage of isolation meant that the costs to participate regularly were higher than for the eastern states. For Tasmania, its size disadvantage made the prospect of competing against the mainland states a difficult, but not less appealing, challenge.

For Western Australia, the experience of playing international lacrosse against Canada in 1907 provided a great lead-in to an expanded program of Interstate lacrosse. In 1909, South Australia sent a team to

Perth for matches against Western Australia and a Combined Goldfields team.[13] The South Australians were victorious by 8 goals to 3 against WALA and by 25-3 against the Goldfields. Western Australia subsequently played in Australian Carnivals in 1910 in Adelaide and 1912 in Melbourne.

West Australia versus South Australia in Perth 1909

13 – CLUB DEVELOPMENT, CHAMPIONSHIPS AND WOMEN'S LACROSSE

In 1909, Interstate lacrosse gained some unscheduled notoriety in Sydney.

The New South Wales versus Queensland Interstate contest on 17th July, at Petersham Oval, produced good lacrosse and a win for Queensland, but the most newsworthy feature was the referees. Among the referee group was Tommy Burns, the celebrated World Heavyweight boxing champion.[14] Burns, a Canadian, was a skilled and passionate lacrosse player who famously played in the Vancouver Greenshirts team that defeated New Westminster for the Canadian "Championship of the World" in September, 1910.[15] Although he had come to Australia in 1909 to put his world title on the line in a fight against Jack Johnson in Sydney, Burns happily put his hand up to connect with lacrosse and blow the whistle in the Interstate match.

Tommy Burns and Jack Johnson

Subsequently, Burns announced plans to bring an "All Indian" lacrosse team to Australia in 1911 but this venture did not proceed. When interviewed about lacrosse, Burns claimed that it was rougher and tougher than boxing and that the element of danger was appealing, quoting lines from the Australian poet, Adam Lindsay Gordon:

> *"No game is ever yet worth a rap*
> *For a rational man to play,*
> *Into which no accident, no mishap,*
> *Could possibly find its way".*

Burns did not blame his Sydney lacrosse adventure when he lost to Johnson on points after previous successes in defending his heavyweight title against thirteen challenges over a period of four years.

Tasmania was not left out of the Interstate action. In 1907 a Victorian "B" team visited Tasmania and was beaten by the locals in both Hobart and Launceston.[17] In the following year the Northern Tasmanian Association again sent a team to play in Melbourne. In 1909 South Australia visited the "Apple Isle" and played matches in both Launceston and Hobart. This was the first occasion on which Tasmania competed in any sport against South Australia.[1] The Tasmanians were no match for the might of the SALA but the experience against better players was what Tasmania was seeking.

The full representative experience for Tasmania came in the 1912 Australian Carnival in Melbourne, when Tasmania competed against every other Australian state. Later, in 1914, a Victorian development team visited Tasmania and played matches in both Launceston and Hobart.[18]

Tasmania and South Australia Teams at Launceston 1909

Junior Interstate Competitions

The first official junior interstate contest in Australia occurred in Sydney in September, 1911 when Petersham, the premier NSW junior team played against the visiting Brighton Wanderers team from

Melbourne. The Wanderers won by 11 goals to 8. Neville Beech, the son of George Beech who helped to found lacrosse in New South Wales, scored 7 goals for the Wanderers. Further Interstate junior competition came in 1912 when a Queensland Schoolboys team visited Sydney in July and played matches at the Sydney Cricket Ground against the NSW juniors and the Victorian Wanderers.

Brisbane became the venue for a three-round contest in June, 1913 when a New South Wales Schoolboys Team visited Queensland. The match results were in favour of the Queensland Schoolboys.

National Championships

Commencing in 1910, lacrosse brought a significant and long-lasting innovation to sport in Australia. Rather than arranging single contests between two states, or sometimes, three states coming together at one location to play interstate fixtures, the concept of an Australian Carnival was born. The South Australian Lacrosse Association invited, and where necessary, subsidized every state to send teams to Adelaide for a concentrated week of lacrosse during July and all but Tasmania took up the new format.[19]

The 1910 Carnival Series in Adelaide was a gala affair and produced a feast of lacrosse, the likes of which had never before been experienced in one place. Other sporting codes looked on with interest and a touch of jealousy and it was not long before the idea of Australian Championships was taken up more widely.

SALA invested considerable planning and funds into the 1910 Carnival to ensure that it was a success and to showcase South Australian lacrosse.[20] Excitement built in the few days before the week of 7-15 July which had been set aside for the games. With 60-100 visiting lacrosseurs and multiple matches compressed into a single week, the logistics of accommodation, transport, grounds, practice arrangements, referees, media and hospitality required a make-over. SALA appointed a special Carnival Committee for the task, headed by Harry Hodgetts, the SALA Secretary.

Western Australian Team, 1910 Carnival in Adelaide

The Carnival matches opened in front of 2000 spectators at the Adelaide Oval on Saturday, 2nd, July and the teams were entertained in the evening at a Smoke Social before a Horndale Winery visit the next day.[21]

When South Australia drew with Victoria in the main game, the result was decided on percentages and Victoria took the honours. At the conclusion of play, the team standings were as follows:

	Points	Goals For	Goals Against
Victoria	7	36	11
South Australia	7	34	14
Queensland	4	26	18
Western Australia	2	11	29
New South Wales	0	4	33

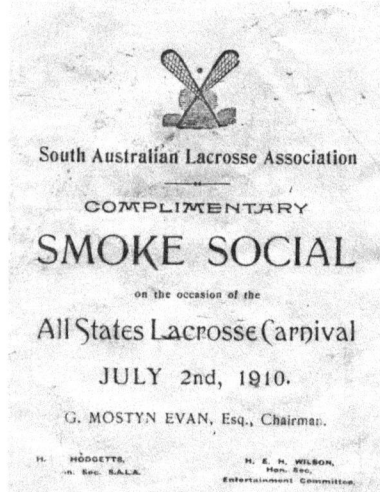
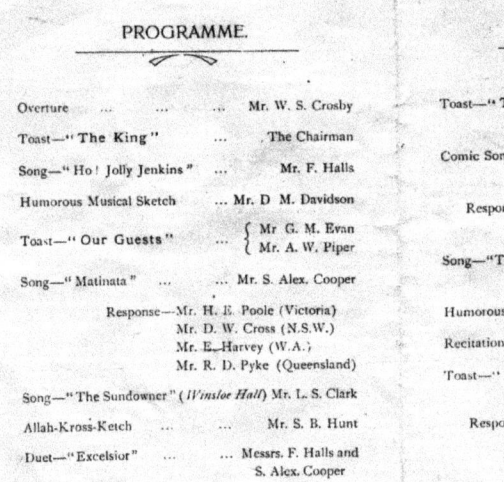

The 1912, Melbourne built on the success of the 1910 Australian Carnival in Adelaide, this time achieving a fully-national participation with every state represented. The Carnival was held over the period 10-17 August At the Melbourne Cricket Ground and St Kilda Cricket Ground. with the following teams representing their respective States:[22]

New South Wales: C. Thomas (goalkeeper), H.E. Dawson, H.L. Dawson, W. O'Neill,
Colours: Light blue   H. Eeg, E. Miller, J. Turnbull (centre), W. Stillman, A. Fulwood, H. Mallett, A. Thomas, R. Rowe (home)

Queensland: A. Davidson (goalkeeper), R. Sheppard, R. Macdonald, W.
Colours: Maroon   Blakey, R. Gore, T. Neill, N. Ridgway (centre), R. Ulcoq, J. Sheppard, O. Thorpe, R. Darvall, E. Thorpe (home), P. King, W. Armstrong, I. Woods

South Australia: G.C. Campell (goalkeeper), R.L. Hammond, R.R. Pinch, H.B.
Colours: Brown &   Hocking, A. Tonkin, H.A. Wicks, W. Noal (centre), R. Flett, W.C.
turquoise blue   Noblet, E. Mann, N.C. Moffat, E. Farrell, (home), J. Gower, H.C. Rennie, J. Thompson, H. Hill, J. Gower

13 – CLUB DEVELOPMENT, CHAMPIONSHIPS AND WOMEN'S LACROSSE

Tasmania:
Colours: Dark green & primrose, white knickers

F. Green (goalkeeper), W. Ratcliffe, J. Lack, F. H. Hanton, L. Gill, H. Green, C. Barwick (centre), B.C. Littler (capt), W. Kilroy, J.G. Littler, G.A. Bowe, L. Green (home), J. Horne, R. Packer, H. Bowe, S. Hopwood, Gatenby

Victoria:
Colours: Dark blue & white facings

H. Gursanscky, (goalkeeper), F. Smythe, B. Clements, G. Flood, W. Russell, S. Benwell, C Graham (centre), V. Boldeman, A. Dean, W. Swan, H. Doyle, V. Rawsthorne (home), J. Beattie, F. Johnson, C.Hurley

Western Australia:
Colours: Dark green & yellow

J.J. Taylor (goalkeeper), G. Clarke (capt), W.H. Tickell, R.C. Hooper, E.C. Smith, D.G. Brown, C. Hickey (centre), F. Knight, A.S. Mason, H.A. Sands, P. le Cornu, R.K. Miller, (home)W. Peters, W. Rodgers, C. Clark

At the conclusion of the busy week, the following results were recorded for the 1912 Carnival:

	Games played	Won	Lost
Victoria	5	5	-
South Australia	5	4	1
New South Wales	5	3	2
Western Australia	5	2	3
Queensland	5	1	4
Tasmania	5	-	5

The Labor Call newspaper in Melbourne had a journalist attend the Carnival and was surprised with the level of sportsmanship displayed in lacrosse compared with Australian Football, commenting [23].....

"The lacrosse carnival opened on the Melbourne Ground, and there was a big crowd of well-dressed people, for the Canadian game is more toney than hoof-ball. Certainly, it possesses this advantage, that though there were one or two collisions and a few cracks over the head with sticks, there was not the slightest indication of the remotest inclination to "stoush". The general tendency was to bear the crosse meekly".

They Don't Do That at Lacrosse

When the champion toeballers are playing a match
To decide which team is the boss,
A pugilist's picnic can't hold it a patch.
But that's not the case at lacrosse.

When the umpire's decisions are deemed quite unfair,
The players resort to brute force;
To 'biffling" and kicking the man then and there;
But they don't do that at lacrosse.

The Garland-McHarg Trophy

The Garland McHarg Trophy

From 1912, the Garland-McHarg Trophy was born as the prize to be competed for in men's national championships. Victoria followed its previous narrow win in Adelaide to place its name on the new trophy.

Initially, the trophy had been presented by Dick Garland and Andy McHarg for competition between Victoria and South Australia in their annual Interstate contests. The VLA sought the agreement of the donors, and the agreement of SALA, to have the trophy re-purposed to become the prize for the winning team at the Australian Championship Carnivals.

This exquisite sterling silver trophy remains to this day as the premier trophy in Australian men's lacrosse. Andrew McHarg was an ex-player with Melbourne University and Carlton and also a member of the Victorian team for its first Interstate contest against South Australia in Adelaide in 1889.

Andrew McHarg

Dick Garland was the Managing Director of the Dunlop Rubber Tyre Company, based in Melbourne. His interest in lacrosse came from many years in Canada where he was, for a time, President of the Toronto Lacrosse Club. He became an active and generous benefactor and contributor to lacrosse in Australia and, with support from George Beech, established a junior club at Brighton in Victoria, known as the Wanderers.

Junior International Lacrosse in Australia

Australia got its second taste of international lacrosse from an unexpected source in August 1912. A party of 65 schoolboy Canadian Cadets from Vancouver High School toured Australia and visited all states except Queensland.[24]

The Cadets program in Canada was a long-established, national organization designed to provide dynamic and structured citizenship activities for Canadian youth aged between 14 and 18 years. The Cadets were billeted in Australian homes as they toured from state to state, giving performances of bugle band, fife and drum band and military manoeuvres as well as playing sports. They were given Government and Mayoral receptions and hospitality at the highest levels wherever they visited. On Friday, 23rd August, 1912 the Cadets played a lacrosse match on the Melbourne Cricket Ground against

Canadian Cadets versus the Brighton Wanderers, MCG 23 August 1912

a team of schoolboys drawn from the Brighton Wanderers Lacrosse Club, and watched by students from Wesley College and Brighton and Melbourne Grammar Schools.[25] The Wanderers team included centreman, Alex Beech, a son of the first Australian lacrosse player, George Beech and attack player Charles Garland, a son of Dick Garland.

This was the first-ever junior international lacrosse played in Australia.[26] The Cadets, disadvantaged by the use of borrowed sticks, put up a strong game but were narrowly beaten by the Wanderers by 4 goals to 3. The Australasian Newspaper ran a major pictorial spread to mark the occasion. Two weeks later, the Cadets took on a team of young Australians from the 92nd Battalion Senior Cadets in Launceston, with Canada triumphing this time by 12 goals to 1. This was the first-ever experience of international lacrosse played in Tasmania.[27]

Garland and Beech were responsible for forming the Wanderers club in 1909 with schoolmates of their sons from Brighton Grammar School. The club's name derived from the Wanderers Cycling Club that Garland was previously involved with in Toronto. They played home games on the Brighton Grammar School oval and, following the world war, combined with the Brighton Presbyterians club to form the highly successful Brighton Lacrosse Club.[28]

Brighton Wanderers Team 1912
George Beech is standing on the left and Dick Garland on the right

Key Players, Administrators and Referees

Across the period from 1901 to 1914, the leading players of the day identified themselves by gaining selection for their State in one or more Interstate matches.

Beyond this group, the pinnacle players were the eighteen men who gained selection in one or more of the four teams assembled in 1907 to represent Australia in Test Matches against Canada. The first-ever Australian representative players were:

Fred Delves (Victoria)	– Goalkeeper	Ern Gooden (S A.)	– Point
Bill Bryning (Victoria)	– Home	Charlie Graham (Victoria)	– Left Defense
Bill Noblet (S.A)	– Right Attack	Les Jones (S.A)	– Cover Point
Vic Steet (Victoria)	– Right Defense	Alby Taylor (S.A)	– Right Home
Fred Kell (S.A)	– Centre	Lou Humphris (S.A)	– Left Home
Bert Mann (S.A)	– Left Attack	Charlie Hughes (S.A)	– Third Man
Albert Box (Victoria)	– Attack	Jack Hutcheon (QLD)	– Attack
Bert Bryning (Victoria)	– Defense	Ollie Thorpe (Queensland)	– Attack
Allan Presgrave (SA)	– Attack	Arthur Rudd (S A)	– Defense

13 – CLUB DEVELOPMENT, CHAMPIONSHIPS AND WOMEN'S LACROSSE

In 1905, Phillip L. Smith from Adelaide became the first player from Australia to play in the USA when he joined the San Jose Lacrosse Club in California as a goalkeeper and subsequently played with San Jose against the Canadian team prior to their departure for Australia in early 1907. Writing to a friend in Australia in 1907, Smith commented: [29]

> *"There are plenty of men in Australia, if given the advantages of the training that the American club members have, would easily out-general the best Canadian players in science and speed. One item the Yankees attach a great deal of importance to is standing a few yards from a brick wall or side of a house and shooting the ball thereon, and catching it as it rebounds. This quickens one's eye to a remarkable degree".*

Among the administrators of this period, the standout contributors who occupied key Executive positions in honorary capacities were:

New South Wales:	Clive Gurnett, Cullen-Ward
Queensland:	Frank Hambleton, Bill Morrison, James Thorpe, Ted Macartney
South Australia:	G. Moyston Evans, George Auld, Henry Hodgetts, R.F Wyly
Tasmania:	J A Huston, Dr L. Grey Thompson, H.T Barry, H.C Littler George Bowe, H. Ford, G.W.R Ife, F.S Hanton,
Victoria:	Phil Shappere, Dan White, Walter Forster, Joel Fox, Bill Lampard
Western Australia:	Wilfred Stow. Fred Wingrove, Ernie Harvey, Gil Clarke, Ike Taylor and Clive Hickey.

Referee Associations were formed in each State during the period prior to the World War, almost without exception comprising retired players. Playing Rules were a subject for regular discussion during this period, although they remained relatively constant from 1903 and any changes came only after discussion and agreement between the states at conferences held in conjunction with Interstate events. An overview of Playing Rules between 1876-1920 is contained in Appendix 1 along with a copy of the original rules.

Beginnings of Women's Lacrosse in Australia

When lacrosse was introduced into Great Britain in 1862, it quickly began to be taken up as a sport for men. Educationists and some media commentators saw a broader role for the sport and recognized that the unique combination of skills and attributes were equally valid for girls and women.

The 1863 Chambers Journal article (see Appendix 2), praised the sport and supported the case for its adoption by women.

Some time passed before the call to lacrosse was heard and taken up by females, but the start came in a somewhat cloistered way in girls' schools, where girls could enjoy the running athleticism of the game away from the prying gaze of males. This fitted the social mores and political correctness of the

Choice of Sports for Women

times. The thinking was that active outdoor team sports were important for the physical and social development of girls but were not suitable to be overtly displayed to the opposite gender. Accordingly, lacrosse, and other 'non-genteel' sports, were fine for girls while at school but should be abandoned once they left school for more demure recreations such as tennis, golf and bowls. Some commentators considered sports such as lacrosse and hockey to be too rough and boisterous for girls.

In an article reprinted in the Sydney Mail in July, 1914, Clementina Cornbloom, an English columnist, reviewed the choice of sports available to women at the time, noting the *'fervent shout of the lacrosse player as she valiantly and feverishly propounds her many and definite reasons for the superiority of lacrosse'*.[30] After arguing the pros and cons of the various sports, Cornbloom concluded that golf was the ideal game for women.

In Australia, there are un-documented reports of lacrosse being played as an activity within the sports curricula in private girl's schools during the late colonial years in Melbourne and possibly elsewhere.

What is clear, is that Miss Gwynneth Morris, an English woman physical educationist, did introduce lacrosse into the Melbourne Church of England Girls' Grammar School in 1906. She is quoted in later years as recalling [31]....

> *"There was in my sport's kit a cherished 'crosse' with which I had played for my college in England. I had just completed a course of training at Kingsfield, Kent. Having had hockey firmly established at the M.C.E.G.G.S, I next turned my attention to lacrosse. I obtained 24 crosses from Canada and soon the senior girls were really keen. Among those who played regularly and keenly at the school were the Percy sisters, Vera Deakin and several others. As none of the other girls' schools in Melbourne took the game up, and I did not consider it advisable to allow mixed matches, the game was dropped after some years.... Though to my mind it is the most strenuous, it is my first choice among all the games in which we were trained as students. We had professional coaches in England. For lacrosse our coach was a Canadian, who came to Kent every winter. The game was played with enthusiasm by the Southern Counties Club (women) and by some of the girls' schools long before the war".*

Morris had been exposed to lacrosse when she studied physical education in London under Madame Osterberg, the famed physical educationist and women's suffrage advocate. In Melbourne, Morris became the pioneer of the Swedish 'gymnastic system' in Victoria. Under her guidance, MCEGGS adopted the policy of organized games as an important part of the development of a girl's character,

13 – CLUB DEVELOPMENT, CHAMPIONSHIPS AND WOMEN'S LACROSSE

promoting self-reliance, self-control and teamwork. Speaking at the 25th Anniversary of the school in 1928, Morris recalled:

> *"In those days the girls played lacrosse and cricket in front of Old Fairlie, the old wooden bungalow with heavy wooden shutters which stood next to Merton Hall, and had been acquired as an overflow house for boarders"* [32]

From time to time, newspaper reports were published in Australia about girls playing lacrosse in England and, in May, 1911, an action photograph of women's lacrosse appeared in the Sydney 'Sun'.[33]

In 1913, an account was given in the 'Saturday Arrow and Referee' in Sydney featuring the first Women's International lacrosse contest played between England and Scotland at Richmond, England. England won the match 7 goals to 3. An indication of the relative size of various sports in the south of England at this time can be gauged from a survey of men's and women's games played on the open spaces under the control of the London County Council during the year ended 30 September, 1912: [34]

Ladies Lacrosse in England 1911
Bedford College versus Southern Ladies Lacrosse Club

Bowls	12,314	Hockey	1988
Cricket	19,730	Lacrosse	69
Croquet	1508	Lawn Tennis	136
Football	13,231	Quoits	4,060

Lacrosse for girls and women was introduced in Scotland at St Andrews College in 1890 and became well-patronized in the Independent Girls Schools of England, Wales and Scotland during the 1890's. There was considerable media debate about the most appropriate sports for females and many regarded lacrosse as too physical and dangerous. Others labelled lacrosse as the ideal sport for females due to its dexterity, all-round athleticism and other qualities.

The first Women's Lacrosse Club in Australia was established at Kogarah in south Sydney, New South Wales in August of 1913.[35] This was the St Georges Ladies Lacrosse Club, pioneered by young women who had been supporters, spectators and family members of the St George men's team. The women were helped by three local men from the St George club, Cec Hatfield, Stan Meyer and Phil Larbalestier. Meyer was a NSW representative player and experienced coach. Hatfield had played with Marrickville before helping to found the St George Club in 1911.

From the outset, women's lacrosse faced disbelief and resistance from some men players who regarded the game as too strenuous and rough for women.

LACROSSE IN AUSTRALIA

The National Advocate reported on the formation of the new ladies' team at Kogarah saying [36] ...

> *"The costume consists of very short pleated crimson skirts and bloomers, and cream blouses. It is not certain that the club will continue on its way serenely, as lacrosse is not a very suitable game for girls. Heads get knocked, and tempers get ruffled".*

Writing as "Maple", in the *St George Call*, one commentator, who was a member of the St George men's club, commented disparagingly about the "Skirts" competition being suspended due to wet weather. [37]

"Point", writing in the Referee newspaper commented that [38]...

> *"Sydney claims the doubtful distinction of pioneers in ladies" lacrosse. ....'Point' wishes the ladies the best of success, but has grave doubts as to whether a strenuous field game like lacrosse is adapted to the requirements of a ladies' pastime."*

Molly Bates, the Treasurer and Press Secretary of the newly formed St Georges Ladies Club responded with an assertive retort, making it very clear that the women were determined to play lacrosse and were committed to running their own affairs.[39]

> *To the Editor of "The Call"*
>
> *Sir,*
>
> *One wonders after reading his occasional remark upon the local ladies' lacrosse club, whether 'Maple' would classify himself as a "sport". Certainly, his remarks are not of the encouraging, go-in-and-win variety that one would expect an enthusiast like 'Maple' to display towards the first ladies' team in the Commonwealth.*
>
> *Until this season the members of the ladies' club have followed up the St George team as barrackers, and supported them in every way possible. It seems strange that when the ladies take up the game themselves, they are not met with the unanimous support and approval from the team they so ably supported.*
>
> *In its modified form, lacrosse is an excellent game for girls- we quote a well-known medico – and though public opinion was at first against us, we are gradually adding to our supporters. 'Maple' would be well advised, therefore, to cease his pessimistic remarks and join the majority.*
>
> *His recent remarks reflect on the membership roll. As we have seventeen members enrolled, we fail to see why we are not entitled to help in the formation of an association.*
>
> *Should 'Maple' doubt this, I will forward a list of the members' names and addresses. He can then add a little Sherlock Holmes brilliance to his many (?) abilities and verify my statement.*
>
> *Yours, etc.,*
>
> *MOLLY M BATES*
>
> *Hon. Sec.*
>
> *St George Ladies' Lacrosse Club*

13 – CLUB DEVELOPMENT, CHAMPIONSHIPS AND WOMEN'S LACROSSE

A second ladies club in Sydney followed soon after at Manly and the two ladies' clubs commenced practice sessions to build their stick skills. When the opportunity come to play a match as a curtain-raiser to the men's Sydney v Mosman match at Hampden Oval on the 23rd August, 1913, the women agreed despite being given very short notice.

Active publicity suddenly brought them a dream opportunity. Pathe's Gazette, an international company which produced newsreel documentaries for screening in public cinemas, listed the first ladies' lacrosse match played in Australia on its program for Monday, 28th August 1913 at the Sydney Crystal Palace.[40]

This had the hallmarks of a Cinderella start. The Crystal Palace, modelled on its famous London counterpart, was a wonderous new entertainment venue in central Sydney. The Palace was opened in June, 1912 and drew large audiences to a diverse range of public entertainments, including movie films. For women's lacrosse to get on the Pathe's billing for its very first game in Australia was an extraordinary coup. Unhappily, it did not happen as the match had to be postponed when the ladies could not get sufficient players together at the short notice.

This was not the first movie screening of lacrosse in Australia as the Brittania Theatre in Melbourne had screened action images from the Australian Carnival in August, 1912 and the Princes Theatre in Launceston, Tasmania, had featured a Pathe's Gazette news clip showing images from the 1913 Men's Interstate lacrosse between South Australia and New South Wales on 15th October 1913.[41] Other men's lacrosse matches were screened around Australia in 1913 and 1914. Disappointingly, none of this historic film footage has been preserved.

When the Sydney Ladies' match was played a few weeks later, the result was a 2-all draw. This was the first-ever known club match between women's lacrosse teams in Australia.[42] The Manly women kept practicing until November before going into a summer recess, determined to return stronger for a competition season in 1914.

During April of 1914, two ladies' teams were practising at Manly and Annie Hatfield was developing a new team at Fort Street Girls High School, a prominent public secondary school located at Observatory Hill in central Sydney, close to the later Sydney Harbour Bridge.[42] The 'Fortians' soon developed a club under the name of Karweens, a locality name in Kogarah. Lacrosse was making a mark and media commentary indicated that it was becoming fashionable for girls to own and carry a lacrosse stick, whether or not they played. Practice matches were arranged between these groups and the St George ladies during June and, with five teams assured, the time had come to establish a coordinating association.

The New South Wales Ladies Lacrosse Association (NSWLLA) was formed at a meeting on Wednesday, 12, May, 1914, with five teams affiliated.[43] The elected officials were:

Chairman: Miss Jessie Walker

Treasurer: Miss Maloney

Secretary: Miss Slater

Press Secretary: Miss M. Bates

The nomenclature of 'Ladies Association', rather than 'Women's Association', pointedly reflected the sensitivities around the branding of female sport in this era. The five teams affiliated with the inaugural NSWLLA were St George, Manly 1, Manly 2, Kareens and Bexley. The playing rules of the NSWLA were adopted with two amendments: the field shortened to 80 yards between the goals and the playing time shortened to two halves of 20 minutes.[44] A weekly competition to commence on Saturday, 11th July was agreed, comprising one round of matches followed by a semi-final and a final. By the time the competition started, a new group at the Cleveland Street, Sydney Girls' High School had formed and chose to play the team having a bye rather than formally joining the competition. The Ladies' matches were played at Moore Park, in central Sydney, and at Manly Oval and Hampden Oval. The Kareens Club quickly established itself as the competition leaders and went unbeaten to win Australia's inaugural premiership in women's lacrosse by 8 goals to 4 over Manly, on Saturday 5th, September. Brief reports and results of ladies matches during the season were included in Sydney newspapers, generally as additions to the reporting of men's lacrosse.

Good cooperation existed between the ladies and the NSWLA, and in July of 1914, joint communications were had with lacrosse in New Zealand where an active women's section had been developed in 1911. Arrangements were made for men's and women's teams from New South Wales to tour New Zealand for international competition in July.[45] This would have been the first-ever women's international lacrosse activity for Australia. Ultimately, this tour did not proceed due to difficulties in securing ship passages as the world became unsettled in the lead up to war.

Later, in August, the ladies played an exhibition match during the half-time interval at the men's interstate match between NSW and Queensland. Queensland lacrosseurs expressed interest in starting the sport for ladies in Brisbane and the prospect of NSW visiting Brisbane in 1915 for Interstate Ladies matches was discussed.[46]

The Ladies Association competition continued in 1914 with teams from Manly, St George, Olympians and Kareens (2 teams). Matches commenced in June but newspaper accounts were scant and the competition fizzled to a conclusion in July as national attention turned to the war effort. The sport had been taken up as a girl's sport in some secondary schools at this time and persisted between 1917 and 1919. During May of 1917, a Field Day for girls' winter sports, organized by educational authorities,

13 – CLUB DEVELOPMENT, CHAMPIONSHIPS AND WOMEN'S LACROSSE

included lacrosse matches involving Fort Street Girls High School and North Sydney High School. Later, the Girls' High Schools Sports Association conducted a promotional day on Wednesday 16, July 1919 in which the following girls' lacrosse matches featured:[47]

> Sydney versus Petersham at Undercliffe
>
> St George versus Cleveland Street (Sydney Girls High School) at the Domain
>
> Fort Street High School versus North Sydney at Birchgrove Oval
>
> Parramatta - bye

War put a hold on the ambitious plans of the NSW Ladies but they had demonstrated how energetic they could be in advancing the sport. Regrettably, the New South Wales activity failed to spur other Australian states and failed to replicate the success achieved in British schools where lacrosse grew as a popular sport of choice for schoolgirls. Unfortunately, no known photographs of the Ladies' Club teams of this era have been preserved. Queensland showed interest in starting women's lacrosse in 1914 but nothing eventuated. Far away in Jamestown, South Australia, attempts were made to establish lacrosse for women. A club was formed in 1914 and a set of lacrosse sticks were passed over to this club by the men's team. Some practice sessions took place but there were insufficient players and the war came to dry up interest.[48]

It seems likely that, without the intervention of the war, women's lacrosse may have grown out of the New South Wales nucleus in 1913 and spread into other states and into international competition. Another twenty years passed before women's lacrosse was revived in New South Wales and initiated in Victoria and South Australia. Another fifty years would pass before Interstate Women's competition was established. International lacrosse for Australian women took sixty years to come.

Notes

1. Australasian (Melbourne) 20/06/1908 p.37
2. Ruddell, Trevor. Little Brother of War, Lacrosse at the MCG. The Yorker, Journal of the Melbourne Cricket Club Library, Autumn 2017 p.27
3. The Argus (Melbourne) 18/03/1909 p.7
4. Letter to the VLA from Ronald Gibbs,1991
5. Letter from Ronald Gibbs to the VLA,1991
6. The Age 6/06/1894 p.6
7. Advertiser (Footscray) 9/05/1914 p.2
8. Independent (Footscray) 23/05/1914 p.3
9. Advertiser (Footscray) 27/03/1915 p.4
10. Winner (Melbourne) 16/06/1915 p.4
11. VLA Annual Report 1935
12. Observer (Adelaide) 3/08/1912 p.30
13. The Mirror (Perth) 20/08/1909 p.15
14. The Sunday Sun (Sydney) 18/07/1909 p.1
15. The Sydney Mail & NSW Advertiser 30/12/1908 p. 1708
16. Examiner (Launceston) 16/09/1907 p.3
17. The Mercury (Hobart) 16/08/1909 p.6
18. The Mercury (Hobart) 31/08/1914 p.3
19. Express & Telegraph (Adelaide) 15/07/1910 p.6
20. The Advertiser (Adelaide) 11/06/1910 p.18
21. The Advertiser (Adelaide) 04/07/1910 p.8
22. The Herald (Melbourne) 23/08/1912 p.3
23. Labor Call (Melbourne) 15/08/1912 p.9
24. The Herald (Melbourne) 22/08/1912 p.2
25. The Age (Melbourne) 24/08/1912 p.6
26. Australasian 31/08/1912 p.67
27. Examiner (Launceston) 16/10/1912 p.7
28. Punch (Melbourne) 16/09/1919 p.30

29. Daily Telegraph (Launceston) 24/07/1908 p.7
30. Sydney Mail 29/07/1914 p.9
31. Argus (Melbourne) 11/06/1936 p.4
32. Argus (Melbourne) 14/04/1928 p.8
33. Sun (Sydney) 12/05/1911 p.9
34. Newcastle Mining Herald & Miner's Advocate 10/05/1913 p.15
35. The Sydney Morning Herald 18/08/1913 p.11
36. National Advocate (Bathurst) 12/09/1913 P.1
37. St George Call (Kogarah) 25/07/1914 p.5
38. Referee (Sydney) 24/06/1914 p.4
39. St George Call (Kogarah) 27/06/1914 p.2
40. The Sun (Sydney) 24/08/1913 p.12
41. St George Call (Kogarah) 16/08/1913 p.7
42. The St George Call (Kogarah) 16/05/1914 p.4
43. The Daily Telegraph (Sydney) 22/05/1914 p.7
44. The Sydney Morning Herald 25/05/1914 p.12
45. Referee 19/08/1914
46. Referee 2/09/1914 p.9
47. Evening News (Sydney) 18/05/1917 p.4
48. Critic (Adelaide) 23/06/1915 p.11

14

The Wartime Years

When war on Germany was declared by Britain on the 4th of August, 1914, Australia and other countries that were part of the British Empire, were drawn into the conflict.

By this time of the year, the various State-based club competitions for lacrosse were advancing towards their finals and their season conclusions. Some clubs lost players to the war effort late in the 1914 playing season but there was little disruption to the competitions and the year was, in general, a vibrant one for lacrosse. Interstate lacrosse continued in August, 1914 when a team from Victoria visited Tasmania and played matches in Launceston and Hobart, but the VLA was shocked and unhappy when the SALA announced in August that it was abandoning the proposed visit of a South Australian team to Melbourne.

Recruitment

Young men who enlisted in the Australian Forces for World War 1, did so of their own choosing. There was no conscription although there was considerable community expectation that able-bodied young men should join the cause in the interests of supporting their country. For many, the prospect of joining with their mates to travel overseas and fight for Australia and The Empire, seemed like an enticing adventure. That rosy picture changed as the war progressed and reports came home of the suffering, injuries and deaths being experienced.

Sportsman were especially targeted for enlistment by the Australian Government as they contained physically fit young men with athletic skills. Special "Sportsmen's Posters", as displayed below, were used in recruiting drives. Lacrosse is depicted in each of these posters, either with a player using a lacrosse stick or by a lacrosse stick incorporated into a logo.

On the 10th of February, 1915, the Melbourne Cricket Club convened a meeting of all sporting organizations at the Melbourne Town Hall. The purpose of the meeting was to support the Australian Government and rouse sporting bodies to get their able-bodied members to enlist. The outcome of this meeting was the formation of a Recruitment Committee, on which lacrosse was represented, with a target to recruit six units of 150 men under the banner of the Sportsmen's 1000.[1] The advantage of recruits joining this program was that friends could enlist together, train together, embark together and fight together.

Lacrosse pride came to the fore when reports came home from the battlefields that Canadian lacrosse players were prized for their skills in launching grenades at German troop positions using their lacrosse sticks. The lacrosse stick, in the hands of an experienced player, enabled grenades to be thrown accurately over long distances. This news was widely reported around Australia and even featured in the Charters Towers "Evening Telegraph", in North Queensland on the 17th of July, 1915: [2]

> *"The sporting proclivities of the young men of the British Empire amaze the Germans, who pretend to see in the Anglo-Saxon love of sport a sign of national degeneration. But sport has its uses, even at the front. It is interesting to learn that some of the Canadian troops at the front use lacrosse sticks for throwing hand grenades into the German trenches, and are able in this way to throw them further and more accurately, and with less risk than otherwise. This is a fine testimony to the practical value of lacrosse, which is the national game of Canada".*

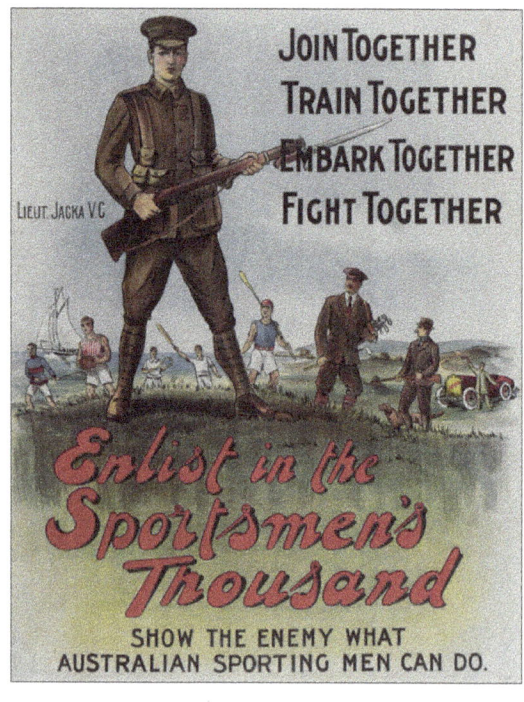

Enlistments

Lacrosse experienced high levels of enlistment by comparison with most sports. A proportion in the order of 70%-80% of players of military age, who were classed as fit for service, responded to the call in each State. In these circumstances, the capacity for clubs to field teams for club competitions was severely stretched.

For the State Associations after 1914, the question of whether, and in what form, club and other lacrosse competitions would be continued, was a question for each Association.

The South Australian Lacrosse Association made an early decision to abandon its club competition midway into 1915 and did not play again until the end of hostilities. Early in the enlistment process, the North Adelaide and Port Adelaide clubs were hit hard with player losses and elected not to enter senior teams in the SALA competition for 1915. The five remaining clubs for the senior competition were East Torrens, Sturt, University, Holdfast Bay and Goodwood. After eleven rounds of matches, with teams playing short or giving walkovers, the SALA resolved to abandon all premiership matches and not award a premiership for 1915.[3] Sturt, the powerhouse club of the SALA, remained unbeaten and missed out on what would have been its 11th senior premiership since Federation. The decision to not conduct competitions was re-confirmed in 1916 and lasted until the war had finished. Seventy players had enlisted before the commencement of the 1915 season in April and, by the time the decision to abandon came, the number had grown to 170. Ultimately, in excess of 240 players out of South Australia's 350 players joined the war effort.

During April, 1916 the SALA compiled and published a listing of players who had enlisted for war service. The list contained 159 metropolitan players from Adelaide's nine clubs and a further 29 players from the various country-based clubs.

In Queensland, the player losses to enlistment were around 80% and the QLA followed South Australia in abandoning all competition from 1915 onwards.[4] The Chelmer Lacrosse Club had 8 of its 14 players enlist. Similar enlistment proportions were experienced in New South Wales but the NSWLA persisted with a reduced club competition in 1915 before deciding not to continue when the Hurstville club requested that the competition be abandoned in July, 1915.[5] In the Federal Lacrosse Club, one junior team reported 8 of its 12 players had enlisted and the remaining 4 had been prevented from joining due to the withholding of parental consent as they were under military age.

Western Australia maintained a skeleton competition for 1915 and abandoned its competitions afterwards until 1919. Lacrosse in Tasmania continued in 1915 with three teams playing in the Northern Association competition and three in the south. Launceston, the founding club of the Northern Association, was unable to field a team. The Northern competition was closed prematurely on the 31st July with unbeaten Tamar awarded the premiership.[6] The traditional North versus South match was played but the State club premiership between the North and South premier teams did not proceed.

14 – THE WARTIME YEARS

Circumstances in Victoria were different. The VLA, with some 800 participants, had the largest population of players in Australia, including a body of school-aged juniors. Two schools of thought emerged as to whether a competition should be conducted, causing some robust debates at the 1915 VLA Annual General Meeting in April. A motion to discontinue games was defeated on the grounds that there were junior and other players available and the best interests of keeping the game alive would be served by mounting a competition.[7] The matter was further considered at the 1916 Annual General Meeting of the VLA when it was decided that all matches would not be "premiership" games. A motion was passed at this meeting which introduced a series of restrictions on players and teams as follows: [8]

> "(1) During the season 1916, and for the currency of the present European war, or any extension thereof, no person shall be allowed to take part in any matches arranged by the Association if over the age of 21 years, unless such person has volunteered for active service with the Australian Expeditionary Forces, and has been rejected by the defence authorities, or, unless, in the opinion of a sub-committee of the Association, to be appointed for that purpose, the circumstances of such person are a sufficient justification for his failure to volunteer for active service when such sub-committee shall give to such person a certificate of permission to play for any period to be stated in such certificate. The period stated may, on application, be extended at the discretion of the sub-committee. The sub-committee shall observe secrecy in all respects concerning the circumstances of every applicant for a certificate.
>
> (2) Every club entering a team or teams for competitions arranged by the Association, shall supply with its nominations a list of the members proposed to constitute such team or teams, and shall state separately the names of proposed players who are over the age of 21 years, and state whether such have been rejected for active service with the Australian Expeditionary Forces.
>
> (3) Every person desiring a certificate under by-law (Resolution 1) shall make application therefor to the sub-committee in writing, and shall in such application state willingness to narrate his circumstances to such sub-committee."

Ultimately, over the course of the war years, some 600 players enlisted from Victoria, representing almost 80% of the military age members. A detailed, but incomplete, listing of players in each Victorian club who enlisted, and those who were killed or died, is contained in the 1919 VLA Annual Report. It records 590 enlistments and 62 deaths. [9] The clubs with the largest numbers of enlistments over the course of the war were Brighton Presbyterians (64), Canterbury (57), South Yarra (38), Hawthorn (38), Kooyong (36), Williamstown (35), Malvern (33), Coburg (27), Maribyrnong (26), Kew (26), Wanderers (25), University (25), Box Hill (21), Essendon (19), MCC (18) and Caulfield (16).

Impact and Aftermath

The extent of decline in player numbers arising from the World War is shown in Figure 1.

The steady expansion of the sport following Federation was suddenly and dramatically reversed by the war. The total population of participating players dropped from 2192 in 1914 to just 225 in

1918, a decline of 90%. The 225 players participating in 1918 were all in Victoria where the VLA had maintained a largely junior, skeleton competition.

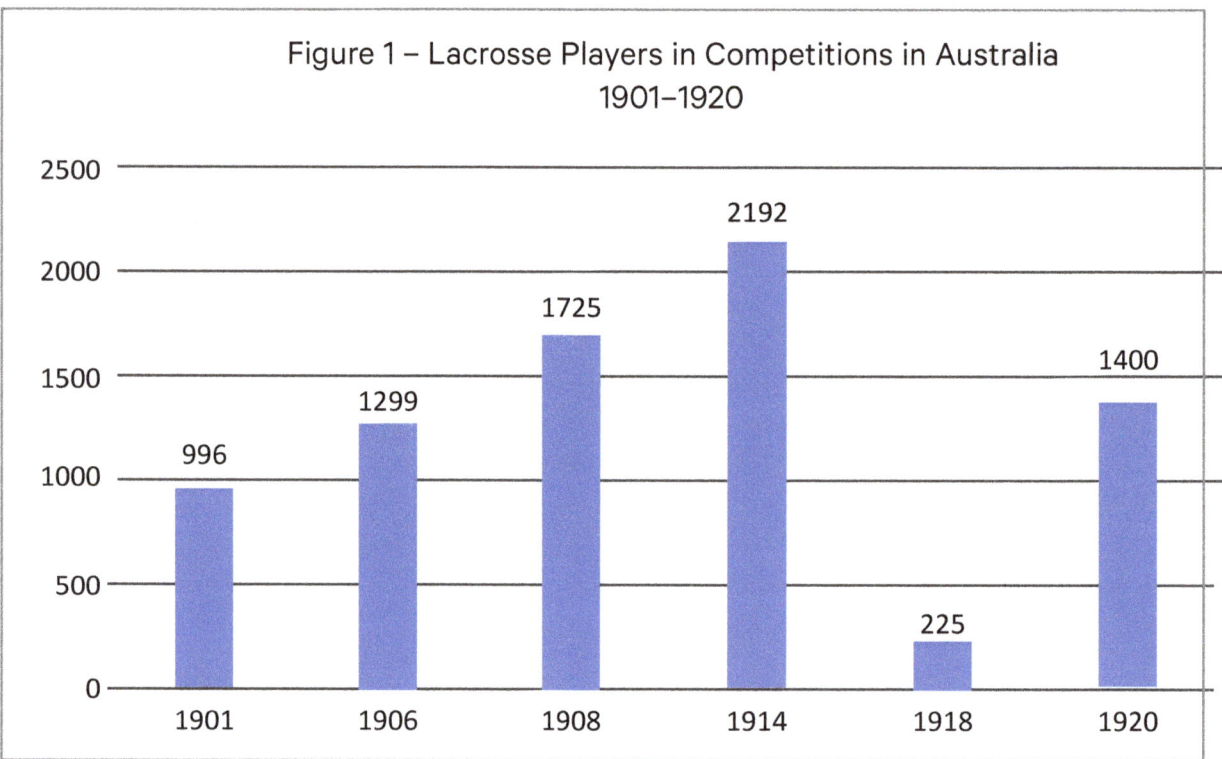

When the war ended on the 11th of November, 1918, the State Associations set about reviving the sport. The logistics of re-patriating soldiers from Europe, coupled with quarantine restrictions linked to a major European influenza outbreak, meant that the return home of soldiers and the rebuilding of the sport was hampered during 1919. As shown in Figure 1, 1400 players were again participating in competitions in 1920. The sport was alive again but the bounce-back had not been stunning. In essence, the game had been set back fifteen years.

Similarly, all clubs were set back and some were crippled, but the impact varied between the states. Table 1 and 2 reveal a severe impact on New South Wales, Queensland and Western Australia with a surprising resilience in South Australia, Tasmania and Victoria. The significant growth of new clubs shown for Victoria in 1920, was coupled with a major loss in team numbers, indicating a structural change rather than expansion. The club competition which the VLA maintained in 1915 comprised three senior sections with 23 teams and two junior sections with 10 teams. Lacrosse continued to be played in Melbourne throughout the remaining war years but the competition had dwindled to 11 teams by 1917. The Essendon and Coburg clubs were disbanded as a result of the war and other clubs were weakened, leading to amalgamations during the post-war years.

14 – THE WARTIME YEARS

	1901	1906	1908	1914	1918	1920
New South Wales	9 (13)	7 (7)	8 (8)	15 (22)	0	7 (12)
Broken Hill	4 (4)	3 (3)	6 (6)	4 (4)	0	0
Queensland	0	6 (6)	8 (13)	4 (4)	0	9 (12)
South Australia	8 (18)	7 (17)	8 (21)	10 (18)	0	10 (20)
SA Country	6 (6)	6 (6)	7 (7)	5 (5)	0	2 (2)
Tasmania	0	6 (6)	7 (8)	7 (7)	0	6 (6)
Victoria	9 (18)	9 (26)	13 (29)	15 (54)	9 (15)	19 (38)
Vic Country	0	0	1 (1)	1 (1)	0	0
Western Australia	5 (9)	9 (15)	9 (18)	6 (8)	0	4 (4)
WA Goldfields	2 (2)	4 (4)	4 (5)	0	0	0
Total	43 (70)	57 (90)	71 (116)	74 (140)	9 (15)	57 (94)

Table 1: Total Number of Lacrosse Clubs and Teams in Australia, 1901-1920

	1901	1906	1908	1914	1918	1920
NSW Men	255	150	210	390	0	180
NSW Women	0	0	0	85	0	60
Queensland	0	90	195	315	0	180
South Australia	306	345	420	345	0	330
Tasmania	0	90	120	105	0	90
Victoria	270	339	450	832	225	500
Western Australia	165	285	330	120	0	60
Total	996	1299	1725	2192	225	1400

Table 2: Lacrosse Players in Competitions in Australia 1901-1920

One of the most pleasing aspects of the post-war rebuilding was the early return of Interstate competition in 1920 after an absence of five years.

Four states embraced the opportunity of an Australian Lacrosse Carnival in Sydney in August 1920 and the team colours of Queensland, South Australia and Victoria once again graced the playing field alongside the host state.[10] South Australia showed they had lost nothing of their pre-war dominance by winning the Carnival with scores of 5 to 4 against Victoria, 8 to 6 against New South Wales and 8 to 6 against Queensland. Most of the premier pre-war players had been replaced and a new set of talent was presented by each state.

South Australia lacrosse Team – 1920 in Sydney

While Tasmania was not able to assemble a team for the 1920 Sydney Carnival, all but one of the former clubs in the island state were functioning again in Hobart and Launceston. The photograph below records the use of the marked centre circle during the face-off between Hobart and University in Hobart in 1920. The centre circle remained as part of the playing rules in Australia until the 1960's.

Hobart versus University 1920

14 – THE WARTIME YEARS

Recognition

Every State Association took steps after the war to acknowledge the sacrifices made by lacrosse players who enlisted to fight, and in so many cases, gave their lives.

Lists of players were published in newspapers and Annual Reports in each State and some states marked their recognition with impressive timber Honour Boards which recorded in gold leaf the names of lost and returned players from the various clubs.

Detailed listings for Victoria are recorded in the VLA Annual Report for 1919 and the main South Australian newspapers for the SALA. In Queensland, a project was undertaken to publish a booklet containing the photographs and brief war biographies for all enlisted members. The Western Australia, Honour Board (photograph courtesy of WALA) records the names of the 24 players who lost their lives and the total of 136 men who enlisted.[11]

At official Australian Government level, all men who served were awarded the Victory Medal and many received valour and other higher awards. These are all recorded in the records of the Australian War Museum, based in Canberra.

Also, a custom was established in 1919 of opening each new playing season with the assembled teams observing one minute of silence in honour of past players killed in protecting their country. This custom remains in Australian lacrosse today.

Western Australian Lacrosse Association Honour Board 1914-1918

Case Studies

Many lacrosse clubs lost players who were killed in action, some with outstanding records as players and administrators. Brief case studies of three men who paid the ultimate sacrifice are presented below to provide some further understanding of the impact of the war.

Private Thomas Anderson Whyte

Tom Whyte
Photograph Courtesy
Australian War Museum

Born in Unley, South Australia, in 1886, Tom Whyte was 28 years of age when he became one of the first men from South Australia to enlist in the Australian Infantry Forces on 19th of August, 1914. He was a member of "A" Company of the 10th Australian Battalion, which departed from Adelaide on the 20th of November, 1914. He was fatally wounded in action at Gallipoli during the first landing at the Dardanelles, died on board the HMHS "Gascon" on April 25, 1915 and was buried at sea. He was posthumously awarded the Victory Medal. All that came home from Gallipoli to his only brother was a brown paper parcel containing a safety razor, a cigarette case, a wristlet, some photos, letters and a pen.

Tom started his lacrosse with the Woodville "B" team in 1902 when he was aged 16 years.[12]

He subsequently became a leading player at Port Adelaide (when Woodville changed name) and later played with North Adelaide. Whyte served on his club Committee and on the SALA Committee and was highly regarded within the lacrosse community. Standing just under 6 feet in height and weighing 185 pounds, Whyte used his burly frame to great effect as a centre player and earned Interstate selection for South Australia on four separate occasions. Work commitments as a Sales Agent prevented him from taking up all of the opportunities to play Interstate lacrosse but he did play in 1909 against Victoria in Adelaide and against Tasmania in 1909. He was also an outstanding oarsman with the Mercantile Rowing Club in Adelaide and represented South Australia multiple times in Interstate rowing.

Soon after arriving at the Australian Army's Mena Base Camp in Egypt, Whyte was involved in the formation of a battalion lacrosse club. The club organized a match against a unit comprised mainly of Queenslanders and won by 11 goals to nil. The goals for this match were fashioned from groundsheets tied together and topped with flags.[13]

Whyte can claim to be the first Australian to play and captain Australia in an International lacrosse contest outside of

Aussie Diggers at the Mena Base Camp, Egypt 1915
Photograph Courtesy Australian War Museum

14 – THE WARTIME YEARS

Australia. While in pre-combat training at the Mena Base Camp, located in Egypt almost under the shadows of the Cheops Pyramid, a team of Australians was assembled for a match against an English team which took place in April, 1915. The English team included a number of players from the 1908 England team that competed in lacrosse at the London Olympic Games. They defeated the Aussies 30 goals to 6.[14]

The photograph of Tom Whyte, seated on one of the large stones of the Great Pyramid on the left, was taken at Giza, North Egypt, and is housed at the Australian War Museum.

The names of the players in the previous photograph are not recorded but the player wearing the Victorian State Team jersey is Austin Laughlin, a centre/ attack player from the Melbourne University club, and later Malvern, who represented Victoria in 1913 and scored the only goal in Victoria's 16-1 loss to South Australia. Following the war, Laughlin returned home as an Army Captain and one of the first lot of Australian Prime Minister, Billie Hughes "Anzac Heroes". He returned to lacrosse and played in the 1920 and 1922 Victorian Interstate Teams.

Tom Whyte sitting on the Great Pyramid, Giza, Egypt 1915
Photograph Courtesy Australian War Museum

Sergeant Noel "Bluey" Ridgway

Noel Ridgway a member of the 49th Australian Battalion, AIF was killed in the Battle of Messines in Belgium on the 7th of June 1917.

Aged 29 years at the time of his death, Bluey started lacrosse as an 18-year-old and progressed quickly to become a prominent player with the Buffalo Lacrosse Club in Brisbane from 1906-14, and a premiership player with the club in 1909. He was a high scoring attackman and also played in the centre. A Commercial Traveler by profession, Ridgway was a member of Queensland State Teams for five years between 1909, -1913, playing twelve games for his State, including participation in the first Australian Carnival in Adelaide in 1910 and the 1912 Melbourne Carnival series.

Among his teammates at Buffalo and in Queensland teams, were the best of Queensland's superstars of the time – Owen Thorpe, Jim Thorpe, Ray Darvall, Ron Pyke and others. Ridgway enlisted in the Army on the 14th of September 1915, was married on the 15th of October, and embarked for war duties on the 31st of January, 1916, never to return.

Noel 'Bluey' Ridgway

Sergeant-Major Harold George "Dick" Woodman

*Harold "Dick" Woodman
Image courtesy of Caulfield Lacrosse Club*

Dick Woodman was born on October 2, 1886 and enlisted in the Australian Infantry Forces on the July 5, 1915 with the 31st Battalion. He was killed in action at Fromelles in France on 21st of July, 1916. His body, along with a grave containing some 250 others, was only discovered recently and he was interred and re-buried at Villers-Brettoneux, France.

Woodman was an accountant by profession and one of the pioneer players in the 1909 team when the Caulfield Lacrosse Club was formed for the second time after lapsing in 1896. He served on the club committee and as a delegate to the VLA in 1914-15 and was appointed as a member of the VLA Rough Play Committee. When war forced the temporary merger of Caulfield with Malvern in 1915, Woodman became the club Secretary. The attached portrait was commissioned by work colleagues of his father and created by artist, Andrew Plant. It was presented to the Caulfield Lacrosse Club in 2017 and hangs today in the Caulfield clubrooms.

In the year before his enlistment, Woodman played in the Junior "A" premiership team for Caulfield and was regularly named in the best players for his role in defense. The group psyche of the times led large numbers of young men, who were mates in sporting teams and community settings, to make their decisions to enlist. This, and the devastating impact of the war on lacrosse clubs, is illustrated by the extraordinary circumstances of the Caulfield club which had eleven of Woodman's team-mates enlist for service during 1914-1916. Seven of this 1914 Caulfield team were killed in action.

None of this Caulfield group were career military men. All were citizens going about their regular jobs and enjoying the mate-ship of lacrosse on Saturdays. They all lived in Caulfield or neighboring Melbourne suburbs and started their military involvement with the enlisted rank of "Private". Each gained military rank promotions according to their experience and leadership as the war progressed. Each were awarded the Victory Medal and some received higher awards for bravery and leadership. Included in this lacrosse-playing group at Caulfield were:

Lance-Corporal Keith Looker, a 29-year-old bank clerk and the Caulfield team captain and goalkeeper. He enlisted on March 3, 1915, served at Gallipoli in the 22nd Battalion, became ill, and died of jaundice in Malta in November of 1915.

Lieutenant Ivon Carlston Bromilow, (attack player) of the 21st Battalion, Field Artillery Brigade, a 20-year-old railways clerk who followed his elder brother and enlisted on September 3, 1915. He died from wounds received in action on the Somme in France in November, 1916.

14 – THE WARTIME YEARS

Lieutenant Garnet Bainbridge, (midfield player), a 21-year-old clerk, enlisted December 11, 1914 and was severely wounded in action when serving with the 4th Battalion in France in September 1917. Garnet was returned to Australia in June, 1919.

Lieutenant Charles James Fulton, M.C., (attack player), 24 years, who enlisted on February 8, 1915 as a member of the 22nd Battalion. He served at Gallipoli and was awarded the Military Cross for gallantry and brave leadership when his Company was caught in heavy machine-gun fire during an attack. Later he served in France and was wounded and returned home in 1919.

Sergeant Charles William Alder, (centre player), 23-year-old motor mechanic who enlisted on September 17, 1914 and served in France with the 9th Battalion, 1st Anzac Supply Column. He returned home in November 1918 and was Mentioned in Dispatches for conspicuous service.

Private Joseph Stanley Bainbridge, a railways signal porter, enlisted on August 17, 1914 at 24 years of age and served with the 6th Battalion. He was killed at Gallipoli on May 8, 1915.

2nd Lieutenant, Alexander Roy Fulton, (attack player), 22- year-old clerk who enlisted on July 6, 1915. He served with the 8th Battalion in Alexandria and then in France and Belgium and was killed instantly in action when hit by a shell. He was initially buried in Ghuluvelt, Belgium and later re-buried at the New Irish Farm British Cemetery.

Corporal Allan Harrison, (midfield player), 19- year-old stoker who enlisted in September, 1914 and served in Egypt and France with the 14th Battalion. He was wounded in action at Gallipoli, died at sea on the 27th of May, 1915 and was buried at East Mudros Military Cemetery, Lemnos.

Corporal George Thomas Browne, a 27- year-old commercial traveler and crack attack player for the Caulfield team, who enlisted in September, 1915 and served with the 23rd Battalion before being discharged with a lung illness in June 1916.

Lance Corporal James Thorold Bromilow, (attack player), a bank clerk and elder brother of Ivon, enlisted on August 17, 1915 at 25 years of age. He served with the 7th Battalion and in the 1st Artillery Field Brigade in France before becoming ill and was returned to Australia and discharged in April, 1918.

2nd Lieutenant Norman Charles Nation, (defense player), a clerk who enlisted at the age of 27 years on December 3, 1915. He was assigned to the 24th Battalion and served in France and then Belgium where he was killed in action after being sniped in the head. He was buried at the British Cemetery at Passchendaele, Belgium.

A Player's Story

In 1972, the author, while holding office as Honorary Secretary of the Victorian Lacrosse Association, received two letters addressed to the Association from 90- year-old W.F (Bill) Furneaux, a past player. The letters, which are reproduced on the next page, provide a glimpse of the past and recount the story of a man who played continuously for 32 years, commencing in colonial times and extending through the Federation and war years. They capture, in a chatty and personal way, the essence of what it was like to play lacrosse in the pioneering years and the importance of the lifelong friendships and memories which lacrosse brings to many people.

Dear Sir

I am giving you an account of my association with the game of La Crosse which I played for about 32 years. I think this is a record, of which I am very proud. I think La Crosse the finest of any of the outdoor games. I had the honour of being associated with many wonderful sportsmen over a number of years. I would like to mention a few which come to mind. I have met, on and off the field, Sir John Latham, Hon. Harold Holt, W.B House, Phil Shappere, Joel Fox, Geo Beech, Rev Redhead, Watty Forster, Doctors Bruce Sutherland, Wally Summons, Hugh Murray, Sir Victor Hurley, Les Hurley, and also Geo Gay, Crom Hurley, Bob Coldstream, Beattie brothers, Captain Fearon, Alf Rudd, Dan White, Wally Lampard, Vern Ransford, Colonel J.E Jones, Noel Murray, Sid Wilson, Frank Smythe, Vic Bolderman and the Johnson brothers.

Bill Furneaux

I first played with Collingwood Club outside the Zoo in the Royal Park in 1895. I was 14 years old at that time. My father played with that team previous to this. I played with that Club for two years before they disbanded. I went to St Kilda Club who had just changed from South Melbourne. I was in the "B" team and in the first year I played with them we won the Premiership and the VLA Silver Badge. That was in 1897. Later I was promoted to the "A" team. I played with them at Albert Park where the present Middle Park Bowling Club is now situated. We used to undress in a room at the Hotel opposite the Middle Park Station. No showers or other facilities. Later we transferred to St Kilda Football Ground and played there for a few years until we lost the use of the ground. While playing here I was picked to play for Victoria against South Australia in Adelaide. That was 1911. Watty Forster was the VLA Secretary at that time, a wonderful worker although a cripple.

We then transferred to Hawksburn (later Prahran) Cricket Ground and changed our name to Hawksburn. I played there for a couple of years until they decided to go back to Middle Park to play. I was living in Prahran at that time. When I first played with St Kilda we were living near the corner of Chapel Street and Malvern Road and I used to walk from there around the Albert Park Lagoon (at the St Kilda end) to Middle Park and walk home again after playing the match. Transport was difficult in those days. I don't think they would do it these days.

I decided to join South Yarra Club who played in Fawkner Park opposite the Alfred Hospital. We used to strip in the Christ Church gymnasium at the corner of Punt Road and Toorak Roads and walk across the park to the playing ground. The first year I played I was fortunate to be a member of the premiership team in 1912. For several years we held the Championship until the war broke out. A couple of years later we found it impossible to form one team although we had had six, so many of the members had volunteered

14 – THE WARTIME YEARS

for service. At that time, it was understood La Crosse players had the biggest percentage of volunteers of any sport who had volunteered for Service.

It looked as though this would be the end of my La Crosse career. I was married and had a family. Malvern La Crosse Club approached me and asked if I would be interested in assisting to keep the game alive. So many of the Clubs had disbanded it was difficult to keep the game going. I was with Malvern for a few years having played in premiership teams a couple of times. At that time, I was living in Caulfield and had an opportunity of going to the Caulfield Club who played in the Caulfield Park and was very near where I was living so I decided to join up with them. I played on for a few more years and then decided I was getting too old to play such a strenuous game, so I gave it away after playing continuously for 32 years. I can look back and think what a wonderful time I had playing with a wonderful lot of sportsmen.

Yours,

Will Furneaux

PS. I have turned 90 years and still play Pennant bowls

Victorian Lacrosse Team in Sydney 1904
Furneaux is seated in the front row, second from the left

Dear Sir

About 1909, St Kilda was playing University on the University Oval. I was playing First Home. Jack Latham (afterwards Sir John and Australia's Attorney-General), was playing Point. During the week I was training and sprained my ankle. I went on to the ground with my ankle well strapped up. The referee, Wally Lampard, cautioned me he would not equalize the sides (which was the rule) if my ankle broke down. It did, at which time of the game I don't remember. He blew the whistle and stopped the game. He told Jack there was no need for him to go off as he had warned me before the game started. Jack insisted to take me to the dressing room and get the ankle bandaged but he did not return to play – Good sport!

Bill Furneaux.

Bill Furneaux was a prolific scoring attackman in Victoria and enjoyed a successful career spanning more than three decades. He followed his father in becoming an Interstate player for Victoria and played with five different clubs. Along the journey he collected multiple VLA premiership medals which varied in design and colour from year to year, as shown below.

His story, as contained in these letters, epitomizes the qualities and experiences of the many people who place high value on the sport of lacrosse. His story provides a fitting finale to this book.

Notes

1. The Argus (Melbourne) 11/02/1915 p.6
2. Evening Telegraph (Charters Towers) 17/02/1915 p.5
3. Referee (Sydney) 19/04/1916 p.10
4. Register (Brisbane) 12/04/1916 p.8
5. Brisbane Courier 26/04/1919 p.11
6. Daily Telegraph (Launceston) 23/07/1915 p.7
7. Minutes of VLA Annual General Meeting 1915
8. Minutes of VLA Annual General Meeting 1916
9. VLA Annual Report 1919
10. Observer (Adelaide) 4/09/1920 p.17
11. Toy I. 2016 A History of the Western Australian Lacrosse Association p.19
12. Observer (Adelaide) 8/05/1915 p.39
13. The Express & Telegraph (Adelaide) 25/03/1915 p.7
14. The Mail (Adelaide) 15/05/1915 p.5

Postscript

By the time that the wartime years concluded in 1918 and lacrosse began an unsteady recovery, the national framework for the sport was well-established.

Participation had been established in the city capitals of each Australian State and some populous regional areas. Winter club competitions coordinated by autonomous associations were operating efficiently and a vibrant program of Interstate contests were regularly played. International lacrosse came to Australia in 1907 when a team from Canada toured for almost three months. Women's lacrosse had made a small, but significant, start in 1913 and appeared set for national expansion before the World War came to interrupt the momentum. More than one attempt had been made to establish a national body to coordinate the sport but the formula was never right and that challenge remained.

The story of the foundation years of lacrosse in Australia is one of passionate and gritty pioneers who stuck with lacrosse for the love of this unique sport.

This account of those first forty-five years is, of course, the prelude to a further century of amazing changes and development in the sport since 1920. That story remains to be documented.

For a time, around the early years of Australian Federation, lacrosse showed signs of out-positioning Australian football as the premier outdoor team game. Circumstances, and two world wars, combined to interrupt the advancement and prevent this from becoming reality.

Unfortunately, by the mid-1950s the sport had died out in the States of Queensland, New South Wales and Tasmania. Since then, spasmodic periods of revival have occurred and now these States, together with the Australian Capital Territory, each have small pockets of keen men's and women's participation. The southern States of Western Australia, South Australia and Victoria continue to have the bulk of the nation's lacrosse players.

Along the way, the hard-working administrators who guided the directions and growth of the sport missed some key opportunities that, with hindsight, may have propelled lacrosse to much higher prominence. The most telling of these were the decisions to not take up invitations for Australia to compete in the Olympic Games in 1908 and again in 1928. These decisions, made at the time on financial grounds, have cost the sport many millions of dollars of government support and the exposure and media promotions that have flowed to other sports in the modern era.

Since the 1960's, Australian lacrosse has steadily built a vibrant and respected international presence and is poised to be part of the Olympics. On 20 July 2021, the International Olympic Committee granted Full Recognition to World Lacrosse and cleared the way for lacrosse to take its place in the Olympic family. The indications are that the sport will be included in the program for the 2028 Games in Los Angeles, with competitions for both male and female teams. Our lacrosse communities look forward to this prospect with expectation and great hopes.

Although the main principles and excitement of lacrosse have remained largely constant throughout the years, the images of modern international lacrosse, both women's and men's, make a stark contrast to those of its colonial beginnings in Australia.

Sarah Mollison in a dodging attack for Australia against England

Ben Newman in action for Australia against the USA

APPENDIX 1

Playing Rules for Lacrosse

The playing rules of the Victorian Lacrosse Association as adopted in 1879 are reproduced below. These rules were based on the original rules developed by George Beers and adopted for play in Canada by the Montreal Lacrosse Club in 1867.

The VLA made some later amendments to playing rules in 1885 which are also reproduced below. As lacrosse spread to other colonies, the VLA rules were used with some minor amendments as determined by each colonial Association.

Following Australian Federation, meetings were held between the State Associations during gatherings for Interstate matches. A new set of rules was agreed nationally in 1903 and regular revisions have continued since that time, coordinated by the national Parent association since 1932.

The Original VLA Playing Rules of 1879
Reproduced courtesy of the Mitchell Library, State Library of New South Wales

THE
LAWS OF LA CROSSE

AS ADOPTED BY THE

VICTORIAN LA CROSSE ASSOCIATION,

Melbourne, 8th April, 1879.

Melbourne:
M'CARRON, BIRD & CO., PRINTERS, 37 FLINDERS LANE WEST.

APPENDIX 1 – PLAYING RULES FOR LACROSSE

THE LAWS OF LA CROSSE.

As Adopted by The Victorian La Crosse Association,
Melbourne, 8th April, 1879.

Rule 1.—THE CROSSE.

Sec. 1.—The Crosse may be any length to suit the player, woven with cat-gut, which must not be bagged. (Cat-gut is intended to mean raw hide, gut, or clock strings; not cord or soft leather). The netting must be flat when the ball is not in it. In its widest part the Crosse shall not exceed one foot. No string must be brought through any hole at the side of the tip of the turn. A leading string may be used, but must not be fastened so as to form a pocket lower down the stick than to the end of the length strings. The length strings must be woven to within two inches of their termination, so that the ball cannot catch in the meshes.

Sec. 2.—Players may change their Crosse during a match.

Rule II.—THE BALL.

The Ball must be India-rubber sponge, not less than eight and not more than nine inches in circumference. In matches it must be furnished by the Club on whose ground the match is to be played.

Rule III.—THE GOALS.

The goals may be placed any distance from each other, and in any position agreeable to the Captains of both sides. The top of the flag poles must be six feet above the ground, including any top ornaments, and six feet apart. In matches they must be furnished by the Club on whose ground the match is to be played.

4

Rule IV.—THE GOAL-CREASE.

There shall be a line or crease, to be called a goal-crease, drawn in front of each goal, six feet from the flag poles, within which no opponent must stand unless the ball has passed cover-point.

Rule 5.—UMPIRES.

Sec. 1.—There must be one Umpire at each goal, who must stand behind the flags when the ball is near or nearing the goal, and at the end opposite to that to which the side he is representing are throwing. Unless otherwise agreed upon by the Captains, they must not be members of either Club engaged in a match; nor shall they be changed during a match except for reasons of illness or injury. They must see that the regulations are complied with respecting the goals and goal-crease, and in deciding any of these points shall take the opinions of the Captains and the Referee. The jurisdiction of the Umpires shall not extend beyond deciding when a goal has been made, unless the Referee shall call upon them to decide, with him, a point in dispute.

Sec. 2.—No Umpire shall, either directly or indirectly, be interested in any bet upon the result of the match. No person shall be allowed to speak to the Umpires, or in any way distract their attention when the ball is near or nearing their goal.

Sec. 3.—Should time be called by the Referee, and after Umpire has left his post the ball should enter the goal, it will not count.

Sec. 4.—The Umpire's decision in all matters over which he has control, shall be final.

Rule VI.—THE REFEREE.

The Captains shall select a Referee, whose duty it shall be, at the commencement of a match, to see that all the regulations respecting the ball, crosse, spiked soles, &c., are complied with, and shall indicate a place as near the centre of the ground as can be arrived at, where the ball shall be "faced" for. He must know before the commencement of a match up to what time the game is to be played, and punctually at the time decided upon he shall call "*Time.*" The Referee shall be on the ground during the match, and shall have power to settle all matters in dispute, and shall enforce the strict observance of the Rules hereinbefore and hereinafter contained; but in case a disturbance or an infringement of any of the Rules may occur at a time when his attention is otherwhere directed, he may, if he deems the matter of sufficient importance, call in the aid of the Umpires and the Captains to settle such dispute. The Referee has no right to express an opinion, and any expressed opinion must be taken as his decision. His first decision must in all cases be final.

Rule VII.—CAPTAINS.

Captains to superintend play may be appointed by each side previous to the commencement of a match. They shall be members of the Club by whom they are appointed, and no other. They may or may not be players in a match; if not, they shall not carry a crosse, nor shall they be dressed in La Crosse uniform. They shall select Umpires, and toss up for choice of goals. They shall report any infringement of the laws during a match to the Referee.

Rule VIII.—NAME OF PLAYERS.

The players of each side shall be designated as follows:—"Goal-keeper," who defends the goal; "Point," first man out from goal; "Cover-point," in front of point; "Centre," who faces; "Home." nearest opponent's goal. Others shall be termed fielders.

The Game.

Rule IX.—MISCELLANEOUS.

Sec. 1.—Thirteen players shall constitute a full field; but Secretaries of the Clubs engaged to play a match may agree between themselves to play a larger number of players.

Sec. 2.—A match shall be decided by the greatest number of goals got during the time the Captains have agreed upon to play.

Sec. 3.—The game shall be suspended for a rest of ten minutes by the Referee calling "Time" at five minutes to half the time agreed upon to play.

Sec. 4.—At the resumption of the game the players must change sides, and the ball shall be "faced for" in the centre of the ground as at the commencement of a match.

Sec. 5.—No change of players must be made after a match has commenced, except for reasons of accident or injury during a match, or upon an agreement made between the Captains. In case of one side being deficient in the number of players, their opponents may either limit their own numbers to equalize sides, or compel the other side to fill up the complement.

Rule X.—SPIKED SOLES.

No player must wear spiked soles.

Rule XI.—UNIFORM.

No player shall be allowed to take part in a match unless he be dressed in the uniform of his Club.

Rule XII.—TOUCHING THE BALL WITH THE HAND.

The ball must not be touched with the hand, save in case of Rules XIII. and XIV.

Rule XIII.—GOAL-KEEPER.

Goal-keeper, while defending goal within the goal-crease, may pat away with his hand or block the ball in any manner.

Rule XIV.—BALL IN AN INACCESSIBLE PLACE.

Should the ball lodge in any place inaccessible to the Crosse, it may be taken out by the hand, and the party picking it up must "face" with his nearest opponent.

Rule XV.—BALL OUT OF BOUNDS.

Ball thrown out of bounds must be picked up with the hand, and "faced" for at the nearest spot within bounds.

APPENDIX 1 – PLAYING RULES FOR LACROSSE

RULE XVI.—THROWING THE CROSSE.

No player shall throw his Crosse at a player or at the ball, under any circumstances.

RULE XVII.—ACCIDENTAL GAME.

Should the ball be accidentally put through a goal, by one of the players defending it, it is game for the side attacking that goal. Should it be put through a goal by any one not actually a player, it shall not count.

RULE XVIII.—BALLS CATCHING IN THE NETTING.

Should the ball catch in the netting, the Crosse must immediately be struck on the ground so as to dislodge it.

RULE XIX.—ROUGH PLAY, &c.

No player shall hold another with his Crosse, nor shall he grasp an opponent's stick with his hands, under his arms, or between his legs; nor shall any player hold his opponent's Crosse with his Crosse in any way, to keep him from the ball until another player reaches it. No player shall deliberately strike or trip another, nor push with the hand; nor must any player jump at to shoulder an opponent, nor wrestle with the legs entwined so as to throw his opponent.

RULE XX.—THREATENING TO STRIKE.

Any player raising his fist to strike another, shall immediately be ruled out of the match.

RULE XXI.—FOUL PLAY.

Sec. 1.—Any player considering himself purposely injured during play, must report to his Captain, who must report to the Referee, who shall warn the players complained of.

Sec. 2.—In the event of persistent fouling, after cautioning by the Referee, the latter may request the Captain to remove the offending player or players, and compel the side to finish the match short-handed.

Rule XXII.—INTERRUPTED MATCHES.

In the event of a match being interrupted by darkness, bad weather, or any circumstance whereby the Captains and Referee think it inadvisable to continue playing, such match shall be considered as drawn.

Rule XXIII.—FLAG-POLE KNOCKED DOWN.

In the event of a flag-pole being knocked down during the game; and if, in the opinion of the Umpire, the ball shall pass through what would be the goal, were the flag-pole standing, it will count for the side who are putting to that goal.

Rule XXIV.—DISPUTES NOT PROVIDED FOR.

In the event of any dispute arising not provided for in these Rules, the Referee shall, at the time and place of the occurrence of such dispute, decide thereon. Either of the parties to the dispute, considering such decision not to be in accordance with the facts of the case, may, however, appeal, by handing to the Secretary of of the Association, within at least seven days from the occurrence such dispute, a written document setting forth the nature of the dispute, and all particulars thereto appertaining. The Association shall, at their first meeting after receipt of such document, or at any subsequent meeting as they may decide, proceed to adjudicate thereon.

Rule XXV.—AMENDMENTS.

Any amendment or alteration proposed to be made in any part of these Laws shall be made only at a meeting of the Association specially called for the purpose; and by a three-fourths vote of the members present at such meeting.

M'Carron, Bird and Co. Printers, 37 Flinders Lane West, Melbourne.

APPENDIX 1 – PLAYING RULES FOR LACROSSE

The VLA Playing Rules adopted in 1885

6

THE LAWS OF LACROSSE.

As adopted by the Association, 8th April, 1879, and revised, 2nd March, 1885.

RULE I.—THE CROSSE.

Sec. 1.—The Crosse may be any length to suit the player, woven with cat-gut, which must not be bagged. (Cat-gut is intended to mean raw hide, gut, or clock strings; not cord or soft leather). The netting must be flat when the ball is not in it. In its widest part the Crosse shall not exceed one foot. A string must be brought through a hole at the side of the tip of the turn. A leading string may be used, but must not be fastened so as to form a pocket lower down the stick than to the end of the length strings. The length strings must be woven to within two inches of their termination, so that the ball cannot catch in the meshes.

Sec. 2.—No kind of metal, either in wire or sheet, nor screws or nails to stretch strings shall be allowed upon the crosse. Splices must be made with either string or gut.

Sec. 3.—Players may change their Crosse during the match

RULE II.—THE BALL.

The Ball must be India-rubber sponge, not less than seven and three-quarters, nor more than eight inches in circumference, and from 4½ to 5 ounces in weight. In matches it must be furnished by the Club on whose ground the match is to be played.

RULE III.—THE GOALS.

The top of the flag poles must be 8 feet above the ground, including any top ornaments, and 6 feet apart. In matches they must be furnished by the Club on whose ground the match is to be played, and shall be placed so that the playing ground shall not be less than 150 yards, nor more than 200 yards in length.

RULE IV.—BOUNDARIES.

The width of the playing ground shall be 100 yards, marked by boundary flags, to be provided by the Club on whose ground the match is played.

RULE V.—THE GOAL-CREASE.

There shall be a line or crease, to be called a goal-crease, drawn in front of each goal, six feet from the flag poles, within which no opponent shall stand unless the ball has passed cover-point's position in the field, which shall be defined by a straight line drawn 18 feet in front of each goal.

RULE VI.—UMPIRES.

Sec. 1.—There must be one Umpire at each goal, who must stand behind the flags when the ball is near or nearing the goal, and at the end opposite to that to which the side he is representing are throwing. Unless otherwise agreed upon by the Captains, they must not be members of either Club engaged in a match; nor shall they be changed during a match except for reasons of illness or with the consent of both Captains. They must see that the regulations are complied with respecting the goals, goal-crease, and cover point-crease, and in deciding any of these points shall take the opinions of the Captains and the Referee. The jurisdiction of the Umpires shall not extend beyond deciding when a goal has been made, unless the Referee shall call upon them to decide, with him, a point in dispute.

Sec. 2.—No Umpire shall, either directly or indirectly, be interested in any bet upon the result of the match. No person shall be allowed to speak to the Umpires, or in any way distract their attention when the ball is near or nearing their goal.

Sec. 3.—No Umpire shall be appointed who is objected to by either Captain, prior to the commencement of a match.

Sec. 4.—Should time be called by the Referee, before the ball enter the goal, it will not count.

Sec. 5. The Association may appoint Umpires and Referees for any match in which it may think fit to do so, and may disqualify any Umpire who, in its opinion, shall have knowingly given an unjust decision, and any Club appointing an Umpire so disqualified, shall be liable to be declared losers of the match for which such appointment was made.

Sec. 6.—The Umpire's decision in all matters over which he has control, shall be final.

RULE VII.—THE REFEREE.

The Captains shall select a Referee, whose duty it shall be, at the commencement of a match, to see that all the regulations respecting the ball, crosse, spiked soles, playing-ground, &c., are complied with and shall indicate a place as near the centre of the ground as can be arrived at, where the ball shall be thrown up. He must know before the commencement of a match up to what time the game is to be played, and punctually at the time decided upon he shall call "*Time.*" The Referee shall be on the ground during the match, and shall have power to settle all matters in dispute, and shall enforce strict observance of the Rules hereinbefore and hereinafter contained; but in case a disturbance or an infringement of any of the Rules should occur, he may, if he deems the matter of sufficient importance, call in the aid of the Umpires and the Captains to settle such dispute. Any proposition or facts that any player may wish brought forward, must be made through the Captains. The Referee has no right to express an opinion, and any expressed opinion must be taken as his decision. His first decision must in all cases be final.

RULE VIII.—CAPTAINS.

Captains to superintend play may be appointed by each side previous to the commencement of a match. They shall be members of the Club by whom they are appointed, and no other. They shall select Umpires, and toss up for choice of goals. They shall report any infringement of the laws during a match to the Referee.

RULE IX.—NAME OF PLAYERS.

The players of each side shall be designated as follows:— "Goal-keeper," who defends the goal; "Point," first man out from goal; "Cover-point," in front of point; "Centre;" "Home," nearest opponent's goal. Others shall be termed fielders.

RULE X.—MISCELLANEOUS.

Sec. 1.—Thirteen players shall constitute a full field; but the Secretaries of the Clubs engaged to play a match may agree between themselves to play a larger number of players.

Sec. 2.—All players shall be bound for the season to the Club they first play with in that season, and shall not play with any other Club without the express consent of the Captain of the opposing team.

Sec. 3.—A match shall be decided by the greatest number of goals got during the time the Captains have agreed upon to play.

Sec. 4.—The game shall be suspended for a rest of ten minutes by the Referee calling "Half-time" at five minutes to half the time agreed upon to play.

Sec. 5.—At the resumption of the game the players must change sides, and the ball shall be "thrown up" in the centre of the ground as at the commencement of a match.

Sec. 6.—No change of players shall be made after a match has commenced, except for reasons of accident or injury during a match, or upon an agreement made between the Captains. In the event of any dispute between the Captains as to the injured player's fitness to continue the Game, the matter shall at once be decided by the Referee. Either side may commence to play with less than their full number, and may complete their team at any time during the game.

Sec. 7.—All matches arranged by the Association shall be commenced at 3 o'clock in the afternoon, and any Club not being ready to start play at 3.15 shall be fined five shillings.

RULE XI.—SPIKED SOLES.

No player shall wear spiked soles.

RULE XII.—UNIFORM.

No player shall be allowed to take part in a match unless he be dressed in the uniform of his Club.

RULE XIII.—TOUCHING THE BALL WITH THE HAND.

The ball must not be touched with the hand, save in case of Rules XIV. and XV.

RULE XIV.—GOAL-KEEPER.

Goal-keeper, while defending goal within the goal-crease, may pat away with his hand or block the ball in any manner.

RULE XV.—BALL IN AN INACCESSIBLE PLACE.

Should the ball lodge in any place inaccessible to the Crosse, it may be taken out by the hand, and "thrown up" by the Referee.

APPENDIX 1 – PLAYING RULES FOR LACROSSE

RULE XVI.—BALL OUT OF BOUNDS.

Ball thrown out of bounds must be thrown in by the Referee at the nearest spot within bounds from the place where it went out of play. The ball behind goal shall still be in play if it remains within the line of the Boundary posts.

RULE XVII.—THROWING THE CROSSE.

No player shall throw his Crosse at a player or at the ball under any circumstances. Should a player lose his Crosse during the game, he shall consider himself out of play, and shall not be allowed to touch the ball in any way until he again recovers it. Kicking the ball is absolutely prohibited to players without a Crosse.

RULE XVIII.—ACCIDENTAL GAME.

Should the ball be accidentally put through a goal, by one of the players defending it, it is game for the side attacking that goal. Should it be put through a goal by any one not actually a player, it shall not count.

RULE XIX.—BALLS CATCHING IN THE NETTING.

Should the ball catch in the netting, the Crosse must immediately be struck on the ground so as to dislodge it.

RULE XX.—ROUGH PLAY.

Sec. 1.—No player shall grasp an opponent's Crosse with his hands, hold it with his arms, or stick or between his legs.

Sec. 2.—No player shall hold an opponent's Crosse with his Crosse, run in front of him, or interfere in any way to keep him from the ball until another player reaches it.

Sec. 3.—No player with his Crosse or otherwise shall hold, strike, or trip an opponent, nor push him with the hand.

Sec. 4.—No player shall be allowed to jump at, or shoulder an opponent from behind while running for, or after reaching the ball.

Sec. 5.—No player shall be allowed to wrestle with the legs entwined, so as to throw an opponent.

Sec. 6.—Any player deliberately striking another with his Crosse or otherwise, shall be immediately ruled out of the match.

Sec. 7.—No player shall charge into another after he has thrown the ball.

Sec. 8.—The check commonly known as the "square" or "cross" check, which consists of one player charging into another with both hands on the Crosse, so as to make the stick meet the body of his opponent, is strictly forbidden.

Sec. 9.—No player shall interfere in any way with another who is in pursuit of an opponent.

RULE XXI.—FOUL PLAY.

Sec. 1.—Any player considering himself purposely injured during play, must report to his Captain, who must report to the Referee, who shall warn the players complained of.

Sec. 2.—In the event of persistent fouling, after cautioning by the Referee, the latter may request the Captain to remove the offending player or players, and compel the side to finish the match shorthanded.

RULE XXII.—INTERRUPTED MATCHES.

In the event of a match being interrupted by darkness, bad weather, or any circumstance whereby the Captains and Referee think it inadvisable to continue playing, such match shall be considered as drawn.

RULE XXIII.—FLAG-POLE KNOCKED DOWN.

In the event of a flag-pole being knocked down during the game; and if, in the opinion of the Umpire, the ball shall pass through what would be the goal, were the flag-pole standing, it will count for the side who are putting to that goal.

RULE XXIV.—DISPUTES NOT PROVIDED FOR.

In the event of any dispute arising not provided for in these Rules, the Referee shall, at the time and place of the occurrence of such dispute, decide thereon. Either of the parties to the dispute, considering such decision not to be in accordance with the facts of the case, may, however, appeal, by handing to the Secretary of the Association, within at least seven days from the occurrence of such dispute, a written document setting forth the nature of the dispute, and all particulars thereto appertaining. The Association shall, at their first meeting after receipt of such document, or at any subsequent meeting as they may decide, proceed to adjudicate thereon.

RULE XXV.—EXTRA TEAMS.

Sec. 1.—Every Club playing two or more teams, shall, be-

APPENDIX 1 – PLAYING RULES FOR LACROSSE

fore the commencement of the Association Matches, send to the Secretary a list of the players in each team, and no Club shall be allowed to play more than three men from one team in any other, on any one Saturday.

Sec. 2.—Any Club commencing during the season to play an extra team must send a list to the Secretary of the players composing such team prior to its taking part in any Association Match.

RULE XXVI.—AMENDMENTS.

Any amendment or alteration proposed to be made in any part of these Laws shall be made only at a Special Meeting of the Association, and by a three-fourths vote of the members present at such meeting.

APPENDIX 2

La Crosse as a Rival to Cricket

The article which is reproduced below was published in the Chambers Journal in England in 1863 and was subsequently published in various newspapers within the Australian colonies.

Chambers's Edinburgh Journal was a weekly magazine started by William Chambers. in 1832. Topics included history, religion, language, and science. In 1854 the title was changed to Chambers's Journal of Popular Literature, Science, and Art, and later changed again to Chambers Journal.

"When the English residents at Boulogne (coastal city in the north of France) played a cricket match for the amusement of the Duchesse de Berry, that lady, after being spectator of some half a dozen innings with extreme ennui (Boredom), sent a gentleman of her retinue to the chief player to beg to know when the game was going to begin, as Madame la Duchesse was "Était terriblement ennuyée"! (The Duchesse was terribly bored!).

The duchesse, good lady, had taken all the desperate fielding and batting of two mortal hours for mere preliminary sport — a prelude to a more exciting and violent competition. Caroline de Bourbon-Sicile, duchesse de Berry (Maria Carolina Ferdinanda Luise; 5 November 1798 – 17 April 1870) was an Italian princess of the House of Bourbon who married into the French royal family. She married Charles Ferdinand, Duke of Berry, nephew of Louis XV11 in 1816. The Duchess 'hit a blot' in our national game when she sent that annoying message!

Cricket, like all other things, has its defects. In the first place, it does not give the player sufficient employment. There are long intervals when a man has nothing to do but stare at the grass, and hope that the ball will come his way. The worse player a cricketer is, the shorter are his innings, and the less he has to do in fielding. On a very cold or very hot day, an hour's fielding is dull work, especially to the men furthest from the wicket. Another drawback of cricket is, that the dress and implements grow daily more expensive; and the greatest disadvantage of all is, that it cannot be played in winter, which is just the time most adapted for running and violent exercise.

Now, lacrosse, the national game of Canada, has none of those defects. It can be played even on the snow, and as well in winter as in summer. It can be played by any number of persons. The ground needs no preparation. The materials for the game are cheap and simple. It employs nearly every player at once, and is capable of infinite varieties, while it furnishes opportunities for the greatest skill and agility. Lacrosse is a game of extreme antiquity, and was borrowed from the American Indians by the Canadians. It is mentioned by Charleroix (1682-1761), that early French Jesuit priest, traveller and historian, who saw the Algonquins playing it on the shores of the St. Lawrence, somewhere between Quebec and The Three Rivers.

It was at a great game of lacrosse, between three Indian tribes— the Shawnees, the Ottawas, and the Delawares — that an attempt was once made to surprise Fort Detroit. Catlin (French painter of Native Americans and traveller) describes thousands of men joining in the game. A few years ago, the young men of Montreal learned the game from the Iroquois of Caughnawaga, and already the Beaver Club of Montreal boast of players who can beat the Indians who taught them. Lacrosse is a game so wild and exciting, so varied, and so dramatic, that it interests the spectator as much as the player, and this cannot be so truly said of any other game. It is also a simple game, and one easily understood. Above all, in lacrosse the muscles of the body are brought into exertion equally and at the same time there is no danger of losing an eye or splitting a thumb. Unlike cricket, lacrosse is a game suited for girls, and might be introduced into girls' schools with great advantage, as the crosse bat is scarcely heavier than a battledore, and there is plenty of healthy running, without any danger of blows.

Lacrosse is generally played by twelve competitors on a side. The players wear flannel shirts and caps, belts or sashes, and light shoes or deer-skin moccasins, which leave the feet unconstrained and pliant. The crosse, or bat, requires careful description. It may be either of ash or hickory ; the former bends easier, the latter is stronger. It is generally about three feet long, but its size and weight may be proportioned to the height and strength of the player. It is bent into the shape of an unbarbed fish-hook, or a bishop's crozier; a net of catgut, or strings of moose skin is then strained across the curve to the width of a racket bat. The netted surface is made rather baggy in the centre, in order to better catch the ball and carry it when required. The ball used at lacrosse is of solid India rubber, as it can be thrown farther, and is harder to stop than the less elastic sponge ball. The ground needs no preparation, but is better when level, and where the grass is short and the stones are few. The goals through which the ball has to be driven are generally about six feet high, and consist of poles bearing colored flags, placed about six feet apart. The rival goals should face each other, and be about half a mile apart.

The game consists in a struggle of the one party to pass the ball through the goal of the other. The party that first drives the ball through the opposite goal is victorious. The excitement and fun consists in the alternate attack and defence. If there are twenty-four players present, twelve for each side,

APPENDIX 2 – LA CROSSE AS A RIVAL TO CRICKET

the two 'captains', or leading men, toss up for the first pick. They then choose their men, and post them over the field, selecting for each his place according to age, strength, skill, and peculiar faculty. The following rules are enforced - ' No swiping' allowed. No tripping or holding your adversary. No throwing the ball with the hand; though in a struggle, and when a player is surrounded it may be kicked with the foot. No picking up the ball with the hand, except in extreme cases, as when it gets into a pool, or in a sand- hole. After every game the players shall change sides. If a ball flung at the goal is caught by the crosse of the goal-keeper, but still breaks in or falls in, the game is still won by the attacking party.

There are many ways of posting your men - according as you are a cautious or an impetuous captain, more aggressive or more defensive: some leaders run their men in a straight wall across the goal; others cluster half their men round the flags, and send the rest afield! Others leave their men to take their own positions, and to trust to the instinct of the moment. The over-cautious captain, who hoards his men too fondly round the fortress of the goal, generally saves himself for a time, but makes little progress towards victory till he grows more adventurous. The over rash player, on the other hand, who leaves his home scantily guarded, is always in danger even in moments of success, if the enemy break from him and make a dash on his home.

The twelve men of each side consist of six field men, ordinary field hands, and six more expert players, to whom the places of honor are reserved. These six are thus subdivided: The goal-keeper, who stands cool and imperturbable, to ward off the ball from the little gateway between the flags. Point, who should be a skilful checker in dangerous moments, stands twelve feet in front of him. Cover-point, who should be a very good player, should never leave his post except to cautiously push a palpable advantage. The home-men, stand near the enemy's goal, to pass the ball quickly in when thrown up to them; they should be specially prompt, yet cool men.

The facers are the two players who begin the game by standing in front of each other, half-way between the goals, and 'three' being counted, trying which by strength or art can obtain the ball. Sometimes it is thrown up and struck at. The ' dodges' at this moment are numerous. Some twist the ball between their legs and the man behind them; others press the ball away by main force. A common method is as ' three' is cried to suddenly turn your back on your adversary, and giving your crosse a twist, to send the ball to your centre man. The moment of- this duel is one of the most beautiful in the game. Every man is standing silent, ready and anxious, more like statues than men; but the instant the ball starts in the air, there is a rush of athletic men, and a whirl of bats, which never ceases, but only grows wilder and fiercer, till the ball is passed between the flag- wands. The ball in lacrosse should seldom be rudely struck, only thrown and tipped.

The good player's object is to catch it as soon as possible in the bag of his net, and if he is fleet enough, or is a swift runner and dodger, to carry it at once through the goal; but as this is rather difficult with twelve opponents, checking him, crossing him, beating at his bat, and waiting to snap him at every wind and turn, the true play is to throw the ball on to the nearest or most accessible and least surrounded man of his party. As it is part of the game to strike the ball that an opponent is carrying to the goal out of his crosse, it requires great practice before you learn how to avoid these blows, and how to catch and carry the ball safest and in the quickest way between the flags. The skilful player can catch the ball at full flight, by holding his crosse almost perpendicular; then by a dip and rise again he turns the crosse to a horizontal position, and runs off with the ball towards the goal.

When closely pursued by checkers, the good player throws the ball at once with care and good aim to the nearest or most accessible man of his party, who nurses it, passes it on, or runs with it, as the case may require. The 'dodging' or avoiding the competitors who would stop you, or take the ball from you, and the 'checking' or stopping the dodger, are the two most subtle, varied, and amusing branches of the game. It is wonderful what room there is in lacrosse for invention, ingenuity, artifice, and dexterity. An Indian dodger will put up his crosse perpendicularly, and then, by a dip and horizontal turn, catch and run off with the swiftest ball; or he will bear the ball to the ground, and catch it after it bounces; or he will catch it between his feet, or under his arms, and toss it on to his crosse, and then run. If closely pursued, the good player throws the ball back over the checker's head to his nearest friend, or he will wave his crosse to and fro to escape the blow of his opponent, or keep whirling round ready for a bolt, or will pretend to fall, and then rise up and dart off on the checker's weakest side; or he keeps changing his crosse from hand to hand, and parrying his opponent's blows with the disengaged hand. The checker is, however, generally too much for the dodger, unless he has a swift pair of legs.

The checker must never let the dodger pass him with the ball, but snatch it from him before he has time to throw, or at least before he has time to throw judiciously or between the flags. He must learn all possible feints, and anticipate every movement of his antagonist. If the dodger has his back towards the checker, the latter must slip his crosse over the dodger's head, and strike the ball from him, or tip it, if possible, into his own crosse; or he can bear up his arm, or tip the end of his rival's bat, and then directly the ball falls, run and lift it off towards one of his own party, who, if un-attacked, can bear it off between the flags. The goal keeper must be specially quick of eye, serpentine in body, and cool of head, without which qualifications he will either lose the game for his side, or receive some injury from the ball. He must never think of special players, but keep his eye un-deviatingly fixed on the ball. He must beware of the dodger throwing the ball between his legs. When he can get a good cut at the ball, he must learn to strike it with the wood-work of his crosse. He must always tip the ball away to the side of the goal, as otherwise the enemy in front might instantly drive it home by a return-blow. There are times when the ball is coming in, but far above the flags, when it is better to let it pass, as otherwise it might be caught and sent in by a straight throw of one of the enemy's advanced-guard.

The player who would excel at lacrosse must not mind an occasional blow on the head or fingers, and if he does, must wear cricket gloves and a thick cap. He must also constantly practice running and dodging. He should run on uneven and even ground, and up and down hill, especially the latter. He must learn to do the mile in as much less than ten minutes, and the six miles in as much less than the hour as possible. A quarter of a mile in a minute, or a mile in five minutes, is good running.

As a game, I rank lacrosse far above cricket or golf. It does not require attendants and special ground, like golf, and it boasts more un-intermittent amusement and more simultaneous competition than cricket. The materials, too, are cheaper, and you require no 'hog-in-armor' costume. It is more varied, more ingenious, more subtle than cricket, and, above all, it can be played in all seasons of the year without danger, expense or preparation. No marquees required, no grass rolling, no expensive bats or balls, no spiked shoes, and no padded leggings to preserve you from the cannon shots of fast bowlers, who seem determined to maim or lame somebody! Above all there is not that tiresome and wearisome waiting for the innings.

The whole twenty-four men have their innings simultaneously, and have both an equal chance and unequal certainty of amusement and employment; while in cricket a beginner gets perhaps ten strokes at a ball, and that is all in the whole game. I admit the pleasure of the good swipe in cricket, the excitement of the runs, the delight of blocking a treacherous slow ball, the rapture of catching out a good player, and the feverish anxiety of a close-run game, but still I hold that cricket cannot hold a candle to lacrosse for variety, ingenuity, and interest.

 The last time I saw it played was in a fine green meadow outside Montreal, not far from the Haunted House, at the foot of a hill from which a fine view is obtained. The shining and uncovered steeples were hid from sight; we were among trees slightly crimsoned with the October frosts. The young Beaver Club of Montreal was playing a party of Indians, who had just arrived by steamer from some river near the Rapids of the St. Lawrence. The Montreal stripplings were dressed in flannel shirts and trousers, and had donned scarlet boating caps and belts. The Indians were dark skinned and older men, with broad chests, and thin, sinewy limbs. They wore feather head-dresses and ornamented loin-clothes, and moved over the field with a restless panther-like freedom. They expressed little pleasure at their double victory, and their stolid stoical features were fixed like those of bronze statues. It was marvellous to see, as the ball for the first time flew up into the air, these statues spring into life instantly. The field was dotted with groups of struggling figures, now running into jostling knots, now fanning out in swift lines like skirmishers before a grand army. Every now and then there would break away from the rest some sinewy subtle runner, who, winding and twisting like a serpent, would dash between the eager rallies of his rivals, avoiding every blow, now stooping, now leaping, now turning, quick as a greyhound, and artful as a fox; and then as the ball was shot between the crimson flags of the Montreal men, the Indians would give a war yell that echoed again.

I only trust that some English country gentleman, who is fond of field-sports, and has a wish to increase the honest and healthy out-door pleasures of his over-worked countrymen, only just awakening to a sense of the importance of gymnastic exercises, will introduce this delightful and exciting game into Great Britain, where it would soon become a formidable rival to cricket, which is itself only a parvenu (Social climber or upstart) of the last two hundred years. It could be played on any of our suburban commons, and the bat could easily be procured from Canada, or made here from a good model"

Bibliography

A. Publications

A Souvenir of Lacrosse in New South Wales, New South Wales Lacrosse Association, Sydney 1907

A Souvenir of Lacrosse in Queensland, Queensland Lacrosse Association, Brisbane, July 1907

Bate Weston. Lucky City: The First Generation at Ballarat. 1851-1901. Melbourne University Press. 1978.

Blainey G. The Rush That Never Ended: A History of Australian Mining, Melbourne University Press. 2003.

Bowden K.M. Goldrush Doctors at Ballarat. Magellan Press, Mulgrave 1977.

Calder Jim and Fletcher Ron. Lacrosse, The Ancient Game. Ancient Game Press, Toronto 2011.

Dingle Tony. The Victorians- Settling. Fairfax, Syme & Weldon, Melbourne. 1984.

Fisher Donald M. Lacrosse: A History of the Game 2002 The Johns Hopkins University Press

Forrest Kay. The Challenge and the Chance: The colonization and settlement of north west Australia, 1861-1914. Hesperian Press, 1996.

Fowler A.J. Lacrosse in Australia. Unpublished Manuscript. Australian Lacrosse Council. 1933.

Frauenfelder P. The Eureka Stockade (Second edition) 1998.

Garden Don. Victoria – A History. Thomas Nelson Australia. 1984.

Harrop Mal. Good Things Came from Glass, The History of Glassmaking in Australia 1812-1987, Melbourne University Press. 2008.

Hyslop Anthea. Sovereign Remedies. A History of Ballarat Base Hospital. Allen & Unwin, Sydney 1980

Jenkin John G. William Bragg and Lacrosse in Adelaide. The Australian Physicist vol 17 no.5 June 1980 pp.75-78.

Mancini A. and Hibbins M. Running with The Ball 1987 Lynedoch Publications, Melbourne.

Moloney J. Eureka. Penguin Books, Victoria 1984.

North American Indian Travelling College. Tewaarathon- Akwesasne's Story of Our National Game. 1978

Poynter John. Alfred Felton. Oxford University Press 1974.

Published posthumously in digital format as 'A History of Lacrosse in Australia' with editing and additions by John Nolan and Bill Gray. Melbourne 2015.

Ruddell Trevor. The Little Brother of War, Lacrosse at the MCG. The Yorker: Journal of the Melbourne Cricket Club Library Issue 62, Autumn 2017 pp.18-27.

Scott Bob. Lacrosse – Technique and Tradition. The Johns Hopkins University Press, Baltimore. 1976.

Senyard June E. The Ties That Bind. A History of Sport at the University of Melbourne. Walla Walla Press, Petersham, New South Wales. 2004.

Serle Geoffrey. The Golden Age – A History of the Colony of Victoria, 1851-1861. Melbourne University Press 1963.

Sladen Douglas. Twenty Years of My Life. Kessinger Publishing. 2004.

Strange A.W. Ballarat: A Brief History. Lowder Publishing, Victoria. 1972.

Templeton I and McDonald B. The Fields: The Kalgoolie and Coolgardie Goldfields 1892-1912 Fremantle Arts Press 1988.

Town David. Orillia's Remarkable Lacrosse World Tour of 1907. Orillia, Ontario, 2015

Toy Ian. A History of the Western Australian Lacrosse Association 1896-2010. Quality Press, Welshpool, Western Australia. 2016

Vennum Thomas Jnr. American Indian Lacrosse. The Smithsonian Institute Press, Washington, USA. 1994.

Webber, Horrie. The History of Lacrosse in Victoria. 1994. (Unpublished). Published posthumously in digital format as "A History of Lacrosse in Australia, 1876-1994" with editing and additions by John Nolan and Bill Gray.

Weyand Alexander M. and Roberts Milton R. The Lacrosse Story. H&A Herman, Baltimore, USA. 1965.

Wilmot R.W.E (ed). The Victorian Sporting Record. McCarron, Bird & Co. Melbourne. 1903.

B. Newspapers

Advertiser (Adelaide)

Advertiser (Footscray, Victoria)

Australasian (Melbourne)

Australasian Sketcher (Adelaide Edition)

Australian Star (Sydney)

Australian Town & Country Journal (Sydney)

Ballarat Star (Victoria)

Barrier Miner (Broken Hill, New South Wales)

Bell's Life & Sporting Chronicle (Melbourne)

Bendigo Advertiser (Victoria)

BIBLIOGRAPHY

Brisbane Courier
Bunbury Herald (Western Australia)
Chronicle (Adelaide)
Coburg Leader (Melbourne)
Coolgardie Miner (Western Australia)
Cornwall Chronicle (Launceston, Tasmania)
Critic (Adelaide)
Cumberland Mercury (Parramatta, New South Wales)
Daily News (Perth)
Daily Telegraph (Launceston)
Daily Telegraph (Sydney)
Echuca & Moama Advertiser (Victoria)
Evening Journal (Adelaide)
Evening News (Sydney)
Examiner (Launceston)
Express & Telegraph (Adelaide)
Gadfly (Adelaide)
Geelong Advertiser (Victoria)
Goldfields Morning Chronicle (Western Australia)
Illustrated Australasian News (Melbourne)
Illustrated Melbourne Post
Illustrated Sydney News
Independent (Footscray, Victoria)
Inquirer and Commercial News (Perth)
Kalgoorlie & Boulder Standard (Western Australia)
Labor Call (Melbourne)
Leader (Melbourne)
Maitland Mercury & Hunter River General Advertiser (New South Wales)
Mercury (Hobart)
Mirror (Perth)
Morning Bulletin (Rockhampton, Queensland)
New Call (Perth)
Newcastle Mining Herald & Miners Advocate (New South Wales)
North Melbourne Advertiser
Observer (Adelaide)
Port Augusta Dispatch (South Australia)
Port Phillip Herald (Melbourne)
Punch (Melbourne)

Queensland Figaro & Punch

Queensland Times, Ipswich Herald & General Advertiser

Quiz & Lantern (Adelaide)

Referee (Sydney)

Register (Adelaide)

Sporting Globe (Melbourne)

Sportsman (Melbourne)

St George Call (Kogarah, New South Wales)

Sunday Sun (Sydney)

Sunday Times (Perth)

Sydney Daily Telegraph

Sydney Morning Herald

Table Talk (Melbourne)

Tasmanian

Tasmanian News (Hobart)

Telegraph (Brisbane)

The Age (Melbourne)

The Argus (Melbourne)

The Golden Age (Coolgardie, Western Australia)

The Journal (Adelaide)

The Queenslander (Brisbane)

The Sydney Mail & New South Wales Advertiser

The Telegraph, St Kilda, Prahran & South Yarra Guardian (Melbourne)

The Week (Brisbane)

The West Australian

Umpire (Fremantle)

Western Mail (Perth)

Williamstown Chronicle (Melbourne)

Winner (Melbourne)

Index

A

Adams, Sam 116, 120
Adelaide Lacrosse Club 89-94
Adelaide Oval 95, 228 ,259
Adelaide University Lacrosse Club 92, 100, 101, 105, 111
Adult Deaf-Mute Lacrosse Club (NSW) 81
Adult-Deaf Lacrosse Club (SA) 190
Advertiser Shield 105
Albert Park 42, 44, 45, 46, 51, 58
Alcock & Co 41
Alcock Henry Upton 40
Alder, Charles 285
Allan, Frank 44
Angel, Jack 150
Appleby, Phil 193-4
Ashburton River 20
Atkins, Charlie 143, 144
Auburn Lacrosse Club 170, 180
Auld, George 107
Australian Infantry Forces
Australian Lacrosse Union 145,192, 196-7, 205, 209
Australian Lacrosse Council 192, 197
Australian Rules Football 55, 64
Ayers, Julian 110

B

Bainbridge, Garnet 285
Bainbridge, Joseph 285
Ball, Robert Walker 116, 117, 118, 120
Ballarat 4-6, 57
Ballarat Athletics Club 10,11
Ballarat Glass Bottle Company 24
Ballarat Lacrosse Club 57-58, 166

Balmain Lacrosse Club 73, 74,76, 254
Banks Lacrosse Club (NSW) 108
Banks Lacrosse Club (WA) 157
Barclay, Jim 41, 48, 53-54, 62, 64, 168
Bates, Molly 268, 270
Beattie, Jack 195
Beech, George 40, 48,53-4, 57, 64, 66, 71-2, 75, 202, 259, 263, 264
Beechworth 14
Beers, George 37, 39, 48, 70
Belgrave Terrace 27-8
Belt, Francis 95
Bendigo Lacrosse Club 60-61
Bexley Ladies Lacrosse Club 270
Big John Baptiste 39
Bohemians Lacrosse Club 62-3, 152,170
Bonnin, Fred 95
Boulder Lacrosse Club 155
Box, Albert 230, 264
Box Hill Lacrosse Club 254
Boyd, William 10, 43
Boyle, Harry 43, 58, 131
Bragg, William 93,100,110
Brighton Grammar School 263
Brighton Presbyterians Lacrosse Club 263
Brighton Wanderers Lacrosse Club 259, 263
Brisbane Lacrosse Club 118, 121, 122, 124, 125
Broken Hill 83, 108-9
Broken Hill Lacrosse Association 83, 108-9
Broken Hill Lacrosse Club 108
Bromilow, Ivon 284
Bromilow, James 285
Browne, George 285
Bryning, Bert 230, 264

Bryning Will 220-221, 228, 233, 264
Bunbury 17, 22
Burke and Wills 7
Burns, Tommy 257
Burr, Thomas 12, 18
Burwood Lacrosse Club 82
Byard, Doug 89
Byfield, John 133

C
Camberwell Lacrosse Club 253
Cambridge University 93, 117, 200
Camden Harbour Pastoral Association 19-20
Canadian Cadets 262
Canadian Lacrosse Team 207-247
Canadian Stag 8-10
Canham Charlie 90
Canterbury Lacrosse Club 253
Carlton Lacrosse Club 53-54, 55, 152
Caulfield Lacrosse Club 60, 64, 131, 168-9, 170, 172, 179, 251
Caughnawaga Indians 37-8, 39, 54
Cavenagh-Mainwaring, Gordon 100, 104, 110, 111, 197
Challenge Cup 11
Championship of Victoria 13-14
Chepmell, Havilland le Messieur 116, 118, 121
Claremont Lacrosse Club 191
Clarence Hotel 53, 57
Coburg Lacrosse Club 192, 278
Coldstream, Bob 134
Collingwood Lacrosse Club 57, 71, 152, 170, 192
Colton, Jack 89
Combined Goldfields 155, 235, 246
Conigrave, Harry 89
Conway, Jack 42-3, 51
Coolgardie Lacrosse Club 154
Copenhagen Grounds 10-12
Cornish, Charlie 107, 110
Cossins, George 95, 110
Cottesloe Lacrosse Club 151, 157
Crystal Brook Lacrosse Club 102

D
Darvall, Roy 188
Davenport, Alf 94, 110
De Grey River 20
Deakin, Alfred 219
Delaware Lacrosse Club 188

Delves, Fred 220-223, 225, 233, 264
Deniliquin 163
Deniliquin Lacrosse Club 74, 119, 163
Dingley Dell 22
Domain Cricket Ground 76
Donnelly River 18, 22 -24
Donovan, John 43
Dungey, John 90
Dunlop Tyre Company 231

E
East Adelaide Lacrosse Club 99, 103
East Fremantle Lacrosse Club 62, 156, 191
East Melbourne Cricket Club 44
East Melbourne Lacrosse Club 58
East Torrens Lacrosse Club 93, 103, 111, 220
Echuca 163-4
Electorate system 104
Eltham Lacrosse Club 143
Emerald Hill 25, 28, 40, 42, 48, 168
England Lacrosse Association 37
Esk Lacrosse Club 136, 138
Essendon Lacrosse Club 168, 220, 254, 278
Eureka Stockade 7, 20
Eyre, John 22

F
Fead, George 90
Felton, Alfred 25-6, 28, 39
Finlay, Charlie 54, 57, 116, 118, 120-22
Fitzroy Lacrosse Club 53-5, 57, 116, 168, 249
Fletcher, Jack 227-9
Fookes, Bill 48, 53-4, 57, 64, 179
Footscray Lacrosse Club 251-53
Forster, Walter 202, 265
Fort Street Girls High School 269, 271
Fotheringham, Charlie 110
Fowler, David 100, 102, 110, 111
Fox, David 52-3, 64
Fox, Joel 48, 57, 64, 66, 167, 179, 182, 202, 265
Fremantle Lacrosse Club 143, 147-9, 150, 154, 156-7, 254
Fulton, Alexander 285
Fulton, Charles 285
Furneaux, Will 285-88

G
Gaggin, William 44
Gallipoli 282, 284, 295

INDEX

Garland, Richard 181-2, 198, 202, 231, 262-64
Garland-McHarg Cup 183, 262
Gibson, Jack 116, 118, 120, 123, 188
Glass Making 24
Glebe Lacrosse Club 80, 190
Glenelg lacrosse Club 103
Glynn, Mary 27
Gooden, Ern 220-21, 225, 229, 233, 264
Gordon, Adam Lindsay 17-18, 21-23, 34
Gordon, George 58, 88, 129-31, 167
Gordon, Weymyss 58, 88
Graham, Charlie 172, 220, 221, 228, 233, 264
Granville Lacrosse Club 78
Grimwade, Frederick 25, 26, 28, 39

H
Hahndorf College 89
Hambridge, Frank 187
Handfield, Theo 172
Hannan's Farm 177
Harrison, Allan 285
Harrison Henry Colton 12-14, 24, 26, 38, 41
Hatfield, Annie 269
Hatfield, Cecil 267
Hawksburn Lacrosse Club 188, 192, 220
Hawthorn Lacrosse Club 170, 172, 180, 225
Heale, Bill 48, 64
Henderson, Doug 110-11, 150, 159
Hill, Herb 100, 158
Hill, Reg 100, 110
Hobart Lacrosse Club 132, 134, 138, 280
Hobart University Lacrosse Club 134, 138, 280
Holdfast Bay Lacrosse Club 103
Honour Boards 281
Hotham Glass Works 38
House, Walter 64, 172, 178, 182, 202, 220
Hughes, Charlie 201, 220, 221, 225, 227, 229, 233, 264
Humphris, Lou 110, 201, 218, 220, 221, 227, 229, 233, 264
Hutcheon, Jack 230, 232, 264
Hyam Cup 74, 75

I
Indooropilly Lacrosse Club 188
Inman, Frederick de Couray 108
Intercolonial competition 75-76
Ipswich Lacrosse Club 118-121, 123
Iroquois Lacrosse Club (NSW) 74, 118
Iroquois Lacrosse Club (SA) 100, 187
Iroquois Lacrosse Club (Qld) 188, 254
Iroquois Lacrosse Club (WA) 191, 254

J
Jamestown Lacrosse Club 97-8, 232, 255, 271
Jones, Les 201, 220, 221, 225, 227, 229, 264

K
Kalgoolie 141, 234-5
Kalgoolie Lacrosse Club 154-5
Karweens Ladies" Lacrosse Club 269
Kaufmann, Robert 51
Kell, Fred 110, 220, 221, 222, 223, 229, 233, 264
Kelly, Thomas 43
Kew lacrosse Club 171, 180
Kewney, Arthur 153
King Edward V11 198-9
Kirribilli Lacrosse Club 78
Knightsbridge Lacrosse Club 95-6
Kogarah Ladies" Lacrosse Club 267
Kooyong Lacrosse Club 253
Kyneton 57

L
Lacrosse race 82, 118, 124
Lassetter, Major Harry 80
Latham, John 60, 202, 221, 223
Laughlin, Austin 283
Launceston Lacrosse Club 133-4, 276
London Chartered Bank Lacrosse Club 79
Looker, Keith 284
Lords Cricket Ground 198-9
Lyne, Sir William 219
Lyons, Bill 45,48, 49, 53-4, 57, 64, 75

M
Macartney, Edward 116, 118, 120, 121, 123, 125, 188, 219, 265
Madden, Sir John 179, 202
Malvern Lacrosse Club 192-96
Manly Ladies' lacrosse Club 269
Mann, A.220, 221, 227, 229, 264
Maribyrnong Lacrosse Club 64
MCC Lacrosse Club 60, 131, 170, 171, 173, 179, 188, 220, 249
McCormack, George 42
McHarg Andrew 231, 262
Melbourne Centennial Exhibition 27

Melbourne Church of England Girls Grammar School 266-7
Melbourne Cricket Club 13, 26,38, 44, 172, 202, 209-10, 231, 273
Melbourne Cricket Club Library 172
Melbourne Cricket Ground (MCG) 10, 55, 172, 174, 181, 201, 222, 249, 260-3
Melbourne Cup 23
Melbourne Glass Bottle Works 25-27, 28, 39, 43
Melbourne Grammar School 263
Melbourne International Exhibition 27
Melbourne Lacrosse Club 43-6, 54-5, 57, 71
Melbourne Sports Depot 193
Melbourne University Lacrosse Club 59, 60-1, 143, 166-7, 169, 170, 179, 180, 188, 200, 225
Mercantile Lacrosse Club 150-52
Miller, John C. 219, 236-7
Millett, John 72
Mines Lacrosse Club 153
Mitchell, George 41, 48
Mohicans Lacrosse Club 78, 125, 188, 190
Montreal Lacrosse Club 37-38
Moonah Lacrosse Club 254
Moore Park 72, 73
Morrison, Bill 83, 181, 187-8, 197, 209, 265
Morrison, Len 134
Mount, Dr Henry Edward 3-4, 7
Mount, Emily Catherine 3
Mount, Emma 3
Mount, Francis 3, 7, 18, 19, 21
Mount, Harry 3, 7
Mount, Julius 3, 7
Mount, Lambton;
    family 3-6
    employment 6
    athletics 8-14
    glass manufacturing 24-28
    lacrosse initiation 33-42
    lacrosse coordinating committee 42-46
    Reds v Blues 47-53, VLA 53-56
Mount, Violet 29
Mount, William 3, 168
Mountain, Bill 54, 182
Mudie, Charles 89
Murray, Cecil 60, 168, 170, 173, 179, 182
Murray, Noel 60, 131, 133, 170, 193, 195
Muscular Christianity 8, 10, 11

N
Nation, Norman 285
New South Wales Lacrosse Association 73-5, 78-9, 80, 82, 124, 208-9, 276
New South Wales Ladies Lacrosse Association 270
Newland, Phil 110
Newtown lacrosse Club
New Zealand 270
Noarlunga Lacrosse Club
Noblett, W.C 201, 220-3, 227, 233, 264
Norcott, Amos 44, 48, 53-4, 64
North Adelaide Lacrosse Club 95, 96, 98, 111, 112, 145, 220
North Broken Hill Lacrosse Club 108
North Perth Lacrosse Club 191, 254
North Sydney Lacrosse Club 82
Northern Tasmanian Lacrosse Association 137-40, 188, 201, 257, 276
Nullarbor Desert 22

O
Oaklands School 73
Ochiltree John 153
Olympian Ladies' Lacrosse Club 270
Olympic Games 200
Oriental Bank 12, 14
Orkney James 19-20
Oxford University 89, 134, 200

P
Paddington Lacrosse Club 78
Paris International Exhibition 27
Parker, George 150, 159
Parkes, Sir Henry 76
Parnell John 59-60
Parsons, Charles 41, 48, 54, 145, 150, 159
Paterson, William 85, 88, 110
Pathe's Gazette 269
Pedestrianism 8, 11
Perth lacrosse Club 143, 146-7, 149, 150, 154, 157-8, 191-2, 254
Petersham Ladies' Lacrosse Club 254, 258
Playing Rules 48-9, 56, 61, 226, 291-306
Port Adelaide lacrosse Club 103, 104, 140, 228, 255, 282
Port Augusta Lacrosse Club 97, 98
Port Germein 97
Port Phillip Club Hotel 42, 44
Presgrave, Alan 201, 227, 228, 229, 264

INDEX

Prince Alfred College 92, 105, 117, 143
Prince, Lloyd 88-89, 110
Prince of Wales 198-9

Q
Queen Victoria 39
Queensland Lacrosse Association (QLA) 187, 209, 219, 254
Queensland Lacrosse Union (QLU) 121, 122, 124, 125-7, 276

R
Radford, Harry 176-7
Redfern Lacrosse Club 73, 79
Redhead, Reverend Thomas 193-4
Rhodes Scholar 134
Richmond Lacrosse Club 54
Ridgway, Noel 283
Riggall William 43
Robin, Percy 116, 118, 120, 123
Rockhampton Lacrosse Club 187
Rounsvell, Horace 153
Rudd, Arthur 220, 227, 229, 232, 264
Ruddell, Trevor 172, 249
Runting, William 44
Russell, Dr Fred 110

S
Sandhurst Lacrosse Club 60, 74, 119, 164
Sandridge 24, 42
Savages Lacrosse Club 121, 123-4
Schafe, Jack 193-5
Scott, Fred 177
Shappere, Phillip 57-8, 62, 64, 66, 169, 171-2, 178-9, 182, 202, 222, 223, 265
Sholl, Reg 104, 107, 111
Smith, Phillip 265
Smith, Seymour 100
Smith, Sidney Talbot 93
South Australian Cricket Association 209-10
South Australian Junior Lacrosse Association 85, 104
South Australian Lacrosse Association (SALA) 95, 97, 100, 101-2, 125, 145, 164-5, 208-0, 230, 259, 262, 273, 276, 281
South Brisbane Lacrosse Club 122-3, 125
South Melbourne Cricket Club 44, 116, 131, 169
South Melbourne Lacrosse Club 53-4, 55, 58, 74, 95-6, 119, 130, 162, 164-8

South Yarra Lacrosse Club 57-8, 254
Southern Tasmanian Lacrosse Association 132-35, 137-40
Sportsmen's 1000 274-5
Sportsmen's Posters 274-5
Spring Road School 195
Spurling, Stephen 134, 136
St Clair 38
St Andrew's College 267
St Georges Ladies' Lacrosse Club 267-8
St Kilda Cricket Ground 51
St Kilda Lacrosse Club 58, 192-4
St Leonard's Lacrosse Club 75
St Peter's College 92, 105
Statter, James 41, 48, 52, 54, 57
Statter, William 41, 48, 52
Steet, Vic 220, 221, 227, 229, 233, 264
Sturt Lacrosse Club 103, 111, 220, 228, 255
Surrey Park Lacrosse Club 253
Swan Lacrosse Club 191
Swan River Colony 71, 141
Sydney Girls High School 270, 271
Sydney Grammar School 79
Sydney Lacrosse Club 16, 71-2, 73, 80-2, 116

T
Tamar Lacrosse Club 136-7, 254, 276
Taylor, Ike 192, 265
Taylor, Alby 220, 221, 227, 229, 233, 264
Thorpe, Jim 188, 217, 265
Thorpe, Ollie 188, 217, 230, 264
Tooronga Road School 195
Toowong Lacrosse Club 123, 125
Tortoise Lacrosse Club 168-70
Tramways Lacrosse Club 132
Tribe, Reg 88-89
Turner, Syd 95, 97

U
Union Bank 18
University of Sydney 82
USA Naval Fleet 200

V
Victoria Flint Glass Works 24
Victorian Chamber of Manufacturers 27
Victorian Football League 222
Victorian Lacrosse Association (VLA) 48-9, 53, 56-7, 134, 165, 167-8, 208-9, 262, 273, 276, 281

Victorian Woolen Manufacturing Company 51

W

Wainwright, Jack 85, 90-92, 94, 97, 110-11
Wall, Robert 116, 118
Ward, Sam 134
Wardill, Major Thomas 179, 202
Warehouseman's Oval 173
Wattle Park Lacrosse Club 254
Waugh, David 116, 118
Webber, Horrie 33
Wentworth Lacrosse Club 190
Western Australian Cricket Association 201, 234
Western Australian Lacrosse Association (WALA) 150, 155, 192, 209, 281
Winham College 92
White, Dan 169, 172-4, 178, 180, 182, 197, 265
Whitney, Arthur
Whyte, Thomas 282-3
Wicksteed, Lew 156, 159
Wilke, Les 150
Wilkinson, Alf 59, 85, 87-9, 97, 110, 111
Wilkinson, Charles 88
Williams, Owen 43
Williamstown 19, 167
Williamstown Cricket Ground
Williamstown Lacrosse Club 171, 176-9
Wills, Tom 24
Willyamas Lacrosse Club 108
Wingrove, Frederick 60, 143, 145, 150, 265
Women's Lacrosse 266- 271
Woodman Harold 284
Woodville Lacrosse Club 103, 111, 113, 190, 282
Wright, Cecil "Bonner" O'Halloran 104, 144-5, 150, 152
Wood, Stan 134, 156, 159
World Lacrosse 290

X

Xavier College 107

Y

YMCA Lacrosse Club (Qld) 188
YMCA Lacrosse Club (Tas) 134
YMCA Lacrosse Club (SA) 102

www.ingramcontent.com/pod-product-compliance
Lightning Source LLC
Chambersburg PA
CBHW041123020526
44107CB00089B/2904